The College and University Counseling Manual

Shannon J. Hodges, PhD, LMHC, ACS, is an associate professor of counseling at Niagara University. He has over 20 years of experience counseling in community agencies, university counseling centers, and residential living communities. He is a former director of a university counseling center and clinical director of a county mental health clinic. In addition, he has over 20 years of teaching experience and has authored numerous books, book chapters, journal articles, and essays, including *The Counseling Practicum and Internship Manual: A Resource for Graduate Counseling Students,* Second Edition; *A Job Search Manual for Counselors and Counselor Educators: How to Navigate and Promote Your Counseling Career;* and *101 Careers in Counseling.* He has also authored a mystery novel with a counselor as the protagonist (*City of Shadows*) and is completing a follow-up novel (*The Lonely Void: A Bob Gifford Counselor Mystery*). Dr. Hodges has received awards for his research and his teaching. He has also served on national committees, most notably the American Counseling Association (ACA) Publications Committee and the ACA Ethics Revision Task Force, along with serving on the editorial review boards of several journals, including the *Journal of Counseling & Development, Counseling and Values, Journal of Mental Health Counseling,* and *Journal of College Counseling.* He has written a monthly column for *Counseling Today* ("Through a Glass Darkly") and is a longtime member of the ACA, the American Mental Health Counselors Association (AMHCA), and several ACA affiliate divisions. Dr. Hodges has taught and counseled overseas, most recently in Australia, and enjoys travel to remote regions of the globe, most especially in the Southern Hemisphere. He is married to Shoshanna Cogan, a former counselor and current international trainer and consultant.

Kimber Shelton, PhD, is a private practitioner and owner of KLS Counseling & Consulting Services in Dallas, Texas. Dr. Shelton has worked in college counseling for 8 years, most recently serving as a staff psychologist and coordinator of diversity programming at the Georgia Institute of Technology Counseling Center. Dr. Shelton has a PhD in counseling psychology from the University of Georgia and a master's degree from Niagara University. She is a member of the American Psychological Association (APA) Committee on Sexual Orientation and Gender Diversity, an APA Minority Fellowship fellow, cochair of the Texas Psychological Association Diversity Division, and received the 2014 Professional Achievement Award from the University of Georgia College of Education. Dr. Shelton has contributed to approximately 20 publications including articles in top-tier, peer-reviewed journals, book chapters, and encyclopedia entries. Her clinical and scholarly interests include cultural diversity, sexual orientation and gender diversity, and relationships and couples counseling.

Michelle M. King Lyn, PhD, is a licensed psychologist and has 16 years of experience working in college counseling. In her current position, she serves as associate director of clinical services at the Georgia Institute of Technology Counseling Center. She has worked in the past at other counseling centers coordinating group psychotherapy, outreach, and post-doctoral training. Dr. Lyn has presented at several national conferences including NASPA (Student Affairs Administrators in Higher Education) and the American Psychological Association (APA) on issues related to collegiate mental health. In her years of experience, Dr. Lyn has provided direct service to hundreds of students and supervised the clinical work of many aspiring psychologists. Other past professional service includes serving on the executive board of the Council on the Psychology of Women and Girls, which is a former division of the Georgia Psychological Association. Dr. Lyn has a PhD in counseling psychology from the University of Georgia and obtained her master's degree from the University of Missouri–Columbia in educational psychology with an emphasis in career counseling. Her undergraduate degree in psychology is from Xavier University of Louisiana. Dr. Lyn currently maintains a private practice and participates in a consultation group for women psychologists in the Atlanta area. As a wife and mother of two, her personal interests include volunteering at community schools, music, comedy, and travel.

The College and University Counseling Manual

INTEGRATING ESSENTIAL SERVICES ACROSS THE CAMPUS

Shannon J. Hodges, PhD, LMHC, ACS

Kimber Shelton, PhD

Michelle M. King Lyn, PhD

SPRINGER PUBLISHING COMPANY
NEW YORK

Springer Publishing Company, LLC
11 West 42nd Street
New York, NY 10036
www.springerpub.com

Acquisitions Editor: Nancy S. Hale
Compositor: diacriTech

ISBN: 978-0-8261-9978-2
e-book ISBN: 978-0-8261-9979-9

16 17 18 19 20 / 5 4 3 2 1

The author and the publisher of this Work have made every effort to use sources believed to be reliable to provide information that is accurate and compatible with the standards generally accepted at the time of publication. The author and publisher shall not be liable for any special, consequential, or exemplary damages resulting, in whole or in part, from the readers' use of, or reliance on, the information contained in this book. The publisher has no responsibility for the persistence or accuracy of URLs for external or third-party Internet websites referred to in this publication and does not guarantee that any content on such websites is, or will remain, accurate or appropriate.

Library of Congress Cataloging-in-Publication Data

Names: Hodges, Shannon, author. | Shelton, Kimber, author. | King Lyn, Michelle M., author.
Title: The college and university counseling manual : integrating essential services across the campus / authors: Shannon J. Hodges, PhD, LMHC, ACS; Kimber Shelton, PhD; Michelle M. King Lyn, PhD.
Description: New York, NY : Springer Publishing Company, LLC, 2016. | Includes bibliographical references and index.
Identifiers: LCCN 2016015497 | ISBN 9780826199782
Subjects: LCSH: Counseling in higher education. | College students–Services for. | College students–Mental health services.
Classification: LCC LB2343 .H528 2016 | DDC 378.1/94–dc23 LC record available at https://lccn.loc.gov/2016015497.

Special discounts on bulk quantities of our books are available to corporations, professional associations, pharmaceutical companies, health care organizations, and other qualifying groups. If you are interested in a custom book, including chapters from more than one of our titles, we can provide that service as well.
For details, please contact:
Special Sales Department, Springer Publishing Company, LLC
11 West 42nd Street, 15th Floor, New York, NY 10036-8002
Phone: 877-687-7476 or 212-431-4370; Fax: 212-941-7842
E-mail: sales@springerpub.com

Printed in the United States of America by McNaughton & Gunn.

This text is dedicated to Dr. Eric Klinger, Professor Emeritus of Psychology at the University of Minnesota Morris, and the late Samuel Schuman, PhD, Chancellor Emeritus at the University of Minnesota Morris, two luminaries who enlightened the paths of many college students.

CONTENTS

CONTRIBUTORS

Geoff Bathje, **PhD**, Associate Professor, Adler University, Department of Counseling and Counselor Education, Chicago, Illinois

Evelyn Hunter, **PhD**, Licensed Psychologist, Assistant Professor, Psychology Department, Presbyterian College, Clinton, South Carolina

FOREWORD

A half century ago, I was a callow undergraduate at a good, small private liberal arts college in Iowa. Recently, I excavated in my library the 1961 yearbook (*The Cyclone*) from Grinnell, a volume which now seems a veritable time capsule of that bygone era in American higher education. My goal was to compare the counseling services available then with those being offered by institutions of a similar size and sort today. My expectation was that I would be able to document significant growth in collegiate attention to this important area over the past five decades. I did not expect to discover that such growth began from a baseline of zero. My old yearbook details what today seems a very slim administration, even for a relatively small college of about 1,000 students. There are the president, the deans (a dean of the college, a dean of men, and a dean of women), a treasurer, a director of food service, a library director and seven library staff, and the like. I found an activities director, bookstore manager, executive housekeeper, and three nurses. What I did not find was anything resembling a professional counseling service.

Does this mean that the 1960s were some sort of golden age of collegiate mental health, and nobody at Grinnell at that time had any problems that might have benefited from contact with a trained professional? Hardly. My friends and I were pretty much like most college-age young women and men today, in both our strengths and our weaknesses. We experienced stress and anxiety, about our work in school and in our extracurricular lives. We had family issues and tumultuous interpersonal relationships. In spite of Iowa's then-rigid liquor laws (state ABC stores; 3.2 beer; no liquor-by-the-drink), there was a discernible problem of substance abuse. There must have been gender issues, although these were not much out in the open, even in student culture. We exhibited a pretty full range of psychological needs. Where, I now wonder, were we supposed to go? To our faculty academic advisors? To the dean of men (a stern figure of behavioral discipline)? To the college chaplain (a professor of religious studies)? It was not clear, and in retrospect, I believe that most of my peers who were in need of counseling either did not get it, or got it from amateurs: friends, teachers, or staff. I can recall an ample handful of students who left college for obvious psychological reasons. A cynic might say that in the mid-20th century, college counseling services consisted of separation or expulsion.

Today, happily, we know better. As I have evolved from undergraduate to graduate student, to professor, provost, and chancellor of two fine public liberal arts colleges, my awareness of the centrality of counseling services to the contemporary college has sharpened and grown dramatically. Grinnell's three nurses have morphed into a Student Health and Counseling Service, which is headed by a "lead psychologist." In addition to on-site counseling, the college contracts with the local mental health clinic for the services of a psychiatrist, who spends time on campus each week. The college's website lists a range of issues for which students do and should seek counseling, among them relationship issues, sex issues, gender matters, anxiety, depression, and grief.

It is instructive and sobering to review what we now know about the counseling needs of today's college students. Imagine for a moment a professor at my alma mater, or at virtually any other college or university campus today, looking out from the front of a medium-sized lecture hall at a random group of 100 students enrolled in, say, the Biology 101 or Introduction to Psychology or Shakespeare Survey course. Of those 100 students, about 30 have been diagnosed with at least one mental health condition during their lifetimes.[1] The percentage of female students with such a diagnostic history is higher (34.3%) than that of males (22.5%). About 17 of those 100 students report having been diagnosed with two or more mental health conditions during their young lives. If our hypothetical instructor is seeing 10 rows of 10 students each, over a row and a half have been diagnosed with a mental health condition within the past 12 months. Just about 20 students have suffered from depression, 16 have had a diagnosis of anxiety, two members of the class suffer from posttraumatic stress disorder, and about six have attention deficit hyperactivity disorder. If our instructor is well informed, she knows that 18- to 25-year-olds have the highest past-year prevalence of serious mental illness, with 7.4% having suffered functional impairment and 8.7% at least one major depressive episode (University of Minnesota, 2010).

Looking out over those 100 eager faces, it is difficult to believe that nearly half (44%) will have engaged in high risk/binge drinking. That behavior would have consequences, of course, for personal health and safety. Nearly a quarter of the students (24) will report they have at some time had a memory loss caused by excessive drinking. Of particular consequence to our hypothetical professor charged with teaching these students, this behavior would also impact their academic careers: 20 of them would report that they had performed poorly on a test or assignment and 22 would have missed class due to alcohol consumption.

Are these numbers and percentages higher than they were in the misty golden era of my undergraduate days? Perhaps a bit. Advances in psychotropic pharmacology have made it possible for young people with what might once have been debilitating mental illnesses to function well enough to attend college.

---

[1] These statistics are from the *2010 College Student Health Survey Report* of health and health-related behaviors of Minnesota postsecondary students. I assume Minnesota students are typical of those across the nation.

Advances in the law, such as the Americans with Disabilities Act, have mandated that colleges and universities cease barring entry to students because of prior mental disablements. These are, in my opinion, happy and good developments. Moreover, frankly, a need to enroll as many students as possible to fill classrooms and coffers has encouraged college admissions offices to open their doors wider than was probably the case in the mid-20th century. But it is not credible to imagine that my classmates (or, for that matter, the binge-drinking medieval undergraduates at Oxford or Cambridge nearly 1,000 years ago) were dramatically less prone to depression, anxiety, or substance abuse than today's students. What has changed is not the nature of college-age young women and men; it is our awareness of that nature, and our willingness to deal with it.

In the pages that follow, three experienced and highly credentialed counseling professionals, writing from both the clinical and research perspectives, demonstrate that awareness and willingness. Shannon J. Hodges, Kimber Shelton, and Michelle M. King Lyn cover an impressive range of issues here. They begin by positioning counseling services within the university context and trace the development of the profession; they conclude by suggesting the future directions, needs, and challenges for counseling services of the future. The authors note the many and important ways in which counselors and counseling centers do more than respond to students' mental problems: Today they also focus upon prevention, self-help and peer counseling, and, perhaps most importantly, education across the spectrum of counseling-related topics. The midsection and core of the book looks at a wide range of specific mental health issues in today's collegiate culture: depression and anxiety, addictions, crisis counseling, and sexual attacks. And it surveys, comprehensively, the increasingly diverse populations of today's institutions of higher education, and the special needs each of those many populations brings to college. This book will provide an almost encyclopedic survey for counseling professionals. It also maps out an expanding and urgently important territory for those of us who teach or manage at 21st-century colleges and universities.

Not infrequently, a prefatory few words such as those herein are misspelled by students as "forward," rather than the correct "foreword." But in this case, such a spelling would not be an error, but a wise play on words. Hodges, Shelton, and Lyn chronicle the advances of collegiate counseling in the past half-century, and present a compelling case for the need to continue moving "forward."

Samuel Schuman, PhD (1942–2014)
Chancellor Emeritus
University of Minnesota, Morris, Minnesota

REFERENCE

University of Minnesota. (2010). *College student health survey report: Health and health-related behaviors.* Duluth, MN: Author.

CHAPTER ONE

COLLEGE COUNSELING: PAST, PRESENT, AND FUTURE

Shannon J. Hodges

The last decade in college student research suggests college students are under considerable stress, exhibit a number of mental disorders, and take medication (Gallagher, 2011) as routinely as previous generations consumed coffee. Regardless of the fact that most college students are relatively well adjusted, the perception in the public seems to be mental illness is rampant among the college population (Gabriel, 2010). Now, college students experiencing emotional difficulty is nothing new. More than 70 years ago E. G. Williamson, a major scholar in counseling psychology, noted almost that all college students have academic and personal issues that colleges should help them address (1939). Wrenn, a notable student affairs scholar argues that "the only justification for student personnel services is they can be shown to meet the needs of students ... These include both the basic psychological needs of all young people and the specific needs that are the direct results of the college experience" (1951, pp. 26–27). Adjustment to college was often viewed through the lens of *in loco parentis* (literally, in the place of parents) and support usually targeted "homesickness," career, or academic concerns. Despite the support of such luminaries as Wrenn and Williamson, college counseling was certainly rudimentary in its origins, with debate regarding who should provide it, qualifications to be a counselor, and whether it should be focused on academic support or more personal and developmental issues.

College and university counseling has evolved considerably in the roughly 80 years since its arrival in higher education. Initially, many educators argued that faculty were the best professionals to provide counseling to students. In addition to teaching classes, faculty provided academic and even personal advising to their students (Patterson, 1928). Others at the college level held that faculty ought to receive general training in counseling to address normal developmental and academic concerns and that only trained professionals could most appropriately respond to students grappling with psychological issues (Lloyd-Jones & Smith, 1938). On religiously affiliated campuses, clerical professionals provided most personal counsel, particularly as it related to sectarian matters (Lloyd-Jones & Smith, 1938). Thus, in the first part of the 20th century, disagreement and confusion persisted regarding both the nature of counseling and precisely who was best suited to provide it. Specific duties of the counselor, the required degree, and specific training were under debate (Tyler, 1969).

During the years following World War II, large numbers of former servicemen flocked to U.S. campuses courtesy of the GI Bill. Previously, college had almost exclusively been the domain of 18- to 22-year old, White, unmarried, male students and the institution they attended effectively served an *in loco parentis* function. College rules and regulations were very paternalistic as students were given curfews, prohibited to live off campus except under extenuating circumstances, and were sometimes prohibited from marrying. (This author [Hodges] had an aunt who was dismissed from college because she got married at the end of her freshman year!) Racial and gender quotas were imposed by many colleges and disabled students often were simply not admitted (Hodges, 2001). Due to federal legislation, students previously denied access to a college education matriculated to campus; many had a spouse and children in tow and, having experienced World War II, were generally unwilling to be dictated to by college officials (Forest, 1989). Due to the large influx of nontraditional students and their families, campuses strained to address vocational, academic, and personal needs former servicemen presented. The counseling movement assisted with this transition by providing academic and career services to veterans new to the college campus. With the Veterans Administration's emphasis on vocational preparation and job training, university "guidance" services expanded to assist in both academic and vocational development (Forest, 1989). The GI Bill provided a springboard for increasing counseling services on campus and sparked a debate regarding training and degree required to provide counseling services.

The expansion of vocational services paved the way for college counselors to begin addressing social and personal concerns in a counseling context and provided momentum for universities to expand the role of college and university counseling centers (Aubrey, 1977). The following decades gave birth to the Civil Rights and Women's movements, and many of the long held social barriers to higher education for ethnic minorities and women were recognized and revised in most regions of the United States (Aubrey, 1977). Students with families—once prohibited on many campuses—were increasing and the influx of these populations represented a major demographic shift for colleges and universities. Changing social demographics also brought about a sense of pluralism and a much more complex social and cultural atmosphere on campuses. Faculty were now suddenly teaching and advising an older, more diverse student body less hesitant to question authority and its established policies and practices.

CHANGES IN STUDENT AFFAIRS: GROWTH IN COUNSELING AND PSYCHOLOGICAL SERVICES

During this period of expanding and changing populations, additional student affairs professionals were hired in an effort to keep pace with the challenges such growth presented. Administrative roles and functions traditionally performed by the faculty were reassigned to student affairs. Formerly part of the faculty domain, counseling had evolved into a separate professional service. Broader responsibility meant changes to a former vocational guidance role, and the counseling center evolved into providing personal counseling and psychological services offered only by professionals with specialized, graduate training in psychology. Because of the increased emphasis on sensitive issues (e.g., depression, anxiety, sexual concerns), counseling professionals in general as well as those on college campuses began advocating for the developing of ethical standards as well (Forster, 1977).

No longer could the office of the dean of women or the dean of men or campus ministers provide all necessary personal services for students. Campus counseling centers established protocols for addressing specific mental and emotional issues. The need for specialized training for college counselors that went beyond vocational and academic concerns became paramount. This growth in the college counseling profession and the increasingly complex mental health issues counselors were addressing led to a campus identity separate and distinct from other student affairs departments and programs. Though still under the student affairs "umbrella," this diversification and professionalization of the field represented a new direction for counselors and created increased professional opportunities at the college and university level (Forest, 1989).

While changes were occurring in higher education, parallel changes were taking place in psychology and the newly separate profession of counseling. In particular, the emergence and popularity of the vocational guidance movement of the 1950s, which also incorporated "personal" concerns, strongly influenced the college counseling profession (Whiteley, 1984). This emphasis in vocational and personal guidance was instrumental in the development of research-based assessment instruments and in bringing counseling into the mainstream of higher education (Morrill, Oetting, & Hurst, 1974). As "professionalization" of college counseling continued, counseling services continued to change with increasing specialization, representing a significant deviation from its faculty-driven origins. The growth and development of counseling theories also proliferated during this era, with humanistic and behavioral approaches becoming increasingly popular on campuses. An increased sophistication in counseling, assessment, diagnosis, and treatment planning became more developed in the professional literature and more common on college campuses (Morrill et al., 1974).

The growth and increased prestige of the American Psychological Association (APA) also attracted many people to the counseling profession. Counseling psychology emerged as a distinct division of APA in the 1950s (Whiteley, 1984). As the psychology profession grew and became more popular and established, APA developed accreditation guidelines for graduate programs in counseling psychology (APA, 1986). In addition, counselor education and training programs emerged as a separate and distinct field from APA and developed their own graduate programs, ethical standards, and credentialing guidelines (American Association for Counseling and Development [AACD], 1981). This differentiation between counseling psychology and counselor education, two very similar professions with different national memberships, credentialing, ethical standards, and degrees, established the practice of different mental health professionals staffing college counseling centers. Clinical social workers would also began to be hired in greater numbers, while psychiatrists, usually staffing university medical centers, became more common in large university's counseling centers. This multiprofessional approach to staffing college and university counseling centers has proliferated since the 1950s and is evident on the 21st-century campus as college and university counseling centers hire psychologists, counselors, social workers, psychiatrists, and so on. While the term "counselor" is often the operative term, "counselor" can refer to any one of the several mental health professionals. This author (Hodges) will generally use the term counselor though it is acknowledged the term is generic and not specifically referring to any one mental health profession.

So, what had begun a generalist training program for faculty of any discipline working with college students in all aspects of their development gradually had grown and emerged into a specialized field. College and university counselors were becoming more likely to self-identify with their specific field of psychology of counseling as they were the general profession of students affairs. College counseling centers had taken over the role of career/vocational counseling and personal counseling. Most counseling centers increasingly required their staff to hold a doctorate degree in psychology (PhD, PsyD, EdD), a master's in counseling (MS, MA) or in social work (MSW; Hodges, 2001; Morrill et al., 1974). Exceptions to psychologists, counselors, and social workers in college counseling centers still were evident, especially in sectarian colleges, but those were becoming the exception as opposed to the general rule by the late 1950s (Aubrey, 1977). These distinctions among college counseling professionals have become more disparate and increasingly complex and have fostered a keen sense of competition among the professional organizations (e.g., APA, American Counseling Association [ACA], National Association of Social Workers [NASW]).

The Turbulent 1960s

During the 1960s, the face of U.S. college campuses was in the midst of a dramatic shift. Formerly the campus was seen to take on the role of parents, and many institutions were very directive in where students lived, their social life, speech codes, and regulation of off-campus activities (Brubacher & Rudy, 1997). The *in loco parentis* approach had already been strained by ex-servicemen who matriculated to college campuses in the post–World War II period. Former World War II veterans, older and many with spouses and children, were less willing to accept the dominant paternal role college administrators enforced. The institutional solution was to keep older, married students separated from traditional-age college students outside the classroom. Separate living quarters, separate clubs and organizations, and even separate functions were established by many colleges to address older students' different needs and to limit contact with their younger counterparts (Brubacher & Rudy, 1997).

This approach to segregation worked well enough until traditional-age students began to demand more freedoms. In the 1960s, the United States was embroiled in an increasingly unpopular war in Vietnam and many college campuses became settings for conflict among administration, students, and the police. The most egregious campus strife likely took place at the University of California, Berkeley, in the late 1960s and at Kent State in 1970, the latter where several students were shot by National Guardsmen in a protest march. It was also during the 1960s when campuses across the country were becoming more gender balanced and racially integrated. This continued demographic transition from an almost exclusive White, upper middle class, male, Protestant student to a more culturally, ethnically, gender balanced, pluralistic one occurred in a crucible of conflict leading to significant changes for college campuses and subsequently college counseling services.

Changes in Counseling

While changes were occurring in higher education all across the country, concurrent changes were taking place in the fields of counseling and psychology. The desire of colleges to select students with the capacity for academic success and also to help retain students had become paramount at colleges and universities (Forest, 1989). Assessment procedures were fast becoming standard in college and university counseling centers. Clinical assessments such as the Minnesota Multiphasic Personality Inventory (MMPI), Beck Depression Inventory (BDI), and other psychological tests designed to gauge psychological issues were becoming increasingly popular in college counseling centers. Assessments to measure alcohol abuse were also being added to the list of standardized assessments, as colleges realized their students were under increased stress and often self-medicated with alcohol.

Rogers (1957, 1961) initiated significant debate that has continued to the present regarding critical ingredients for successful counseling outcomes. Rogers coined what he called the necessary and sufficient characteristic for counseling success (Rogers, 1961). These optimal conditions are: genuineness, empathy, and unconditional positive regard. Genuineness is the degree to which the counselor is authentic and nondefensive with the client. Genuine counselors are sincere, open with their clients, and do not have hidden agendas. Empathy means understanding the client's world as if it were one's own, but always remembering that it is the client's issue. Unconditional positive regard, sometimes called warmth, refers to the extent to which counselors communicate an attitude of nonjudgmental caring and respect for the client. Rogers (1961) acknowledged the reality that counselors would often encounter clients holding contrary values systems. Counselors, Rogers maintained, must be aware of their own values in order not to try and impose their values onto their clients. At the same time, counselors must not pretend agreement with the client's values, otherwise artificiality can destroy the counselor's authenticity and harm the therapeutic relationship.

Rogers's approach contrasted significantly with earlier Freudian and behavioral models to psychotherapy. Perhaps due to the zeitgeist of the 1960s, humanistic approaches such as that articulated by Rogers and Maslow were becoming increasingly popular on college campuses. Other notable theorists (Carkhuff, 1969; Gazda, 1984) also outlined necessary conditions for creating a therapeutic relationship. They departed somewhat from Rogers's philosophy by maintaining that effective counselors must be intentional in their choice of specific skills in the therapeutic encounter. Many of these skills had a cognitive and behavioral frame of reference (Ellis, 1962). Unlike Rogers, who emphasized the primacy of being a particular type of counselor, they argued that successful counseling involves behaving in particular ways and employing certain measurable goals. These skills, techniques, and goals involved self-disclosure, reframing, treatment plans, and homework outside the session.

Techniques for intervention and counseling had become more common and college counseling had likewise increasingly become more specialized. In psychology, distinctions were made between master's and doctoral degrees. Greater efforts toward requiring credentials of those who practiced psychology had begun. State licensing laws had become more common, with many university counseling centers requiring psychologists to be licensed or license eligible in order to be hired. The growth in size and influence of the APA had a dramatic impact on the face and direction of college counseling (Forest, 1989). As counseling psychology grew from its infancy in the 1950s into a strong movement, counseling center staff also evolved. The influence of the APA was that psychologists would be on the doctorate degree, a specific curriculum, and formal criteria for practicum and internships. At roughly the same time, the American Association for Counseling and Development (later renamed as the ACA), also developed criteria for counselor education training programs that eventually evolved into the Council for the Accreditation for Counseling and Related Educational Programs (CACREP).

Though college counseling had begun with faculty providing the service, it had evolved into a separate and distinct profession by the late 1950s. While specialization (psychologist, counselor, social worker, etc.), degree (doctorate and masters in psychology, counseling, etc.), and credential (licensure and/or national certification) were the lynchpins of the college counseling field, counseling centers remained well within the "family" of student affairs. Furthermore, many student affairs professionals staffing residential life, Dean of Students offices, and career services were trained with a strong counseling emphasis (Brammer, 1977; Parker, 1966; Warnath, 1971). The advantages of counseling training both for the counseling center and throughout student affairs had become well recognized. The American College and Personnel Association (ACPA) had developed a branch of their membership devoted to counseling and psychological concerns and even affiliated with the ACA for several years.

The result of credentialing and specialization was that the college counseling profession emerged as a distinct specialty within student affairs (Forest, 1989; Warnath, 1971). The changes have continued steadily through the 21st century (Bishop, 2006; Hodges, 2001). While specific training in a mental health profession has been standardized for some five decades, the professions representing college counseling have become quite diverse: clinical psychology, counseling psychology, counseling, social work, marriage and family therapy, psychiatry, psychiatric nursing, and so on. Furthermore, college counseling centers vary considerably from large university centers of 50 or more with some attached to a medical center, to small college counseling "offices" staffed by one counselor. With the advent of the community college, and subsequent counseling centers at 2-year institutions, traditionally with a focus on career, vocational, academic and some personal counseling, the profession has, ironically, become more diverse while simultaneously requiring strict credentialing guidelines. In fact, a "counselor" may well be a psychologist or social worker depending on the size and type of institution. Female counseling professionals, who were grossly underrepresented in college counseling until the 1980s, now outnumber men (Gallagher, 2011). As professionalization of the college counseling center has become de rigueur, competition among the various professional organizations representing counseling center staff (e.g., APA, ACA, NASW) has likely increased (Hodges, 2001). The current scenario being played out among the competing mental health professions staffing college counseling centers likely is confusing to most faculty, general student affairs, and certainly students. Though the quality in curriculum, training, and credentialing has certainly improved the strength and quality of the college counseling field, one wonders about the utility of infighting among the disparate professions staffing college counseling.

THE CHANGING FOCUS OF COLLEGE COUNSELING: FROM DEVELOPMENTAL APPROACH TO MEDICAL MODEL

The basic elements of college counseling have changed considerably from the origin of college counseling to the present time. Originally, college counseling was primarily concerned with academic issues (Winston, 1989). This focus shifted to career, personal, and developmental issues over the decades as professional counselors replaced faculty as the primary providers of mental health services on college campuses (Morrill et al., 1974). The last great "phase" of change in college counseling has clearly been away from a developmental model toward a strong mental health focus, with the use of the *Diagnostic and Statistical Manual of Mental Disorders* (*DSM-5* as of 2013) (Kay & Schwartz, 2010). While career counseling continues to be practiced in many college counseling centers, personal and career services have been split on many campuses. The percentage of college students on psychoactive medications has increased dramatically in the past decade (Kay & Schwartz, 2010). While developmental concerns, such as inability to select an academic major, and relationship issues remain common concerns, more serious psychological issues such as anorexia, depression, suicide ideation, and anxiety have risen sharply and show little signs of abating. In fact, depression, along with anxiety, has become the most common psychological ailment on college campuses (Gallagher, 2011). Students presenting at college counseling centers with posttraumatic stress disorder (PTSD) have also increased exponentially, leaving critics to ponder if there is anyone in college who has not been traumatized.

Counseling Director Surveys

There has been a decided shift in the focus of college counseling away from a historical developmental perspective (Forest, 1989) to that of a mental health focus (Kay & Schwartz, 2010). A National Survey of Directors has been conducted annually since 1981 by Robert Gallagher, formerly of the University of Pittsburgh. Each year Gallagher surveys directors of college counseling centers to gauge changes in college mental health issues. Some of the findings from Gallagher's 2011 survey follow:

- 69% of counseling center staff are women
- 64% of centers have access to on-campus psychiatric services
- 91% of directors reported that severe psychological problems continue to be on the rise
- 78% reported crises requiring immediate attention
- 77% reported psychiatric medication issues
- 42% reported self-injury issues
- 42% reported alcohol abuse
- 30% reported problems related to earlier sexual abuse
- 23% reported on-campus sexual assault concerns
- 25% reported career planning issues (2011, pp. 4–5)

These statistics from the longest running survey of college counseling center directors provide a snapshot of the changing focus of the college counseling center. While some college counseling centers, particularly community colleges and small institutions, will continue with career counseling and advising and providing counseling and assessment for undecided majors, most college counseling centers seem almost entirely focused on in-depth psychopathological concerns. Gallagher's survey (2011) is illustrative of the continued shift. Though I (Hodges) have yet to seen any data on the percentage of college counseling centers that have split into a separate office, my sense in dialoging with counseling center staff is that career services are increasingly becoming a separate function on a growing number of campuses. Thus, a traditional branch, if not the very foundation, of college counseling services is increasingly divorced from the counseling center. This may be neither "good" nor "bad" per se, but rather a reality of a much stressed collegiate populace and an overburdened counseling staff.

In addition, Gallagher's survey may provide impetus for the merging of counseling and medical services and this dynamic has also, in my experience, become more common on college campuses. Gallagher has documented that regular psychiatric services have increased significantly over the past two decades (2011), as well as the percentage of students on psychoactive medication, especially selective serotonin reuptake inhibitors (SSRIs; e.g., Prozac, Zoloft, Celexa); there has even been an increase in select antipsychotic medications (e.g., Haldol, Stelazine, Mellaril). An interesting side note to this initial chapter was reviewing two publications on college counseling centers from different eras. Warnath's (1971) *New Myths and Old Realities* certainly was prescient regarding forecasting an age where psychoactive medications would be commonplace among college students. Still, Warnath's text continued to chronicle a college counseling center with a strong developmental focus at the core of its mission. In Delworth, Hanson, and Associates' *Student Services: A Handbook for the Profession,* Forest and Winston wrote separate chapters on the function of college Counselors. Their chapters, "Guiding, Supporting, and Advising Students: The Counselor's Role" (Forest, 1989) and "Counseling and Advising" (Winston, 1989), read like quaint anachronisms of a simpler, more innocent era of higher education. It is not that the topics of Forest and Winston's eminently readable chapters have become extinct on campuses around the country; rather, on an increasing number of campuses, many of the guiding, supporting, and advising functions have likely been farmed out to other campus services to free up counselors to address more in-depth psychological maladies (i.e., major depression, PTSD, bipolar disorder, even schizophrenia).

An Integrative Approach to College Counseling

There are numerous biological, social, and cultural factors that impact the development and functioning of college students. From a biological perspective, the adolescent brain is one in transitional development. The most important of these changes likely relate to cognitive development and emotionality and are found in the prefrontal cortices, hippocampus, and the amygdala (Kay, 2010). The amygdala is responsible for storing emotional "memories" (Van der Kolk & McFarlane, 1996), including traumatic events. The hippocampus is the central learning and memory section of the brain. The maturation of the prefrontal cortex is essential in cognitive processing and executive functioning such as abstract reasoning and self-reflection. The continuing development of these sections of the brain in late adolescents (traditional-age college students) may help explain risk-taking behavior such as unprotected sex, binge drinking, aggression (e.g., fights), and the lack of self-reflection often seen in many college students. Coincidentally, the adolescent period of life-span development is the physically healthiest time in the life span (Kay, 2010), yet incident rates of binge drinking, sexual assault, and risky sexual behavior are real concerns on any college campus (Grayson & Meilman, 2006). There can be little doubt that incomplete late adolescent–early adult brain development plays an important role in the aforementioned maladies (Medina, 2008), though it cannot explain all behavior as many college students have healthy sexual interactions (Granello, Welsh, & Harper, 2006), most do not binge drink (Meilman, Lewis, & Gerstein, 2006), and the majority of college students do not exhibit violent behavior (Van Brunt, 2012).

The documented success in cognitive approaches to counseling would also seem to support the importance of the environment as an important component in addition to biology and genetics. While college counselors must of necessity take into account and screen for psychiatric issues (e.g., major depression, PTSD, bipolar disorder), nonmedical cognitive strategies must also be coupled with medical model treatment so as to maximize student coping strategies and lessen dependence on medication. The "quaint" development approach outlined in this chapter also remains relevant as college students of different ages progress through stages during their undergraduate and graduate school years. Students age, gain weight and muscle mass, have sexual relationships, get married and divorced, have children, graduate and move on to graduate or professional school, or straight into careers. Culture also has been well documented as an exerting important influence on social and even career development (Sue, Arrendondo, & McDavis, 1992) and scarcely anyone in this postmodern age would argue in omitting multicultural considerations such as ethnicity, spirituality, disability, and socioeconomic status. Furthermore, a "wellness" approach focused on identifying client strengths should be employed as clearly it is as important for holistic considerations (Duncan, Miller, Wampold, & Hubble, 2009; Hattie, Myers, & Sweeney, 2004). Thus, the forces impacting a student's emotional well-being are multiple and realistically should be approached from a treatment model that addresses the brain, social and cultural development, and wellness and resiliency factors. For this text, an integrated approach incorporates a broad range of the previously mentioned considerations with regard to counseling college students of all ages.

Ethical and Legal Issues

This chapter began by addressing historical foundations of college counseling, originating with faculty providing services to that of a specialized, highly trained staff of mental health professionals composed of psychiatrists, psychologists, counselors, social workers, psychiatric nurses, and others. The incidence rate of serious traumatic events such as college student suicides, high profile mass killing tragedies such as that at Virginia Tech, Northern Illinois University, and others have spurred campus administrators to push for stronger mental health services, more two-way communication between the counseling center and central administration, and increased effectiveness at recognizing and providing early intervention with high-needs students potentially capable of violence. A practice of suspending potentially suicidal students has been roundly criticized (Grayson & Meilman, 2006; Kay & Schwartz, 2010) and many professionals in the field believe such practice may run afoul of the Americans with Disabilities Act of 1990, which includes mental disorders (Hodges, 2001). Regardless of how professionals in the counseling centers feel, due to potential liability and fears of Virginia Tech–like traumas, this practice is likely to continue if not increase in the future. A more in-depth, detailed review of ethical and legal issues will be chronicled in Chapter 5.

CONCLUSION

This chapter has provided an overview of the historical, developmental, medical, and contemporary considerations regarding college student development (e.g., academic, career, psychological, medical, and wellness) as they apply to college counseling centers. Information from research and national surveys has been included to underscore the important changes in college mental health. College administrators and college counseling center professionals are keenly aware of the need to stay current with changing collegiate mental health issues. Additional complexities such as the emergence of students attending college through the Internet will be explored in a later chapter. Though this chapter has documented significant transition from who provided counseling, to the focus of counseling (e.g., from faculty to professional counselors, from academic and career to the medical model approach) what remains constant is the need to remain current with regard to continuing changes in higher education. Furthermore, as college counseling is provided by numerous members of the mental health professions such as psychiatrists, psychologists, counselors, social workers, and so on, it becomes imperative for such professionals to work across disciplinary lines in order to deliver the best possible mental health treatment. Subsequent chapters highlight additional areas of college counseling.

REFERENCES

American Association for Counseling and Development. (1981). *Ethical standards.* Alexandria, VA: Author.

American Psychological Association. (1986). *The accreditation handbook.* Washington, DC: Author.

Aubrey, R. F. (1977). Historical development of guidance and counseling and implications for the future. *Personnel and Guidance Journal, 55,* 288–295.

Bishop, J. B. (2006). College and university counseling centers: Questions in search of answers. *Journal of College Counseling, 9*(1), 6–19. doi:10.102/j.2161-1882.2006 .tb00088.x

Brammer, L. M. (1977). Who can be a helper? *Personnel and Guidance Journal, 55,* 303–308.

Brubacher, J. S., & Rudy, W. (1997). *Higher education in transition: A history of American colleges and universities.* New Brunswick, NJ: Transaction Books.

Carkhuff, R. R. (1969). *Helping and human relations: A primer for lay and professional helpers* (2nd ed.). New York, NY: Holt, Rinehart, & Winston.

Duncan, B. L., Miller, S. D., Wampold, B. L., & Hubble, M. A. (2009). *The heart and soul of change: What works in therapy.* Washington, DC: American Psychological Association.

Ellis, A. E. (1962). *Reason and emotion in psychotherapy.* New York, NY: Stuart.

Forest, L. (1989). Guiding, supporting, and advising students: The counselor's role. In U. Delworth & G. R. Hanson (Eds.), *Student services: A handbook for the profession* (pp. 265–283). San Francisco, CA: Jossey-Bass.

Forster, J. R. (1977). An introduction to the standards for the preparation of counselors and other personnel services specialists. *Personnel and Guidance Journal, 35,* 596–601.

Gabriel, T. (2010, December 19). Mental health needs seen growing at colleges. *New York Times.* Retrieved from http://www.nytimes.com/2011/us.html?pagewanted=all&_r=o

Gallagher, R. P. (2011). *National survey of counseling center directors.* Alexandria, VA: International Association of Counseling Services, Inc.

Gazda, G. M., Asbury, F. A., Balzer, F. J., Childers, W. C., Phelps, R. E., & Walters, R. P. (1984). *Human relations development: A manual for educators* (3rd ed.). Newton, MA: Allyn & Bacon.

Granello, C. M., Welsh, D. P., & Harper, M. S. (2006). No strings attached: The nature of casual sex in college students. *Journal of Sex Research, 43*(2), 255–267.

Grayson, P. A., & Meilman, P. W. (Eds.). (2006). *College mental health practice.* New York, NY: Routledge.

Hattie, J. A., Myers, J. E., & Sweeney, T. J. (2004). A factor structure of wellness: Theory, assessment, analysis, and practice. *Journal of Counseling and Development, 84,* 354–364.

Hodges, S. (2001). University counseling centers in the twenty-first century: Looking forward, looking back. *Journal of College Counseling, 14*, 65–77.

Kay, J. (2010). The rising prominence of college and university mental health issues. In J. Kay & V. Schwartz (Eds.), *Mental health care in the college community* (pp. 1–20). Chichester, UK: Wiley-Blackwell.

Kay, J., & Schwartz, V. (Eds.). (2010). *Mental health care in the college community.* Chichester, UK: John Wiley.

Lloyd-Jones, E. M., & Smith, M. R. (1938). *A student personnel program for higher education.* New York, NY: McGraw-Hill.

Medina, J. (2008). *Brain rules: 12 principles for surviving and thriving at work, home, and school.* Seattle, WA: Pear Press.

Meilman, P. W., Lewis, D. K., & Gerstein, L. (2006). Alcohol, drugs, and other addictions. In P. Grayson & P. Meilman (Eds.), *College mental health practice* (pp. 195–214). New York, NY: Taylor & Francis.

Morrill, W. H., Oetting, E. R., & Hurst, J. C. (1974). Dimensions of counselor functioning. *Personnel and Guidance Journal, 52*, 254–359.

Parker, C. A. (1966). The place of counseling in the preparation of student personnel workers. *Personnel and Guidance Journal, 45*, 254–261.

Patterson, D. G. (1928). The Minnesota Student Personnel Program. *Educational Record, 9*, 3–40.

Rogers, C. R. (1957). The necessary and sufficient conditions of therapeutic personality change. *Journal of Consulting Psychology, 21*, 95–103.

Rogers, C. R. (1961). *On becoming a person.* Boston, MA: Houghton Mifflin.

Sue, D. W., Arrendondo, P., & McDavis, R. J. (1992). Multicultural competencies and standards: A call to the profession. *Journal of Counseling & Development, 70*, 477–486.

Tyler, L. F. (1969). *The work of the counselor* (3rd ed.). Englewood Cliffs, NJ: Prentice-Hall.

Van Brunt, B. (2012). *Ending campus violence: New approaches to prevention.* New York, NY: Routledge.

Van der Kolk, B. A., & McFarlane, A. C. (1996). *Traumatic stress: The effects of overwhelming experience on mind, body, and society.* New York, NY: Guilford.

Warnath, C. F. (1971). *New myths and old realities.* New York, NY: Free Press.

Whiteley, J. (1984). Counseling psychology: A historical perspective. *The Counseling Psychologist, 12*(1), 1–25.

Williamson, E. G. (1939). *How to counsel students: A manual of techniques for clinical counselors.* New York, NY: McGraw-Hill.

Winston, R. B., Jr. (1989). Counseling and advising. In U. Delworth & G. R. Hanson (Eds.), *Student services: A handbook for the profession* (pp. 371–400). San Francisco, CA: Jossey-Bass.

Wrenn, C. G. (1951). *Student personnel work in college: With emphasis on counseling and group experiences.* New York, NY: Ronald Press.

CHAPTER TWO

MULTICULTURAL COUNSELING COMPETENCY AND DIVERSITY ISSUES

Kimber Shelton

"Multicultural Counseling Competencies = Ethical Practice" (*Arredondo & Toporek, 2004, p. 44*)

The title of Arredondo and Toporek's commentary on the purpose and necessity of multicultural counseling competence is well-suited to begin a discussion on multiculturalism, diversity, and inclusivity in college counseling. Colleges and universities are enjoying a greater diversity of students, staff, and faculty than ever before in U.S. history. To ethically meet the demands of increased diversity on college campuses and within college counseling centers (CCCs), counseling centers must demonstrate multiculturally competent practice.

Definitions for multicultural competence, diversity, and inclusivity are as diverse as what they represent. However, most definitions of multicultural counseling competence are based on the multicultural counseling competencies (MCC) articulated by Sue, Arredondo, and McDavis (1992), which focus on multicultural awareness, knowledge, and skills regarding one's own culture and the culture of the other individuals with whom one works. Simply stated, diversity is "all the ways in which people are different" (Bucher, 2004, p. 1). Directly relevant to the diversity of clients and clinical issues presenting to CCCs, inclusivity emphasizes the necessity of attending to multiple forms of diversity, identities, and culture. Rather than the dominant focus on race and ethnicity, inclusive definitions of multiculturalism and diversity encompass identities such as sex, sexual identity, gender identity, ability, socioeconomic status, spirituality, and acculturation.

More recently, the multicultural literature has highlighted the necessity of attending to multiple identity statuses and intersectionality. For example, the identities of a 30-year-old, divorced, Latina graduate student who is a mother cannot be separated. The combination of this student's identities impacts her lived experiences; therefore, cultural competent therapy accounts for how her intersecting identities impact her reality in the world. Similarly, multicultural competence cannot be viewed as an area of independent practice in counseling centers (i.e., one multicultural seminar, having one person in charge of multicultural initiatives, or only focusing on areas of diversity with certain cultural groups). Furthermore, multiculturally competent practice is not to be viewed as a subordinate, substandard, or menial task relegated to entry-level staff and trainees. Ethical practice within service delivery, peer relationships, research, and training requires the integration of multicultural competence within all CCC operations. Thus, multiculturalism, diversity, and inclusivity are more than additive tasks—they are essential to the provision of ethical, responsible, and quality services to clients, center staff, and the entire campus environment. This chapter briefly explores the diversity composite of U.S. colleges and counseling centers, articulates the standards and requirements of ethics as related to diversity, and provides readers with information and tools for expanded attention to diversity and inclusivity excellence within CCCs.

DIVERSITY ON THE COLLEGE CAMPUS

Today's U.S. colleges and universities appear very different from the appearance 50 or even 25 years ago. Legislation and a changing cultural landscape have opened the doors of higher education to a diverse pool of participants that had previously been excluded from university enrollment. Furthermore, the advances in technology and increased intercultural communication demonstrate a need for universities to prepare students to compete in a global marketplace, thus prompting a greater need for focusing on diversity.

Ethnic minorities represent approximately 40% of the overall population (U.S. Census Bureau: State and County Quick Facts, 2011) and are projected to show a significant increase in population by year 2050 (Ortman & Guarneri, 2010). Asian and Hispanic populations are projected to more than double their 2000 population size by year 2050. In fact, all racial and ethnic populations are expected to grow by 2050, with the exception of the White, non-Hispanic population, which is projected to experience a decline in population (Ortman & Guarneri, 2010). Similar to the overall U.S. ethnic demographic changes, colleges, and universities show increased populations of ethnic minority students. Over the past 20 years or so, the percentage of Asian/Pacific Islander students rose from 2% to 7%, Black students rose from 9% to 14%, and, with the most significant increase in student enrollment, the percentage of Hispanics students rose from 3% to 12% (U.S. Department of Education, National Center for Education Statistics, 2011). The increasing rate of student enrollment of ethnic minorities is in contrast with White students who showed a decreased enrollment status from 83% to 62% (U.S. Department of Education, National Center for Education Statistics, 2011).

International students demonstrate an ever-increasing contribution to the diversity on college campuses. With students coming primarily from India, China, and South Korea, the number of international students studying in the United States continues to rise, comprising approximately 3% of overall enrollment in U.S. colleges and universities (undergraduate 2%; graduate 10%) (U.S. Department of Education, 2009). This is highlighted at the institution of two of the authors in which 127 countries are represented in the overall student body (Georgia Institute of Technology Office of Institutional Research and Planning, 2011). Over the last three decades, there is also increased linguistic diversity within the overall population and U.S. colleges. In 2007, approximately 20% of the population spoke a language other than English at home; of that population, 62% were Spanish speakers. Other languages with over 1 million speakers included Chinese, French, Tagalog, Vietnamese, German, and Korean (Shin & Kominski, 2010).

College campuses show increased diversity in gender, age, and ability status. Since the late 1980s, women have dominated postbaccalaureate enrollment and the rates between 2000 and 2010 steadily increased (62% in contrast to the increased rate of males at 38%). From 2000 to 2010, the enrollment status of adults over age 25 increased 42% and is projected to increase by another 20% by 2020 (U.S. Department of Education, National Center for Education Statistics, 2012). We also see increased rates of individuals with disabilities enrolling in college. Twenty percent of Americans report having some form of disability (Freedman, Martin, & Schoeni, 2004) and many of these individuals are enrolled in college. In 2007, the U.S. Department of Education (2011) reported 11% of undergraduate students reporting having a disability.

Race, ethnicity, nationality, language, sex, age, and ability only touch the surface of diversity on college campuses. Socioeconomic status, political affiliation, religion, sexual identity, gender identity, health status, physical appearance, immigrational status, acculturation, and geographical location among many other identity statuses account for the richness of diversity on campuses. Furthermore, although measurement-related issues exist (see Kettmann et al., 2007; Schwartz, 2006), research and anecdotal data suggest that as well as increased diversity in cultural identities, CCCs are seeing an increased diversity in presenting clinical concerns and increased severity in mental health issues. In their 13-year review of services, Benton, Robertson, Tseng, Newton, and Benton (2003) noted significant increases in the number of students presenting to counseling centers with anxiety, depression, suicidal ideation, sexual assault, abuse, and personality disorders. In another more recent study, it was found that students enter CCCs with multiple presenting concerns and indicated significant disturbance to social and academic functioning (Krumrei, Newton, & Eunhee, 2010). Twenge et al.'s (2010) meta-analysis of MMPI and MMPI-2 scores found an increase in psychopathology in college students in the years 1938 to 2007. Thus, as well as attending to cultural aspects of diversity, multiculturally competent counseling centers must also attend to the diversity of clinical issues appearing in counseling centers and must recognize how culture impacts the presentation of symptomology and how students utilize counseling center services (Smith et al., 2007).

MULTICULTURAL COUNSELING COMPETENCE AND ETHICS

> The provision of professional services to persons of culturally diverse backgrounds by persons not competent in understanding and providing professional services to such groups shall be considered unethical. (Korman, 1974, p. 105, as cited in Sue et al., 1992, p. 480)

There is extensive research on the deleterious impact of providing culturally insensitive counseling services, particularly to groups who have been historically marginalized (for review, see the American Psychological Association [APA], 2003b; Guthrie, 1998/2004; U.S. Department of Health and Human Services [DHHS], 2001). In summary, clinician and systemic cultural incompetence have been related to delayed entry into treatment, premature termination, perpetuation of distrust in mental and physical health care, internal and external stigmization, and emotional scarring of clients. U.S. colleges' history of mistreatment of minority groups combined with the bias and unethical treatment within psychological research and clinical practices may act as significant barriers to mental health services for underrepresented college students.

To better protect and serve vulnerable populations, licensure, accreditation, and professional organizational bodies developed multicultural competence standards of care and guidelines. CCCs are thus required to follow the multicultural ethical guidelines set by the broader psychological community and guidelines specific to college counseling.

Multicultural Counseling Guidelines

Being the most prolific of existing general multicultural guidelines, counseling centers are wise to make use of the MCC model (Sue et al., 1992), which is comprised of a 3 × 3 matrix of characteristics and dimensions. Characteristics are (a) counselor awareness of his or her own assumptions, values, and biases; (b) understanding the worldview of culturally different clients; and (c) developing appropriate intervention strategies and techniques. Dimensions within each characteristic consist of (a) beliefs and attitudes; (b) knowledge; and (c) skill. Although Sue and colleagues did not articulate their model as a stage model, it is commonly considered that counselor development involves, first, understanding one's own identity through engagement in self-awareness and reflective processing; second, building one's knowledge of one's own culture and the culture of others; and, third, demonstrating a skill set of cultural competent interventions.

The APA's 2003 Guidelines on Multicultural Education, Training, Research, Practice and Organizational Change for Psychologists (aka the Multicultural Guidelines) has an established presence in CCCs. The Multicultural Guidelines provides 10 guidelines to aid psychologists in their work with diverse groups across multiple professional settings. In their application of the Multicultural Guidelines to CCC settings, Perez, Fukuyama, and Coleman (2005) note the importance of inclusion of Multicultural Guidelines in direct service, training, and organizational change. They express counseling centers' responsibility to reflect a commitment to multiculturalism in both individual and systemic adherence to the guidelines. In addition to broader guidelines regarding diversity, a number of population-specific guidelines serve as resources for counseling centers. Population-specific guidelines draw attention to the unique issues and experiences particular groups encounter and the importance of addressing individual diversity. Counseling centers that demonstrate proficiency in awareness of both systemic and individual diversity issues place themselves in a position to be culturally responsive to students they serve. Although it is not an exhaustive list, a compilation of multicultural competence and diversity-focused guidelines are presented in Table 2.1.

Ethical Guidelines

Those working within counseling centers are required to abide by the ethical principles of their profession. The relationship between ethical practice and multicultural competence is so aligned that every major counseling/psychological ethics code articulates the necessity of multicultural competence. Of all psychological organizations, the American Counseling Association (ACA) *Code of Ethics* (2005) most directly addresses diversity. The term *diversity* is used 18 times in the ACA *Code of Ethics* and the terms *culture* and *culturally* are used over 40 times (Doverspike, 2007). In fact, the very first paragraph of Section One reads, "Counselors actively attempt to understand the diverse cultural backgrounds of the clients they serve. Counselors also explore their own cultural identities and how these affect their values and beliefs about the

---

TABLE 2.1   Multicultural and Diversity-Related Guidelines

- Advocacy Competencies (Lewis, Arnold, House, & Toporek, 2002)
- Competencies for Counseling With Transgender Clients (American Counseling Association, 2010)
- Guidelines for Assessment of and Intervention With Persons With Disabilities (American Psychological Association, 2012)
- Guidelines for Providers of Psychological Services to Ethnic, Linguistic, and Culturally Diverse Populations (American Psychological Association, 2003a)
- Guidelines on Multicultural Education, Training, Research, Practice and Organizational Change for Psychologists (American Psychological Association, 2003b)
- Guidelines for Psychological Practice With Girls and Women (American Psychological Association, 2007)
- Guidelines for Psychological Practice With Older Adults (American Psychological Association, 2014)
- Guidelines for Psychotherapy With Lesbian, Gay, and Bisexual Clients (American Psychological Association, Division 44/Committee on Lesbian, Gay, and Bisexual Concerns Joint Task Force on Guidelines for Psychotherapy With Lesbian, Gay, and Bisexual Clients, 2000)
- Guidelines for Psychological Practice with Transgender and Gender Nonconforming People (American Psychological Association, 2015)
- Multicultural Counseling Competences and Standards (Sue et al., 1992)
- Association for Specialists in Group Work: Multicultural and Social Justice Competence Principles for Group Workers (Singh, Merchant, Skudrzyk, & Ingene, 2012)
- Strategies for Building Multicultural Competence in Mental Health and Educational Settings (Sue & Constantine, 2005)

Note: Full citations are available in the References section.

counseling process" (ACA, 2005, p. 4). To better respond to individual and cultural differences, revisions were made to the 2002 APA Ethical Standards and Code of Conduct for Psychologists. Language changes to the code's preamble express psychologists' responsibility to "protect civil and human rights," the principle "justice" was created to address fairness, justice, and equality, and changes were made to Principle E: Respect for People's Rights and Dignity, to more directly address psychologists' aspirational behaviors regarding respecting culture and not condoning prejudice. The National Association of Social Workers also made revisions to their ethics code (2008) to better address multiple aspects of diversity. These revisions include Sections 1.05–Cultural Competence and Social Diversity, 2.01–Respect, 4.02–Discrimination, and 6.04–Social and Political Action. Similar language and mandates are present within the American Psychiatric Association Principles of Medical Ethics (2001), and the American Association for Marriage and Family Therapy *Code of Ethics* (2012). Thus, adherence to ethical guidelines requires adherence to multicultural principles.

CCC-Specific Diversity Guidelines

The International Association of Counseling Services, Inc. (IACS) is the accrediting body for CCCs. According to IACS's (2010) Standards for University and College Counseling Services, multicultural competence in intervention and training, and diversity in staff, are requirements for obtainment and retainment of accreditation. CCCs operating within Departments of Student Affairs may also be responsible for adhering to guidelines posed by the Council for the Advancement of Standards in Higher Education (CAS). The mission of CAS includes "promot[ing] the improvement of programs and services to enhance the quality of student learning and development" (CAS, 2008, p. 1), which includes those services provided by CCCs. As well as developing general guidelines for higher education professionals (CAS, 2012), CAS developed specific standards for CCCs, the CAS (2012) Counseling Services Standards. Although diversity, equity, and fairness are consistent themes throughout the revised Counseling Services Standards, Part 7: Diversity, Equity, and Access specifically addresses multiculturalism and diversity. In summary, Part 7 expresses CCCs' responsibility in creating and maintaining an inclusive and welcoming environment, and mandates that counseling centers act as agents of social justice. Part 7 of the Counseling Services Standards is presented in Table 2.2.

TABLE 2.2 CAS Counseling Services Standards—Part 7. Diversity, Equity, and Access

Within the context of each institution's unique mission and in accordance with institutional polices and all applicable codes and laws, counseling services (CS) must create and maintain educational and work environments that are

- Welcoming, accessible, and inclusive to persons of diverse backgrounds
- Equitable and nondiscriminatory
- Free from harassment

(continued)

TABLE 2.2   CAS Counseling Services Standards—Part 7. Diversity, Equity, and Access (*continued*)

CS must not discriminate on the basis of ability; age; cultural identity; ethnicity; family educational history (e.g., first generation to attend college); gender identity and expression; nationality; political affiliation; race; religious affiliation; sex; sexual orientation; economic, marital, social, or veteran status; or any other basis included in institutional policies and codes and laws.

CS must

- Advocate for greater sensitivity to multicultural and social justice concerns by the institution and its personnel
- Modify or remove policies, practices, facilities, structures, systems, and technologies that limit access, discriminate, or produce inequities
- Include diversity, equity, and access initiatives within their strategic plans
- Foster communication that deepens understanding of identity, culture, self-expression, and heritage
- Promote respect about commonalities and differences among people within their historical and cultural contexts
- Address the characteristics and needs of a diverse population when establishing and implementing culturally relevant and inclusive programs, services, policies, procedures, and practices
- Provide staff members with access to multicultural training and hold staff members accountable for integrating the training into their work
- Respond to the needs of all students and other populations served when establishing hours of operation and developing methods of delivering programs, services, and resources; ensure physical, program, and resource access for persons with disabilities
- Recognize the needs of distance learning students by providing appropriate and accessible services and resources or by assisting them in gaining access to other appropriate services and resources in their geographic region

Source: CAS Professional Standards for Higher Education (8th ed.). Copyright © 2012 Council for the Advancement of Standards in Higher Education. Reprinted with permission. No part of the CAS Standards and Guidelines may be reproduced or copied in any form, by any means, without written permission of the Council for the Advancement of Standards in Higher Education.

Diversity as a high priority is also present in other organizations typically involved with CCCs (i.e., the Association for University and College Counseling Center Directors [AUCCCD], Association of American Colleges and Universities [AAC&U], and Association of Counseling Center Training Agencies [ACCTA]). In addition to adherence to psychological ethics codes and organization missions, CCCs do well to familiarize themselves with the ethical codes and principles of organizations that they work closely with, such as the American College Personnel Association (ACPA).

INTEGRATING MULTICULTURAL COMPETENCE AND DIVERSITY IN COUNSELING CENTERS

To adequately address the needs of college students, staff, and the larger campus community, CCCs must operate from a systems base in which the CCC operates as a multicultural organization. As per Sue and Constantine (2005), a multicultural organization is:

... committed (action as well as words) to diverse representation throughout all levels, sensitive to maintaining an open, supportive, and responsive environment, working toward and purposefully including elements of diverse cultures in ongoing operations, carefully monitoring organization policies and practices to the goals of equal access and opportunity, and authentic in responding to changing policies and practices that block cultural diversity. (p. 223)

Multicultural organization development is social justice oriented, believes that inequities are due to monopolies of power, and assumes that conflict is inevitable and not necessarily unhealthy (Sue, 1995). The results of a multicultural organization include improvement in services, productivity, and education (Sue, 1995). Sue identified six multicultural organization values: (a) creates a vision that reflects multiculturalism; (b) is reflective of the contributions of diverse cultural and social groups in their mission, operations, products, and services; (c) values diversity and sees it as an asset; (d) seeks equal access and opportunity through envisioning, planning, and problem-solving activities; (e) recognizes that equal access and opportunities are not equal treatment; and (f) values diversity and works to diversify the environment. Such organizations make intentional efforts to reflect multiculturalism; diversity is reflected in their mission, operations, products, and services; diversity is valued and viewed as an asset; equal access and opportunities do not equate to equal treatment; and they work to diversify (Sue, 1995).

The College and University Counseling Center Multicultural Competence Checklist

Fully integrating multicultural competence and diversity and shifting toward a multicultural organization and social justice agency can be a daunting task for which many counseling centers may feel underprepared. Although checklists and guidelines are available for counseling training and student affairs, specific guidelines and checklists for developing a multicultural organization do not exist for the unique needs of CCCs. The College and University Counseling Center Multicultural Competence Checklist (CUCMCC) (Bathje & Shelton, 2013) was developed to provide specific approaches and strategies that CCCs can use to develop, enhance, and assess their multicultural counseling organizational development.

The CUCMCC was created by reviewing extant literature on measures of multicultural competence (clinician level) and several multicultural competence "checklists" that have been developed for different organizational settings. All items that appeared applicable to the organizational level within a university counseling center setting were selected; several additional items were developed to create a comprehensive list of potential competencies. The list was then reviewed by several university counseling center staff members who were identified as experts in multicultural counseling competence by their peers. The experts identified the most salient and important items for the final checklist.

The CUCMCC contains 56 items designed to evaluate the current status and developmental progress of the organization across time. The identified areas of competence on the CUCMCC include (a) diversity vision, mission, and values, (b) physical environment, (c) leadership and policy, (d) staffing, performance evaluation, and promotion, (e) training and supervision, (f) professional development, (g) clinical services, and (h) consultation, outreach, and advocacy. The full CUCMCC is available in Table 2.3. The remaining section of this chapter on integration of multicultural competence practices is organized by the eight CUCMCC themes.

TABLE 2.3 Multicultural Competence Checklist for Counseling Centers

It is recommended that this checklist be used at least annually to evaluate the status of multicultural competence in your counseling center. The following scale is recommended:
1. Goal not met; regressed since last evaluation
2. Goal not met; no change since last evaluation
3. Goal not met; progress since last evaluation
4. Goal met; but regressed since last evaluation
5. Goal met; no change since last evaluation
6. Goal met; progress since last evaluation

Diversity Vision, Mission, and Values	
1. The center's vision, mission, and values statements specifically address diversity and multiculturalism and/or a specific multicultural mission statement outlines the center's commitment to multiculturalism (Reynolds & Pope, 2003).	/6
2. Staff members are able to articulate the center's multicultural values and mission to the university community.	/6
3. Center has yearly and long-term diversity initiatives that are clearly defined and measureable (Reynolds & Pope, 2003).	/6
4. Diversity initiatives are created in a manner that promotes success: four phases (planning, assessment, implementation, reassessment) (Ingle, 2005).	/6
5. Website information is user friendly, accessible, and communicates the center's diversity values and mission statement.	/6
Physical Environment	
6. The environment in both common areas and individual offices is accessible to persons of all ability and body types (Ponterotto, Alexander, & Grieger, 1995).	/6
7. The environment in both common areas and individual offices reflects valuation of diversity (e.g., art work, magazines, books, décor) (Ponterotto et al., 1995).	/6
8. A review of the environment is performed to identify and eliminate culturally offensive materials (Reynolds & Pope, 2003).	/6

(continued)

TABLE 2.3   Multicultural Competence Checklist for Counseling Centers (*continued*)

Leadership and Policy

9. Multicultural counseling competence is a requirement of ethical practice. As such, center staff follows ethical guidelines as established by accrediting bodies.	/6
10. Leadership articulates a commitment to multiculturalism to staff and endorses multicultural work of staff within the counseling center.	
11. Staff leaders are involved in making organizational and institutional changes, including soliciting support and resources from upper administration (Toporek, Lewis, & Crethar, 2009).	/6
12. The policy and procedures manual clearly states the importance of nondiscrimination, the center's commitment to equity and diversity, and the expectation that all staff will regularly seek opportunities to develop their multicultural competence.	/6
13. Center policies are routinely reviewed and updated as needed to reflect diversity and inclusivity, and are congruent with multicultural literature (Reynolds & Pope, 2003).	/6
14. The center is committed to long-term and systemic/strategic plans for enhancing the center's multicultural competence and educating the entire staff on diversity issues (Sue & Constantine, 2005).	/6
15. The center has an active "multicultural committee" with sufficient resources and funding, and composed of staff and trainees to provide leadership and support with regard to multicultural issues (Ponterotto et al., 1995). Or the center has a "diversity coordinator" who initiates diversity programming and is supported by center leadership and staff.	/6
16. Forums are provided to allow "difficult dialogues" on topics of multicultural issues and diversity climate.	/6
17. Policies and procedures are in place to allow staff from historically marginalized and underrepresented groups to safely give feedback about their experiences of the climate of the center and/or make grievances (Ducker & Tori, 2001).	/6

Staffing, Performance Evaluation, and Promotion

18. The center recruits and retains staff and trainees with social identities that mirrors or surpasses the diversity of the campus student population (i.e., race/ethnicity, gender, ability, sexual/gender identity) (Dana, Behn, & Gonwa, 1992; Pontorotto et al., 1995; Reynolds & Pope, 2003).	/6
19. Members of the permanent staff can fluently provide counseling in the native languages of the largest ethnic/national groups on campus (Dana et al., 1992).	/6

(*continued*)

TABLE 2.3 Multicultural Competence Checklist for Counseling Centers (*continued*)	
20. There is a mechanism for evaluating staff and trainee multicultural competency. Expectations for specific multicultural competencies are documented for staff and staff engages in regular assessment/ evaluation of their multicultural competence (Dana et al., 1992; Reynolds & Pope, 2003).	/6
21. Staff members develop individual multicultural goals on a yearly basis that are assessed (Reynolds & Pope, 2003).	/6
22. Multicultural competence is assessed and given priority in all hiring and promotion decisions (Reynolds & Pope, 2003).	/6
23. Multiple sources of assessment are used to evaluate the performance of the center in the area of multiculturalism (i.e., internal assessment by center staff and clients, and external assessment by a consultant, administration, and/or the wider university community). Assessment is performed regularly (Reynolds & Pope, 2003).	/6
Training and Supervision	
24. Recruitment efforts are made to attain representation of each of the major areas of social identity among the trainees (Ponterotto et al., 1995).	/6
25. Multicultural issues are infused into all topics including professional development, training, and seminars (Reynolds & Pope, 2003).	/6
26. Staff can identify how diversity has been integrated into their training seminars and clearly reflected in seminar syllabi (Ponterotto et al., 1995).	/6
27. Trainee evaluations include assessment of multicultural competence and the multicultural values and mission outlined by the center's multicultural goals and objectives (Perez et al., 2005; Ponterotto et al., 1995).	/6
28. Varied assessment strategies are used to assess trainees, e.g., written and oral measures (Ponterotto et al., 1995).	/6
29. Trainees are provided with multiple strategies for providing multicultural feedback to the counseling center (i.e., supervision, seminar, written program evaluation, meeting with training directors).	/6
30. When training issues arise related to diversity or trainees from underrepresented groups, an effort is made to empower trainees in their remediation and remediation is supportive/formative rather than punitive.	/6
Professional Development	
31. Training and professional development opportunities are regularly offered that focus specifically on cultural issues, and include a sufficient self-reflective component that promotes self-awareness, in addition to knowledge and skills (Dana et al., 1992; Resnick, 2006; Reynolds & Pope, 2003).	/6

(*continued*)

TABLE 2.3   Multicultural Competence Checklist for Counseling Centers (*continued*)

32. Staff has an understanding of how historical and present discrimination, prejudice, and bias impact themselves, clients they serve, and trainees they supervise (Resnick, 2006; Reynolds & Pope, 2003).	/6
33. Staff are encouraged, supported, and rewarded for engaging in scholarly (publications, presentations) and external professional diversity development activities (e.g., training or participation in cultural events) (Reynolds & Pope, 2003).	/6
34. Staff engages in regular self-assessment of multicultural competence using previously developed assessment instruments or center-created assessment instruments (Resnick, 2006).	/6
Clinical Services	
35. Clients are asked about their preferences for a counselor based on important aspects of social identity.	/6
36. Intake forms ask clients about important aspects of their identity (e.g., gender, sexual orientation, race, ethnicity, nationality, ability status, family socioeconomic status, and religion/spiritual beliefs) (Dana et al., 1992).	/6
37. Accurate client demographics are obtained and efforts are made to provide appropriate services to ongoing clients and to recruit populations that underutilize counseling center services.	/6
38. If diagnosis is performed, culture-bound syndromes are listed as diagnostic options.	/6
39. Cultural formulations are created for all clients (e.g., p. 749 in the *DSM-5*, American Psychiatric Association, 2013).	/6
40. Treatment is offered in a variety of formats to meet the needs of different groups (e.g., couples counseling, family counseling, group counseling, consultation, outreach, and education) (Dana et al., 1992).	/6
41. A referral/resource list is available to refer clients for alternate treatments or culturally appropriate forms of support on or near the campus (e.g., community organizations, spiritual organizations, alternative medicine, indigenous healers) (Dana et al., 1992).	/6
42. If the counseling center has session limits, a process exists to allow for exceptions to the session limit based on financial need when free and comparable services are not available within the community.	/6
43. Clients are encouraged to provide feedback about their cultural experiences and climate with regard to their interactions with the counseling center (Ducker & Tori, 2001).	/6

(*continued*)

TABLE 2.3 **Multicultural Competence Checklist for Counseling Centers (*continued*)**	
44. Case conceptualizations and treatment planning are framed within the cultural context of the client.	/6
45. All staff are familiar with the most current multicultural competencies for their profession (e.g., social work, counseling, psychiatry, psychology).	/6
46. If assessment is performed, only culturally appropriate measures, norms, and interpretations are used (Dana et al., 1992).	/6
Consultation, Outreach, and Advocacy	
47. Alternative helping roles are supported, including working outside of the office, advocating for environmental change, and increasing prevention activities (Resnick, 2006; Toporek et al., 2009).	/6
48. Specific diversity-focused outreach programs and workshops are designed and implemented on campus (Reynolds & Pope, 2003).	/6
49. All outreach activities are evaluated to identify the need or opportunity to include components of multiculturalism (Toporek et al., 2009).	/6
50. Opportunity for consultation on multicultural issues is integrated into the center's programming and available to the campus community.	/6
51. There is an emphasis on social responsibility, community engagement, and strong relationships between the counseling center and campus organizations that serve and represent historically marginalized or underserved groups (Lucas & Berkel, 2005).	/6
52. The counseling center maintains a list of resources for clients with financial needs, including but not limited to access to emergency loans, low-cost child care services, low-cost medical or psychiatric services, food pantries, and renter's assistance.	/6
53. Leadership provides periodic updates about diversity initiatives to on-campus media (Ingle, 2005).	/6
54. The center is invested in empowering and advocating for individual clients as well as the larger campus community (Toporek et al., 2009).	/6
55. Staff receives ongoing training regarding advocacy and social justice work and measures.	/6
56. Staff engages in social justice and advocacy work at the individual, center, university, and national levels (Toporek et al., 2009).	/6
Note: May be reproduced for individual or counseling center use. Written permission from author is needed for use in research.	

Diversity Vision, Mission, and Values

As a multicultural organization, CCCs must have a vision that reflects multiculturalism and inclusivity, values diversity as an asset, engages in planning to promote equal access, and works to diversify the entire environment (Sue, 1995). The development and use of a diversity vision, mission, and values statement provide multiple diversity-related benefits to CCCs. First, a diversity mission statement "… identifies its [center's] values and priorities and ideally identifies diversity issues as central to the department or division" (Pope, Reynolds, & Mueller, 2004, p. 64). Therefore, those consulting with or utilizing services at the counseling center are informed of the center's stance on diversity. The intended result publicizing the diversity mission statement is to educate the public, create a welcoming environment, and inform constituent that diversity is a priority. Second, the diversity mission statement serves as a guide for the day-to-day functions of center staff, and creates a template for accountability. The diversity mission statement articulates the responsibilities of the staff and center, thus, the center is held accountable for adhering to the diversity mission statement. An example of a diversity and inclusivity vision, mission, and values statement is presented in Table 2.4.

TABLE 2.4 Georgia Tech Counseling Center Diversity and Inclusivity Vision, Mission, and Values Statement

Vision
To create an inclusive and dynamic space of awareness, respect, and appreciation for all forms of diversity wherein all share the responsibility of fostering and nurturing cultural competence in the service of promoting excellence and leadership of global citizens.

Mission
The Georgia Tech Counseling Center (GTCC) has the primary mission to provide the highest quality of multiculturally competent counseling and psychological care to meet the educational, developmental, and social needs of Georgia Tech as an institution.

Our diverse services range from online resources, community outreach, assessment, prevention, education, and therapeutic interventions. The services are offered with compassion, respect for others and appreciation of individual differences.

Our training program affords experiences in providing direct services within a counseling center setting among a culturally diverse campus population. We seek trainees from diverse backgrounds who value and model diversity, sensitivity, and inclusivity.

GTCC recognizes that intersecting identities, internalized oppression, and socio-political and historical factors adversely impact certain populations. Therefore, we are committed to the development of a culturally diverse and competent staff who aim to respect and empower diverse individuals and groups. Furthermore, we take great pride in our efforts to promote social justice, provide corrective emotional experiences, and decrease stigma.

(continued)

TABLE 2.4 Georgia Tech Counseling Center Diversity and Inclusivity Vision, Mission, and Values Statement (*continued*)

Striving for true diversity and inclusivity is our ultimate goal. With our world and students continually changing, our diversity mission and our center will continue to be progressive and open to change.

Values

Excellence: We believe in providing the highest quality services that facilitate students' and trainees' health and development, based on empirically supported principles and a commitment to continual professional and organizational improvement.

Respect: We believe that every person should be accorded fundamental respect and deserves services that are congruent with their worldview. Our staff is committed to developing the knowledge, awareness, and skills necessary to fulfill this value. We provide services that honor diversity and are inclusive and welcoming of everyone.

Justice: We believe in promoting social justice in our community by advocating for fairness and institutional responsiveness. We seek to change conditions that negatively impact equal access to services, resources, and benefits.

Integrity: We believe cultural competence is achieved through individual and collective accountability and responsibility as guided by ethical standards, professional development, and self-assessment.

Reprinted with permission from Georgia Tech Counseling Center.

Developing a Diversity and Inclusivity Mission Statement

1. *Leadership:* Diversity initiatives that are leader initiated and/or supported have a greater change of successful implementation. Articulating the importance of such initiatives, providing space and opportunity for the creation of such an initiative, and fostering morale are essential components to the development of the mission statement.

2. *Mission statement committee:* Create a diversity mission statement committee. Diversity within the committee can assist with the creation of the thoughtful mission statement. A diverse committee is able to provide a range of diverse ideas based on individual experiences, formal education, and clinical and research strengths. As well as clinical staff, committees may also include trainees and administrative professionals.

3. *Assessment and research:* Prior to constructing a mission statement, committee members assess the current culture, policies, and procedures of the counseling center and university. The committee also explores the diversity-related missions and initiatives of sister institutions and is up to date on current diversity-related research and guidelines.

4. *Incorporate staff:* Staff buy-in is important for a successful mission statement, as such staff members are encouraged to provide feedback and ideas for the mission statement. This can be done in a number of ways. As the committee completes drafts of mission sections, staff feedback is directly solicited. Another way to involve staff is using staff meetings or

retreat time to break staff members into teams and work on different components of the mission. The committee then integrates staff feedback and committee drafts to create a unified document.

5. *Present, post, and advertise the mission statement:* As well as presenting the mission statement to center staff, including the mission statement in policy and procedure manuals, and posting it in the center, the mission statement is also advertised to university groups.
6. *Assessment:* Continually reassess the diversity and inclusivity needs; adjusting mission, vision, and values statement accordingly.

Physical Environment

Diversity and inclusivity are related to the physical environment of CCCs in two specific ways, accessibility and aesthetics. CCCs have limited utility if they are not accessible to a wide range of students. Furthermore, CCCs, particularly those at public universities or at universities that receive government funding, must adhere to the requirements of the Americans with Disabilities Act (ADA, 1990; Americans with Disabilities Amendments Act, 2008). This includes being accessible to persons with physical, mental, cognitive, and learning disabilities. Accessibility is enhanced if the center's doors (and building doors) are wheelchair accessible; has accessible restrooms set up to accommodate various body sizes; has signs and paperwork that accommodate individuals with vision disabilities; and has established emergency evacuation plans for those with physical disabilities. Additional aspects of diversity within the physical environment include having gender neutral or all gender restrooms, and access to restrooms with diaper changing tables.

The aesthetics of the counseling center environment, including waiting areas, hallways, group rooms, and individual counseling offices, should be reflective of the overall value of diversity. This includes magazines, books, artwork, and décor that reflect multiculturalism and is absent of materials that are culturally offensive. CCCs do well to know the populations they serve and should obtain décor that is reflective of their campus community while also being inviting to members who may shy away from obtaining therapeutic services. Waiting rooms that also provide a level of privacy (e.g., placing chairs so that they are not all facing one another or having a private room for students presenting distraught) is another way to demonstrate respect for individual diversity.

Leadership and Policy

Successful integration of diversity, multiculturalism, and inclusivity is challenged without effective leadership and policy. Those in positions of power within the counseling center (e.g., center director) must demonstrate effective multicultural leadership, expect and support diversity competence of staff, create avenues for rectifying areas of multicultural lag, and advocate for the multicultural organization to extend to the larger campus community. Furthermore, leadership is responsible for creating positions aimed at enhancing the center's overall multicultural competence, prioritizing multiculturalism with budget decisions, and rewarding staff who fully participate in cultural development. The presence of ineffective leadership does not negate staff responsibility. Staff may act within their sphere of influence (Pope et al., 2004) and support one another's diversity leadership development.

As well as adherence to professional and ethical guidelines and policies, specific policies are created in the counseling center to promote diversity and inclusivity excellence. Policy and procedure manuals are designed to create an environment of social justice, respect, and change. Considering that the college campus environment is ever changing, policy and procedure manuals are treated as living documents evolving as the counseling center and university change. At a minimum, the policy and procedure manual is current; however, optimally it is progressive in effecting multicultural change.

Intentionality in multicultural competence and diversity excellence is achieved through the creation of a multicultural strategic plan. A strong multicultural strategic plan develops out of a comprehensive needs assessment (i.e., noting current diversity strengths and growth areas) and includes creating specific strategies for addressing individual, group, and institutional dynamics that promote diversity and remove bias. The plan provides strategies for eliminating systemic barriers and discriminatory power structures, building center-wide cultural competence, and advancing policies and practices that enhance diversity. Short-term and long-range goals are concrete, measurable, and sustainable and aligned with the mission of the center and university-wide diversity initiatives. The strategic plan and goal attainment are regularly assessed and staff members are appropriately awarded for their participation and contribution to strategic plan goals and diversity initiatives.

Several options are available to assist CCCs in creating and maintaining multiculturally competent policies and procedures. A multicultural committee that has appropriate authority, funding, and support can help CCCs create and implement diversity initiatives. As well as policies and procedures, multicultural committees may address university-wide diversity initiatives and/or programs, and staff and trainee training. Another option for supporting multicultural excellence is establishing a diversity coordinator position. According to the needs of the university and counseling center, diversity coordinators serve different roles. Diversity coordinator responsibilities may include (a) chairing multicultural and strategic planning committees; (b) consultation with university constituents to enhance diversity-focused relations; (c) development of training and educational opportunities for staff, trainees, and the university population; (d) assessment of the center's diversity needs; and (e) provide expertise in providing services to underrepresented groups. While establishing such a position highlights the center's value of diversity and assists the center's achievement of a higher level of multicultural competence and diversity excellence, the diversity coordinator position does not negate other staff members' multicultural responsibilities. Just as a counseling center may have a training coordinator or group coordinator, all staff are expected to participate in training or leading the groups. The same principle applies to diversity; even with a diversity coordinator position, all staff are required to participate in diversity initiatives.

Staffing, Performance Evaluation, and Promotion

Building a multicultural organization is not only beneficial to those served at the counseling center, but is also highly beneficial for those employed within the center and the counseling center as a whole. Higher levels of job satisfaction, organization commitment, trust, positive evaluation of management, lower turnover, and absenteeism are correlated with perceived fairness and organizational justice (Bratton, Callinan, Forshaw, & Sawchuk, 2007). Similarly to the experience of clients, staff also appreciate when their identities are valued and respected.

From an efficiency standpoint, the center benefits overall from staff diversity and cultural competence. Many counseling centers struggle with an unbalanced ratio of clinical staff to clients. This struggle places counseling centers in a position in which they are unlikely to meet the needs of a significant population of students and referral becomes a primary treatment modality. In an effort to meet the needs of students who present to counseling centers, centers may not have the physical resources to reach out to communities of students that are in need of services yet are less likely to directly seek counseling services. A diverse staff offers opportunity for innovative solution-finding and unique service and treatment ideas, which can lead to creative strategies for better meeting student needs or resolving the staff-to-student imbalance.

As multiculturally competent practice is to be infused throughout all center policies and practices, multicultural competence must be considered in recruitment, retainment, and promotion of staff. Also specific to recruitment, retainment, and promotion, a multicultural organization is aware of systems of oppression that have historically kept certain communities out of employment positions and aims to rectify such practices if they exist within the center. The counseling center should employ clear procedures for routine evaluation of staff multicultural competency and initiatives. Staff members should work with administration to develop attainable multicultural goals (Reynolds & Pope, 2003) and the center should reward staff for their multicultural leadership. Some counseling centers may wish to invite outside agencies to help assess the center's and staff's overall level of adherence to multicultural organizational development (Reynolds & Pope, 2003).

Training and Supervision

CCCs have a responsibility for providing multicultural training and supervision to trainees. This includes infusing multicultural principles in training seminars, case conference meetings, clinical staff meetings, and supervision, and recruiting a diverse cohort of trainees to add to the richness of the center. Multicultural training focuses on increasing trainees' self-awareness and knowledge regarding different cultures, and helps build skills for working with diverse populations (Resnick, 2006; Reynolds & Pope, 2003).

In order for staff to provide trainees with such training, staff must first demonstrate multicultural counseling competence and recognition of how biases may impact their work with supervisees (Resnick, 2006). This can be acquired through staff consultations, as well as continued diversity education.

Trainees' orientation to the counseling center's multicultural mission and diversity values can occur prior to their practicum or internship start date. The center's website, statements regarding training, and practicum and internship interviews should all exhibit the center's commitment to multiculturalism and diversity. During orientation, staff explicitly share the center's multicultural expectations by discussing policy and procedure manuals, providing detailed multicultural objectives in training manuals, and providing syllabi that clearly articulate multicultural expectations (Ponterotto, Casas, Suzuki, & Alexander, 1995).

Like other staff members, trainees are evaluated for their multicultural competence and adherance to policies and principles presented in the mission and vision statements (Perez et al., 2005). Staff members are expected to take the lead in addressing and initiating conversations regarding diversity-related issues (Constantine, 1997), and for providing trainees with both written and oral feedback that is attentive to the learning style of trainees. Multicultural competence can be evaluated at a developmental level and, when needed, remediation interventions are provided in a manner that empowers cultural competence and are void of being unnecessarily punitive.

It is unrealistic to assume that staff will have superior multicultural knowledge and competence in all areas. In fact, trainees have much to offer CCCs in terms of multicultural development and can be respected as a benefit to the center. Therefore, as well as providing trainees with feedback, feedback is regularly elicited from trainees and they are provided with multiple ways to provide such feedback in a way that is safe and without repercussion.

Professional Development

Effective counseling requires that practitioners are well versed in the historical and sociopolitical realities and cultures of their clients, trainees, and themselves. Considering that complete and full multicultural competence is never completely attained and development of multicultural competence is a continuous process, counseling center staff engage in ongoing multiculturally oriented professional development opportunities. At the individual level, staff can focus on multiculturally competent professional development through journal and book reading, and being afforded the opportunity to attend diversity-related conferences and workshops. As well as administrative assessment of multicultural competency, staff must intentionally enhance their cultural competence through regular self-assessment of their competence levels, which can be assisted by center-created assessments of previously developed assessment instruments (Resnick, 2006).

Organizational structures can also be developed to improve the multicultural competence of those within the counseling center. For one, staff should be encouraged and rewarded for their multicultural scholarship, excellence in training, and professional development. Additionally, centers can provide specific diversity-focused training. Centers can invite experts in the area of diversity to provide specific trainings to center staff and staff are encouraged to provide trainings in their area of diversity expertise.

In addition, centers can implement regular and on going multicultural training. For example, Florida State University's Counseling Center created clinical teams that regularly engaged in "difficult dialogues," with the purpose of building multicultural competence (Fukuyama & Delgado-Romero, 2003). Georgia Tech's Counseling Center has a similar series titled "Invited Dialogues," where, during a monthly meeting, senior staff engage in self-awareness and multicultural competence–building activities. At the end of each year, the Invited Dialogues series is assessed through use of confidential online surveys and changes are made to improve next year's series.

A 1-hour talk is typically insufficient for providing in-depth understanding of any diversity-related issues. Centers can enhance specific diversity under-standing through creation of a year-long cultural concentration. As well as gen-eral diversity-related content, staff and trainees are encouraged to focus on a specific diversity theme in case presentations, journal discussions, seminars, and supervision. For example, Georgia Tech recently completed a theme focused on improving the services provided to transgender identifying students. Over the course of the year, staff completed a Safe Space training, attended an in-house workshop led by an expert in working with transgender clients, arranged a panel discussion with transgender individuals, presented clinical cases focused on transgender clients, and watched a documentary and read journal articles related to transgender issues. By the end of the year, center staff expressed a significant increase in knowledge and skills for providing affirmative services to transgender identifying students.

Clinical Services

Culture impacts clients' view of therapy, help-seeking behavior, expectations, and communication style. Given this, cultural considerations and conceptual-izations are instrumental in helping clients reach their goals and increase self-efficacy. To assist in destigimization and to demonstrate the center's focus on culture, client paperwork and forms must be culturally appropriate (Dana, Behn, & Gonwa, 1992). This includes being accessible to students with vision or learning difficulties, using nonbiased language, and providing multiple identity indicators. A secondary goal of inquiring about identity characteristics is to prime college students to consider their multiple identities and help to prepare them for work and to thrive in a global marketplace. To further estab-lish an environment in which clients feel open and accepted, clients are asked their counselor preference in terms of specific individuals or identity statuses. If clinically appropriate and available, such preferences are honored.

To create an appropriate cultural case conceptualization, clinicians must obtain adequate information about the background and identity of cli-ents. This involves using assessments that have been culturally normed and clinical interviews that prompt for diversity-related discussions. Since staff should be knowledgeable about the history of overpathologizing minority groups and the Western ideals in which psychotherapy is based, efforts should be made to identify and appropriately utilize culture in therapy and acknowledge culturally bound diagnoses to properly treat students. Interventions are also culturally informed and appropriate for the individual student being served. Several models exist for helping clinicians assess and address culture within the therapeutic environment. For example, the ADDRESSING Model was developed to assist counselors in organizing and addressing complex cultural issues in therapy (Hayes, 1996). ADDRESSING is an acronym for age and generational influences, disability, religion, ethnicity, social status, sexual orientation, indigenous heritage, national origin, and gender. The model can be used to "(a) raise awareness of and challenge one's own biases and areas of inexperience, and (b) consider the salience of multiple cultural influences on clients of minority cultures" (p. 334).

To best meet the needs of a diverse student population, multiple modes of treatment should be made available. This includes providing individual, group, couples, and family counseling (Dana et al., 1992). When the counseling center is the not the best venue for supporting students, appropriate referrals are made to community providers or options given for alternative treatments (Dana et al., 1992). This may involve connecting students with community organizations, providers with specific identities preferred by students, ingenious healers, spiritual organizations, and medical professionals. A primary stressor and cause for premature dropping out of college is financial limitations (Public Agenda, 2011); CCCs should make efforts to provide adequate services to students experiencing financial hardship or who have limited financial resources and make referrals to community resources. This may mean making appropriate adjustments to session limit requirements if free or if comparable and accessible services are not available in the community, as well as referrals for access to emergency loans, low-cost child care services, low-cost medical or psychiatric services, food pantries, and renter's assistance.

CCCs can also improve their multicultural competency by soliciting ongoing feedback from clients (Ducker & Tori, 2001). Centers can provide confidential means for providing feedback, as well as encouraging direct feedback throughout therapy. Using a Likert scale, such assessment questions may include, "How satisfied are you with how your counselor respects your background, culture, and identity (e.g., ethnicity, gender, sexual orientation, religion, nationality, ability status)?" and "How satisfied are you with how your group counselor(s) respect(s) your background, culture and identity (e.g., ethnicity, gender, sexual orientation, religion, nationality, ability status)?" This feedback is used to further the multicultural organization's development, and evaluate staff competence in individual and group therapy.

Consultation, Outreach, and Advocacy

CCCs as multicultural organizations strive to be places of prevention and change, and are leaders in advocacy and support to the campus community. This requires staff to step outside of their therapy offices and use alternative modalities to engage with the broader community. As such, staff engage in multiculturally focused consultation, outreach, and advocacy. Counseling centers that are leaders in diversity work will likely be a sought-after resource by other campus groups such as housing, Greek life, faculty members, parents and/or student groups, and organizations. Counseling centers should be prepared to provide multicultural consultation regarding addressing cultural or cross-cultural issues with students, handling acts of intolerance or hate, invited speakers to the campus, and updating policies or completing diversity-focused assessment.

Outreach programming serves many functions on the college campus. For one, many counseling centers are understaffed; providing outreach allows CCCs to provide services to students who may not be able to access services offered within the center. Additionally, outreach programming and education may be sufficient in addressing the mental health needs of particular students, thus reducing the necessity for them to enter treatment later. Providing outreach serves to normalize counseling, destigmatize therapy, and can provide students with a specific contact for further consultation. Multicultural awareness is present in outreach activities in two ways. First, multicultural principles should be visible in all outreaches; for example, stress management outreaches acknowledge how culture impacts our perception and coping abilities. Second, specific diversity-focused outreaches can be constructed to reach identified populations or to provide general multicultural skill building. As per IACS, outreach "... programs should be responsive to sexual/relational orientation, gender identity, racial, cultural, disability and ethnic diversity among students, and reach students who are less likely to make use of traditional counseling services" (p. 5). As with any strong marketing, diversity-focused outreaches are likely to do better with catchy, innovative titles to keep the audience's attention. Keeping in mind cultural stigma related to counseling, titles that are depathologizing are most appropriate. For instance, students may be less likely to attend "Interracial Relationships" and more likely to attend a program titled "#interraciallovin!"

When areas of injustice are present on the campus, the CCC provides individual therapy and support, as well as acting as an advocate and ally by engaging in social justice work. Social justice has been described as:

> Social justice is both a process and a goal. The goal of social justice is full equal participation of all groups in a society that is mutually shaped to meet their needs. Social justice includes a vision of society in which the distribution of resources is equitable and all members are physically and psychologically safe and secure. (Bell, 2007, p. 1)

A social justice framework is applicable to all functions of CCCs including therapist's self-awareness, the provision of clinical services and training, working within the university community, and the relationship with the civic community (Smith, Baluch, Bernabei, Robohm, & Sheehy, 2003). Take the situation of Justus for example. Justus is a busy PhD student with mild depressive symptoms who is struggling to find time during the week to exercise and spend quality time with his partner, Dominic. Justus's therapist is aware of the therapeutic benefits of exercise on mood, and would ideally encourage Justus to invite Dominic to work out with him at the university gym, thus allowing them to spend quality time together before Justus must return to his lab. His therapist is aware that their university does not provide domestic partner benefits; therefore, Dominic is not able to access the university gymnasium. Justus's therapist empathizes with his presenting concerns and provides tools for mood enhancement, expresses her frustration regarding university policy, and encourages Justus to find creative ways of working out with Dominic during the day (e.g., going for runs on campus). Justus's therapist then organizes with other campus allies to address university policies that are discriminatory to same-sex couples. In doing such, Justus's therapist has attempted to be responsive to Justus's presenting concerns, while also confronting systemic issues that jeopardize the mental well-being of clients in same-sex relationships.

Within the university setting, other counseling centers' social justice initiatives may be related to:

1. Addressing oppressive relationships between international graduate students and advisors
2. Lack of access to mental health services and inadequate service delivery to minority groups (e.g., veterans, student athletes, ethnic minorities, LGBTQ students, students with disabilities)
3. Producing culturally informed marketing and advertisement aimed at stigma reduction
4. Advocating for policies that encourage student safety (e.g., Good Samaritan policies)
5. Providing diversity-related consultation, outreach and training (e.g., Safe Space trainings, "difficult dialogue" meetings, intercultural communication, sexual assault, and violence training)
6. Evaluating the climate of the counseling center and university community
7. Responding to societal, political and geographical needs of students (e.g., immigration reform, gun violence)
8. Serving on committees and creating policy to assist the university's transition in effectively meeting the needs of diverse student groups

Practitioners may not be trained in advocacy work, thus leadership improves the overall multicultural effectiveness of the center by providing advocacy and social justice skill training opportunities. In regard to evaluation, leadership also ensures that all staff participates in multicultural focused consultation, outreach, and advocacy work and that outreaches are evaluated.

CONCLUSION

Multicultural initiatives should not be seen as only a means for helping minority or marginalized groups, but instead should be viewed as a means for improving the overall campus climate for all students, staff, and faculty. Research demonstrates that increased diversity sensitivity on college campuses positively impacts the experience of targeted groups and majority groups alike (Smith, 1997). CCCs can establish themselves as diversity campus leaders by striving for diversity excellence in counseling center staff and trainees, responding to clients in culturally appropriate manners, and creating systemic change on campus to produce a welcoming cultural climate.

REFERENCES

American Association for Marriage and Family Therapy. (2012). *Code of ethics.* Washington, DC: Author.

American Counseling Association. (2005). *Code of ethics.* Alexandria, VA: Author.

American Counseling Association. (2010). American Counseling Association competencies for counseling with transgender clients. *Journal of LGBT Issues in Counseling,* 4(3–4), 135–159. doi:10.1080/15538605.2010.524839

American Psychiatric Association. (2000). *Diagnostic and statistical manual of mental disorders* (4th ed., text revision). Washington, DC: Author.

American Psychiatric Association. (2001). *The principles of medical ethics with annotations especially applicable to psychiatry.* Washington, DC: Author.

American Psychiatric Association. (2013). *Diagnostic and statistical manual of mental disorders* (5th ed.). Arlington, VA: Author.

American Psychological Association. (2002). Ethical principles of psychologists and code of conduct. *American Psychologist, 47,* 1597–1611.

American Psychological Association. (2003a). *APA Guidelines for providers of psychological services to ethnic, linguistic, and culturally diverse populations.* American Psychological Association (APA), Public Interest Directorate. doi:10.1037/e305082003-001

American Psychological Association. (2003b). Guidelines on multicultural education, training, research, practice, and organizational change for psychologists. *American Psychologist, 58*(5), 377–402. doi:10.1037/0003-066X.58.5.377

American Psychological Association. (2007). Guidelines for psychological practice with girls and women. *American Psychologist, 62*(9), 949–979. doi:10.1037/0003-066X.62.9.949

American Psychological Association. (2012). Guidelines for assessment of and intervention with persons with disabilities. *American Psychologist, 67*(1), 43–62. doi:10.1037/a0025892

American Psychological Association. (2014). Guidelines for psychological practice with older adults. *American Psychologist, 69*(1), 34–65. doi:10.1037/a0035063

American Psychological Association. (2015). *Guidelines for psychological practice with transgender and gender nonconforming people.* Retrieved from http://www.apa.org/practice/guidelines/transgender.pdf

American Psychological Association, Division 44/Committee on Lesbian, Gay, and Bisexual Concerns Joint Task Force on Guidelines for Psychotherapy With Lesbian,

Gay, and Bisexual Clients. (2000). Guidelines for psychotherapy with lesbian, gay, and bisexual clients. *American Psychologist, 55*, 1440–1451.

Americans with Disabilities Act of 1990, 42 U.S.C. § 12111(9).

Americans with Disabilities Amendments Act of 2008, § 2(b)(5), 122 Stat. at 3554.

Arredondo, P., & Toporek, R. (2004). Multicultural counseling competencies = ethical practice. *Journal of Mental Health Counseling, 26*, 44–55.

Bathje, G. A., & Shelton, K. (2013). *The College and University Counseling Center Multicultural Competence Checklist.* Unpublished manuscript.

Bell, L. A. (2007). Theoretical foundations for social justice education. In M. Adams, L. A. Bell, & P. Griffin (Eds.), *Teaching for social justice: A sourcebook* (2nd ed., pp. 1–14). New York, NY: Routledge.

Benton, S. A., Robertson, J. M., Tseng, W.-C., Newton, F. B., & Benton, S. L. (2003). Changes in counseling center client problems across 13 years. *Professional Psychology: Research and Practice, 34*(1), 66–72.

Bratton, J., Callinan, M., Forshaw, C., & Sawchuk, P. (2007). *Work and organization behaviour.* New York, NY: Palgrave Macmillan.

Bucher, R. D. (2004). *Diversity consciousness: Opening our minds to people culture and opportunities.* Upper Saddle River, NJ: Pearson.

Constantine, M. G. (1997). Facilitating multicultural competency in counseling supervision: Operationalizing a practical framework. In D. B. Pope-Davis & H. L. K. Coleman (Eds.), *Multicultural counseling competencies: Assessment, education, and training, and supervision* (pp. 310–324). Thousand Oaks, CA: Sage.

Council for the Advancement of Standards in Higher Education. (2008). *General CAS standards.* Retrieved from http://www.cas.edu/getpdf.cfm?PDF=E868395C-F784-2293-129ED7842334B22A

Council for the Advancement of Standards in Higher Education. (2012). *CAS Professional Standards for Higher Education.* Retrieved from http://www.collegecoun seling.org/cas-counseling-standards

Council for the Advancement of Standards in Higher Education. (2012). *Standards and guidelines.* Retrieved from http://www.collegecounseling.org/cas-counseling -standards

Dana, R. H., Behn, J. D., & Gonwa, T. (1992). A checklist for the examination of cultural competence in social service agencies. *Research on Social Work Practice, 2*(2), 220–233.

Doverspike, W. F. (2007). Ethics and diversity. *Georgia Psychologist, 61*(3), 3.

Ducker, D., & Tori, C. (2001). The reliability and validity of a multicultural assessment instrument developed for a graduate program in psychology. *Professional Psychology: Research and Practice, 32*, 425–432.

Freedman, V. A., Martin, L. G., & Schoeni, R. F. (2004, September). Disability in America. *Population Bulletin, 5*(3), 3–32.

Fukuyama, M. A., & Delgado-Romero, E. A. (2003). Against the odds: Implementing multicultural competencies in a counseling center on a predominantly White campus. In G. Roysircar-Sodowsky, D. S. Sandhu, & V. E. Bibbins (Eds.), *A guide-book: Practices of multicultural competencies* (pp. 205–216). Alexandria, VA: Association for Multicultural Counseling & Development.

Georgia Institute of Technology Office of Institutional Research and Planning. (2011). *2011 Georgia Tech mini fact book.* Retrieved from www.irp.gatech.edu, http://www.irp.gatech.edu/wp-content/themes/GeorgiaTech/MFB-Archive/MFB11.pdf

Guthrie, R. V. (1998/2004). *Even the rat was White: A historical view of psychology.* Upper Saddle River, NJ: Pearson Education.

Hayes, P. A. (1996). Addressing the complexities of culture and gender in counseling. *Journal of Counseling and Development, 74,* 332–338.

Ingle, G. (2005). Will your campus diversity initiative work? *Academe, 91*(5), 13–16.

International Association of Counseling Services, Inc. (2010). *Standards for university and college counseling services.* Retrieved from http://www.iacsinc.org/IACS%20STANDARDS%20rev%2010-3-11.pdf

Kettmann, J. D. J., Schoen, E. G., Moel, J. E., Cochran, S. V., Greenberg, S. T., & Corkery, J. M. (2007). Increasing severity of psychopathology at counseling centers: A new look. *Professional Psychology: Research and Practice, 38,* 523–529.

Korman, M. (1974). National conference on levels and patterns of professional training in psychology: Major themes. *American Psychologist, 29,* 301–313.

Krumrei, E. J., Newton, F. B., & Eunhee, K. (2010). A multi-institution look at college students seeking counseling: Nature and severity of concerns. *Journal of College Student Psychotherapy, 2*(4), 261–283. doi:10.1080/87568225.2010.509223

Lewis, J., Arnold, M. S., House, R., & Toporek, R. L. (2002). *Advocacy competencies: Task Force on Advocacy Competencies.* Alexandria, VA: American Counseling Association.

Lucas, M. S., & Berkel, L. A. (2005). Counseling needs of students who seek help at a university counseling center: A closer look at gender and multicultural issues. *Journal of College Student Development, 46,* 251–266.

National Association of Social Workers. (2008). *Code of ethics.* Washington, DC: Author.

Ortman, J. M., & Guarneri, C. E. (2010). *United States population projections: 2000 to 2050.* Retrieved from http://www.census.gov/population/projections/files/analytical-document09.pdf

Perez, R. M., Fukuyama, M. A., & Coleman, N. C. (2005). Using the multicultural guidelines in college counseling centers. In M. E. Constantine & D. W. Sue (Eds.), *Strategies for building multicultural competence in mental health and educational settings* (pp. 160–179). Hoboken, NJ: Wiley.

Ponterotto, J. G., Alexander, C. M., & Grieger, I. (1995). A multicultural competency checklist for counseling training programs. *Journal of Multicultural Counseling & Development, 23*(1), 11–20.

Ponterotto, J. G., Casas, J. M., Suzuki, L. A., & Alexander, C. M. (1995). *Handbook of multicultural counseling.* Thousand Oaks, CA: Sage.

Pope, R. L., Reynolds, A. L., & Mueller, J. A. (2004). *Multicultural competence in student affairs*. San Francisco, CA: Jossey-Bass.

Public Agenda. (2011). *With their whole lives ahead of them: Myths and realities about why so many students fail to finish college*. Retrieved from http://www.publicagenda.org/files/theirwholelivesaheadofthem.pdf

Resnick, J. L. (2006). Strategies for implementation of the multicultural guidelines in university and college counseling centers. *Professional Psychology: Research and Practice, 37*(1), 14–20. doi:10.1037/0735-7028.37.1.14

Reynolds, A. L., & Pope, R. L. (2003). Multicultural competence in college counseling centers. In D. B. Pope-Davis, H. L. K. Coleman, W. M. Liu, & R. L. Toporek (Eds.), *Handbook of multicultural competencies*. Thousand Oaks, CA: Sage.

Schwartz, A. J. (2006). Are college students more disturbed today? Stability in the acuity and qualitative character of psychopathology of college counseling center clients: 1992–1993 through 2001–2002. *Journal of American College Health, 54*, 327–337.

Shin, H. B., & Kominski, R. A. (2010). *Language use in the United States: 2007*. American Community Survey Reports, ACS-12. Washington, DC: U.S. Census Bureau. Retrieved from http://www.census.gov/hhes/socdemo/language/data/acs/ACS-12.pdf

Singh, A. A., Merchant, N., Skudrzyk, B., & Ingene, D. (2012). Association for specialists in group work: Multicultural and social justice competence principles for group workers. *Journal for Specialists in Group Work, 37*(4), 312–325.

Smith, D. G. (1997). *Diversity works: The emerging picture of how students benefit*. Washington, DC: Association of American Colleges and Universities.

Smith, L., Baluch, S., Bernabei, S., Robohm, J., & Sheehy, J. (2003). Applying a social justice framework to college counseling center practice. *Journal of College Counseling, 6*(1), 3–14.

Smith, T. B., Dean, B., Floyd, S., Silva, C., Yamashita, M., Durtschi, J., & Heaps, R. A. (2007). Pressing issues in college counseling: A survey of American College Counseling Association members. *Journal of College Counseling, 10*, 64–78.

Sue, D. W. (1995). Multicultural organization development: Implications for the counseling profession. In J. G. Ponterotto, J. M. Casas, L. A. Suzuki, & C. M. Alexander (Eds.), *Handbook of multicultural counseling* (pp. 474–492). Thousand Oaks, CA: Sage.

Sue, D. W., Arredondo, P., & McDavis, R. J. (1992). Multicultural counseling competencies and standards: A call to the profession. *Journal of Multicultural Counseling and Development, 20*(2), 64–88. doi:10.1002/j.2161-1912.1992.tb00563.x

Sue, D. W., & Constantine, M. G. (2005). Effective multicultural consultation and organizational development. In M. G. Constantine & D. W. Sue (Eds.), *Strategies for building multicultural competence in mental health and educational settings* (pp. 212–226). Hoboken, NJ: Wiley.

Toporek, R. L., Lewis, J. A., & Crethar, H. C. (2009). Promoting systemic change through the ACA Advocacy Competencies. *Journal of Counseling & Development, 87*, 260–268.

Tori, C. D., & Ducker, D. G. (2004). Sustaining the commitment to multiculturalism: A longitudinal study in a graduate psychology program. *Professional Psychology: Research and Practice, 35*(6), 649–657. doi:10.1037/0735-7028.35.6.649

Twenge, J. M., Gentileb, B., DeWall, C. N., Ma, D., Lacefield, K., & Schurtz, D.R. (2010). Birth cohort increase in psychopathology among young Americans, 1938–2007: A cross-temporal meta-analysis of the MMPI. *Clinical Psychology Review, 30,* 145–154.

U.S. Census Bureau: State and County Quick Facts. (2011). *Data derived from population estimates, American community survey, census of population and housing, state and county housing unit estimates, county business patterns, nonemployer statistics, economic census, survey of business owners, building permits, consolidated federal funds report.* Retrieved from http://quickfacts.census.gov/qfd/index.html

U.S. Department of Education. (2009). *International students in the United States.* Retrieved from http://nces.ed.gov/programs/coe/indicator_ins.asp

U.S. Department of Education, National Center for Education Statistics. (2011). *Digest of Education Statistics, 2010* (NCES 2011-015), Chapter 3. Retrieved from nces .ed.gov/pubs2011/2011015.pdf

U.S. Department of Education, National Center for Education Statistics. (2012). *Digest of Education Statistics, 2011* (NCES 2012-001), Chapter 3. Retrieved from http://nces .ed.gov/fastfacts/display.asp?id=98

U.S. Department of Health and Human Services. (2001). *Mental health: Culture, race and ethnicity. A supplement to Mental Health: A Report of the Surgeon General.* Rockville, MD: U.S. Department of Health and Human Services, Public Health Office, Office of the Surgeon General.

CHAPTER THREE

ESSENTIAL SERVICES IN COLLEGE COUNSELING

Michelle M. King Lyn

College counseling centers (CCCs) are an integral part of the campus community regardless of the size and administrative structure of the institution. As such, it is important for centers to provide multifaceted services to students and to the university at large. Counselors in most CCCs serve as important consultants in crisis intervention and crisis management. Counselors also provide consultation to students, faculty, and staff, and educate the campus community about social and psychological issues. However, the most common and essential function of a CCC remains providing direct clinical services to students. The purpose of this chapter is to provide an overview of the essential services in CCCs that are not detailed in other chapters of this book.

Determining the best direct clinical services to provide has been a question raised and addressed by many professional organizations at the national and international level. One leading organization, the International Association of Counseling Services, Inc. (IACS), provides accreditation standards and utilizes well-defined criteria to accredit college and university counseling centers around the world. The most recent IACS standards for accreditation (2012) state that counseling services should serve the following four important functions on a college campus:

1. Provide counseling to students for issues that require professional intervention
2. Assist students in meeting their educational goals by playing a preventive role and teaching new skills to help them be successful in college and beyond
3. Support healthy growth and development of students by providing outreach and consultation to the campus community
4. Contribute to campus safety

This chapter examines essential direct clinical services provided to students to meet the four functions as delineated by IACS, specifically: (a) individual counseling; (b) group counseling; (c) couples and family counseling; and (d) assessment and testing.

INDIVIDUAL COUNSELING

The most recent survey of university and CCC directors indicates that individual counseling is still the primary service provided to students at all counseling centers. However, data suggest that over time, centers have relied less on individual counseling to meet the needs of the campus community (Gallagher, 2012). The context in which university counseling centers provide individual counseling to students on campus has shifted according to trends in the field. Services are consistently in high demand, resources for funding and staffing are limited, and some evidence suggests college students are presenting with more significant pathology and severity of issues. All of these factors, individually and collectively, have impacted the provision of individual counseling services on university campuses.

According to the directors who participated in the most recently published National Survey of College Counseling, 88% believed that the trend of students with more severe issues presenting for services has continued (Gallagher, 2012). The majority of them (55%) indicated using specific strategies to address the higher demand for services and the increased severity of problems. The most commonly reported strategies of the directors include (a) identifying student with significant issues early and forming interdisciplinary committees to intervene with these students (e.g., Students of Concern Committees); (b) spending more time training faculty to recognize and refer students in distress; (c) providing targeted skills training for students to provide them with coping strategies; (d) expanding external referral networks; (e) training faculty and other campus staff working with students to normalize emotional distress for students; and (f) increasing training for counseling center staff to work with difficult cases.

It can be especially challenging to meet the needs of students seeking individual therapy in the context described earlier, especially when the number of counseling center staff is limited relative to the number of students on campus. Most college and university centers find it difficult to stretch resources to meet the needs of the student body with regard to providing individual counseling (Gallagher, 2012). The IACS standard for the optimal student-to-staff ratio in CCCs is 1 full-time equivalency (FTE) staff member for every 1,000 to 1,500 students (IACS, 2012). While the standard is defined by IACS as "aspirational," many centers fall short of the standard and are motivated to find ways to "do more with less." Some common ways of serving students under the constraint of limited staff resources include the following: (a) offering short-term counseling and imposing session limits; (b) providing brief and targeted interventions other than individual psychotherapy; and (c) developing nontraditional models of delivering clinical services, which might combine both strategies given in (a) and (b).

Short-Term Individual Counseling

Offering time-limited and short-term counseling is how most contemporary counseling centers meet the needs for individual counseling as a primary intervention. Over the past 15 years, there has been some discussion in the college counseling literature about the implementation of session limits (Wolgast et al., 2005). In 2012, Gallagher reported that 77% of directors either promoted their services as short-term or utilized session limits. In addition, the national mean number of sessions in the same survey was 6.2 with a range of 0 to 60. The mean number of sessions has been consistently close to six in the directors' survey and in counseling center outcome studies for several years (Choi, Buskey, & Johnson, 2010; Wolgast et al., 2005). The trend suggests students generally elect short-term counseling over long-term options.

The primary goal of imposing session limits was to maximize resources and limit wait times for individual counseling services. However, beyond the practical reasons related to demand for services, time-limited counseling offers benefits specific to the college population. Eichler and Schwartz (2010) proposed several reasons that brief therapy might be considered optimal for CCCs:

1. Students often have a focus on the here and now and present situational concerns
2. Culturally diverse clients may consider counseling as a mechanism for seeking expert input on addressing a specific problem and may be less interested in insight-oriented therapy
3. Developmental issues may be addressed using psychoeducation in combination with brief therapy as intervention

Furthermore, Carlson (2004) offers the following perspective on the use of short-term therapy with college students:

The toddler finds exploration of the external world exciting for a while, but then needs a respite. Similarly, the undergraduate student is often fascinated with exploring his or her internal world, but frequently has a fluctuating capability to stay with the exploration. Although this need for a respite to "refuel" varies for each individual depending on his or her separation-individuation from parental figures, it is particularly common among first year and sophomore students who often return to the counseling center to continue their exploration later in their stay at college. (p. 48)

Even considering the potential benefits of short-term counseling in CCCs, there are still potential problems, barriers, and challenges to implementing time-limited or brief therapy. Eichler and Schwartz (2010) noted that assessment of clinical need is an important aspect of determining appropriateness for brief counseling. Some important traits to look for when assessing potential fit for brief therapy are students who express positive use of therapy in the past, state a desire for a reduction in symptoms, present with situational issues, show a capacity toward internalization and introspection, and have the ability to establish rapport, openness, and trust in relationships (Eichler & Schwartz, 2010). It is clear not all students presenting to CCCs will meet such criteria. For those who do not, the dilemma often becomes whether more harm than good may be done if a student is only seen for a few sessions. Eichler and Schwartz (2010) further point out the potential for students feeling a "false sense of hope" or abandonment if termination and transfer for continued care is not handled appropriately.

Students may also present with different levels of motivation and readiness for change that will also impact the benefit received from short-term counseling. The four-stage transtheoretical model presented most recently by Norcross, Krebs, and Prochaska (2011) is widely cited and outlines varying stages at which individuals are willing to address their concerns. The first stage, *precontemplation*, occurs prior to one's acknowledgment of problem. The next stage, *contemplation* involves one acknowledging the existence of a problem and exploring actions that will bring the desired change. *Preparation* is the third stage, which involves further identifying changes that need to be made. Next, the *action* stage is the phase where actions are taken to make change. The final stage, *maintenance*, involves revisiting previous changes and solidifying change.

Most counseling techniques are designed to help individuals presenting in the *action* phase of change. Students may be best suited for brief counseling or counseling center interventions when they are prepared to take action and make changes. Counselors working with students in earlier stages may attempt to move the student to the next level of change by providing psychoeducational information. It is also helpful to move students toward the action stage by raising their awareness about the problems they are just beginning to acknowledge. The application of the Norcross et al. (2011) model or a similar model of change in stages is an important tool in the assessment of fit for time-limited services. College counselors may be trained to use stages of change and appropriate therapeutic interventions. Such training would streamline the process of meeting students where they are while providing efficient and effective time-limited individual counseling.

Session Limits in CCCs

It has been established that many CCCs limit the number of individual sessions students can have in a given time frame. According to the Gallagher (2012) study, most counseling centers offer session limits in the 6- to 15-session range. Contrary to this trend, Lunardi, Webb, and Widseth (2006) offer an alternative approach where sessions are unlimited. In a study of 404 students using the counseling center, they found that 75% of their sample utilized less than 20 sessions during their matriculation time at the college. They assert that the majority of students in the developmental stage of late adolescence prefer to take breaks from therapy where they can test what has been learned in therapy on their own. The data from both Gallagher (2012) and Lunardi et al. (2006) suggest that students will self-select a time-limited approach, thus it is not imperative for centers to impose strict session limits.

The movement toward session limits is reactionary to the demand for services, yet some research has emerged substantiating session limits may have clinical significance as well. For example, Wolgast et al. (2005) examined the number of sessions at a CCC that were required for students to see significant change in their symptoms. They examined students taking the Outcome Questionnaire-45 (OQ-45) pre- and postcounseling. Only those students who were significantly impaired prior to counseling and then scored in the functional score range after counseling were included in the final analysis. A total of 914 counseling center clients were included in the study.

The purpose of the study was to develop guidelines based on clinical evidence for decision making with regard to session limits. Furthermore, the authors challenged counseling center administrators to balance session limit decisions with demands on counseling center resources. The findings indicated that students with less severe symptoms at intake required 14 sessions to show clinically significant change. Students with moderate to severe symptoms at intake required 20 sessions to demonstrate clinically significant change. Thus, centers with session limits less than 14 may consider whether they offer sufficient services for even those students presenting with mild symptoms.

Wolgast et al. (2005) offer several interesting implications for their study that are applicable today and may provide solutions for the challenges created by session limits. For one, they indicated the need for centers to hire more therapists to meet clinical demands. In addition, outreach can be used as a preventive intervention to address mental health concerns before students come to the counseling center. They also suggest the need for graduate training programs to adequately prepare aspiring college counselors to provide short-term therapy within the current environment of CCCs. Finally, they suggest that more empirical research is needed in CCCs to inform decisions about services and staffing.

Some authors have presented specific theoretical models that are effective with college students in time-limited therapy. In one example, Carlson (2004) outlines a time-limited approach of working with college students from a psychodynamic perspective—intensive short-term dynamic psychotherapy (ISTDP). Before using this approach with students, an assessment of their ego strength, defenses, and reality testing must be done. Other criteria in determining goodness of fit for this approach include having a history of meaningful attachments, ability to relate well with the therapist, being psychologically minded and motivated, and performing at a reasonably high level socially and academically. Carlson (2004) purports that many college students will meet these criteria and thus could benefit from this approach. The process of therapy includes identifying and breaking down defenses, identifying and expressing repressed emotions, altering relational patterns between self and others, making behavior changes in the identified problems areas, and restructuring thoughts about self and feelings. Carlson (2004) maintains that college counselors have brief time windows to make lasting impacts on the lives of students and the ISTD approach takes full advantage of those opportunities.

Regardless of the short-term model used or the exact number of sessions allowed, most agree on the importance of absolutely the best treatment possible while understanding the limitations of brief approaches. Strategies for ensuring the highest quality of short-term care include the following:

1. Staying updated with literature on college counseling trends and models for services delivery.
2. Being aware of the needs on a specific campus. A needs assessment can help determine what the particular campus wants or needs from the perspectives of faculty, staff, and students.
3. Providing professional development for staff to attend conferences focused on college mental health and counseling center administrative best practices.
4. Obtaining client feedback regarding their experiences of brief intervention.

Nontraditional Models of Clinical Service Delivery

Single Session

It is very common for students to attend one counseling session and then terminate services. Research has consistently indicated that one is the modal number of sessions for most CCCs. Minami et al. (2009) found 39% of students attended only one session across an 8-year study between 1999 and 2007. In addition, Choi et al. (2010) reported 19% of 78 students in their sample attended one session, creating a mode of one session.

Due the mode of one trend, it is important for the first session to involve not only assessment and understanding of the problem for the student but providing some level of intervention. Traditional intakes involve the clinician gathering data from clients in a 60- to 90-minute session. A single session model of brief therapy encourages the therapist to provide intervention in the first session. Students may expect to receive suggestions from the counselor and recommendations during the first and potentially only session. Students in college today are more likely to be knowledgeable and experienced and comfortable with counseling. They are thus more likely to be consumers with expectations during the first session. The expectation lends itself to counselors being more proactive during initial sessions, especially in brief and time-limited models.

Stepped-Care Model of Service

The process for traditional clinical services models usually entails a student coming in to fill out initial paperwork and then meet with a counselor for an intake appointment or equivalent. The first appointment (initial assessment, initial consultation, intake, etc.) can range in time from 60 to 120 minutes depending on the center. After the intake, the student may be assigned to weekly individual counseling, group counseling, or couples counseling if appropriate. Students may also be placed on a waitlist if the preferred mode of treatment is unavailable due to high demand for treatment. In order to meet higher service demands, it is important for centers to develop alternative and innovative service models different from traditional service models where all students are assigned to an individual counselor.

Another problem with the traditional model is that not all students are suited for weekly individual counseling for a variety of reasons. Also, not all students are seeking individual counseling and this may not be a preferred method of treatment for them. For example, research indicates that ethnic minority students prefer more informal counseling modalities such as advising or mentoring over traditional psychotherapy. Cultural competency requires that such alternatives may be provided when clinically appropriate rather than insisting that students participate in weekly individual counseling. Another reason that weekly one-on-one counseling may not be the best option for some students is that their presenting issues may be more immediate or situational requiring crisis intervention or brief consultation about specific question or issues. In this scenario, the clinical need of the student may not rise to the level of needing ongoing individual counseling. Finally, it may also be the case that group counseling is indicated as a better method for the presenting concern, such as students with interpersonal and relational concerns who have the capacity to tolerate the anxiety that may come from being in group.

Two of the three authors of this book work full-time in a university counseling center implementing an innovative model designed to initially assign students to the least intensive level of care. It was employed due to the increased demand for individual counseling and the lack of growth in the number of staff counselors. Data were gathered by the center staff over a several year period to determine a more efficient way of delivering clinical services to students. The model that emerged is called the "stepped-care model" in which students are evaluated initially and then assigned to the least resource intensive service that meets their needs.

The first "step" and level of intervention consists of psychoeducational workshops provided by the counseling center staff. The workshop topics were selected according to the most common presenting problems of students seeking services at the center. Specifically, it was determined that the primary workshops would address anxiety symptoms, depression, relationship issues, and academic concerns. Psychoeducational workshops focus on providing information and context for the presenting problem, building skills for coping, and providing opportunities for interactive and experiential learning and growth related to the topic. Some topics that seem to be popular are stress management, cognitive behavioral principles for dealing with anxiety and depression, and relationship issues.

For students assigned to individual counseling, they are allowed up to 16 sessions. Pinkerton, Talley, and Cooper (2009) suggested about 16 sessions being optimal, based on national data.

Evidence-Based Practice and Effectiveness of College Counseling

Research on evidence-based practice (EBP) saw a surge in the 1990s and early 2000s. The research was used to validate and standardize treatment for certain diagnostic categories such as anxiety, depression, and eating disorders. Many of the studies were performed in clinical settings other than university and CCCs. The literature validating treatment and investigating EBP in university and CCCs is just beginning to emerge.

Cooper, Benton, Benton, and Phillips (2008) noted reasons that EBP research has not been well suited for CCCs. One reason that seems to be consistent with other counseling center literature suggests counselors of college students tend to be eclectic in their treatment styles. Thus, college counselors were less likely to subscribe to manualized treatments. This assertion led to an examination of university counselors' perceptions and use of EBP. It was found that counselors at centers in different cities and states, regardless of years in practice, gender, and primary profession, utilized research to inform their practice. Furthermore, there was slight difference in ethnicity where non-White counselors relied less on EBP than their White counterparts. The authors thought this was due to less EBP for non-White groups. The findings support the scientist practitioner models on which most training programs are based.

Treatment Effectiveness in Counseling Centers

Treatment effectiveness in a counseling center is typically measured by using a valid and reliable clinical assessment pre- and postcounseling. Counseling centers must conduct outcome studies to demonstrate the utility and significance of their services, especially when budgets are tight in higher educational settings. The financial security of some counseling centers and center staff may be tied to good counseling outcome assessment and demonstrated effectiveness of treatment.

Researchers such as Choi et al. (2010) have examined counseling outcomes for students and the impact on academic functioning. Beyond retention rate and grade point average (GPA), Choi et al. examined the usefulness of counseling by looking at student improvement in three areas: symptom reduction, problem-solving ability, and academic function as defined by measures of academic adjustment (AA) and institutional attachment/goal commitment (IA/GC), which were chosen by the authors instead of GPA or another measure of academic functioning. The assessments were chosen by Choi et al. because they differ from the retention data gathered in past studies. Of the 78 students in their sample, the results were strong in showing improvement in all three areas. The authors propose there is significant overlap in personal and academic functioning. Their results indicated that for the students who showed the most significant reduction in symptoms pre- and postcounseling, those students were the most committed to achieving their academic function. The study results, although limited in generalizability, provide support for the benefits of counseling on multiple aspects of student success and functioning.

Another recent study looking at outcome data and effectiveness of CCC services yielded positive results indicating effective treatment for that center (Minami et al., 2009). The results suggested that students presenting with higher symptomology on the Outcome Questionnaire (OQ-45) showed improvement after two or more sessions in counseling. In terms of those clients that were difficult to treat, students with substance abuse issues and those with physical symptoms accompanying psychological symptoms were found to be more treatment resistant and those with intimacy issues took more sessions to treat. There were also some demographic trends, such as students who indicated their relationship status was separated or divorced had poorer outcomes than students who were partnered or married. Minami and colleagues emphasize the need for more research on effectiveness of college counseling services.

Research on ethnic minority students seeking assistance in college counseling settings is also limited. One such study examining the effectiveness of counseling for ethnic minority students also utilized the OQ-45 pre- and posttreatment to investigate outcomes for a large nationwide sample of African American, Asian American, Caucasian, and Latino students seeking services in counseling centers (Kearney, Draper, & Baron, 2005). The study found that cross-ethnicity students benefited from counseling, though Caucasian students attended more sessions than the other ethnic groups. These findings suggest the need for continued work in stigma reduction for students of color seeking counseling.

Despite higher utilization by Caucasian students, Asian American students presented with more serious symptomology at intake. Latino and African American students followed and Caucasian students were last. Regarding ethnic minorities, Kearney et al. (2005) conclude that counseling center services are effective. In particular, African American students presented as the least distressed of students of color but utilized counseling services more than other students of color. This suggests some centers are providing helpful services to African American students. However, centers need to continue to work toward providing culturally competent services including outreach and interventions designed to address stressors faced by ethnic minorities in the campus environment (e.g., discrimination, lack of support, social isolation).

Additional Considerations in Individual Interventions With College Students

Staff Training in Alternative Models

It is essential for college counselors to have a wide repertoire of clinical assessment and intervention skills. Some recent authors suggest that all CCC staff should be trained in providing brief or time-limited individual counseling (Eichler & Schwartz, 2010). Furthermore, therapists providing traditional intakes and long-term therapy and those counselors providing single session and brief therapy utilize a very different set of skills. If trained in the former model, additional training for staff would assist counselors in adopting skills specifically for the college counseling setting. Offering or attending frequent staff trainings and providing opportunities for staff to be up to date with counseling treatment needs and trends would be considered best practices.

In both long-term and short-term therapy, gathering historical data about early childhood and adolescent experiences must be done skillfully by asking open-ended questions, guiding clients through developmental milestones in their lives, and inviting clients to engage in story telling about themselves. Additional training for staff to work in a short-term framework might focus on how to balance detailed information gathering with rapport building to put the client at ease relatively quickly. In a brief therapy model, clinicians are building rapport initially and at the same time reviewing symptoms with the clients. Information is focused on the present concerns and issues rather than on historical data. Brief therapy clinicians have to be selective and knowledgeable about the potential impact of historical data such as family mental health history, past occurrence of current symptoms, and the impact of substance use and traumatic events.

Instead of gathering a full history, such a focused history aids in conceptualization and formulating a potential diagnostic picture and treatment recommendations to share with clients during the first session. It is important to provide feedback or direction during the first meeting, particularly since college students may not return for a second session. Thus, taking advantage of each session to offer clear direction ensures the student has some type of take away from the initial contact, which may be their only contact. In addition to feedback and suggestions, clinicians may even elect to provide information about diagnostic impressions and treatment recommendations at the end of the first session.

Consideration of Client–Therapist Relationship in Brief Counseling With College Students

The strength and nature of the relationship between client and counselor facilitates successful brief therapeutic intervention. Gelso et al. (2012) have developed a model outlining three aspects of the relationship that have equal importance but serve different functions. The model, called the Tripartite Model of the Psychotherapy Relationship, includes a working alliance, a transference–countertransference configuration, and a real relationship (Gelso et al., 2012). Relatively speaking, the working alliance and transference/countertransference have received more attention in the literature than the real relationship. Thus, Gelso et al. (2012) developed an instrument to assess and better understand the real relationship. The instrument looks at the "real relationship" between client and therapist and measures genuineness and realism as aspects of this relationship. In a fast-paced CCC setting, the development of the "real relationship" may be important in retaining clients and getting them to buy into the counseling process. With so many students only attending counseling once and then not returning, it seems important that a genuine connection with a counselor would allow for a greater sense of meaning and commitment to resolving issues. In the actual study by Gelso et al. (2012), the results showed that when clients and therapists both had strong perceptions of the real relationship, counseling outcomes in brief therapy were stronger.

A key implication of the present results is that therapists should pay close attention to their personal or real relationships with their clients. If they sense that the client is not developing a personal connection early in treatment, or if the therapist is not developing an increasingly sound real relationship from his or her perspective, it may be wise to explore this with clients or make efforts to strengthen the relationship. Kivlighan (2012) has theorized about the process of strengthening the real relationship. Although cautioning against a prescriptive approach, he suggests generally that the therapist focus on being truly himself or herself with the client and avoid an impersonal, so-called professional front. Similarly, the real relationship is fostered by the therapist's ongoing attempt to grasp empathically what is going on inside the client. However, to date no empirical research exists on ways of strengthening the real relationship, especially when it appears to be weak. This is a research topic that would seem to be of particular importance.

Referrals and Scope of Services

The process of making effective referrals is a skill that requires the implementation of important components. One important component of making referrals is to clearly define eligibility and scope of services for students utilizing the counseling center. Some centers utilize a contract to clarify the nature of brief services including session limits and expectations of client and counselor. It is also important for counselors to be consistent in the message and limits given to students in order to provide equitable access to services. The utmost consideration to ethical principles and best practices for CCCs providing brief therapy should be given. Furthermore, policies, procedures, and guidelines about brief services should be developed by clinicians in different positions of influence and power within the center. Campus stakeholders and referral sources also need to be as aware of the counseling center policies in order to accurately represent to students what might happen when referred to the counseling center.

In addition to campus partnership, counseling centers must work to establish a wide-reaching network of clinicians in the geographical area of the campus. The outside clinicians should optimally range in specialization and clinical expertise and have working knowledge of CCC clients or understanding of higher education environments. Barriers for students seeking off-campus referrals may be no health care insurance or limited income. In consideration of keeping costs low for students being referred, some counseling centers try to find clinicians who offer pro bono services to clients and may make this a criterion for all referral resources.

Reasons for providing referral might include a clinical need for intensive work, which would include sessions more often than once a week, reaching session limit, preference of the student to see someone off campus, desire for long-term ongoing work, or a need for highly specialized treatment. Clear policies and procedures regarding scope of services and guidelines for making referrals help simplify the referral process for both students and staff. Staff may have varying degrees of comfort with making referrals but can consult written policy or one another as needed. It also is important for staff to be consistent in their rationales for making referrals so students will not feel dismissed.

Providing appropriate and good referrals is an important service to offer students. Students may be intimidated or overwhelmed by the process of finding a therapist and having the guidance of counseling center staff may improve their overall comfort level with seeking therapy. Staff can reassure students by referring them to a known clinician. It can be helpful to let students know about the therapist's approach or whether the clinician himself or herself once worked at the counseling center making the referral. Some of these techniques build a personal connection, which makes it more likely for the student to follow through with referral. Students may also be inclined to provide a release of information (ROI) allowing two-way communication between the referring center and the clinician.

GROUP COUNSELING

Group therapy is considered by many to be an optimal mode of treatment for college students (Johnson, 2009; Rutan & Stone, 2001). These authors note that group therapy can be utilized to help college students achieve important developmental tasks in college such as forming a sense of one's identity, forming intimate relationships, and finding an appropriate balance between independence and dependence. Furthermore, it is important and healthy for college students to broaden their worldview and seek out new experiences with diversity.

Group therapy offers an ideal format for accomplishing many of the developmental tasks of late adolescence and young adulthood. Group should be a safe place for students to practice and develop interpersonal skills such as setting boundaries, learning coping skills, and building self-awareness. Finally, group can serve as the family away from home for many students and provide a corrective experience for students seeking to distance themselves from maladaptive patterns in their family of origin (FOO). Essentially, group therapy can offer students a better understanding of themselves in relationship to others.

Ribeiro (2013) discusses group therapy for college students as a rich environment to explore multiple aspects of identity such as race, ethnicity, gender, class, ability, and sexual orientation among others. Groups serve as a mirror image to larger societal dynamics in which college students can discover more dimensions of their own identity and better understand their impact on the world. The goal of a group is to facilitate all of these processes in a healthy, challenging, and affirming environment. Students often feel vulnerable revealing hidden or apparent aspects of their identity, thus safety is of great importance.

In addition to general and identity development, group offers many other benefits for college students. One can argue there is a direct match between the common developmental needs of college students and the curative factors of group most notably outlined by Yalon and Leszcz (2005). Specifically the experience of the curative factors—altruism, catharsis, development of socializing techniques, existential factors, group cohesiveness, imitative behavior, imparting information, installation of hope, interpersonal learning, universality, and the corrective recapitulation of the primary family group—facilitate the achievement of intimacy in relationships over social isolation. Thus, it is not surprising many studies have documented the efficacy of group for several college student issues.

The Efficacy of Group Therapy With College Students

Some clinical issues of students in group therapy in a CCC might include relationship problems, social anxiety, fear of intimacy, abandonment issues, and low self-esteem. Some group interventions are manualized and have a pre-scribed process of treatment. For example, Kilman, Urbaniak, and Parnell (2006) examined a manualized treatment for attachment problems in relation-ships as well as a skills-focused relationship group program. In the study, two groups of undergraduate students participated in the two different types of treatments. The authors compared each program's effectiveness with treating unhealthy relationship beliefs, self-esteem issues, anger issues, and patterns of relationship problems. At the end of the treatments, students in both groups changed unhealthy relationship beliefs to healthier ones, reported fewer rela-tionship problems and tested higher on self-awareness. In addition, those in the attachment-focused group had higher self-esteem and improved their anger management skills (Kilman et al., 2006). The study suggests both the manual-ized attachment group and the skills-focused relationship group are beneficial for college students presenting with a variety of issues and provides further support for the effectiveness of group intervention for college students.

Specific types of group therapy have also been examined in terms of effectiveness with college-age students with social anxiety. In order to explore the best treatment method for students presenting with social anxiety, Bjornsson et al. (2011) examined cognitive behavioral group therapy (CBGT) and group psycho-therapy treatments in several groups. The pre- and post-group measures indicated that both types of group were found to be effective, and one was not more effective than the other regarding results. In comparison to one another, CBGT had more attrition as compared to the general psychotherapy group. Bjornsson et al. (2011) suggest this may be due to a lesser focus on group dynamics and relationships among group members, leading to less commitment. The authors suggest that CBGT has shown good results with social anxiety in the past, but it can perhaps be modified to attend to relationships in the group as a way to decrease attrition.

Administration and Coordination of a Group Program

College counselors come from a variety of fields and training programs includ-ing social work, marriage and family therapy, professional and rehabilitation counseling, and psychology. As such, they are an eclectic group of professionals who borrow from different theoretical approaches to group therapy such as systems theory, cognitive behavioral theory, and psychodynamic theory. Also, counseling centers may be innovative in the types of groups offered according to the student population at respective schools. For example, one counseling center model combines the benefits of expressive arts with group therapy for students (Boldt & Paul, 2011). Group members are encouraged to explore their emotions and express themselves through art assignments such as family genograms, self-metaphors, and other "artistic prompts" that emerge from the students' goals and themes from the group. The authors note the importance of using screenings to assess the proper fit of the group members as well as the balance of process and structure so students have time for creating, connecting, and sharing. One mode or type of group will not work in all centers; therefore, it is helpful to have a team of staff, typically led by a group coordinator, to brainstorm and bring to life ways of utilizing group therapy to serve students.

Group therapy is a proven effective treatment modality. In addition to providing an effective way of addressing common student concerns, group therapy is also an efficient way of meeting the demand for services. Depending on the focus and goals of the group, group therapy can allow 8 to 12 students to be seen during a 60- to 90-minute therapy hour. Group may offer a solution to the counselor-to-student ratio problem faced by most centers as discussed earlier in this chapter.

While IACS maintains that group therapy "should" be offered at CCCs, there are some common barriers to the administration and coordination of a successful group program. One common challenge is that students come to the counseling center most often expecting to receive individual counseling services. They are usually unaware of group therapy as an option for treatment and even less aware of the benefits of group therapy. Due to the lack of knowledge and understanding about group therapy as a more effective mode of treatment for some issues as outlined in the previous section, counseling center clinicians are placed in the role of educating students about group.

Hahn (2009) noted that some clinicians may be uncomfortable with group, thus they may not recommend it to students coming to the counseling center for help. Resistance to making group referrals can be a competence issue where therapists are not as well trained in group as they are in individual counseling. They may be uncertain about how to handle clinical issues such as shame faced by students in group. Hahn (2009) proposes that group elicits uneasiness in both group members and group therapists thus making it difficult to start and maintain healthy and viable groups in a CCC. Thus, CCC group therapists need constant training and updating of skills.

Several centers are running thriving group programs and providing a variety of groups. One way to promote group in the center is to provide group peer supervision weekly or monthly to all group coleaders. A format such as this provides an opportunity for on going training and exploration of current group therapy literature. Furthermore, there are opportunities for exploring parallel processes in group supervision and group therapy. Coleading groups offers benefits to counselors and students alike. Kivlighan, London, and Miles (2012) found that group members tended to be more satisfied with co-led groups. Leaders benefit from seeing another therapist work with clients. Coleading is another method of professional development for staff by being exposed to different theoretical approaches in therapy.

Preparing Clients for Group

Proper preparation for group therapy leads to greater satisfaction with one's group experience. In other words, group works best when students are prepared for it. Bownman and DeLucia (1993) note that one of the best predictors for achieving therapeutic goals in group is how prepared someone is for it. If students have little exposure or inaccurate information (e.g., myths vs. truth about groups), they are likely to find group not helpful. Again, clinicians are charged with the task of adequately preparing students for group by dispelling myths about and making appropriate group referrals.

Resistance to joining group is a natural reaction, thus it is best to start with normalizing the student's concerns. It also helps to hear the student's specific concerns in order to address the resistance head on. For example, the student may have misperceptions about group based on distorted or inaccurate media representations of group therapy. Many counseling centers have developed brochures that explore the benefits of group as well as common myths and truths about group. In addition to these suggestions, Rutan and Stone (2001) suggest the following method for adequately preparing students for joining group:

1. Build initial rapport
2. State client goals and expectations
3. Outline specifics of the group format, time, place, number of members, and so forth
4. Deal with initial anxiety that comes with joining a group
5. Discuss and accept group guidelines

Group Member Selection

In addition to proper orientation to group, the selection of appropriate group members is another important aspect to maintaining an effective group. Burlingame, Cox, Davies, Layne, and Gleave (2011) designed the group selection questionnaire (GSQ) to assess three factors: (a) expectancy—how much a potential group member believes group will help them; (b) participation—assessment of appropriate skills and attitudes about group interactions; and (c) demeanor—measurement of potentially problematic group member behaviors. The three subscale scores were used in an empirical study and were found to be predictive of group member success in some cases and premature drop out in other cases. The GSQ or similar instrument would be of great use to counseling center staff in identifying potential group members. Because students are often referred to a group screening before joining a group right after intake, additional data to use before or after a group screening would be beneficial. Those students who seem less appropriate for group after reviewing assessment scores, or those exhibiting intended or unintended deviant behaviors such as monopolizing, attacking other members or group leaders, frequent lateness, or infrequent attendance, may be considered for referrals to other inside or outside resources. Essentially, group success for students does not have to be a hit or miss scenario and it is possible to reserve group for those students who will be most successful in this treatment modality.

Types of Groups Offered in a CCC

General Interpersonal Process Groups

The focus on group process is intended to help move students toward their goals for joining group. Using a semistructured format is recommended to facilitate cohesion and engagement. The group leaders must create a balance in the group process so the therapists are not held solely responsible for the group (Johnson, 2009). Group cohesiveness is facilitated by members taking responsibility for the group. Marmarosh, Holtz, and Schottenbauer (2005) indicated the benefits of group for college students with respect to group cohesiveness. They reported group cohesiveness facilitated group-derived self-esteem and personal self-esteem in CCC group members. The students also showed improvement in overall psychological well-being from being part of the group process. The Marmarosh et al. (2005) article points to group cohesiveness as that which facilitates curative factors of group as outlined by Yalon and Leszcz (2005).

Furthermore, Kivlighan (2012) studied the experience of curative factors by group members. His results indicate that group leaders' primary function in a group is to create a therapeutic group culture and not to focus on individual group member change. The focus on the group is a unique aspect of the interpersonal process. Student who benefit from being a part of an interpersonal process find the group itself is the main conduit of change for them, rather than pointing to specific interventions or techniques as change agents.

Theme Groups

Theme groups (also referred to as support groups) are well-established psychosocial treatment modalities in which clients address issues resulting from particular problems or diagnoses. Theme groups tend to be homogeneous in make up with members having commonality around the theme of the group. For example, a CCC theme group may be a FOO group, depression group, or social anxiety group. Ribeiro (2013) states that theme groups can be tailored to serve the larger campus needs.

Theme groups may be formed for cultural minorities on campus such as nontraditional-age students, students identifying as LGBTQI, students with disabilities, or students of color on predominantly White campuses. As noted in Chapter 2, cultural competence requires that counselors attend to unique experiences of ethnic and sexual minorities, as well as other marginalized or oppressed groups on campus. Group therapy is a good format for attending to the needs of these groups, especially those groups that are homogeneous and theme oriented.

Psychoeducational Groups

Some students with public stigma, self-stigma, or a lack of familiarity with counseling may prefer to engage with the counseling center informally via different psychoeducational workshops and programs (Wade, Post, Cornish, Vogel, & Tucker, 2011). Most counseling centers target specific groups to address popular presenting concerns such as stress management or relationships. These groups tend to be less process oriented and are structured similar to a class or lecture. Attendees may participate as much or little as they feel comfortable.

A group such as this may expose someone to the counseling center's services without that person having to make a commitment to therapy. Such groups also provide a valuable service to the university at large as faculty and staff may elect to attend workshops as well. The groups not only break down stigma but reach larger masses of people (Fende & Anderson, 2007). Sometimes psychoeducational groups can be provided to counseling center clients only as an adjunct to other treatment. In this case, topics are usually chosen according to similar presenting issues.

Several studies have examined the effectiveness of psychoeducational groups on college students. In many of the studies, the students volunteered to participate in the research for extra credit and are not necessarily counseling center clients. These students, although receiving credit for their participation, often benefit from the group interventions being provided. For example, Schwartz, Magee, Griffin, and Dupuis (2004) conducted a psychoeducational group for students focused on reducing dating violence. The intervention involved teaching about gender role stereotyping, conflict management, healthy and unhealthy aspects of entitlement, and anger management skills. After participating in the group, students increased in their protective factors against dating violence and decreased in their risk factors.

Similarly, Cash and Hrabosky (2003) provided psychoeducational intervention to students about body image issues. Students decreased their body dissatisfaction after becoming more familiar with norms for body mass index (BMI) and engaging in self-reflection about their own body dissatisfaction. The information provided to students impacted the way they saw themselves and they incorporated healthier attitudes and behaviors related to body image. Students are a receptive audience in this format since they are generally open to learning and applying new information as a larger part of their college experience.

COUPLES COUNSELING

According to the Standardized Data Set published by the Center for Collegiate Mental Health (CCMH) (2012), a large number of students representing 100 different counseling centers ($N = 75,500$) answered a questionnaire about relationship status. Approximately 37% of students reported being in a serious dating or committed relationship, marriage, or domestic partnership. Though students are engaging in relationships at high numbers and campus culture often has a focus on dating, couples counseling is not always a focus in CCCs.

When resources for providing couples counseling may be limited due to the size and scope of counseling centers, many centers offer psychoeducational options for teaching relationship skills that can enhance students' overall college experience. Studies have found that students can improve their romantic relationship skills by participating in a preventive relationship intervention that is computer based (Braithwaite & Fincham, 2009). The results of the study also indicated improved mental health variables such as anxiety and reduced physical and psychological aggression in the relationships of college students who participated in the computer-based intervention. Topics covered in the intervention included communication and problem solving.

When it comes to couples counseling in a university or CCC, one of the primary tasks is to establish eligibility for services. Many counseling centers will see couples only when both partners are enrolled as students. Other centers will see couples as long as one partner is enrolled as a student. Other issues in couples counseling may center on the way a couple is defined. Friends, romantic partners, and roommates may present as a couple to work on relationship issues such as communication, conflict resolution, or building trust.

Models for Couples Counseling in CCCs

The literature is sparse when it comes to couples counseling with college students. Gibbons and Shurts (2010) offer several suggestions about the lack of focus of couples counseling in CCCs. They state that most college counselors are not focused on working with couples or families in their training. They suggest that one way to more adequately serve couples is by offering couples groups, since most college counselors have more training in group therapy. They further suggest forming a group for couples focused on a common issue for couples in the college population such as career problems faced by couples. Additional problems that may be sources of conflict or stress for student couples include decision making about graduation and pursuing dual career opportunities. Similar to any group in a CCC, goals for the couples group would be facilitating communication, fostering growth for each partner, working through conflict in a healthy manner, and clarifying roles in the relationship. Like other authors, Gibbons and Shurts (2010) suggest that a semistructured format would work best with couples groups, whether career focused or with other themes.

FAMILY COUNSELING

Family counseling in a traditional sense in CCCs is uncommon. Similar to couples counseling, with family counseling the question of eligibility for services must be established. In order to answer these questions, counseling centers will optimally have clear policies and procedures to clearly define who, in addition to the registered student, is considered the client. For this reason some centers do not offer family counseling as a service. If family counseling were offered, the center would have to determine if the student is the client or if the family as a whole is the client. Due to liability concerns and limits to confidentiality, it may be too risky and complicated to consider the family as the client. It is less confusing if only the student is defined as the client and family is limited to the role of providing collateral client information.

Despite the difficulties of offering family counseling as a service, counseling center staff recognize that the influence of family on the life, attitudes, and functioning of a college student is very significant. As part of the development from late adolescent to young adult, students are in the process of establishing themselves as independent adults. Students tend to feel the challenge of defining themselves whether living at home or living on campus. The family's reaction to these changes is sometimes the presenting issue that brings a student in for services at a counseling center. Furthermore, students may be focusing on FOO issues without ever bringing another family member to session.

The influence of the family relationship is paramount to most college students, yet family counseling would be for most centers too resource intensive and considered beyond the scope of a CCC.

One specific way the family impacts college counseling relates to students and their attitudes toward seeking help and mental health counseling. Vogel, Michaels, and Gruss (2009) conducted a study to examine the impact of parental help-seeking behaviors on the likelihood of the student to seek help for mental health concerns. The authors found that parental attitudes did influence help-seeking behaviors in college students. In particular, those parents and children with definite goals for higher achievement were most closely correlated and had similar attitudes about seeking help. Thus overall, parents, according to the authors, can play a key role in whether or not a student that needs counseling may come to the center.

Parents may also consult with counseling center staff on general questions or specific scenarios. Typically, a concerned parent may call or contact a center clinician and ask for guidance on how to deal with a problem with a son or daughter. Questions may focus on signs of distress in a student or the past history of mental health problems that are resurfacing. In this scenario, counseling center staff can act as consultants without divulging whether the student in question is a client at the center or not, thereby offering support to the family while maintaining the student's confidentiality.

In cases where students have signed a release allowing the counselor to talk to parents, more specific information can be shared. Parents and family may also be brought in as consultants to help a student in counseling. Counselors will generally speak with the student initially, and explain to him or her what will happen during the session with parents in the room. There are several advantages to conducting a session this way including: (a) empowering the student; (b) helping to build and maintain rapport between the counselor and student; and (c) establishing the difference between family counseling and consultation with family. For example, a student at risk for harming self or others may give consent for a counselor to talk to his or her parents about treatment planning and referrals for continuity of care. Having this open communication among the student, parents, and clinician may empower the student by providing a supportive space in which the student can openly discuss feelings with the parents or by creating a space in which the student feels she or he is part of the treatment planning rather than just being the topic of discussion. This type of communication may also increase feelings of trust between the student and the clinician and it provides an opportunity for the family to participate in the treatment process without engaging in family counseling. Partnerships with parents can be reassuring to the family involved and sessions involving parents may be particularly helpful with facilitating communication among students, parents, and clinicians.

Treating Minors

When students are under the age of 18, consent must be obtained from parents in order to treat them as clients. Students whose parents refuse to give consent are advised to wait until they turn 18 before being seen at a CCC.

TESTING AND PSYCHOLOGICAL ASSESSMENT

Weissberg (1987) made the following observation regarding the availability of information about coordinating a testing program in a CCC: "Although testing services have clearly been a part of many counseling center operations since their inception, information on the nature and scope of such services is very scarce in the literature" (p. 253). The same appears to be true in more recent literature. In fact, in the 2012 survey of counseling center directors, there were no items about psychological testing. There were, however, questions focused on assessment, specifically risk assessment and suicide assessment. For the purposes of this chapter, the focus of this section is on the types and ways that formal psychological testing and assessment is incorporated into the CCC environment. Specifically, personality assessment, outcome assessment, psychoeducational testing, and national testing programs are explored.

Personality Assessment

Personality assessment may be offered as part of a battery or in conjunction with a detailed clinical interview to determine psychopathology or clarify diagnostic questions. Training centers may offer more extensive personality testing to help trainees hone their diagnostic skills and learn how to integrate testing data with data gathered from structured interviews. In particular, those centers with training programs for psychology doctoral students may have more extensive personality assessment options since psychological testing is a core competency for psychologists.

A variety of studies have been conducted using personality assessments in college students. The two assessments most often found in the literature are the Minnesota Multiphasic Personality Inventory-2 (MMPI-2) and Personality Assessment Inventory (PAI). In the research, personality assessments are used to explore personality traits of particular types of clients presenting at CCCs such as self-injurious behavior (Kerr & Muehlenkamp, 2010) and malingering (Blanchard, McGrath, Pogge, & Khadivi, 2003). Others have studied the psychometric properties of the MMPI-2 and PAI in college counseling settings (Forbey, Lee, & Handel, 2010). One criticism is that while these two assessments show somewhat consistent validity and reliability with college students, they were not developed specifically to assess clinical issues in the college counseling setting.

Clinical Outcome Assessment

Outcome Questionnaire-45

As noted earlier in this chapter, the OQ-45 has previously been used for outcome assessments in CCCs. Locke et al. (2011) point out that the OQ-45 is a global measure of functioning and does not look specifically at the types of problems with which college students often present in counseling. However, one advantage of the OQ-45 is that it requires 2 to 3 minutes to administer and is easy to score. Thus, taking repeated measures on a weekly basis or every time a client presents for therapy is very manageable for both clients and clinicians.

Counseling Center Assessment of Psychological Symptoms

Recent articles on psychological testing in the counseling center literature have focused on the Counseling Center Assessment of Psychological Symptoms (CCAPS) instrument developed by Locke et al. (2011) specifically for use in the CCC setting. The instrument is designed for and normed on college students. In addition, it is offered at no cost for counseling centers, seeks to balance strong statistical properties with clinical relevance to the college population, and can be used for clinical and research purposes (Locke et al., 2011).

It was reported by McAleavey et al. (2012) that over 100 counseling centers are using the CCAPS-62 or the short form of the instrument. Part of the popularity stems from its compatibility with most electronic scheduling and clinical databases (e.g., Titanium) used in contemporary centers. Furthermore, the CCAPS was developed utilizing the data collected from a large sample of college center clients ($n = 22,060$) by the CCMH (2012).

As part of the process of establishing the psychometrics for the CCAPS, concurrent validity was measured by comparing results of the CCAPS with other well-established assessments such as the Beck Depression Index, Beck Anxiety Inventory, Eating Attitudes Test-26, and others (McAleavey et al., 2012). Ultimately, the CCAPS offers the following subscales for assessing symptoms in college students presenting at counseling centers: depression, eating concerns, substance use, generalized anxiety, hostility, social anxiety, family distress, and academic distress. McAleavey et al. (2012) found that the subscales may not distinguish between students in treatment and those not in treatment; however, elevated scores on a particular subscale tend to be indicative of a diagnosable disorder, as established by interrater studies. Clinically, subscale scores can be used to further assess elevations during intake interviews.

The CCAPS may also be used to determine counseling outcomes. Thus, it can be used at repeated intervals for measuring change in symptoms over time. McAleavey et al. (2012) indicate this is done by looking at an elevated score on a subscale at the beginning of treatment and comparing it to the subscale score weekly or at the end of treatment. One of the clinical uses is that therapists can track client progress. McAleavey et al. suggest engaging students in the discussion about their progress and getting them invested in the process of completing the CCAPS before each session. Given the widespread use of the CCAPS in counseling centers, the potential for data collection regarding outcome and clinical trends in the CCC is promising. To date, the CCAPS appears to be the most useful instrument developed specifically for college populations, although a few others have been developed within a much smaller framework and used in specific counseling centers (e.g., College Adjustment Scales, K-State Problem Identification Rating Scales).

Psychoeducational Assessment

Students with symptoms of a learning disability (LD) or attention deficit hyperactivity disorder (ADHD) may present to a CCC for assistance. The problems may be overlapping with anxiety and or depression, causing academic problems and/or disruption. Some centers may be equipped to provide a full battery of tests to assess for and formally diagnose ADHD or LD. The process is time and labor intensive and requires proper training and background for the clinicians doing such work. Due to the fast-paced nature of contemporary counseling centers, the majority of centers may not be able to offer full battery assessments. It is more likely clinicians would be able to determine or rule out the need for more extensive testing and then make appropriate referrals.

National Testing Programs: Testing as Income Source for Centers

Several counseling centers are called "counseling and testing" centers because they offer some type of testing services to the community at large. Some examples might include national tests such as the ACT, SAT, or GRE. By offering such options, centers can generate revenue to purchase supplies and other goods. In addition, students may find it convenient to take national tests on their home campus. Another example of tests offered might include distance learning testing for correspondence courses. The testing center located within a CCC is typically staffed by one FTE psychometrist and a clerical worker. In most situations, the testing service is ancillary to the counseling center, but is important to the overall functioning of the center due to income-earning potential.

REFERENCES

Bjornsson, A. S., Bidwell, C., Brosse, A. L., Carey, G., Hauser, M., Mackiewicz, K. L., & Craighead, W. E. (2011). Cognitive-behavioral group therapy versus group psychotherapy for social anxiety disorder among college students: A randomized controlled trial. *Depression and Anxiety, 28,* 1034–1042.

Blanchard, D. D., McGrath, R. E., Pogge, D. L., & Khadivi, A. (2003). A comparison of the PAI and MMPI-2 as predictors of faking bad in college students. *Journal of Personality Assessment, 80,* 197–205.

Boldt, R. W., & Paul, S. (2011). Building a creative-arts therapy group at a university counseling center. *Journal of College Student Psychotherapy, 25,* 39–52.

Bownman, V. E., & DeLucia, J. L. (1993). Preparation for group therapy: The effects of preparer and modality on group process and individual functioning. *Journal for Specialists in Group Work, 18,* 67–79.

Braithwaite, S. R., & Fincham, F. D. (2009). A randomized clinical trial of a computer based preventive intervention: Replication and extension of ePREP. *Journal of Family Psychology, 23,* 32–38.

Burlingame, G. M., Cox, J. C., Davies, D. R., Layne, C. M., & Gleave, R. (2011). The group selection questionnaire: Further refinements in group member selection. *Group Dynamics: Theory, Research, and Practice, 15,* 60–74.

Carlson, T. M. (2004). A short-term dynamic psychotherapy approach for college students. *Journal of College Student Psychotherapy, 18,* 47–67.

Cash, T. F., & Hrabosky, J. I. (2003). The effects of psychoeducation and self-monitoring in a cognitive-behavioral program for body-image improvement. *Eating Disorders, 11,* 255–270.

Center for Collegiate Mental Health. (2012). *Annual report*. Retrieved from http://ccmh .psu.edu/wp-content/uploads/sites/3058/2014/07/2012_CCMH_Report-Reduced -Size.pdf

Choi, K. H., Buskey, W., & Johnson, B. (2010). Evaluation of counseling outcomes at a university counseling center: The impact of clinically significant change on problem resolution and academic functioning. *Journal of Counseling Psychology, 57,* 297–303.

Cooper, S. E., Benton, S. A., Benton, S. L., & Phillips, J. C. (2008). Evidence-based practice in psychology among college counseling center clinicians. *Journal of College Student Psychotherapy, 22,* 28–50.

Eichler, R. J., & Schwartz, V. (2010). Essential services in college counseling. In J. Kay & V. Schwartz (Eds.), *Mental health care in the college community* (pp. 57–93). Hoboken, NJ: Wiley.

Fende, J. M., & Anderson, T. (2007). An investigation of psychoeducational interventions about therapy. *Psychotherapy Research, 17,* 120–127.

Forbey, J. D., Lee, T., & Handel, R. W. (2010). Correlates of the MMPI-2-RF in a college setting. *Psychological Assessment, 22,* 737–744.

Gallagher, R. P. (2012). *National survey of college counseling*. Retrieved from http:// www.iacsinc.org

Gelso, C. J., Kivlighan, D. M., Busa-Knepp, J., Spiegel, E. B., Ain, S., Hummel, A. M., … Markin, R. D. (2012). The unfolding of the real relationship and the outcome of brief psychotherapy. *Journal of Counseling Psychology, 59,* 495–506.

Gibbons, M. M., & Shurts, W. M. (2010). Combining career and couples counseling for college students: A narrative approach. *Journal of College Counseling, 13,* 169–181.

Hahn, W. K. (2009). Ingenuity and uneasiness about group psychotherapy in university counseling centers. *International Journal of Group Psychotherapy, 59,* 543–552.

International Association of Counseling Services, Inc. (2012). *Standards for university and college counseling centers*. Retrieved from http://www.iacsinc.org

Johnson, C. V. (2009). A process-oriented group model for university students: A semi-structured approach. *International Journal of Group Psychotherapy, 59,* 511–528.

Kerr, P. L., & Muehlenkamp, J. J. (2010). Features of psychopathology in self-injuring female college students. *Journal of Mental Health Counseling, 32,* 290–308.

Kearney, L. K., Draper, M., & Baron, A. (2005). Counseling utilization by ethnic minority college students. *Cultural Diversity and Ethnic Minority Psychology, 11,* 272–285.

Kilman, P. R., Urbaniak, G. C., & Parnell, M. M. (2006). Effects of attachment-focused versus relationship skills-focused group interventions for college students with insecure attachment patterns. *Attachment and Human Development, 8,* 47–62.

Kivlighan, D. M. (2012). Individual and group perceptions of therapeutic factors and session evaluation: An actor–partner interdependence analysis. *Group Dynamics: Theory, Research, and Practice, 15,* 147–160.

Kivlighan, D. M., London, K., & Miles, J. R. (2012). Are two heads better than one? The relationship between number of group leaders and group members, and group climate and group member benefit from therapy. *Group Dynamics: Theory, Research, and Practice, 16*, 1–13.

Locke, B. D., Buzolitz, J. S., Pui-Wa, L., Boswell, J. F., McAleavey, A. A., Sevig, T. D., ... Hayes, J. A. (2011). Development of the Counseling Center Assessment of Psychological Symptoms-62 (CCAPS-62). *Journal of Counseling Psychology, 58*, 97–109.

Lunardi, P. M., Webb, R. E., & Widseth, J. C. (2006). If we open the door, how long will they stay? The use of personal counseling in a small college. *Journal of College Student Psychotherapy, 21*, 15–24.

Marmarosh, C., Holtz, A., & Schottenbauer, M. (2005). Group cohesiveness, group-derived collective self-esteem, group-derived hope, and the well-being of group therapy members. *Group Dynamics: Theory, Research, and Practice, 9*, 32–44.

McAleavey, A. A., Nordberg, S. S., Hayes, J. A., Castonguay, L. G., Locke, B. D., & Lockhard, A. J. (2012). Clinical validity of the Counseling Center Assessment of Psychological Symptoms-62 (CCAPS-62): Further evaluation and clinical applications. *Journal of Counseling Psychology, 59*, 575–590.

Minami, T., Davies, D. R., Tierney, S. C., Bettmann, J. E., McAward, S. M., Averill, L. A., ... Wampold, B. E. (2009). Preliminary evidence on the effectiveness of psychological treatments delivered at a university counseling center. *Journal of Counseling Psychology, 56*, 309–320.

Norcross, J. C., Krebs, P. M., & Prochaska, J. O. (2011). Stages of change. *Journal of Clinical Psychology, 67*, 143–154.

Pinkerton, R., Talley, J. E., & Cooper, S. L. (2009). Reflections on individual psychotherapy with university students: What seems to work. *Journal of College Student Psychotherapy, 23*, 153–171.

Ribeiro, M. D. (2013). Groups in college counseling centers. *The Group Psychologist.* Retrieved from http://www.apadivisions.org/division-49/publications/newsletter/group-psychologist/2013/04/college-counseling-groups.aspx

Rutan, J., & Stone, W. (2001). *Psychodynamic group psychotherapy.* New York, NY: Guilford Press.

Schwartz, J. P., Magee, M., Griffin, L. D., & Dupuis, C. W. (2004). Effects of group preventative intervention on risk and protective factors related to dating violence. *Group Dynamics: Theory, Research, and Practice, 8*, 221–231.

Vogel, D. L., Michaels, M. L., & Gruss, N. J. (2009). Parental attitudes and college students' intentions to seek therapy. *Journal of Social and Clinical Psychology, 28*, 689–713.

Wade, N. G., Post, B. C., Cornish, M. A., Vogel, D. L., & Tucker, J. R. (2011). Predictors of the change in self-stigma following a single session of group counseling. *Journal of Counseling Psychology, 58*, 170–182.

Weissberg, M. (1987). Testing services in college and university counseling centers. *Journal of Counseling and Development, 65*, 253–256.

Wolgast, B. M., Rader, J., Roche, D., Thompson, C. P., von Zuben, F. C., & Goldberg, A. (2005). Investigation of clinically significant change by severity levels of college counseling center clients. *Journal of College Counseling, 8*, 140–152.

Yalon, I., & Leszcz, M. I. (2005). *The theory and practice of group psychotherapy* (5th ed.). New York, NY: Basic Books.

CHAPTER FOUR

CAREER AND ACADEMIC COUNSELING AND AUXILIARY SERVICES

Shannon J. Hodges

As was noted in Chapter 1, career counseling and academic advising were functions previously provided by faculty (Winston, 1989). As the curriculum expanded and diversified, the need for more specialized knowledge and individual attention became necessary. There is also little doubt that demands placed on faculty (e.g., scholarship, committee service, writing grants) left precious little time for academic advising. Although college faculty certainly understand their profession and its demands, academic advisors and career counselors possessing the knowledge, skills, and professional dispositions can provide comprehensive services in the way of assessment and counseling that faculty may have neither the time nor qualifications to carry out. While academic advising may not be part of many counseling centers, in community colleges and in small colleges and universities, advising may be paired with career counseling as there is a natural fit between these two student services.

A BRIEF HISTORY OF CAREER COUNSELING

Similar to advising, career counseling at the college level has had a long and varied history (Pope, 2000). Frank Parsons's 1909 *Choosing a Vocation* was the first publication to utilize a formal approach to career assessment and counseling. In 1922, Viteles (1974) established the first vocational guidance clinic in an effort to provide more systematic assistance to adults struggling to find a career. Shortly thereafter, Carl Rogers broadened the idea of career counseling as an important psychological concept and incorporated it into his theory and practice (Gordon, 2006). Professionals in the mental health field were beginning to view career counseling, or "guidance" as it was often termed, as a developmental construct equal in importance to that of personal counseling.

Donald Super's *Career Pattern Study*, launched in 1951, was the first longitudinal study on career behavior (Gordon, 2006). Super drew on the broader influences of economics, sociology, and family influence and integrated them into his theory (Crites, 1981). College administrators used the work of

Super and Rogers to develop a more systematic approach to career counseling and advising. Granted, the student body of the 1950s represented a demographic far different than that of 21st-century U.S. college students. In the 1950s, college students were almost exclusively White, Protestant, male, and from more affluent families, as opposed to the more broad cultural and socioeconomic demographic of students today. Regardless, career theory paved the way for development of standardized tests to assess career interest and aptitude. Career assessments helped provide more in-depth information to the student and the counselor. Career theory likely helped to cement the need for specially trained student services professionals who could give and interpret career assessments. It is well worth noting that career counselors possessing advanced degrees in counseling or a related field and trained in the use and interpretation of career tests have a decided advantage over student services professionals who lack such a background. While the paths of career counseling and career advising diverged from one another decades ago, merging these disparate student services is well worth considering. As previously mentioned, many 2-year colleges and small 4-year institutions have already combined career counseling and academic advising.

INTEGRATING CAREER AND ACADEMIC SERVICES

The need to integrate career and academic advising would appear vital on college campuses (Gordon, 2006). A growing number of citizens seem disenchanted with colleges due to cost and whether institutions prepare graduates for the workforce. Academic and career decisions are seldom made in isolation as numerous factors influence students' choices of a major, coursework, and preparing for future careers. Such factors could include personal and career interest, career and academic aptitude, family and cultural considerations, and so forth. The evolution of academic disciplines and proliferation of courses of study require a broad approach to advising. Academic advisors need to be prepared to counsel on how academic performance, career interest, aptitude, and work ethic impact selection of a future career. Given the debate regarding the escalating costs of a college education and the concerns about student debt, colleges must of necessity assist students in career selection and placement. Beyond testing or evaluating academic performance, advisors must understand the importance of changing career trends as reflected in the Bureau of Labor Statistics's *Occupational Outlook Handbook* (*OOH*, www.bls.gov/ooh), an online publication that tracks the job outlook in thousands of career fields. Every career counselor and advisor should make students aware of this resource so that students will better understand their chances of career viability. Furthermore, career counselors should advise clients that the *OOH* is updated every few years to reflect market changes in occupations.

A significant intent of this book and this chapter is to provide basic career counseling and advising information for college counselors, advisors, and student affairs professionals. Naturally, career advisors likely come from a variety of disciplines other than the field of counseling. For noncounselors working in career advising who may be reading this text, we wish to stress the importance of developing a working understanding of career theory. Career advisors will also need to be able to articulate the importance and limitations of career assessment. For example, I (Hodges) have often counseled college students who have asked, "What does the test tell me I should do for a career?" It is critical for the advisee's to understand that tests are at best "resources" that offer additional information for consideration. For example, the Self-Directed Search (SDS), developed by Holland, Fritzche, and Powell (1994), assesses career interest in a variety of vocational areas and provides a three-letter occupational code based on six variables: realistic (R), investigative (I), artistic (A), social (S), enterprising (E), and conventional (C). A sample occupational profile might be SEA for a "social–enterprising–artistic" occupational profile. Such a profile would be consistent with occupations in education, counseling, social work, the ministry, teaching drama, and so forth (Holland et al., 1994). The SDS is not "telling" the student to go into one of the identified careers, something students and parents often mistakenly assume, but is merely illustrating careers the test taker may have an interest in. A student would not necessarily change his or her major due to results of the SDS or any other career assessment, but the advisor and student should consider and discuss the results of the assessment. Making sense of the test results to a college student who is undecided regarding a major or who is considering switching majors is where the ingenuity of the career counselor or advisor comes in.

A significant change to the college population in the past 20 years is that older adult students now make up a large part of the student population today. For our purposes, older than average or nontraditional students (e.g., undergraduate students 25 years of age or older) have become the norm on many campuses across the country, especially at urban campuses, community colleges, and web-based institutions (e.g., University of Phoenix, Walden University, Cappella University). Some nontraditional students may be starting second or even third careers with the intention of upgrading skills (especially in community colleges) or landing a better paying or more secure career. Still others may have a bachelor's or even graduate degree and are interested in additional education in a related field (e.g., a student with a 2-year degree in human services is going for a bachelor's in psychology). While nontraditional students usually have more life and work experience due to their age and years in the workforce, they also have greater stressors and needs, such as child care, more financial aid concerns, wider range of evening and weekend class availability, and so forth. Given the life demands of older adult learners, and many traditional universities' lack of academic and cultural "fit," it is a small wonder that older adults have started to enroll in nontraditional, virtual institutions. This demographic shift away from 4-year colleges represents a serious challenge to traditional colleges and their services and functions such as those afforded by the counseling center. For example, the University of Phoenix, the largest of the virtual, nontraditional universities, has an enrollment exceeding 250,000 students (Gillespie, 2015). Nontraditional institutions such as the University of Phoenix typically deliver education at a significantly reduced cost than traditional, residential institutions. Thus, it is no stretch of the imagination to understand the very real threat upstart institutions pose to traditional institutions. To counter this, many residential institutions commonly offer more online courses in undergraduate and graduate degree programs (Ericae, n.d.).

Additional special student populations, such as those from culturally different backgrounds, require career counselors and advisors to be educated and sensitive to issues that will influence their academic and vocational choices. Family and cultural influences may have a profound impact on the academic majors and careers students choose to go into. Career counselors and advisors should also be aware of how collectivist cultures may in effect predetermine a student's career choice. For example, while mainstream U.S. culture upholds the belief in autonomy of a given student to freely select her or his major or career, in many cultures the student's family may play an active role in selecting the son's or daughter's career (DeVaney & Hughey, 2000). In addition, many students come from backgrounds where religious, tribal, or community leaders have a significant influence and serve as ad hoc counselors and advisors. Independent decision making on the part of the student may not be appreciated or even tolerated in such a family or culture. Family and cultural influences can play a supportive or depressive role in the manner in which students engage in the academic major or career selection process. Career counselors and advisors, particularly those of the majority culture, must be aware of and sensitive to the impact cultural tradition plays in influencing academic and career exploration.

College students, regardless of age, gender, and culture, need good, up-to-date information on career possibilities, job search information, and the skills needed to be marketable in an ever-evolving 21st century, globally interconnected world (Freedman, 2004). Students need career counseling and advising that is appropriate to their developmental needs. This means that counselors and advisors will need to evaluate and modify their strategy with students depending on the age and experience of the student. Clearly, counseling or advising a 40-year old, single-parent female holding two part-time jobs while attending college is significantly different than counseling an 18-year-old freshman struggling to decide on a major and career direction.

DEFINING CAREER ADVISING AND CAREER COUNSELING

This chapter acknowledges that some institutions will employ professionally trained counselors (i.e., those with a graduate degree in counseling or a related field) to provide career and academic counseling to students while other institutions will hire staff trained in a variety of disciplines (e.g., English, philosophy, business). Career advisors with a counseling background will have a broader and deeper understanding of career assessment and developmental theory than faculty or staff educated in other fields, as counselor education includes a background in career testing and most nontherapeutic fields do not. This chapter is not arguing that academic advisors with degrees in, say, history are unqualified. The point is that professionally trained academic counselors have an advantage in that they truly are "counselors" in every sense of the term.

Although counselors would appear to be a natural profession to provide academic as well as career counseling under one campus resource (the counseling center), a recent survey by the National Academic Advising Association (NACADA, 2004) revealed that more than 70% of the nearly 1,700 advisors responding to the survey did not have a counseling degree.

Because most academic advisors are not trained counselors, they must of necessity establish a good relationship with the career or counseling center so that adequately trained professionals can provide career assessment when it becomes necessary. This chapter does acknowledge that while academic advising and career counseling are similar and have over lapping responsibilities, they also are distinctly different functions. Career advising is here defined as a process whereby an academic advisor or counselor assists college students in the selection of an appropriate academic major based on a good understanding of student interests, needs, and abilities. Career counseling is here defined as a professional, confidential relationship involving a trained counselor who is licensed or certified (or in the process of becoming licensed or certified) and may involve counseling, advising, and career testing and interpretation to explore career possibilities. Some major differences between advising and career counseling may involve the type of information discussed, degree, training, and qualifications of the professional advisor or career counselor, where the career counselor is likely able to provide more in-depth information and additional privacy.

Career counseling services include career counseling, testing, career planning and development interventions, cooperative education and experiential career education, and job placement and employment services. Academic advising is likely to be more narrowly focused on academic issues, choosing a major, advising students experiencing academic difficulty, and making referrals to the counseling/career center or an academic unit. O'Banion defined academic advising as a process that helps students develop their full potential (1972). He illustrated five dimensions of the academic advising process:

1. Exploration of life goals
2. Exploration of vocational goals
3. Program choice
4. Course choice
5. Scheduling choice (Gordon, 2006, p. 10)

O'Banion asserted that student exploration of life goals and vocational goals must be completed prior to selection of course work and college major. He also emphasized the need to identify the knowledge, skills, and attitudes of academic advisors for completing the five steps in the advising process that he outlined. It is interesting to note that introductory courses such as "College 101," emphasizing study skills and career testing for undecided majors, have become commonplace on college campuses. But students who enter college with a selected major, who make up the majority of college students, may have had little career testing. Some career assessment is conducted in high schools using the Armed Services Vocational Assessment Battery (ASVAB) that the armed services offer high school juniors and seniors for free. School counselors may also offer the SDS or another similar tests to assess career aptitude or interest, though most high school assessments are likely geared toward academic achievement (e.g., PSAT, SAT, ACT, Iowa Test).

Crookston used the term *developmental advising* to indicate congruence between the college student's age, social-developmental level, and academic advising. He defined "developmental" as a systematic process through which students set and achieve their academic, career, and personal goals with the aid of an academic advisor (Gordon, 2006). His idea was that advising should address these areas in order to maximize the advising relationship. Pardee (1994), on the contrary, pointed out the complex web of constraints that conspire against "developmental advising" (p. 59); these include student behavior (how independent or dependent), the advisor's skills and motivation, and the institutional constraints such as quality and type of services, enrollment levels, and who is doing the advising (faculty or professional staff). It is essential to note as well the significant changes in Western society and in higher education that likely have impacted advising. For example, in the Internet age, with student communicating with family and friends via their mobile devices (e.g., texting, e-mail, Facebook), taking classes through the Internet, and accessing advising information on the institution's website, this has profound implications for delivery of academic advising, career counseling, personal counseling, and higher education overall. At this point with technological advances moving so rapidly, it is difficult to predict with any degree of confidence what advising and counseling will look like in 10 years. It is likely, however, that in-person, face-to-face contact will decline and advising and counseling delivery via technology will increase.

In light of technological advances, professional organizations such as the NACADA, the American Psychological Association (APA), and the American Counseling Association (ACA) have and will continue to revise their ethics and internships/externships to reflect the technological revolution sweeping through higher education and societies at large. In point of fact, ACA just completed the revision of their ethical code and a large part of the revision related to technology and social media (ACA, 2014). The goal of academic advising, however, remains to "teach students to understand the meaning of higher education, teach students to understand the purpose of the curriculum, and to foster students' intellectual and personal development toward academic success and lifelong learning" (NACADA, 2012).

USE OF ASSESSMENTS IN CAREER COUNSELING AND ADVISING

Since the early 1900s, when Frank Parsons published his classic opus, *Choosing a Vocation*, career counselors have worked to devise methods of assessing clients' career interests. Interest inventories that ask clients to report their "likes" and "dislikes" for various activities have proved to be very helpful for this purpose. Several interest inventories that career counselors commonly use are briefly discussed in this section of the chapter.

Spokane asserted that the purpose of career testing is to provide career information, highlight particular interests and aptitudes, provide motivation and purpose to the student, clarify expectations, and plan interventions (1991). Use of career assessments will likely unearth important information to enhance the advising or career counseling relationship. While the research is more limited than one would like, it does suggest that career testing is helpful to the advising and counseling process. Ideally, a student would be assessed using the SDS, Strong Interest Inventory (SII), SIGI PLUS (System of Interactive Guidance and Information), or another such test in order to provide the counselor/advisor and the student baseline information they would otherwise not have. Interest inventories are commonly used assessment tools in career counseling and advising. Betsworth and Fouad (1997) investigated several decades of research on career interest and found they were correlated with career choice. In addition, they found that the relationship between interest and satisfaction was relatively weak, though they speculated this could be due to methodological problems. Randahl, Hansen, and Haverkamp (1993) found that students who used an interest inventory were more likely to take an active role in career exploration than students who were not tested on career interests. Thus, interest inventories are highly recommended in the career counseling and advising process, particularly with undecided majors or students with majors who are questioning their current career focus.

Naturally, interest inventories are not "stand alone" tests for career counseling and advising. First of all, interest inventories assess interests and not aptitude, and are therefore not valid measures of future career success (Hood & Johnson, 2007). Yet, as interest inventories are the starting point for students struggling to identify viable careers, interest identification likely is the first step toward possible career identification. Furthermore, people are unlikely to prosper in careers for which they are disinterested. For this reason interest inventories are often administered together with aptitude tests in order to get an accurate picture of interests and potential skills.

Second, it is essential that career counselors explain the nature of the interest assessment to the student; namely, that the test assesses interest and can provide helpful information about how their identified interests match up with potential careers. Students need to know the test won't "tell them what career to go into" but rather will provide additional "food for thought." The information gleaned from career counseling sessions and career testing can be linked to the *OOH* to examine future viability of a student's careers of interest. After counseling, assessment, use of the *OOH*, and individual career exploration, college students likely will have gained significant information about career options available to them. Such information certainly is no guarantee to future career or academic success though it certainly provides a realistic foundation upon which the student can begin to construct his or her own career scaffolding. Failure to utilize a career strategy incorporating counseling, testing, and use of the *OOH* could lead to a more arbitrary, "scattershot" approach likely yielding less desirable results.

Career interest inventories are of limited value in making finer distinctions within specific fields. For example, an interest inventory may reveal a student has a high interest in the profession of engineering, but will not identify which specific engineering field would be the best fit (e.g., chemical engineering, electrical engineering, mechanical engineering). Particular inventories geared for the engineering field such as the Purdue Interest Questionnaire for engineering and technical students would be an example of an interest inventory that makes finer distinctions within a particular field (Shell, LeBold, & Ward, 1991).

Career interest inventories may be inappropriate for students with severe mental or emotional disturbances. Depressed and highly anxious clients are likely to select more negative responses and endorse more passive interests than people who do not have a documented mental disorder. Career counselors should screen for the presence of mental disorders as part of the initial intake and interview prior to commencing career assessment and counseling. Once again, this is another important reason for counselors to serve in an academic advising as well as career counseling role.

Another important consideration lies in understanding that interest inventories may evidence significant changes for younger clients, especially the traditional college-age population. Career counselors should consider readministering an interest inventory if it has been longer than 6 months since the client last completed one (Hood & Johnson, 2007). Interests are most likely to change in students under the age of 20 who have experienced significant changes in their situation (e.g., transferred to a different college or changed their major).

Finally, career counselors may choose to use an interest card sort in the place of an interest inventory if they are interested in the underlying reasons for the client's choices (Slaney & MacKinnon-Slaney, 2000). A card sort functions as a type of structured interview between the counselor and client. Students would be instructed to sort cards with occupational titles into piles of "would choose," "would not choose," and "no opinion." Next, they would be instructed to subdivide the three piles into smaller piles based on their reasons for placing the cards into those piles. The card sort is an assessment technique to assist the career counselor and client in understanding the rationale for the career choice. Then, the career counselor and student can look for themes in the student's preferences that can then guide the career exploration process. Examples of card sorts include the Missouri Occupational Card Sort, Missouri Occupational Preference Inventory, Nonsexist Vocational Card Sort, Occ-U-Sort, and Slaney's Vocational Card Sort (Slaney & MacKinnon-Slaney, 2000). The Vocational Exploration and Insight Kit, which includes an 84-item card sort together with other career exploration activities, is especially appropriate for highly motivated clients who wish to consider their career choices in a more in-depth manner (Hood & Johnson, 2007).

POPULAR INTEREST INVENTORIES

Several of the most popular inventories used for career and academic planning are briefly discussed in this chapter. These inventories include the Campbell Interest and Skill Survey (CISS), SDS, and SII. All these inventories include a measure of self-rated competencies as part of the inventory itself or as a parallel instrument (Betz & Rottinghaus, 2006). These types of career interest assessments can often predict occupational interest more than career counseling or advising alone (Hood & Johnson, 2007). Furthermore, this author's opinion is that as counselors and psychologists receive extensive training in career assessments, they likely make ideal career advisors and certainly career "counselors." Though hard figures are difficult to come by, this author (Hodges) has noticed anecdotally that many college career centers are often staffed with noncounselors. It will be interesting to note the manner in which college career centers evolve over the next decade.

Campbell Interest and Skill Survey

The Campbell Interest and Skill Survey was developed by Campbell (2002). The CISS provides interest and skills scores for 7 orientation scales, 29 basic scales, 60 occupational scales, and 3 special scales (academic focus, extroversion, and variety). The seven orientation scales are similar to the six Holland scales on the SII. In contrast with the SII, the CISS uses unisex occupational scales instead of separate scores for men and women (Campbell, 2002).

The Self-Directed Search

The SDS (4th edition), which can be self-administered in traditional pen-and-paper form or online, is based on Holland's (1997) theory of vocational choice. Holland's theory can be summarized as a "person–environment congruence" theory (Spokane & Catalano, 2000, p. 137) that theorizes people will be more satisfied and successful if they live and work in an environment that is compatible with their interests and skills. As previously mentioned, the SDS classifies an individual into six different personality–work typologies. The six are realistic (R), investigative (I), artistic (A), social (S), enterprising (E), and conventional (C), and the SDS provides the career counselor and student with a three-letter occupational profile (e.g., SEA, RIE, AES).

Although the SDS is classified as an interest inventory, it is an inventory of both interests and abilities. The current version of the SDS consists of:

- Four sections: two that inquire about activities liked (66 items) or occupations (84 occupations) and two that inquire about competencies (66 items) and abilities (12 rating scales)
- There are four versions:
  - The Regular Form (Form R) for high school students, college students, and adults
  - The Easy Form (Form E) for adults or high school students with limited educational backgrounds
  - The Career Planning Form (Form CP) for adults in career transition
  - The SDS Career Explorer for middle school students

The *Occupations Finder*, a booklet that accompanies the SDS, lists over 1,300 occupations according to their Holland code and the amount of education required. When the student completes the SDS, the counselor can explain the results and provide further recommendations to the student. Further recommendation could be to explore the identified careers of interest. Exploration could involve looking up information on a particular career in online resources or interviewing someone working in a career of high interest.

Other helpful resources for college students who have completed the SDS to consult are the Bureau of Labor Statistics' *OOH* either in the traditional print version or online at www.bls.gov/ooh. The *OOH* lists the occupational demand for all occupations the Bureau of Labor Statistics tracks. Students who take the SDS should review the *OOH* to see the projected demand for the careers of interest. The *OOH* along with the SDS and good career counseling and advising can help an undecided major or one contemplating career change with very helpful information. Clearly, students should not use the *OOH* as an absolute authority on careers, as career outlooks change due to varying societal norms and workforce demands, but it provides important information regarding the extended occupational outlook. Students do need to be educated and aware of the current and extended occupational outlook for the particular careers of interest.

Strong Interest Inventory

The 2004 version of the SII is the most recent version in a series that began with the publication of the Strong Vocational Interest Blank (SVIB) by E. K. Strong, Jr., in 1927 (Hood & Johnson, 2007). The SVIB was ultimately revised and is now the SII. The SII is especially noteworthy due to its popularity, strong research base, and its prominent role in career assessment (Hood & Johnson, 2007). The current version of the Strong is composed of:

- 291 items with a 5-point response format for each item
- 30 Basic Interest Scales (BISs)
- 244 Occupational Scales (OSs, 122 for each gender)
- A Personal Style Score titled Team Orientation

The 291 items of the SII are divided into six sections (occupations, subject areas, activities, leisure activities, people, and your characteristics). In the first five sections, clients indicate whether they *strongly like*, are *indifferent to, dislike,* or *strongly dislike* the activity represented by that particular item. For the last section, they indicate to what degree a characteristic is like them on a five-point scale. Most clients taking the SII will complete it in 25 to 30 minutes. The SII is scored on a computer and the results are reported on a multipage profile or a computerized narrative interpretation. The SII is offered in three different forms: high school, college, and standard. The standard form is geared for adult learners with a less robust educational background. The SII produces scores on four sets of scales: General Occupational Themes (GOT), BISs, OSs, and Personal Style Scales (PSSs).

The SII also contains three administrative indices that provide valuable information for interpreting the client's profile. These indices are (a) item response percentages, illustrating the percentages of *strongly like, like, indifferent, strongly dislike, dislike,* for the different sections of the SII; (b) total response index, which indicates number of items completed (unless the number falls below 276, and then it is not scored); and (c) typicality index, a measure that reveals the consistency with which a person has responded to the items. The typicality index tallies the number of inconsistent responses to 24 pairs of items that possess similar content (Donnay, Morris, Schaubhut, & Thompson, 2005). For example, if the client likes accounting as a career but not a subject, the responses would be scored as inconsistent.

GOTs and BISs are two sets of homogeneous scales that provide an overview of the SII profile as well as a framework for interpretation of the other scales. Each of the six GOTs contains items selected to fit Holland's (1997) description of six occupational types (see previous Holland RIASEC codes). As in Holland's SDS, the GOTs are applied to BISs, OSs, and PSSs. Unlike the SDS, the SII will provide a two-dimension GOT code: realistic–investigative (R-I), or social–enterprising (S-E).

The BISs function as subscales for the six GOTs. Like the SDS, they are grouped into six GOT categories on the basis of correlations between the two sets of scales. The BIS are relatively short, six to 12 items (Donnay et al., 2005). Scores of these scales can be significantly affected by responses to a few items.

The GOTs and BISs have been standardized so that the combined group of men and women in the GRS will obtain a mean *T* score of 50 and a standard deviation score of 10 for each scale. Higher scores indicate a stronger correlation to the particular theme. Gender differences are most noticeable on scales in the realistic category, particularly in the categories of mechanics and construction, military, computer hardware and electronics, athletics, and protective services BISs (Donnay et al., 2005). Counselors should take such differences into account when interpreting scores on these scales, particularly for women or men considering nontraditional careers.

The SII profile also provides scores for 122 pairs of OSs for women and men. The OSs were developed by selecting items that significantly differentiated between the interests of women or men in the particular occupation and women and men in general. The typical scale contains 25 to 30 items selected in this manner (Hood & Johnson, 2007). As with other SII scores, the OSs has a mean *T* score of 50 and a standard deviation of 10 and higher scores indicate stronger correlations.

PSSs include five PSSs that assess personality factors related to educational and career planning. These five scales, each of which is bipolar in nature, are briefly described as follows:

- Work style: High scorers prefer to work with people; low scores prefer to work with ideas, data, or things.
- Learning environment: High scorers possess academic interests associated with advanced degrees; low scorers possess practical interests associated with technical or trade school attendance.
- Leadership style: High scorers prefer to direct others; low scorers prefer to lead by example.
- Risk takers/adventure: High scorers prefer to take chances; low scorers prefer to play it safe.
- Team orientation: High scorers prefer to accomplish tasks as a team; low scorers prefer to accomplish tasks independently.

Interpretation of the SII

The career counselor should review the entire profile the SII provides to ensure the client understands what high and low scores mean. Many students, particularly traditional-age college students, may occasionally express "the test told me to be a nurse." The career counselor should carefully explain that a high score indicates an "interest" in the field of nursing. Students should be encouraged to research careers in which they have a strong interest. Research could include checking the *OOH* to see about projected job growth in an interest area, interviewing someone in the field of their career interest area (e.g., interviewing a nurse), and then examine the academic and training requirements for nursing.

Naturally, no career assessment is going to answer all of the student's questions regarding career selection. But standardized career assessments provide important information for the student who can then set about narrowing career choices using an academic focus. Career counselors should caution students that a high score on a particular occupational or interest scale does not necessarily mean that it would be a good career fit. This is where the counseling and advising phase becomes critical. Some nonstandard assessment resources, most of which are self-guided, are provided in the following sections of this chapter.

Computer-Based Programs

A number of computer-based programs have been developed to assist clients and students in career exploration. Two very popular computer programs are SIGI PLUS, developed by the Educational Testing Service, and DISCOVER, developed by ACT (formerly the American College Testing Service). Both programs are comprehensive, interactive, easy to use, and available on the Internet. A comprehensive review of research on the effectiveness of DISCOVER found it increased users vocational identity, level of career development, and self-confidence in career decision making (Luzzo, 2002). The programs are most effective when used in conjunction with counseling (Eveland, Conye, & Blakney, 1998). These interactive programs appear to be helpful for all clients regardless of gender, age, or culture (Eveland et al., 1998).

Career Planning Resource Books

Career planning resources have become very popular and can play a helpful role in providing additional information regarding career choice. Career planning guides, whether books or workbooks (many available on Kindle or other e-book platforms) provide self-guided exercises clients can utilize outside the career counseling session. Many, such as Bolles (2011), use a decision-making model as a conceptual framework. Exercises in these resources tend to be qualitative and experiential in nature and easy to apply in daily life. Examples of some of the more popular books are *What Color Is Your Parachute? 2016: A Practical Manual for Job-Hunters and Career-Changers* (Bolles, 2016) and *Making Career Decisions That Count: A Practical Guide* (Luzzo, 2002). There are numerous additional resources available at major book retailers or though purchase on the Internet.

Another career planning resource is a helpful book titled *Career Tests: 25 Revealing Self-Tests to Help You Find and Succeed at the Perfect Career* (Janda, 1999). Janda's text contains numerous rapid career assessment inventories testing areas such as career search activities, career concerns, career values, procrastination, and numerous additional career assessments. The tests are brief, self-report types that can provide basic information and direction to the client and counselor in a short period of time. Some of the most helpful of the tests involve career search activities, procrastination, and job interviewing self-statements. Because the tests in Janda's book are all Level A tests regarding test user qualifications, any career counselor or advisor could make use of them. Students will easily be able to understand the information and potentially take the test at different times to chart progress in the desired areas. The brief assessments in Janda's book are no substitute for normed, comprehensive career interest inventories such as SDS, SII, or others but can serve as additional, cost-effective resources to them.

Self-Assessment

The following Self-Assessment for Undecided Majors and Students Seeking Career Counseling is in a conceptual format to help students explore careers. Like all such exercises, it should be paired with career assessment and a trained counselor.

Sample Self-Assessment for Undecided Majors and Students Seeking Career Counseling:

1. What are your current academic and career interests?
2. How motivated are you to select a major? (Circle one):
   Unmotivated   Somewhat Motivated   Highly Motivated
3. Regarding the previous question, cite specific steps you have taken to select an academic major (e.g., met with a career counselor, taken career and academic interest inventories, spoken with an academic advisor, talked with friends in majors you are interested in).
4. Imagine you are suddenly 10 years older. What career/job do you most wish to be doing? What do you most like about that particular job/career (e.g., specific job duties, work environment, training/education required, skills required)? Then, what would it take to achieve that vision?
5. Some people find their hobbies provide them helpful career insight. What are five of your hobbies? Would you be interested in exploring one (or more) of those hobbies as a career?
6. If you were to ask someone who knows you well, what would that person cite as your top three personal strengths?
7. With reference to the previous question, if you were to ask that same person "What careers do you think I might be good at?" what might that person suggest?
8. If you have met with a career counselor and taken the SII, SDS, or another interest assessment, what were the five occupations that most interested you?

9. What clubs and organizations are you active in? What drew you to these clubs and organizations?
10. What have the three most interesting classes you have taken? What made them so engaging? How could the information in these classes be helpful in career selection (if at all)?

The following Career Functioning Assessment (CFA) is a conceptual framework for career counselors to use when counseling students. The CFA also includes the Career Functioning Scale (CFS) to provide the career counselor a means of assessing the client's current career functioning level. Although this is a subjective-type measure, it provides the career counselor some method of pulling together career or academic information in a comprehensive manner. The CFA should be completed after an intake interview and career assessments have been conducted. The career counselor should also review any additional documents (related to work history, career assessment, etc.). Career counseling would then follow after the intake, assessment, and CFA have been completed. Ideally, after a few sessions of career counseling, the client's CFS score should increase. Should the client score below 30 on the CFS, the career counselor or advisor should refer the client for mental health counseling.

CAREER FUNCTIONING ASSESSMENT

Shannon J. Hodges, PhD, LMHC, ACS

The CFA provides a conceptual framework to assess a client's current occupational functioning and serves as a starting point for assessing future career success. The CFA's multilevel structure, along with the CFS (range 1–100), are designed to provide a more comprehensive picture of a client's occupational outlook. The CFA and CFS should always be used in conjunction with standardized, normative referenced, career assessments (e.g., SII, ASVAB, SDS), review of previous records, and sessions in career counseling. Counselors should take the client's age, gender, culture, and mental health (e.g., depression, anxiety, posttraumatic stress disorder [PTSD]) into consideration when using the CFA and CFS.

Level I: Employment Status: The counselor should circle one of these categories:

1. Client is working in desired career (or studying/training for desired career).
2. Client is working in a career that is related to the desired career (e.g., teacher's aide when desired career is that of teaching).
3. Client is working in a survival job (e.g., fast-food industry type job) or is underemployed in some capacity (e.g., client has advanced degree or specialized training and is working for lower or minimum wage).
4. Client is unemployed.

Level II: Career Goals: The counselor should circle one of the following categories:

1. Client has clear and attainable career goals.
2. Client's career goals are somewhat clear and/or attainable.
3. Client has not fully developed clear goals or the goals appear unrealistic.
4. Client is unable to articulate career goals at present.

Occupational Optimism–Pessimism Scale

On the scale that follows, circle the number that best approximates the client's level of optimism or pessimism related to career success. Depending on the nature of the interaction with the client (client's mood, motivation, responsiveness, etc.), the counselor may simply select a number or ask the client: *"On a scale of 1 to 10, with 1 being pessimistic and 10 very optimistic, what number represents your confidence level regarding having a successful career?"*

1	2	3	4	5	6	7	8	9	10
Pessimistic			Optimistic				Very Optimistic		

Level III: Motivation: The counselor assesses the client's motivation to work toward the goals or to find career goals.

Client's current motivation to achieve career goals or to develop career goals: Depending on the nature of the counselor–client interaction (e.g., client's mood, motivation, responsiveness), the counselor may select a number that best approximates the client's level of motivation, or simply ask the client, *"On a scale of 1 to 10, what number best represents your motivation to achieve/develop career goals?"*

1	2	3	4	5	6	7	8	9	10
Unmotivated			Moderately Motivated				Highly Motivated		

Level IV: Supports (e.g., social, familial, spiritual, financial): The counselor should circle all support systems the client identifies as present in his or her life:

1. Client has a social support network (at least 1 or 2 close friends).
2. Client has family support (at least 1 or 2 supportive family members).
3. Client has adequate financial support (e.g., can pay rent, bills, support self/family).
4. Client has support from a spiritual network or some other support system (e.g., church, synagogue, 12-step community, support group).

Level V: Career Functioning Scale (Scored 1 to 100)

The CFS is a subjective assessment representing the counselor's best approximation of the client's current occupational functioning on a 1- to 100-point scale. Basic criteria to assess career functioning are provided for CFS scores in each scoring range. It is up to the counselor to assess the client's current functioning based on information gained through testing, an intake interview, and/or a counseling session. Higher scores are expected to be consistent with more positive occupational success (or in the case of an adolescent or young adult, more potential for success), while lower scores are expected to be consistent with less occupational success.

91 to 100: Client's career has been very successful or displays successful potential (e.g., good references, high grades, ability to hold a job, information from aptitude and/or interest testing); articulates clear career goals; is able to meet goals; is able to address workplace challenges; is respected by coworkers, supervisors, and educators; is highly optimistic about future career success; and is motivated and engaged with learning new skills important for continued success. Client appears fully able to reach career goals through training, experience, and work ethic.

81 to 90: Client's career is going very well or has that potential; client articulates clear career goals; is able to address workplace challenges; is respected by coworkers, supervisors, and educators; some concerns about achieving major goals; strong functioning on the job; general overall satisfaction with career/job; and interested in learning new skills for future success, though may express some concerns regarding ability to meet long-term job/career goals.

71 to 80: Moderately successful in career or job or has that potential; respected by coworkers, supervisors, and educators; some concerns about achieving career goals; perhaps some expressed dissatisfaction with current or past career/job.

61 to 70: Client has achieved some level of career/job success, though has difficulty meeting challenges in career/job; may express some disharmony or dissatisfaction in the workplace; may express some frustration or pessimism with career outlook or current job; may have barriers such as incomplete education/training; health or mental health issues may be a concern; may express frustration with many coworkers, supervisors, and educators.

51 to 60: Moderate dissatisfaction with job/career; numerous concerns expressed regarding job/career; job may not be congruent with career goals or desired lifestyle; may have experienced periods of unemployment; may express coworkers, supervisors, and educators are not as respectful as the client would like. Client may have gaps in work history for various reasons (e.g., firing, health or mental health issues, substance abuse, incarceration); may be unable to articulate career goals or articulate unrealistic career goals.

41 to 50: Significant dissatisfaction with job/career; difficulty maintaining employment; may report long history of workplace conflicts with coworkers, supervisors, educators with little insight as to his or her own contribution to conflicts. Mental health, health, and/or substance abuse may have played a role, as well as legal issues, and so forth. May be unable to articulate career goals or articulates unrealistic career goals.

31 to 40: Chronically unemployed or underemployed; unable to articulate career goals or articulates unrealistic career goals; regular conflicts with coworkers, supervisors, and educators; likely expresses pessimism regarding career success. May come from family of origin with multigenerational unemployment; may have lack of appropriate vocational role models; may have health, mental health, substance abuse history, legal difficulties, and so forth.

21 to 30: Chronic unemployment; client evidences a lack of clear career goals or articulates unrealistic career goals, or is unable to meet career goals; feels hopeless regarding career success and may lack motivation to seek employment, or may frequently blame others for lack of success (e.g., former bosses, coworkers, family). Client may present as depressed or lethargic, poorly groomed, irritable, restless, and so forth. Client may have poor insight into nature of struggles; may have health, mental health, substance abuse issues, legal difficulties, moderate to significant dysfunction in family of origin; and so forth.

11 to 20: Chronic unemployment; cannot articulate career goals; feels hopeless regarding career success; lacks understanding of how to plan for a career; and may have had long-term unemployment. Client may appear anxious, depressed, restless, emotionally distant, or hostile; may blame others (e.g., former bosses, family members); and may be resistant to career intervention. Client may have a history of health, mental health, or substance abuse issues, legal difficulties, dysfunctional family of origin, incomplete education, and so forth.

1 to 10: Long-term unemployment; unable to articulate career goals; feels hopeless regarding career success; family of origin may have experienced multigenerational unemployment; lacks motivation to seek employment and is very resistant to intervention. Client may appear anxious, depressed, restless, angry, or behavior may suggest client has given up on envisioning any reasonable career success. Client likely has extensive health, mental health, or substance abuse issues, poor role modeling, and so forth, and has little insight into the nature of his or her career history or occupational outlook.

The Career Values Checklist

Score each of the following items in terms of their importance to you. A score of 1 represents the value of highest importance and 10 the lowest:

1. A job/career that would bring me prestige.
2. A job/career that would bring me personal and professional fulfillment, though not necessarily a high salary.
3. A job/career that would provide a good salary and stable employment but not necessarily be what I love doing.
4. A job/career where I would be of service to others even though I might not make a large salary.

5. A job/career where I have the freedom to make independent decisions, but with the knowledge that could mean a less secure job.
6. A job/career where I could work with a team of colleagues.
7. A job/career where I could work primarily alone.
8. A job/career where I could work overseas with a diverse, multicultural population.
9. A job/career that would offer employment security, benefits, but would not be very fulfilling.
10. A job/career that would provide career satisfaction but little in the way of security.

10 Decision-Making Questions for Career and Life Consideration

1. When you make important decisions are you most likely to make them impulsively, intuitively, or rationally?
2. Think of the biggest decision you have made. How did you arrive at the decision you made? How do you feel about how your decision has turned out?
3. When you are faced with an important decision, how do you go about making it? What strategy is most helpful?
4. Consider a "poor" decision you have made in the past. What did you learn from that experience? How could that knowledge be helpful now?
5. Regarding making decisions, do you tend to seek other's advice before making the decision or make it alone?
6. Everyone makes decisions that work out well and others that turn out to be disappointments. Regardless of success or disappointment in a decision, do you tend to reflect on what went well and what went poorly? Or, would you simply put both out of you mind?
7. Think back to your family of origin (or however you might have been raised); did your parents/guardians tend to demonstrate confidence in your decision-making ability?
8. When you are faced with an important choice, what seems most helpful in that decision-making process?
9. Say a close friend came to you with a big decision to make. How might you advise your friend? What might be important considerations?
10. On a scale of 1 to 10, with 10 being "I have absolute confidence in my decision-making judgment," and 1 being "I have zero confidence in my decision-making ability," where are you at this moment? (If less than 10, ask, "How could you move up one number?")

MODELS OF ASSISTANCE, COPING, AND CLIENT CHANGE

Clients' expectations for change may vary widely depending on their level of insight into the nature of their struggle. Clients will also differ in the extent to which they take personal responsibility for their contribution to whatever struggle or challenge they are encountering. It is likely that clients who are self-referred will have more motivation, insight into the problem, and be more committed to change than clients mandated by various judicial, academic, supervisory, or personal authorities. Brickman et al. (1982) have identified four different orientations toward counseling based on the client's views. Students presenting themselves to the counseling center may subscribe to any one of these four models:

- Moral Model: People are responsible for their problems and solutions. Students who fit this model may look on counselors or advisors as consultants who may recommend self-help resources (e.g., books, personal growth groups). They may perceive themselves as being "lazy" with a need to work harder.
- Compensatory Model: People are not responsible for their problems but are responsible for their own solutions. Students with this point of view may perceive counselors as advocates who can help them overcome a problem they did not cause (e.g., poor education, lack of career guidance in high school). They may view themselves as deprived individuals who must assert themselves. Students in this model may look to the counselor for empowerment to help correct deficits.
- Enlightenment Model: People are responsible for their problems but not for the solutions to the problems. Students endorsing this model may look on counselors as saviors who can provide long-term care for them by means of ongoing support groups or additional coping methods. They may also view themselves as guilty individuals who must submit to a higher authority. Students in this model may expect counselors to help provide them with the discipline they perceive themselves as lacking.
- Medical Model: People are not responsible for problems or solutions. Students who fit this model view counselors as experts able to remedy their problems by external means (e.g., by prescribing a treatment program). They regard themselves as ill people who must accept advice or treatment from the proper authority. Students subscribing to this model may expect counselors to prescribe the solution, which they in turn will follow (Brickman et al., 1982; Hood & Johnson, 2007, p. 40).

Career counselors can typically determine the student's orientation through a standard intake interview. Counselors might ask, "Who is to blame for this problem?" and "Who is responsible for solving this problem?" Career counselors may also consider an "internal" versus "external" locus of control during the intake session. Students who believe they are in control of their destiny (internal locus of control) fit the moral or compensatory models; clients who believe they are the victims of chance or their environment (external locus of control) conform to the enlightenment or medical models. An internal locus of control has been identified as being consistent with resilience, stronger work ethic, and lower rates of anxiety and depression (Rotter, 1966; Seligman, 2002).

STAGES OF CHANGE

Many college students who present themselves to the counseling center for counseling or advising may be resistant to change. Career counselors and career advisors would be well advised to consider the conceptual framework established by Prochaska, DiClemente, and Norcross (1992). The Stages of Change represents a model for career counselors and advisors to use to evaluate where students currently are in the decision-making process. The Stages of Change is a five-step model (sometimes "Relapse" and "Transcendence" are noted as the sixth and seventh steps) you can use for evaluation and later discussion with students with career and academic concerns.

The Stages of Change are as follows:

1. **Precontemplation:** The client or student is unaware there is a problem. For example, a student may be academically at risk of being dismissed from college but remains convinced he or she is doing well. Despite encouragement from the roommate and resident advisor, the student has refused to seek career counseling.
2. **Contemplation:** After the term ends and grades come out, the student begins to entertain the possibility that a 1.94 GPA (4.0 scale) does not bode well for admission to, say, medical school and perhaps a change of major is warranted.
3. **Preparation:** The student, realizing he or she is in academic jeopardy, makes an appointment at the counseling center.
4. **Action:** The student commits to eight sessions of career counseling and agrees to take the SII.
5. **Maintenance:** Six months later the student, who has chosen a different and more appropriate major, has improved grades and reports feeling much better about the choice of major and life direction.

The sixth and seventh stages are offered for further consideration:

6. **Relapse:** The student discovers the new major and potential career also is not a fit and resumes class absenteeism, becomes depressed, and slides back into academic difficulty. The student then returns for continued career counseling and exploration.
7. **Transcendence:** After more counseling and exploration, the student finds a new major and path and is pleased with it. The student attends class regularly, grades improve, and satisfaction with the new academic and career focus goes up significantly. The student even secures an internship in the new area of study.

Perhaps the most helpful aspect of the Stages of Change model is that it has such broad application. Though it is most often applied to clients mandated for addictions counseling, the model is easily applicable to any number of counseling issues college students may present. Students encountering academic struggles and career indecision are also prime candidates for assessing change. It also is worth mentioning that many students and clients will recycle through some or all of the stages several times before achieving any lasting change. The keys to change likely are awareness of a problem and developing the resilience to address that challenge. Researchers at the University of Rhode Island have developed the University of Rhode Island Change Assessment (URICA), a 32-item questionnaire that assesses attitudes and behaviors associated with the different stages of change; it is another good resource for evaluating a student's readiness for change (Cohen, Glaser, & Calhoun, 2005).

SUMMARY

Career counseling represents an opportunity for counselors to assist college students in deciding on a major or a career change. Intake interviews, counseling sessions, and assessment provide students with a wealth of helpful information during periods when they may be struggling to make decisions or when they are simply unsure about the current and future courses of their lives. Because career concerns overlap with depression, anxiety, stress levels, addictions, and overall mental functioning, placing the career center within counseling services is highly recommended.

Academic advising is also very correlated to career counseling and many of the same concerns that apply to career counseling certainly apply to academic advising. While numerous professionals on college campuses provide advising, most notably faculty, counselors are well qualified to staff academic advising centers, as students with undecided majors will likely need career counseling and assessment as well. Academic advisors who understand the nexus between academics, good mental health, and future career success, and who are capable of providing holistic treatment of the student, are in a privileged position to improve students' academic functioning as well as the quality of their lives.

REFERENCES

American Counseling Association. (2014). *2014 code of ethics*. Alexandria, VA: Author.

Betsworth, D. G., & Fouad, N. A. (1997). Vocational interests: A look at the past 70 years and a glance at the future. *Career Development Quarterly, 46*, 23–47.

Betz, N. E., & Rottinghaus, P. J. (2006). Current research on parallel measures of interests and confidence for basic dimensions of vocational activity. *Journal of Career Assessment, 14*, 56–76.

Bolles, R. N. (2016). *What color is your parachute? 2016: A practical manual for job-hunters and career-changers*. Berkeley, CA: Ten Speed Press.

Brickman, P., Rabinowitz, V. C., Karuza, J., Coates, D., Cohn, E., & Kidder, L. (1982). Models of helping and coping. *American Psychologist, 37*, 368–384.

Campbell, D. P. (2002). The history and development of the Campbell Interest and Skill Survey. *Journal of Career Assessment, 10*, 150–168.

Cohen, P. I., Glaser, B. A., & Calhoun, G. B. (2005). Examining readiness for change: A preliminary evaluation of the University of Rhode Island Change Assessment with incarcerated adolescents. *Measurement and Evaluation in Counseling and Development, 38*, 45–62.

Crites, J. O. (1981). *Career counseling: Models, methods, and materials.* New York, NY: McGraw-Hill.

DeVaney, S. B., & Hughey, A. W. (2000). Career development of ethnic minority students. In D. A. Luzzo (Ed.), *Career counseling of college students: An empirical guide to strategies that work* (pp. 233–254). Washington, DC: American Psychological Association.

Donnay, D. A. C., Morris, M. L., Schaubhut, N. A., & Thompson, R. C. (2005). *Strong Interest Inventory manual: Research, development and strategies for interpretation.* Mountain View, CA: CPP.

Ericae.net. (n.d.). *Online degrees.* Retrieved from Ericae.net/published/online-degrees-2.htm

Eveland, A. P., Conyne, R. K., & Blakney, V. L. (1998). University students and career decidedness: Effects of two computer-based career guidance interventions. *Computers in Human Behavior, 14*, 531–541.

Freedman, T. L. (2004). *The world is flat: A brief history of the twenty-first century.* New York, NY: Farrar, Straus, & Giroux.

Gillespie, P. (2015, March 25). *University of Phoenix has lost half its students.* Retrieved from http://money.cnn.com/2015/03/25/investing/university-of-phoenix -apollo-earnings-tank/index.html

Gordon, V. G. (2006). *Career advising: An academic advisor's guide.* San Francisco, CA: Jossey-Bass.

Holland, J. L. (1997). *Making vocational choices: A theory of vocational personalities and work environments* (3rd ed.). Odessa, FL: Psychological Assessment Resources.

Holland, J. L., Fritzche, B. A., & Powell, A. B. (1994). *Self-Directed Search: Technical manual.* Odessa, FL: Psychological Assessment Resources.

Hood, A. B., & Johnson, R. W. (2007). *Assessment in counseling: A guide to the use of psychological assessment procedures* (4th ed.). Alexandria, VA: American Counseling Association.

Janda, L. (1999). *Career tests: 25 revealing self-tests to help you find and succeed at the perfect career.* Avon, MA: Avon Media Corporation.

Luzzo, D. A. (2002). *Making career decisions that count: A practical guide* (2nd ed.). Upper Saddle River, NJ: Prentice Hall.

National Academic Advising Association. (2004). *Statement on the concept of academic advising.* Retrieved from http://www.nacada.ksu.edu/definitions.htm

Pardee, C. F. (1994). We profess developmental advising, but do we practice it? *NACADA Journal, 14*(2), 59–61.

Pope, M. (2000). A brief history of career counseling in the United States. *Career Development Quarterly, 48*(3), 194–211.

Prochaska, J. O., DiClemente, C. C., & Norcross, J. C. (1992). In search of how people change: Applications to addictive behaviors. *American Psychologist, 47,* 1102–1114.

Randahl, G. J., Hansen, J.-I. C., & Haverkamp, B. E. (1993). Instrumental behaviors following test administration and interpretation: Exploration validity of the Strong Interest Inventory. *Journal of Counseling and Development, 71,* 435–439.

Rotter, J. (1966). Generalized expectations for internal versus external control of reinforcement. *Psychological Monographs, 80,* 1–28.

Seligman, M. E. P. (2002). *Authentic happiness: Using the new positive psychology to realize your potential for lasting fulfillment.* New York, NY: Free Press.

Shell, K. D., LeBold, W. K., & Ward, S. (1991). *The Purdue Interest Questionnaire: Helping engineering and technology students make career decisions* (pp. 442–452). Proceedings of the Frontiers in Education Twenty-First Annual Conference, West Lafayette, IN.

Slaney, R. B., & MacKinnon-Slaney, F. (2000). Using vocational card sorts in career counseling. In C. E. Watkins, Jr., & V. L. Campbell (Eds.), *Testing and assessment in counseling practice* (2nd ed., pp. 371–428). Mahwah, NJ: Erlbaum.

Spokane, A. R., & Catalano, M. (2000). The Self-Directed Search: A theory-driven array of self-guided career interpretations. In C. E. Watkins, Jr., & V. L. Campbell (Eds.), *Testing and assessment in counseling practice* (2nd. ed., pp. 339–370). Mahwah, NJ: Erlbaum.

Viteles, M. S. (1974). Industrial psychology: Reminiscences of an academic moonlighter. In T. Krawiec (Ed.), *The psychologist* (Vol. 2, pp. 441–500). New York, NY: Oxford University Press.

Winston, R. B. (1989). Counseling and advising. In U. Delworth, G. Hanson, and Associates (Eds.), *Student services: A handbook for the professions.* San Francisco, CA: Jossey-Bass.

CHAPTER FIVE

PROFESSIONAL ISSUES IN COLLEGE COUNSELING CENTER STAFFING

Michelle M. King Lyn

COUNSELING CENTER STAFFING

Past Staffing Trends of College Counseling Centers: A Historical Perspective

From a historical perspective, staffing trends in college counseling centers have changed over the years. In the earliest research published by a college "mental hygiene" clinic staff member, psychiatrists staffed these offices (May, 2008). During and after World War II (late 1940s–mid 1950s), the field of psychology expanded greatly. As noted in Chapter 1, psychologists began staffing counseling centers on campuses, and the treatment of students shifted from the health services to a focus on vocational and educational problems along with emotional concerns. Social workers were also part of the staff at these early versions of today's counseling centers. Even so, the change over from psychiatrist-led to psychologist-led services continued from college to college, depending on the perspective and preference of the university.

Today, although most counseling center directors are clinical or counseling psychologists, some are psychiatrists and some centers are merged with health services. It is clear from the most recent directors survey (Gallagher, 2012) that counseling center directors are a diverse group of professionals representing many disciplines, as shown in Table 5.1.

Although not many psychiatrists serve as counseling center directors, 57% of directors surveyed in 2012 indicated that on-campus psychiatric consultation was available.

In terms of other staffing trends, it is clear that women by far make up the majority of counseling center directors (59%) and staff counselors (69%) in the field (Gallagher, 2012). The college counseling field, like the field of psychology, is dominated by women. Even in 1987, Whiteley, Mahaffey, and Greer (1987) gathered data from 899 institutions and found that college counselors were mostly women and mostly White (80%), with 20% of counselors identifying as people of color. From the results of the most recent Association for University

TABLE 5.1 Director's Professional Identity	
Clinical psychologist	28.8%
Counseling psychologist	35.3%
Psychiatrist	0.7%
Mental health professional	4.8%
Social worker	9.2%
Student personnel administrator	0.7%
Professional counselor	17.1%
Registered nurse or nurse practitioner	1.4%
Family therapist	1%
Internal medical physician	0.3%
Other	0.7%

Source: Gallagher (2012).

and College Counseling Center Directors (AUCCCD) sample of 293 institutions, college counselors are only slightly more diverse today (22.1% people of color and 77.9% White/Caucasian) (Gallagher, 2012).

In their article, Leventhal and Magoon (1979) outlined the following suggestions for counseling centers as they relate to staffing trends:

1. Counseling centers should have staff who are licensed psychologists.
2. Psychologists on staff should be jointly appointed as faculty.
3. Counseling center staff should practice from diverse theoretical orientations and may even be integrative.
4. Counseling center staff need to attend regularly scheduled training to be up to date with treatment.
5. Counseling center staff need to work through internal issues that might negatively impact their work.

These staffing directives were written decades ago and still offer wisdom for today's counseling center professionals.

Staffing Patterns According to School and Center Characteristics

Some authors have focused on counseling center staffing patterns according to the type of institution. For example, several authors have looked at the staffing and utilization in small schools as well a staff experience in the International Association of Counseling Services (IACS)–accredited schools versus nonaccredited schools (Coll, 1993; Harrar, Affsprung, & Long, 2010; Harris & Kranz, 1991). Harris and Kranz (1991) indicated that in small schools, there was a gradual shift from vocational counseling to personal counseling. Also in the

1980s, staff at counseling centers at small schools began to notice a higher demand for services and greater severity of problems. As a result, nearly half of the centers ended up with waitlists during this time. More outside referrals were made at small schools due to limited or part-time staff, especially for long-term counseling issues.

Staffing trends in the 1980s called for more broad training of staff. For example, it was suggested that counseling center staff at smaller schools need to be especially good at making referrals effectively. Since the need to foster relationships with appropriate referral resources is evident, it was noted that counseling centers at small schools were moving toward a team approach focused on building strong working relationships with college administrators and beyond the campus. Lastly, the authors asserted that small schools were impacted by the trend for more services earlier than larger schools (Harris & Kranz, 1991).

Coll (1993) examined the experiences of college counselors in community colleges, specifically looking at those centers with IACS accreditation and those without. Results indicated that counselors in IACS centers experienced less role conflict than nonaccredited counterparts. This may be due to having better defined roles and expectations for the centers since they are required to have detailed policy and procedural manuals. For the purposes of the study, role conflict was defined as inconsistency of expectations associated with a role. Role strain can lead to less job effectiveness, higher turnover and burnout, and less commitment to the organization.

Coll's (1993) article noted several benefits to being IACS accredited: (a) less role strain and burnout for staff; (b) more resources from the school for the center; and (c) better job effectiveness and clarity for what's expected on the job. This article suggests that IACS-accredited centers function better and have more satisfied staff over time. Whiteley et al. (1987) also found that IACS-accredited centers were more likely to have people of color on staff, more training programs, and more directors with doctoral degrees in counseling or clinical psychology. Accredited centers offered a wide range of personal and career counseling services and outreach services, but were less likely to provide academic advising as part of their services.

In addition to school size and center accreditation, staffing patterns may also follow patterns of primary service delivery and utilization. For example, a center that does mostly intake assessments and subsequent referrals may be able to operate with a smaller staff; however, a center providing individual counseling as its primary service will need more staff. Some centers hire temporary or contract therapists during peak times of the year to meet the demand for services. The contract therapists are usually private practitioners in the community with experience or expertise working with the college population.

Recent Staffing Trends and Changes

In terms of services, in 1987 the primary service was individual counseling followed by career counseling. By contrast, the most essential services today as perceived by counseling center directors are crisis intervention, consultation with faculty and staff, serving on crisis intervention teams with other university officials, training of residential life staff or others who work directly with students, and brief counseling for students (Gallagher, 2012). Not surprisingly, group counseling was rated as more essential by directors at larger schools. Interestingly, vice presidents rated the same services as important and by far saw crisis intervention as the most essential services. These trends highlight the growing emphasis of centers on crisis intervention and related services. Another major shift was that career counseling was rated the second most essential service in 1987, and it was ranked fifth on the 2012 list of essential services by both directors and vice presidents. It was not included in the 2013 list to be ranked. The shift from career to personal to crisis intervention as the focus is noteworthy when considering staffing trends. Counselors with a career counseling focus may not be as good of a fit for counseling centers today as would have been the case in the past.

Other noteworthy staffing and service trends emerged from polling staff counselors whose primarily professional association was with the American College Counseling Association (ACCA; Smith et al., 2007). Of those who responded, 45% were either director or associate director. The majority did not have administrative roles in the center, and the authors were most interested in gathering data from those counselors who did not serve as administrators. Survey questions focused on work load and daily duties. The results demonstrated that staff counselors did a variety of activities (e.g. providing outreach, meeting with campus administrators weekly, and consultation with psychiatry) and thus needed to be broadly trained to be competent at their jobs. In addition, counselors reported having their biggest challenge being students with severe psychopathology and multicultural issues. Again, these areas should be consistently emphasized in training for college counselors. Lastly, it was noted that college counselors need to be well versed in crisis management and offer many services beyond individual counseling. The counselors who responded to the poll mentioned but deemphasized crisis planning as part of their role. This is likely because it was published just prior to the 2007 Virginia Tech and 2008 Northern Illinois State campus shootings.

Staffing in College Counseling Centers

Watson and Schwitzer (2010) noted that "the reach of college counseling professionals is wide." Specifically, every presenting issue from students' adjustments to psychosis to suicidality will present at a college counseling center. The need for well-trained, multidisciplinary staff is clear. There are many overlapping skills and abilities among the professionals working together in the college counseling setting. At the same time, each field has a specific contribution to the overall quality of services.

Psychologists

By far, psychologists are the largest group of counseling center directors, with counseling psychologists still representing the highest percentage within the group. Given the increased focus on crisis intervention, it is likely that more and more clinical psychologists will be members of counseling center staff. Traditional counseling psychologists who may want to focus more on developmental or career concerns may be less likely to choose counseling centers as a primary career option.

Counseling centers are optimal training environments for psychologists since many staff psychologists value supervision and training and see it as an important aspect of their professional development. In addition to providing training in individual, group, and couples counseling, psychologists may provide supervision for training in psychological assessment, another focus of training for clinical and counseling psychology programs.

Many decades ago, the literature often made mention of "turf wars" between clinical and counseling psychologists at counseling centers. Survey data at the time suggested that directors preferred to hire counseling psychologists over clinical psychologists, but there was more of a balance than ever in these practices (Corazzini, May, & Robbins, 1986). Corazzini et al. (1986) suggested more clinical psychologists would be hired in counseling centers over time, which seems to be the case today. Furthermore, the increase of programs offering the doctor of psychology degree (PsyD) have allowed for greater numbers of clinical psychologists in the job market; many may be seeking a counseling center position. Thus, the applicants from PsyD programs may have very similar credentials, especially in regard to practicum and internship training, as the applicants from counseling psychology or clinical psychology doctor of philosophy (PhD) programs.

Counselors and Counselor Educators

Counselors as a professional group may include a wide variety of specializations and academic training such as professional counselor, rehabilitation counselor, certified addictions counselor, and licensed marriage and family therapist (LMFT). In order to be licensed in one of these professions, clinicians must obtain a substantial number of supervised clinical hours after graduation, in addition to passing written certification examinations. Many counselors opt to get their pre-degree practicum and internship experience or their post-degree supervised experience from other licensed clinicians in the respective field working in college counseling settings. This may be one way qualified, licensed clinicians are recruited into a center after completing their post-degree hours.

Counselors may also have subspecialty areas after working under supervision in multiple settings in order to obtain licensures. Some may work in inpatient settings to obtain licensure and can transfer their assessment and treatment skills gained from working with more severe clients into the college counseling setting. An example might be a professional counselor who worked in an inpatient eating disorders clinic during a clinical internship. Certainly, this training would be useful in working with college students. Once licensed, counselors may also choose to work in private practice but may be open to providing services to clients on a contract basis during peak traffic times of the semester.

Licensed marriage and family therapists (LMFTs) also bring a unique skill set into the counseling center setting. Although family counseling may not be readily offered in counseling centers, exploring and working through family dynamics may also be needed when parents are involved in a student's hospitalization, treatment, or referral. LMFTs may also be more adept at group counseling due to training in working with multiple dynamics during family sessions (Simmons & Doherty, 1998).

Social Workers

Social workers are trained from a unique perspective that examines the individual in the context of a larger society and the systems that affect that individual. As such, social workers may be trained in advocacy, building relationships with other providers, and making referrals to adjunct services in order to meet the holistic psychosocial needs of the clients they work with. In a counseling center setting, social workers may enhance the staff by bringing this unique perspective into the college environment. In addition, they have the foundational and theoretical knowledge to explore systems with clients and help clients better navigate those systems.

One recent staffing trend is the hiring of licensed clinical social workers (LCSWs) into the role of client care coordinator or case manager to assist with the referral and continuity of care for more challenging or complex student problems. For example, an LCSW in the role of case manager for a college center might assist a severely anorexic student who has attempted therapy at the college counseling center with limited success. In the role of case manager, the staff member would be sharing resources with the student, contacting outside providers, and, if authorized, coordinating with parents to help the student find the appropriate level of care. In addition to coordinating referral, the LCSW staff member is also assessing the student during each case management meeting for decompensating and the potential for emergency hospitalization. Individuals with a social work background would have better working knowledge of coordinating such care for the student. Similar to counselors, another issue to consider in staffing is, depending on state laws, LSCWs may or may not have hospitalization privileges; however, in most states they do.

Psychiatrists

Campus mental health centers may have originated in student health centers where the mental health staff were mostly psychiatrists. Around the 1950s, most counseling centers were established separately from health centers, thus fewer psychiatrists were on board (Kraft, 2009). More psychologists and social workers staffed counseling centers with psychiatrists providing part-time hours, sometimes in a strictly consultative role. This model is consistent with the majority of today's counseling centers, where psychiatrists are full-time staff at a separate health center or are on staff part-time at the counseling center. There are some counseling centers that are merged with health centers where psychiatrists and other clinicians work under the same administrative umbrella.

Regardless of the structure of collaboration, it is clear that counseling centers are tasked with developing partnerships with psychiatrists on and off campus. More college students are using psychotropic medication to address psychological issues (Kraft, 2009). Many students may have been prescribed medication prior to coming on campus. Given the need for psychiatric evaluations and medication management, it is imperative for counseling centers to maintain relationships with psychiatrists on and off campus.

The current statistics on psychiatric consultations support the idea that centers are meeting the obligation to help students with psychiatric concerns. Gallagher (2012) reported that 57% of directors have access to on-campus psychiatric services. The average number of hours of psychiatric consultation is limited to 2.7 hours a week for every 1,000 students. In addition, in order for students to see a psychiatrist on campus, 44% of centers require that a student is in therapy in the counseling center. Psychiatrists in the centers polled were primarily providing direct services to students but some also attended case conference meetings and staff meetings. Psychiatrists appeared to be integrated with the counseling center staff in varying degrees depending on the center.

Physicians and Nurses

Physicians and nurses are likely to work closely with counseling center staff in centers with a merged model. A white paper published by the American College Health Association (ACHA, 2010) reported the results of a survey of directors from merged or integrated centers conducted to better understand trends and services at merged centers. Of 359 directors invited to participate in the survey, 92 respondents (25.6%) indicated being from merged centers. Of this group, they were asked to complete additional data about their centers. Psychologists made up 23.4% of the 92 directors polled, but 14.9% reported being a nurse, 14.9% reported being a nurse practitioner or physician assistant, and 12.8% reported being physicians. The number of nurses and physicians in director roles was far greater than the directors in the study identifying as psychiatrists (2.1%). The ACHA data indicate that within merged centers, there are more options for who can hold the director position due to access to other health care workers.

The survey participants indicated that the merging occurred via upper administration initiatives. Furthermore, the philosophical underpinnings behind the mergers were rooted in providing better continuity of care for students' holistic health. Cross-training of medical and mental health staff is needed to achieve these philosophical goals. In the context of a merger, nurses and physicians must be cross-trained in knowledge about mental health issues and health in a broader sense, especially for those serving as directors or other administrators in the center. Training may ideally focus on making referrals, differential diagnoses, and adapting the "bedside manner" for students with mental health issues.

Trainees

Similar to staff, trainees at college counseling centers are diverse in educational background and training. Emerging psychologists, counselors, social workers, and psychiatrists may all participate in training at a college counseling center depending on the structure and administration of the center. Trainees provide direct services to students and receive supervision by a licensed professional or more advanced trainee. Depending on the structure of the training program, trainees may be fully integrated into the center staff by attending case conference meetings or staff meetings. Typically, there is a selection process to assist training directors in finding a trainee who is the best fit for a program with respect to clinical skills, interpersonal style, goals for supervision, and training.

IACS has indicated that trainees should not be allowed to see more clients than senior staff. The ratio proposed by IACS exists to protect students and trainees alike. The IACS (2011) standards state that trainees' contact hours should not be 40% of clients at the center. Trainee limitations are needed as a reminder that trainees are students who must find ways to balance school and work. Trainees tend to be integral and effective clinicians and provide valuable services to college counseling centers. Outcome studies comparing pre- and post-data of clients of trainees and those of senior staff have found that some trainees had better pre-/post-outcomes than did staff, although interpretation of this result requires great caution because clients perceived to have complicated issues are actively reassigned to staff (Minami et al., 2009).

Peer Counselors

Peer counselors or educators are usually undergraduate students who provide basic helping services to other students. Examples might include career development paraprofessionals who might assist other students in finding career-related resources, or health educators who provide outreach about topics such as alcohol and drug use on campus. In these examples, the peer counselors are responsible for helping on a basic level that does not surpass their training or position. The students in these roles may also serve as ambassadors for the counseling center to the larger student population. This marketing from students in visible roles is one way for students to learn about the services offered at the counseling center.

Professional Development

Many mental health professionals working at college counseling centers appreciate the benefits afforded to them working in a higher education setting. One benefit is financial support toward professional development and training opportunities. Counseling centers usually have budget amounts set aside for training of its staff. Counselors usually have autonomy to select the workshops and conferences that relate most to their roles in the center. They may also choose workshops in specific clinical interest areas. Centers benefit from having their staff maintain professional licensure by earning continuing education credit and being up to date on the most current and innovative treatment practices.

Professional counseling center staff may also present workshops and trainings at local and national conferences. Some directors offer additional funding to staff presenting at conferences. Staff presentations increase the center's visibility and provide the opportunity for the improvement of services through the exchange of ideas. Preparing for presentations also leads to an objective evaluation of programs and services and an attempt to see your center's initiatives from a fresh perspective.

Many counseling center directors encourage their staff to become members of professional organizations and to become involved in committee work, conference planning, and to take on leadership roles in those respective organizations. Staff members benefit in terms of their own personal and professional growth by acquiring leadership, management, and networking skills. These skills are beneficial to those staff members with an interest in administration within a college counseling center or other mental health setting. Via networking as a member or leader in a professional organization, staff counselors are also exposed to research, clinical interventions, and programming that may be adopted at the home center. Similar to other student affairs professionals, counseling center counselors benefit from gaining notoriety in their respective fields. Doing so helps with job satisfaction and with potential for advancement within or beyond the university.

Research is another area in which staff members are encouraged to participate. Creating original research is an important aspect of professional identity for some college counselors. Often, there is the opportunity to continue with research topics pursued during graduate studies. In addition, counseling center counselors are in a unique position to contribute to the literature for college counseling while they are actively engaged in clinical work. They can observe trends in clinical services and design research to better inform their practice and that of the college mental health field at large.

College counselors may be interested in writing or research but may be faced with barriers regarding time allocation for these activities. Release time to develop, pursue, and write-up empirical research must be considered. Given utilization trends, counselors may already have multiple roles within a center and have limited ability to do research even when they may otherwise desire to do so. The culture of the center and the support of the director varies from center to center with respect to support for scholarly activities of staff counselors.

Limitations on Professional Development and Advancements

The opportunities for advancement in college counseling centers are limited. Although many centers have a multileveled system such as the one described in Figure 5.1 in this chapter, the number of administrative positions relative to the number of staff counselors is small. One solution to the problem is that staff may move outside of an organization to advance. It is typical for staff counselors to remain for 4 to 6 years in an entry-level position (Londono-McConnell & Matthews, 2003). Another solution might be to create a tiered system for nonadministrative staff based on annual evaluations or performance appraisals (see Figure 5.2 for an example). Staff counselors may also advance by taking on an area of coordination within the center or increasing responsibility within their coordination area over time. The advancement of staff needs to be supported by the counseling center director, division administrators, and the

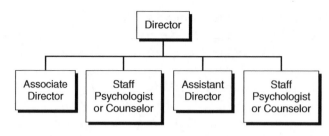

Figure 5.1 Sample organizational chart found in many university and college counseling centers.

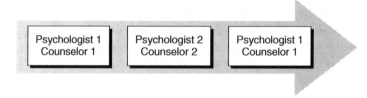

Figure 5.2 Potential path for career advancement for staff clinicians.

appropriate human resources representatives. Advancement of staff would be considered an important aspect of professional development to staff counselors with career aspirations of working in college counseling centers as a career.

Career Development of Counseling Center Staff

Many career development models explore the process of selecting, starting, and ending a career from a life-span approach. This section focuses on an American College Personnel Association (ACPA) Commission on Counseling and Psychological Services (CCAPS) newsletter article by Londono-McConnell and Matthews (2003) that outlines a career development model for counseling center professionals. The model describes counseling center counselors in varying stages of their careers and the process of moving from one stage to the next based on the amount of time working in a counseling center. The model offers a unique perspective on the career trajectory of many counseling center professionals and it is based on the personal experiences of the authors.

Stage 1—"Young Guns"

Counselors at this stage are new professionals transitioning out of their role as student into professional. They typically have a high level of energy and enthusiasm for their positions and try out various professional activities both inside and outside the center. One task at this stage is defining what constitutes a good fit for them with respect to position and work environment. Some areas of professional struggle might include competence, licensure, and developing one's own style as a therapist. In addition, personal issues such as establishing work/life balance and financial difficulties are common. The "young guns" usually stay in this stage for 4 to 6 years.

Stage 2—"Crossroad Counselors"

In the time span of 6 to 10 years of working in a counseling center, counselors are in stage 2 where they begin to question whether to remain in a counseling center setting. This questioning may stem from a need to determine if a better fit for them exists in a different setting. In addition, there are limited opportunities for advancement in counseling centers due to small numbers of administrative positions. In light of the "glass ceiling," the cyclical nature of counseling center work that may be experienced as monotonous, and stresses associated with burnout, "crossroad counselors" have much to evaluate regarding their commitment to staying in or leaving a counseling center. Some other personal issues might challenge counselors in this stage such family commitments and needing to scale back on professional activities.

Stage 3—"The Next Generation"

If counselors remain in a counseling center after the crossroad stage, they would be considered as a part of the "next generation." The third stage begins within the range of 11 to 16 years working in a college counseling center position. They may take on roles as mentors and supervisors of "young guns." One characteristic of this stage is the marked age difference between these counselors and early career counselors. There is also an increased age difference between counselors and students, which makes it more difficult for counselors to relate to students. The counselors at this stage also explore the option of taking on associate director and director positions within a counseling center. This may be a challenge for many since the directors' positions are few and often require geographic mobility. Next-generation counselors engage in a re-visioning of their future and next steps in their career.

Stage 4—"Seasoned Sages"

In the final stage of counseling center professionals' career development, there may be consideration of moving into higher education administration as a career choice. After contributing so much to the field of college counseling through their dedication and commitment, they benefit from a high level of respect. However, there may be contemplation and reflection on one's career and whether the desired goals were achieved. In addition, counselors in stage 4 may feel isolated professionally because mentors have moved on and perhaps passed away. Also some of the professional associations may cater to younger or midstage counseling professionals. One suggested way "seasoned sages" may reinvigorate their careers is by connecting with individuals from earlier stages to gain new energy and ideas while offering the wisdom of their experience.

The stages described in this model will not apply to all counseling center professionals. However, they may shed light on personal and professional development issues impacting the retention of counselors at certain points in their careers. In addition, the model may provide assistance to counseling center professionals seeking validation for their own career experiences. (Of note, the bio for each author was provided at the end of the newsletter article and the authors themselves worked in counseling centers and likely experienced many of the issues described in the model before deciding to pursue private practice and consultation.)

Supervision and Consultations

Staff counselors in college counseling centers benefit from consistent access to peers for peer supervision and consultation. There are many opportunities for both formal and informal consultation within the college counseling center setting. In addition to supervision dyads of counselors at different levels in the center, most centers coordinate a variety of meetings to meet the clinical and administrative needs of the center.

1:1 Supervision Dyads

Depending on hiring requirements, some staff counselors may begin an entry-level position prior to obtaining licensure in a mental health field. Under these circumstances, the staff member would be required to attend weekly supervision with a qualified clinician according to state licensure laws. Formal supervision such as this is typically documented and monitored by the appropriate licensing board. The focus of supervision would be on clinical issues as well as professional development issues or other topics of interest related to the work setting. The supervisor relationship may be time limited and is usually dependent on the unlicensed staff member obtaining licensure.

Less formally, early career professionals might choose to have regular meetings with a more experienced professional or staff member serving as a mentor. Directors and other administrators might serve as mentors to other staff members as well. The focus of these meetings might be on professional decision making, leadership skills, or job effectiveness. The meetings may occur in conjunction with or completely separate from performance evaluations. Inherent in supervision, consultation, or mentorship is the relationship between the two professionals having clearly defined roles. Also, building of trust in these relationships is important. Staff-to-staff supervision and mentoring can enhance working relationships and contribute to staff's understanding of one another's values and strengths as clinicians.

Case Disposition and Assignment Teams

Weekly meetings that are used to review staff cases and attend to client assignment also allow the opportunity for consultation and peer supervision. It is common that centers have more than one team that meets to staff and assign cases. Other centers may elect to have one team that consists of some senior staff and interns or one team with all senior staff and interns. In a group setting, shared decisions can be made about difficult or challenging cases. There may also be times when policies or procedures are reviewed as part of the disposition of a case. Members of the team may learn new information or review information they may need for a similar situation in the future. Another benefit of the team approach is that members are aware of traffic flow in the center and can give students a consistent message during intakes about wait times, referral options, and services available in the center other than individual counseling.

Weekly Case Conference or Case Presentations

In addition to weekly meetings to discuss assignment and disposition of cases, a case conference meeting may be held. All clinicians (practicum students, interns, senior staff, counseling center administrators, and consulting psychiatrists) would be required to attend these meetings and adjust their schedules accordingly. These meetings provide the opportunity for clinicians with varying degrees of experience to meet and discuss clinical issues. It may also be a time to cover outreach needs of the center. A meeting time for all center clinicians fosters collegiality in the work environment and enhances learning and mentorship opportunities where professional behavior is modeled.

For example, in the center where this author is employed the weekly case conference is used for a variety of purposes. The associate director of clinical services or a designee is responsible for setting the agenda for the meetings each week. Meetings usually open with senior staff making announcements pertaining to all clinicians such as which groups are open or closed or outreach coverage needs. The meeting can then continue in a couple of different directions depending on the predetermined schedule. Most staff expressed the preference for having a variety of meeting formats to engage different learning styles and other individual comfort levels in group settings.

One meeting format option is a review and in-depth discussion of preselected journal articles. Another type of meeting would be a predetermined in-house or guest speaker presenting on a clinical issue. An in-house speaker might provide training to clinical staff on a center-wide initiative such as suicide assessment or the use of initial assessment data in working with students. A guest speaker may represent other campus offices or an off-campus mental health agency with a specific focus. Guest speakers are usually invited to speak on clinical issues that are common in the center. The final meeting format is less structured and clinicians are encouraged to discuss a challenging case, themes in their work, successes, or issues around the person of the therapist. Practicum students and interns are encouraged to actively participate and not defer to senior staff to contribute. The goal is to foster confidence in discussing clinical cases in a variety of situations and settings at all levels of training.

The success of these meetings can be attributed to a number of factors. One, having a variety of meeting formats and preplanning the dates for each type of meeting seem to provide both consistency and variety to different types of learning styles. Also, the consistent presence of psychiatry staff has enhanced the meetings and allowed for a strong collaborative relationship with psychiatry even with them being housed in the health center under a different administrative branch of the university. Frequent contact with psychiatry allows the opportunity to discuss shared cases and gain familiarity with treatment approaches of the psychiatrists on staff. Lastly, the meetings assist in team building for the center.

Supervision of Supervision

Most training decisions are made by a training committee in a counseling center. Under the guidance of one or more training directors, depending on the size of the center, the training committee discusses trainee progress, problems, and issues concerning the supervisory relationship. Again, having the collective wisdom of many supervisors with differing degrees of experience and diversity of perspectives is a benefit to all senior staff members, especially those in the role of supervisor.

Managing Conflict Among Staff

Conflict is a natural and healthy part of any relationship. In the workplace, conflict among staff is to be expected where differences of opinion, interests, and ideas are present. When conflict occurs among staff members of the counseling center, the situation is best managed when all parties are invested in working through the conflict and reaching a satisfactory resolution for all. Self-reflection may help a staff member understand the nature of the conflict and, depending on the nature and impact of the conflict, evaluate the degree that it needs to be addressed.

The policy and procedure manual of a center may be used as a resource in working through staff conflict. The Georgia Tech Counseling Center Policy and Procedure Manual (2013) was used as a reference in this section of the chapter. One approach to dealing with conflict is to consult professional guidelines established with mental health clinicians in mind. In keeping with the ethical guidelines of the American Psychological Association and other mental health professional organizations, when a staff member is in conflict with another, one member should initiate a conversation to address the nature of the conflict. The tone of the approach and subsequent conversation should not be overly aggressive or accusatory in nature. Also, the ability to use "I" statements and take ownership of one's feelings and reactions is considered an effective communication skill to help resolve conflict. It is considered effective to listen nondefensively to the other's point of view. Active and reflective listening, similar to what is used in clinical situations, demonstrates that the listener is present and invested in hearing the other person's concerns. Finally, collaborative problem solving between the parties in conflict is suggested and then developing a plan both parties can follow is a final step.

There may be times when staff members elect to involve the director or his or her designee. The goal of the director would be to encourage staff to manage conflict on their own. When this is not possible, the director will attempt to be neutral. If this is not possible, a neutral party will be brought in by the director to work with the parties in conflict.

Again, conflict in the workplace is common. In counseling centers, conflict occurs but the involved parties tend to have basic working knowledge of conflict resolution techniques. However, these skills do not always translate so it is important to have clear policies and procedures in the staff manual or standard operating procedures to address conflict among staff.

Issues Involving Counseling Center Staff and Central Administration

Counseling center staff and administrators do not always agree on student concerns. For example, a staff member may be expected to disclose information about a student outside of confidentiality limitations. Over the years, staff have been more willing to disclose such information, feeling pressure to safeguard the campus from widespread tragedies. There are several other possible misconceptions held by central administration about the counseling center.

Several of these potential issues are discussed by Much, Wagener, and Hellenbrand (2010). At times, counseling centers may be expected to provide a simple and fast solution for a complex student issue. When the process of counseling is unknown or misunderstood, some might assume one meeting can remedy a long-standing problem. In the case of students being referred by administrators to the counseling center, the issues tend to be multilayered, which would require time and effort for the counseling center staff to appropriately assess and intervene. There may be some frustration by administrators with the process (Much et al., 2010).

Counseling center staff, as licensed mental health clinicians, are required to indicate their scope of competence to licensing boards. At times, counseling center staff may be called on to practice outside their competence area (Much et al., 2010). The reason counseling centers refer cases to outside professionals is that there are many instances where student issues are beyond the scope of service or competence. Ethical principles require referral in these situations to avoid potential legal problems. However, the majority of these issues are unknown to central administration, so counseling center staff has to provide education about competency limits, scope of services, and center referral policies and procedures.

Central administration may be more likely to value aspects of the counseling center services that may be least enjoyable to counselors. For example, the AUCCCD surveys from 2010 to 2012 demonstrate the vice president of student affairs sees crisis services as the most essential aspect of the counseling center. However, counseling staff may place more value on other aspects of their roles such as training, group psychotherapy, and multicultural competence. Much et al. (2010) also suggest a conflict in what is valued most by administration (crisis intervention) and counseling center staff (prevention, outreach). The potential for counselor burnout is greater in situations where staff are not engaged in the activities they most enjoy. It is therefore important to balance administration expectations with the areas of greatest work satisfaction by counseling center staff to safeguard against staff burnout.

Counseling center staff are required to have appropriate boundaries between themselves and students as potential clients. The nature of dual relationships can be harmful to students and it is the role of the professional to moderate the potential for such. Other student affairs professionals may not be called upon to maintain the same degree of interpersonal distance between themselves and students. At times, central administration may perceive counseling center staff as being less willing to participate in activities such as welcome week or attending student concerts or performances (e.g., Greek Life step show). Counseling center staff may appear to be unsupportive or aloof when such events occur, but in actuality they are being mindful of the comfort of the students. These dual relationship conflicts are more likely to be an issue on smaller campuses where a lack of staff presence is more evident at various events. On larger campuses, counseling center staff would be less integral to the efforts to demonstrate staff support for student affairs events.

Even with these potential challenges in working with central administration, the role of today's counseling center director is to work closely with central administration to facilitate knowledge and understanding of the counseling center's larger purpose in the campus community. It is clear that the role of counseling centers is seen as an important one, even if consistent refinement of that role is needed through strong and consistent communication between central administration and the center.

Support Staff and Issues

Administrative staff provide support for the operations of the center each day. The configuration of support staff differs greatly from one center to the next. Typically there is at least one person working in the front office responsible for opening and closing the center, answering phone calls and routing them appropriately, and attending to the reception area of the center. The person(s) may also have a fair amount of client interaction and may greet students and other visitors and field their questions. The front office staff in that role also handles confidential documents provided by clients. They may process new client paperwork, make and file client files, and schedule initial appointments.

In addition to clerical and reception work, front office staff may be expected to alert clinicians to unusual, alarming, or disturbing behavior observed in the waiting area. For this reason, support staff chosen in counseling centers are often warm and friendly but also observant and assertive. The personality traits of the individual(s) in the role are helpful in determining fit for the position. At times the person in the role may also supervise other support staff. The title office manager can be used to best describe the position.

Business Manager

A business manager works closely with the director to attend to budgetary issues. The purchases and payments needed to operate the center are monitored by the business manager. Additionally, a business manager may coordinate travel to and from professional workshops for counseling staff and assist with registering clinicians for desired workshops. The business manager also serves as a backup to support and reception staff. Similar to the clerical workers, business managers must be knowledgeable and understanding of how to handle confidential documents and Health Insurance Portability and Accountability Act (HIPAA) regulations.

Boundaries, Self-Care, and Other Issues

The counseling center sees students in distress and the degree the distress is obvious varies greatly. At times, students may come into the center in tears or visibly angry. Sometimes students may "spill" prior to meeting with a counselor and talk about their personal issues with the support staff. When this happens, it is considered a boundary issue and support staff must not cross boundaries with clients and engage in clinical intervention inadvertently. Similarly, support staff may see a student in distress or hear aspects of the student's story while waiting to see a counselor. Healthy boundaries would require the support staff member to be discreet about what was overheard and resist any temptation about getting more information from the student or the therapist. Boundaries exist to protect clients and the center as well from liability.

Boundaries are present to protect the staff, too. For example, the counseling staff member may unintentionally "bring home" aspects of the distress, an important self-care issue for which clinicians receive training. Administrative staff, however, may not be aware of how working with distressed students may impact them, especially those with a personality that is engaging, outgoing, and friendly, and draws students to them. If managed properly, these personality traits can be an asset to the center overall.

Students presenting to the center may be highly anxious or self-conscious and exhibit limited social skills (poor eye contact, awkwardness, and incoherent speech). Support staff is required to be patient with such students, showing compassion for their possible difficulties and respecting their space in getting the help they are seeking.

Another challenge for support staff may come in managing the different personalities of senior staff members and counseling center administrators. Support staff deals with a variety of requests, preferences, and suggestions from professional staff. The front office or support staff typically acclimates to the different styles in order to provide back up and support as needed. Some senior staff may want or need more support than others. Thus, it helps to have clear policies and procedures for all to review along with clearly defined roles for support staff members. A well-trained and efficient support staff contributes a great deal to the overall workings of the center, making it a positive environment for students and staff alike.

Training of Staff

Clinical Staff

IACS-accredited sites are mandated to provide regular opportunities to receive training to enhance existing skills. Continuing education training may occur on or off site. It is also recommended that staff receive training related to policies and procedures for their respective sites. Discussion of ethics as related to center policies and procedures can also be helpful in training senior staff. Training for new professional staff often occurs informally through mentoring or peer-to-peer supervision. Counseling centers often schedule annual or biannual planning retreats as a time for training and reviewing center services.

Support Staff

It is important for front office staff to be trained regarding confidentiality and handling client records. Staff should be trained on what to say over the phone when someone is asking if a particular person is a client. If the caller persists, then it can be helpful to transfer the caller to a counseling center administrator or on-call counselor. Another aspect of confidentiality is for support staff not to read client records beyond what is necessary to make an appointment or gather contact information from the file. Support staff should demonstrate discretion in talking to students by using a low, calm voice rather than calling students' names loudly. In addition, papers with client data should not be in plain sight for other students or visitors to read and should be shredded if discarded rather than placed in the trash. As front-line employees at the center, it is essential that support staff learn to engage in a conscientious manner with students, faculty, and staff.

REFERENCES

American College Health Association. (2010). Considerations for integration of counseling and health services on college and university campuses. *Journal of American College Health, 58,* 583–597.

Coll, K. M. (1993). Role conflict differences between community college counselors from accredited centers and non-accredited centers. *Journal of College Student Development, 34,* 341–345.

Corazzini, J. G., May, T. M., & Robbins, S. B. (1986). Counseling center hiring preferences. *Journal of Counseling Psychology, 33,* 78–80.

Gallagher, R. P. (2012). *National Survey of College Counseling 2012.* Retrieved from http://www.collegecounseling.org/wp-content/uploads/NSCCD_Survey_2012.pdf

Georgia Tech Counseling Center. (2013). *Policy and procedure manual.* Unpublished inhouse manual.

Harrar, W. R., Affsprung, E. H., & Long, J. C. (2010). Assessing campus counseling needs. *Journal of College Student Psychotherapy, 24,* 233–240.

Harris, S. A., & Kranz, P. (1991). Small college counseling centers: Changing trends for a new decade. *Journal of College Student Psychotherapy, 5,* 81–89.

International Association of Counseling Services, Inc. (2011). *Standards for university and college counseling centers.* Retrieved from http://www.iacsinc.org

Kraft, D. P. (2009). Mens sana: The growth of mental health in the American College Health Association. *Journal of American College Health, 58,* 267–276.

Leventhal, A. M., & Magoon, T. (1979). Some general principles for university counseling centers. *Professional Psychology, 10,* 357–364.

Londono-McConnell, A., & Matthew, J. K. (2003). *Seasons of a counselor's life: Career development of professional staff in counseling centers.* Commission on Counseling and Psychological Services (CCAPS) newsletter. Retrieved from http://www.myacpa.org/comm/ccaps/Seasons.htm

May, R. R. (2008). The development of a psychotherapy service at Amherst college. *Journal of College Student Psychotherapy, 22*, 13–49.

Minami, T., Davies, D. R., Tierney, S. C., Bettmann, J. E., McAward, S. M., Averill, L. A., … Wampold, B. E. (2009). Preliminary evidence on the effectiveness of psychological treatments delivered at a university counseling center. *Journal of Counseling Psychology, 56*, 309–320.

Much, K., Wagener, A. M., & Hellenbrand, M. (2010). Practicing in the 21st century college counseling center. *Journal of College Student Psychotherapy, 24*, 32–38.

Simmons, D. S., & Doherty, W. J. (1998). Does academic training background make a difference among practicing marriage and family therapists? *Journal of Marital and Family Therapy, 24*, 321–336.

Smith, T. B., Dean, B., Floyd, S., Silva, C., Yamashita, M., Durtschi, J., & Heaps, R. A. (2007). Pressing issues in college counseling: A survey of American college counseling association members. *Journal of College Counseling, 10*, 64–77.

Watson, J. C., & Schwitzer, A. M. (2010). The wide reach of college counseling. *Journal of College Counseling, 13*, 98–99.

Whiteley, S. M., Mahaffey, P. J., & Geer, C. A. (1987). The campus counseling center: A profile of staffing patterns and services. *Journal of College Student Personnel, 28*, 71–81.

CHAPTER SIX

ETHICAL AND LEGAL ISSUES IN COLLEGE AND UNIVERSITY COUNSELING

Shannon J. Hodges

College counseling and mental health practice have evolved to the point they are considered de rigueur in higher education. Numerous studies, most particularly the National Survey of Counseling Center Directors conducted annually by Gallagher and associates, illustrate the challenges college students and college counselors face. Academic journals such as the *Journal of College Counseling* and the *Journal of College Student Psychotherapy* focus specifically on college counseling. More general journals such as the *Journal of College Student Development* and the *Journal of College Health* have also included articles on college mental health. General periodicals such as *The Chronicle of Higher Education* and monthly periodicals such as *Counseling Today* and *The Monitor* also address collegiate mental health needs and challenges. Scholarly attention from these various publications points to the fact that the mental health needs of college students are front and center in higher education.

But it has been collegiate tragedies that have, to a great extent, defined collegiate mental health needs. As discussed in Chapter 10 (Crisis and Trauma Counseling), high-profile collegiate shootings at Virginia Tech, Northern Illinois University, and others have crystallized the public's attention on college student mental health concerns to a far greater extent than the American Psychological Association (APA), American Counseling Association (ACA), National Association of Social Workers (NASW), and other mental health professional organizations could ever do. But tragedies, though the highest profile aspect of legal and ethical issues in college counseling, are only part of the story. Legal decisions handed down by the courts (e.g., *Tarasoff v. the University of California, Jaffee v. Redmond*) and enacted by Congress (e.g., the Americans with Disabilities Act [ADA]) have had a profound impact both on higher education and the practice of counseling in general (Wheeler & Bertram, 2012) and college counseling in particular (May, 2006).

Ethical standards, like laws, are living documents and subject to political, social, and developmental changes (Remley & Herlihy, 2010). In fact, this author (Hodges) recently served on the ACA's Ethics Revision Task Force charged with rewriting ACA's *Code of Ethics*. ACA's revised *Code of Ethics* was recently approved by ACA's Governing Council and is now in place (ACA, 2014). The APA, NASW, American Association for Marriage and Family Therapy (AAMFT), and so on, codes of ethics also must undergo periodic review and revision in order to remain culturally relevant (Francis, personal communication, 2012). Therefore, my coauthors and I agreed that any text we wrote would need to have a chapter on ethical and legal issues as these may well overshadow clinical concerns in this litigious, 21st- century era. Having made the previous statement, however, it is incumbent upon this author to remind readers that in actually very few mental health professionals get sued (thankfully!). But even the threat of a lawsuit can be quite stressful so it's prudent to know both the risks and the odds of being sued. Some 15 years ago while serving as a director of a university counseling center, I attended a workshop at a national conference. Though I cannot recall the precise title, the workshop focused on liability in college and university counseling centers. The presenter was a long-time director of a university counseling center and was married to an attorney. She informed us that if we considered the literally millions of hours of counseling performed by psychiatrists, psychologists, counselors, social workers, in colleges, K–12 schools, inpatient and outpatient facilities, addiction centers, and so forth, very, very few mental health professionals get sued. But, she reminded us, any one of us could be sued. Because anyone could be sued we need to operate from the mind-set that we're prepared to explain why we offered the treatment we offered. The best defense against litigation therefore is preparation.

To digress a little further, I spent a brief time running a county mental health clinic in Oregon after I completed my doctorate. My job was to oversee all the clinical programs, supervise staff, and be a liaison to outside agencies (e.g., police, state hospital, state prison). The job required a large set of well-defined skills that fell well outside clinical issues and clinical training. Though I felt well versed in professional ethics by virtue of education, training, and experience I was ill prepared to deal with lawyers in a courtroom. Because we were the county clinic, members of our staff were frequently called to provide testimony in court on issues regarding child custody, parole and probation, involuntary commitments to the state psychiatric hospital, and so on. When placed under oath I learned rather quickly lawyers can make mental health professionals look quite bad! In one suppressed experience, an attorney harangued me for nearly 20 minutes on what were essentially semantics. It wasn't that I (actually one of the staff) had done anything illegal or unethical; rather, it was our inability to say conclusively that the attorney's client was no longer a danger to self or others. Fortunately, the county attorney and the judge occasionally intervened and when I stepped down from the witness stand soaked in perspiration the only harm was to my self-esteem. My point in this reminiscing is that we college counseling professionals must be vigilant regarding our ethics, legally sound, and prepared for the worst-case scenario while we hope it never arrives.

Finally, while I have over 20 years counseling experience, 10 years supervising college residential communities, and more than 20 years college teaching experience, I would by no means consider myself an expert on legal issues. Good attorneys are worth what they are paid to help mental health professionals with legal entanglements. All colleges and universities retain legal counsel to represent and protect the institution from liability. Presumably, an institution's lawyers could also represent a counselor being sued. But the Pennsylvania State University (PSU) sex scandal has clouded the issue of just who an institution's lawyers represent. Former Penn State President Graham Spanier thought PSU's lawyer represented him, only to have PSU's lawyer testify against him on statements Spanier assumed were covered by lawyer–client privilege (Dawson, 2013). This high-profile case illustrates a clear reason why college counselors must carry their own separate liability insurance. Moreover, understanding and remaining current on professional ethics also can provide protection for college counselors as can a thorough knowledge of pertinent laws such as the ADA, Family Educational Rights and Privacy Act (FERPA), Section 504 of the Rehabilitation Code, and others. As legal and ethical concerns are paramount, I begin with confidentiality.

CONFIDENTIALITY AND LIMITS

Confidentiality is a professional ethical mandate that the counselor conducts counseling while keeping the client's identity and content of the sessions private. Confidentiality arose as a legal tradition through the principle that absent privacy, counseling could not be conducted given the personal nature of the service (Remley & Herlihy, 2010). In fact, even the Supreme Court has recognized in *Jaffee v. Redmond (1996)* that privacy and confidentiality are critical for effective counseling practice. As counseling provides a benefit to society, the courts have generally upheld a client's right to privacy. While confidentiality is a professional ethic that belongs to the counselor, the right to privacy actually belongs to the client (Wheeler & Bertram, 2012). But confidentiality, naturally, is not without limits. General exceptions to confidentiality are suspected abuse of a minor or vulnerable adult, danger to self and others, when a client waives the right, and so on. Counselors should note that a subpoena from a lawyer is not a protected reason to violate confidentiality and doing so could result in being sued for malpractice (Remley & Herlihy, 2010; Wheeler & Bertram, 2012). When subpoenaed, the counselor should contact his or her attorney and let the legal expert deal with the matter. (A fuller discussion of this and other related issues takes place later in this chapter.)

DUTY TO WARN AND PROTECT: *TARASOFF V. REGENTS OF THE UNIVERSITY OF CALIFORNIA*

The *Tarasoff* case is sometimes referred to as the mental health profession's *Miranda* warning (The famous, "You have the right to remain silent ..." that virtually everyone knows courtesy of TV and films) (Wheeler & Bertram, 2012). The California Supreme Court surprised the mental health profession when it ruled in 1976 that a therapist who knows or should have known if a patient poses a "serious danger of violence to others" and does not exercise reasonable care to protect the intended victim or notify the police can be held liable (*Tarasoff v. Regents*, 1976, p. 345). The case involved a graduate student at the University of California–Berkeley, Prosenjit Podder, who revealed in counseling to a staff psychologist at the university counseling center that he intended to kill Tatiana Tarasoff, because she had broken off their relationship. The university psychologist considered the threat to be serious and contacted the campus police, who questioned then released Mr. Poddar because Ms. Tarasoff was overseas for several months and the police deemed the situation nonthreatening. The psychologist reported his concerns to his supervisor, a psychiatrist, who directed that no further action be taken as Mr. Poddar did not meet criteria for a civil commitment to a psychiatric facility. When Ms. Tarasoff returned to campus a few months later from overseas, Mr. Poddar murdered her. Ms. Tarasoff's parents sued the psychologist, the university, the psychiatrist, the university counseling center, the campus police, and the University of California's Board of Regents. The defendant, the University of California, won the initial case, but upon referral, the plaintiff, the Tarasoff family was awarded damages against the university due to negligence.

The court ruled certain duties and obligations arise on the part of a therapist from the special relationship with the client and that this relationship may create affirmative duties for the benefit of third parties. The court specifically ruled:

> Once a therapist does in fact determine, or under applicable professional standards reasonably should have determined, that a patient poses a serious danger of violence to others, he bears a duty to exercise reasonable care to protect the foreseeable victim of that danger.
> (*Tarasoff v. Regents*, 1976, p. 245)

The court, however, also recognized the confidential nature of the therapeutic relationship is critical to its success and ought to be preserved:

> We realize that the open and confidential character of psychotherapeutic dialogue encourages patients to express threats of violence, few of which are ever executed. Certainly a therapist should not be encouraged to reveal such threats; such disclosures could seriously disrupt the patient's relationship with his therapist and with the persons threatened. To the contrary, the therapist's obligations to his patient require that he not disclose a confidence unless such disclosure is necessary to avert danger to others, and even then that he do so discreetly, and in a fashion that would preserve the privacy of his patient to the fullest extent compatible with the prevention of the threatened danger. (p. 347)

Therefore, the court concluded that the psychotherapist–patient privilege ought to be preserved when possible, though certainly not in cases where a life appears at risk. Naturally, such situations present a serious challenge for a counselor, as verbal threats against a third party are difficult to interpret. Furthermore, the counselor could find himself or herself caught between concern about a *Tarasoff* duty and a client suing for breach of privacy (Wheeler &

Bertram, 2012). Many states have enacted legislation limiting the liability of mental health professionals when they breach a client's confidentiality in order to protect a third party. To minimize potential liability, counselors must understand the limits of the *Tarasoff* ruling and any related court decisions or legislation in the state where the counselor practices.

POST-*TARASOFF* COURT DECISIONS

The *Tarasoff* decision and a number of subsequent cases (e.g., *McIntosh v. Milano*, 1979) held that liability applies when the counselor reasonably believed, or should have believed, that the client posed a serious danger to an identifiable potential victim (Wheeler & Bertram, 2012, p. 103). First of all, the counselor must judge the client poses a serious threat. Second, there must be an identifiable third party at risk. Based on these precedents, a college counselor should consider the following factors when evaluating on whether a client might pose a serious threat to another person:

1. Clinical diagnoses of the client (*Diagnostic and Statistical Manual of Mental Disorders,* fifth edition [DSM-5])
2. Context and manner in which the threat is made
3. The client's ability to act on the threat
4. The client's history of violence
5. Actions that provoked the threat
6. Whether the threats are likely to continue
7. The client's response to treatment
8. The client's relationship with the potential victim

Adapted from Wheeler and Bertram (2012)

College counselors should make three additions to the aforementioned list:

9. What is the gender of the client? (Males are more prone to use violence.)
10. Does the client currently own a handgun or semiautomatic weapon?
11. Does the client tend to self-medicate with alcohol or other drugs (and does the client tend to get violent when drinking or using drugs)?

I make these additions (Questions 9, 10, and 11) to the aforementioned decision-tree list, as males are significantly more likely to use deadly force (O'Toole, 1999) and access to a handgun or semiautomatic weapon has proven devastating in colleges and secondary schools. Alcohol in particular is often the accelerant for this volatile mix, igniting violence.

As I write, the country is scarcely recovered from the shooting spree at Sandy Hook Elementary School in Newtown, Connecticut, where 27 people were gunned down, including 20 children. Other recent high-profile shootings by college students in Colorado and California have magnified the issue of college violence and the important role of mental health assessment and gun control. Sandy Hook represents the worst mass killing in U.S. P–12 school history. As previously noted, universities have experienced similar terrible tragedies (e.g.,

Virginia Tech, Northern Illinois University, among others). Given the situation that currently permeates the country, it is possible that college counselors will be given more leeway in decisions involving risk assessment. An additional aspect from the *Tarasoff* ruling is that a counselor must exercise reasonable care to protect the intended victim or victims. The difficulty, naturally, comes in that assessing risk can be very murky indeed. Consider the following statements:

> Client 1: "I have a handgun and I'm going to take care of that bastard for stealing my girlfriend."
> Client 2: "I'm so upset. I'll get him!"

Client 1 has made a more specific threat involving a deadly weapon and the counselor likely should report the threat to the police. Client 2 has made the type of statement jilted partners worldwide have made. But Client 2's threat is nebulous and doesn't involve anything specific. "Reasonable care" likely would dictate further questioning in both cases and ascertaining whether or not either client has a history of violence as well as determining specificity (e.g., "What does 'I'll get him' mean?"). Client 2 also is female and while there are no guarantees, women are far less likely to use deadly force against a third party. In point of fact, all major shooting sprees in recent history have involved young males with semiautomatic weapons. Despite this, the FBI maintains there is no one profile for a shooting tragedy (FBI, 1998). Thus, counselors must aggregate areas of concerning behavior (i.e., history of violence, access to weapons, alcohol abuse, specific threats) to make the best possible call regarding potential violence.

Regardless, in several cases, courts have declined to impose liability in the absence of a readily identified victim. Other courts have held that the duty to warn is broad and can extend to foreseeable victims of the client who may not be specifically identifiable but nonetheless would be likely targets if the client were to become violent (*Hedlund v. Superior Court*, 1983; *Jablonski v. United States*, 1983). The Arizona Supreme Court upheld this standard and held a psychiatrist liable for failure to protect a potential victim within the "zone of danger" who was probably at risk of harm from the patient's violent conduct (*Hamman v. County of Maricopa*, 1989). With the shooting tragedy at Sandy Hook Elementary School, a push is currently being made for stronger mental health screenings. This type of legal action likely raises the specter of increased accountability for counselors and other mental health professionals. In the event a client of a counselor goes on a shooting spree resulting in injury or death, counselors and former counselors likely will be held more liable. The trouble for college counselors—in fact all mental health professionals—is that predicting violence with any degree of accuracy is very difficult (FBI, 1998), though high-risk indicators would be previous acts of violence, specific threats, possession of a handgun or semiautomatic weapon. Thus, the potential harm that came out of the *Tarasoff* case is a very difficult problem for counselors in a Sandy Hook type of case. Nevertheless, such expectations are likely to be placed on mental health professionals, including college counselors.

But some courts have rejected the foreseeable harm scenario altogether, holding that there is a duty to exercise due care in determining whether a client poses an unreasonable risk of serious bodily harm to others (*Perreira v. Colorado*, 1998). Furthermore, the Florida appeals court declined to follow *Tarasoff* in 1991, ruling that imposing a duty to warn third parties would require a psychiatrist to foresee a patient's dangerousness, which the court deemed near impossible and would undermine psychiatrist–patient confidentiality and trust (Wheeler & Bertram, 2012). The court understood the difficulty of predicting dangerous behavior, comparing it to a therapist using a crystal ball (*Boynton v. Burgess*, 1991). Florida does have a statute permitting psychiatrists to warn third parties, but reporting is nor mandatory according to case law (*Boynton v. Burgess*, 1991; Fla. Stat. 491.0147, 2010). The *Boynton* court specified that the ruling also applied to psychologists, psychotherapists, and other mental health professionals (e.g., licensed counselors, social workers, marriage, and family therapists). Therefore, in Florida, counselors may breach confidentiality to prevent clear and imminent physical harm to a person, but there is no mandatory duty as exists under *Tarasoff*. But counselors in Florida need to be mindful of any new case law that may further define the duty to warn and protect and should be aware of any new law passed by the state legislature.

Texas is another of the few states that have expressly decided not to adopt the *Tarasoff* court decision. In 1999, the Texas Supreme Court held that mental health professionals have no common-law duty to warn readily identifiable third parties of a patient's threats against them (*Tharper v. Zezulka*, 1999). However, by Texas statute, counselors are permitted to make certain disclosures to law enforcement officials or medical professionals in situations potentially involving risk to health and safety of third parties (Wheeler & Bertram, 2012). Complicating the matter, however, Texas offers no specific grant of immunity in the state's statutes, potentially creating a decision-making dilemma for the counselor (Tex. Health & Safety Code 611.004, 2009). Clearly, college counselors may feel caught in an ethical versus legal bind regarding disclosure to third parties. Prior to any such disclosures, college counselors must get good legal advice and carefully document their course of action.

Two additional cases from California, where *Tarasoff* was decided, seem to expand the meaning and intent of the California immunity statute: *Ewing v. Goldstein* (2004) and *Ewing v. Northridge Hospital Medical Center* (2004). In these cases, a California appeals court held that psychotherapists who predicted or actually believed that a patient posed a threat of serious bodily injury or death to a third party have a duty to warn, even if the threat was relayed to the therapist by a patient's relative and not the patient. This ruling raises serious questions for counselors and other mental health professionals if courts interpret the immunity laws in such a broad manner (Wheeler & Bertram, 2012). For example, who should be considered a relative for purposes of deciding whether there is a duty to warn and protect (Wheeler & Bertram, 2012)? Furthermore, what if family members providing information to the counselor disagree on the degree of dangerousness? Moreover, do family members with no mental health training have the background to offer a learned opinion regarding imminent danger? Clearly, when it comes to predicting threats to third parties the counselor is between the proverbial rock and hard place.

The majority of legal cases involving danger to third parties involve personal injury (Wheeler & Bertram, 2012). But, the Vermont Supreme Court ruled that the duty to warn and protect applied in a property damage case. In *Peck v. Counseling Service of Addison County, Inc.* (1985), a counselor was informed by her client he wanted to burn down his father's barn. He promised his therapist he would not carry out the threat, but then he proceeded with his stated intent. The Vermont court was convinced arson posed a grave danger to human life and was unwilling to limit the duty owed by the therapist (Wheeler & Bertram, 2012). The *Peck* case also illustrates that counselors may need to err on the side of action when their clients swear they *will not* carry out a threat. This Vermont case also illustrates the difficulties involved in ascertaining how much trust a counselor should have in a client's word. This author's experience is many counselors frequently "take a client's word for it" mentality. Such practice may be unwise and open the counselor to legal charges.

IMMUNITY FROM LITIGATION

The cases noted in this chapter underline the courts' continued struggles with the issues of confidentiality and the duty to warm and protect potential victims from violence. In the 1980s and 1990s, a majority of state legislatures passed laws providing immunity for mental health professionals who take action to protect potential third-party victims from dangerous clients (Wheeler & Bertram, 2012). These various state immunity laws vary greatly regarding what constitutes a duty, what actions of the mental health professional will fulfill that duty, and specifically who is covered by that statutory duty (Wheeler & Bertram, 2012). Awareness of applicable state liability laws, following the code of ethics (e.g., ACA, APA, NASW), and judicious documentation in the record are all highly recommended actions for college counseling professionals.

In Virginia, an immunity law specifies mental health service providers have a duty to take precautions to protect readily identifiable third parties from violent behavior or serious harm when the client has communicated to the counselor orally, in writing, or by sign language a specific immediate threat to cause serious bodily injury or homicide (Wheeler & Bertram, 2012). The counselor may seek the client's involuntary (or "civil") commitment to a psychiatric center, make reasonable attempts to warn the victim or contact the police without fear of litigation (Va. Code Ann., 54.1-2400.1, 2011).The law also makes health care providers immune from civil suit for breaching confidentiality in communicating such threats, failing to predict harm in the absence of a threat, or failing to take precautions other than those specified in the law. The high-profile shooting tragedy at Virginia Tech several years ago highlights the need for college counselors to feel unfettered to breach confidentiality when they believe a third party may be at serious risk of bodily harm from a client. Naturally, as has been previously stated, predicting violence is a very difficult task. With immunity laws college counselors can disclose to legal authorities and at-risk third parties with more confidence. This author can also state as a former director of a university counseling center, clinical director of a county mental health clinic, veteran of three college counseling centers, and as one who supervised collegiate living groups for 10 years, that breaking confidentiality in matters of perceived imminent danger can leave one feeling personally vulnerable. Immunity laws do help with protection from litigation though they do not protect counselors against violence at the hands of disgruntled former clients.

Laws are always in flux, and in the wake of the Sandy Hook tragedy there is much talk involving mental health screening particularly when citizens wish to purchase weapons. High-profile incidents (e.g., Columbine, Sandy Hook, Virginia Tech) create impetus for evolving legislation and judicial change. College counselors must keep up with the shifting grounds of legal changes regarding mandated disclosure and confidentiality. Subscribing to a legal newsletter (e.g., *Higher Education Alert & Higher Education Law in America, Campus Legal Advisor, Faculty Focus*) can help keep college counselors updated on legal developments and provide concrete information. Naturally, all college and university counseling services must maintain a close relationship with their university legal counsel.

HIV/AIDS AND LIFE-THREATENING ILLNESS

A dilemma since the mid-1980s has been whether counselors should warn partners of HIV-positive AIDS clients. Realizing the potential for transmission of a deadly virus to a third party, which can then be passed to additional unsuspecting persons, college counselors certainly have a right to protect the public. Virtually all states now have statutes governing the reporting of HIV and AIDS cases to public health officials and corresponding confidentiality duties, but many of the laws that either permit or require reporting apply only to physicians. The ACA *Code of Ethics* provides an ethical perspective in Standard B.2.c:

> When clients disclose that they have a disease commonly known to be both communicable and life threatening, counselors may be justified in disclosing information to identifiable third parties, if the parties are known to be at serious and foreseeable risk of contracting the disease. Prior to making a disclosure, counselor's assess the intent of clients to inform the third parties about their disease or to engage in any behavior that may be harmful to an identifiable third party. Counselors adhere to relevant state laws concerning disclosure about disease status.

Problematic in the ACA *Code of Ethics* is the requirement to "confirm that there is such a diagnosis," as confirmation of such may be impossible. How would the counselor confirm the diagnosis? Absent a written release to the client's physician, confirmation likely would not be possible. In this case, erring on the side of action may be necessary should the counselor have a reasonable belief the client with a communicable disease is not being honest with his or her partner. One might also ponder whether this particular section of the ACA *Code of Ethics* might place counselors at some legal risk due to the impossibility of confirmation. Fortunately, as of yet, no counselor or therapist has been successfully sued for failure to "confirm a diagnosis." (*Note:* The current ACA *Code of Ethics* was adopted in 2014.)

College counselors must follow the statutory mandates regarding disclosure. College counselors who are uncertain should contact their university counsel or their state or local public health provider who can help explain state obligations regarding disclosure. Be aware of accurate information regarding safe sex and the transmission of HIV, AIDS, and other transmittable diseases. Speak with clients regarding safe sex practices and legal responsibilities. If a client refuses to inform his or her partner(s) about a communicable disease, then contact the local public health agency to see what the agency is able to do without compromising the client's confidentiality (Wheeler & Bertram, 2012). Yet another possibility is to refer the client for a medical evaluation by a physician who may be able to make a report to the appropriate public health authority without facing liability for breach of confidentiality (Wheeler & Bertram, 2012). Yet another possibility is for the counselor to see whether the client is willing to speak with the public health authority in her or his presence. In the event of legal uncertainty, counselors should always consult an attorney.

LEGAL, ETHICAL, AND RISK MANAGEMENT ISSUES

The risks of encountering violence in the workplace vary considerably depending on the nature of counseling work and setting. For example, counseling in a college or university setting likely holds less risk that in a maximum security prison or an inpatient psychiatric setting. But all counseling occupations, as with any job, carry the risk of violence. Prior to the late 1990s, who would have considered that P–12 settings and colleges and universities would witness high-profile shooting sprees resulting in mass killings? It's fair to say that counselors also tend to see themselves as helpers and as such likely do not often view themselves as being at risk from violent clients and ex-clients. But as more counselors are called upon to handle complex mental health issues (e.g., trauma, crisis intervention, working in correctional facilities, and particularly counseling clients with violent histories), college counselors could face more serious risks. Clearly, tragedies at Virginia Tech, Northern Illinois, and several other institutions likely have stripped away the sense of denial that the campus is a benign, idyllic place of refuge. Because of the dearth of research targeting violence against college and university counseling professionals, this chapter draws from general sources and make recommendations based upon such findings.

Studies of workplace violence against mental health professionals have yielded varying estimates on the potential for a counselor or other therapist to be assaulted (Baird, 2005). Studies conducted by Tully, Kropf, and Price (1993) and Reeser and Wertkin (2001) are among the few in the professional literature. Thackery and Bobbit (1990) reported that among the participants in a regional conference, 50% of clinical staff and 28% of nonclinical staff indicated they had been attacked at least once. Similar findings were reported by Perkins (1990, as cited in Baird, 2005) in a British study where 116 psychologists were surveyed. Of this group, 52% reported having been assaulted in the year prior to the study. Other potentially dangerous and intimidating behaviors have also been reported in the mental health profession. Romans, Hayes, and White (1996) reported that out of a sample of 178 counseling staff, roughly 6% reported being stalked, and 10% had a supervisee who had been stalked. Others suggest that violence against mental health professionals likely is underreported in the field and that therapists are likely to face assault at some point in their careers (Whitman, Armao, & Dent, 1976).

These studies should not be taken to imply that most clients at college or university counseling centers are dangerous. In fact, most clients do not pose a significant risk for assaulting, stalking, harassing, or threatening college counseling staff. It is also worthwhile to mention that driving an automobile over the course of a lifetime is also somewhat risky, yet few people cease driving because of the risks involved. Regardless, the risks are ever present and college and university counseling staff must prepare staff and interns to deal with the threat of violence.

Predictors of Client Violence

Kinney (1995) cites several risk factors as rough predictors to use in assessing the potential for a person to commit violent acts. Naturally, as has been mentioned in this text, predicting violence with any degree of accuracy is very difficult (FBI, 1998). Furthermore, there is no particular profile for "shooters" (FBI, 1998) or other violent people. Nevertheless, the indicators listed in the following are useful when counseling clients who have a predisposition for violence:

- Emotionally disturbed individuals
- People under extreme stress
- History of substance abuse
- Frequent disputes with supervisors or authority figures
- Routine violation of company/agency/school policy rules
- Threats of violence, either verbal or written (including electronic communication)
- Sexual and other harassment/bullying of coworkers or peers
- Preoccupation with weapons and violence (video games, TV, movies, the Internet, etc.)
- An isolated individual with a minimal support system (Kinney, 1995, p. 25)

Also:

- The person has a history of committing violent acts (domestic abuse, dating relationships, etc.)
- An individual with a history of cruelty to animals
- A person with access to a handgun or assault weapon (FBI, 1998)

Managing Aggressive Behaviors

Dealing with the possibility of client assault involves recognizing risks and learning how to deescalate potentially dangerous situations before they become violent. Prevention clearly is the best measure, though challenging as it may be to accurately predict violence in clients. Here are some tips to keep in mind:

- Unusual behavior (e.g., speaking to oneself, hallucinations) likely will be unsettling, but usually does not necessarily indicate violent or dangerous behavior. (Keep in mind that support staff, faculty, students, etc., will be far more threatened by unusual behavior and may request counseling staff to remove such students from campus. Remember, unusual behavior is not against the law.)
- If a client suddenly begins exhibiting unusual behavior such as mentioned earlier, ask the client if he or she has recently gone off prescribed medications. Many clients who discontinue taking antipsychotic medications will exhibit decompensating behavior. Although going off medication does not mean clients will become violent, the risk increases and their behavior may be a danger to themselves.
- Developing strong relationships with clients likely is one of the best ways to lessen the risk of violence. The stronger your relationship with a client, the more likely it is that you will be able to defuse a potentially violent situation.
- Be aware of a client's history and issues so as to notice signs of aggression or social isolation and intervene.
- In residential living communities (e.g., residence halls, co-ops, Greek houses), be aware of bullying and how it may precipitate violence among peers. Develop a strong referral system with collegiate living groups to facilitate referrals. Close relationships with resident directors (RDs), resident advisors (RAs), and other housing staff are essential.
- Naturally, all threats are not equal. A 19-year-old female with no history of violence, who owns no weapons yet who makes a vague threat to "get you!" likely does not carry the same threat as a 35-year-old male student with a violent history who owns numerous guns and other weapons and makes a specific threat of violence: "I'm going to shoot you tomorrow." Regardless, take all threats seriously and follow up on the threat through established and appropriate channels (e.g., supervisor, police, disciplinary committee).
- Know the violence prevention plan/emergency response plan at your counseling center/university.

Defusing Violence

- The best way to deescalate a potentially violent situation is to give the outward perception of calm. (Much easier said than accomplished!) Speaking with calm though firm voice might provide just enough management to defuse a tense situation (Hodges, 2011).
- Assess and define the level of the existing threat by evaluating the nature, severity, and potential for harm inherent in the incident (Zdiarski, Dunkel, & Rollo, 2007).
- The relationship you have with a client could make a difference in a critical situation. Present a demeanor that suggests empathy and encourage the client to sit down and talk the matter over (Hodges, 2011; Kinney, 1995).
- Always have a safety plan in your counseling center and make sure everyone, counselors, support staff, graduate students, and so on, know the plan. To ensure staff know the safety plan, conduct drills each semester (Kinney, 1995; Zdiarski et al., 2007).
- Regarding the previous suggestion about a safety plan, one staff member should be assigned as the safety officer and take responsibility for implementing the plan, running drills, and grading the staff on the drill. The safety officer could also be a liaison to the campus crisis team.
- Provide in-service training on campus safety. In particular, provide outreach to campus housing (residence halls and apartments), fraternity and sorority houses, and cooperative living groups.
- Train RDs and RAs on signs of emerging crisis, intervention (approaching troubled person, referral to counseling center, follow-up, etc.).
- Develop a quick method of notifying campus/community police of a crisis.
- In the aftermath of a crisis, debrief staff and students and provide counseling. Establishing a caring presence is critical. (Adapted from Zdiarski et al., 2007)

Risk Management Guidelines for College Counseling Centers

In the post-*Tarasoff* era, college counselors, like all mental health professionals, have a legal and ethical obligation to prevent clear and imminent danger to the client and others. Counselors must also revisit the ethical mantra of "What's in the best interest of my client?" while simultaneously balancing the need to limit their liability. The good news for college counselors is that despite a litigious society, few counselors actually are sued. Unfortunately, anyone can be sued and even unsuccessful or frivolous lawsuit can be very stressful! Therefore, college counselors must explicitly address confidentiality and its limits during the informed consent phase just prior to treatment. Although there is no absolute protection against liability, there are several suggestions to follow that could help reduce liability.

Some guidelines:

- Apprise clients of the limits of confidentiality at the onset of counseling and give periodic reminders.

● Consult with your supervisor and trusted colleagues when concerning issues are raised regarding clients.
● Know the law in your state and whether it requires a communicated threat against a specifically identified victim or if it encompasses a broader duty. If there is a statute that provides immunity for good faith acts on your part, know what it says about actions you must take. Your state counseling, psychological, social work, and so on, association may be able to help you understand your legal obligations.
● Review your code of ethics (e.g., ACA, APA, NASW) and when you have ethical questions consult with your supervisor or a trusted colleague.
● Consult the campus attorney if you are concerned about liability or if your legal duty is unclear.
● Make referrals where appropriate.
● Obtain prior psychiatric and legal history (if possible). Does the client have a history of violence? What were the circumstances? Does the client react impulsively (e.g., make threats, become easily agitated)? Does the client abuse substances? (If alcohol and other drugs are involved, the risk for violence is increased.) Does the client appear delusional? Has the client recently gone off antipsychotic medication? Has the client's behavior recently become more aggressive or threatening?
● Inquire about the client's access to handguns or other deadly weapons, suicidal or homicidal ideation, and current or future plans for violence. (Does the client speak of violent fantasies?)
● Consider all appropriate clinical responses and the consequences of each (i.e., warning the potential victim if known, contacting the police, referring the client to a psychiatrist for an evaluation, revising the treatment plan, or hospitalizing the client). If appropriate, involve the client in your decision-making process. Do not reveal confidential information that is not necessary to protect potential victim(s).
● Know and follow institutional behavioral policies.
● Document all actions you take, those you reject, and the rationale behind each decision.

Adapted from Wheeler and Bertram (2012)

Following these guidelines does not provide absolute protection for potential victims of violence or absolve a counselor's responsibility or liability. But having a safety plan, safety officer, rehearsing drills, and following a plan to reduce liability (as per the aforementioned suggestions) can establish an atmosphere that may reduce risk of harm and potential liability. As community colleges, colleges, and universities are educational institutions, this chapter and the recommendations herein are examples of the counseling profession's "teachable" moments. Hopefully, safety plans, crisis teams, and such will be used only in safety drills. Recent experiences at P–12 and college campuses serve as a somber reminder that while education must strive for the best outcomes, campuses must prepare for the worst.

REFERENCES

American Counseling Association. (2014). *ACA code of ethics.* Alexandria, VA: Author.

American Psychiatric Association. (2013). *Diagnostic and statistical manual of mental disorders* (5th ed.). Arlington, VA: Author.

Baird, B. N. (2005). *The internship, practicum, and field placement handbook: A guide for the helping professions* (4th ed.). Upper Saddle River, NJ: Pearson/Prentice Hall.

Boynton v. Burglass, 590 So. 2nd 446 (Fla. Dist. Ct. App. 1991).

Dawson, M. (2013, December 22). *Graham Spanier's lawyer accuses former Penn State legal counsel Cynthia Baldwin of "flip-flop"; Baldwin's attorney responds.* Retrieved from http://www.centredaily.com/news/local/education/penn-state/jerry-sandusky/article42837516.html

Ewing v. Goldstein, 120 Cal. App. 4th 807 (2004).

Ewing v. Northridge Hosp. Med. Ctr., 120 Cal. App. 4th 1289 (2004).

Federal Bureau of Investigation. (1998). *The school shooter: A threat assessment.* Washington, DC: Author.

Fla. Stat. 491.0147 (2010).

Hamman v. County of Maricopa, 161 Ariz. 58, 775 P.2d 1122 (1989).

Hedlund v. Superior Court, 34 Cal. 3d 695, 669 P2d 41 (1983).

Hodges, S. (2011). *The counseling practicum and internship manual: A resource for graduate counseling students.* New York, NY: Springer Publishing Company.

Jablonski v. United States, 712 F.2d 391 (9th Cir. 1983).

Jaffee v. Redmond, 518 U.S. 1 (1996).

Kinney, J. A. (1995). *Violence at work: How to make your company safer for employees and customers.* Englewood Cliffs, NJ: Prentice-Hall.

May, R. (2006). Legal and ethical issues. In P. A. Grayson & P. W. Meilman (Eds.), *College mental health practice* (pp. 43–58). New York, NY: Routledge.

McIntosh v. Milano, 403, A.2d 500 (N.J. Super. 1979).

O'Toole, M. (1999). *The school shooter: A threat assessment perspective.* Federal Bureau of Investigation, National Center for the Analysis of Violent Crime (NCAVC). Quantico, VA: Federal Bureau of Investigation.

Peck v. Counseling Service of Addison County, Inc., 499 A.2d 422 (Vt. 1985).

Perreira v. Colorado, 768 P.2d 1198 (Colo. 1989).

Reeser, L. C., & Wertkin, P. A. (2001). Safety training in social work education: A national survey. *Journal of Teaching in Social Work, 21,* 95–114.

Remley, T. P., & Herlihy, B. (2010). *Ethical, legal, and professional issues in counseling* (3rd ed.). Upper Saddle River, NJ: Pearson.

Romans, J. S. C., Hayes, J. R., & White, T. K. (1996). Stalking and related behaviors experienced by counseling center staff members from current or former clients. *Professional Psychology: Research and Practice, 27,* 595–599.

Tarasoff v. Regents of the University of California, 551 P.2d 334 (Cal. 1976).

Tex. Health & Safety Code 611.004 (2009).

Thackery, M., & Babbit, R. G. (1990). Patient aggression against clinical and nonclinical staff in a VA medical center. *Hospital and Community Psychiatry, 41,* 195–197.

Tharper v. Zezulka, 994 S.W.2d 635 (Tex. 1999).

Tully, C. T., Kropf, N. P., & Price, J. L. (1993). Is the field a hard-hat area? A study of violence in field placements. *Journal of Social Work Education, 29,* 191–199.

Va. Code Ann. 54.1-2400.1 (2011).

Wheeler, A. M. N., & Bertram, B. (2012). *The counselor and the law: A guide to legal and ethical practice* (6th ed.). Alexandria, VA: American Counseling Association.

Whitman, R. M., Armao, B. B., & Dent, O. B. (1976). Assault on the therapist. American *Journal of Psychiatry, 133,* 424–429.

Zdiarski, E. L., II, Dunkel, N. W., & Rollo, J. M. (2007). *Campus crisis management: A comprehensive guide to planning, prevention, response, and recovery.* San Francisco, CA: Jossey-Bass.

CHAPTER SEVEN

DEPRESSION- AND ANXIETY-RELATED DISORDERS

Kimber Shelton

Depression and anxiety are the most prominent psychological issues on college campuses and in counseling centers. Each year college counseling center directors report that anxiety and depression exceed all other mental health concerns presented in counseling centers. Of the 400 counseling centers who participated in the Association of University and College Counseling Center Directors (AUCCCD) Annual Survey (Mistler, Reetz, Krylowicz, & Barr, 2012) approximately 42% listed anxiety as the top presenting concern and depression as the second most frequently presented concern (36.4%) (followed by relationship problems, 35.8%; suicidal ideation, 16.1%; and alcohol abuse, 9.9%). Students may arrive on college campuses with preexisting anxiety- and depression-related disorders or may develop anxiety and depression symptoms during their college tenure. Transition issues, problems with roommates, family of origin issues, academic demands, interpersonal conflicts, financial issues, breakups, grief and loss, sexual or physical assault, identity concerns, substance abuse, injury, low self-esteem, and career concerns are among the stressors that can complicate or lead to the development of depression- and anxiety-related disorders.

Depression and anxiety symptoms have the potential to significantly impair students' abilities to be academically successful. National data show that 8.4% of full-time college students aged 18 to 22 experienced a major depressive episode and were totally unable to carry out their normal activities for more than 60 days in the past year (Substance Abuse and Mental Health Services Administration [SAMHSA], 2012). Decreased capacity for concentration and focus, diminished motivation and energy levels, disturbed sleep, changes in appetite, and mood lability can have devastating consequences to students' social, academic, and personal lives. Students may find it increasingly difficult to attend classes and meetings, remain focused in lectures, complete assignments and projects, engage in research, and effectively communicate with others. Additionally, concerning is the fact that depression and anxiety symptoms place students at a higher risk for suicide. Suicide is the third leading cause of death for college students (Centers for Disease Control and Prevention [CDC], 2013) with 7.4% of college students reporting having considered suicide in last 12 months (American College Health Association [ACHA], 2013).

DIAGNOSTIC CONSIDERATIONS AND ETIOLOGY

The most recent edition (fifth) of the *Diagnostic and Statistical Manual of Mental Disorders* (*DSM-5*; American Psychiatric Association [APA], 2013) impacts the diagnosis of depression- and anxiety-related concerns. Once classified together as "mood disorders," bipolar disorder and depressive disorders now have separate categorical sections in the *DSM-5*. Previously classified as "anxiety disorders" in the *DSM-IV-TR* (APA, 2000), the *DSM-5* now provides separate categories for obsessive-compulsive and related disorders (i.e., body dysmorphic and trichotillomania) and trauma- and stress-related disorders (i.e., posttraumatic stress disorder [PTSD] and acute stress disorder). Table 7.1 provides an overview of current *DSM-5* classification system for depression and anxiety. To properly assess and diagnosis, counseling center staff would likely benefit from attending training on the current *DSM-5* or by having the center sponsor an in-house training.

In general, diagnosis of depression- and anxiety-related disorders requires symptoms to be present for at least a 2-week period of time and the presence of the symptoms must cause significant distress and/or impaired functioning (social, occupational, academic, relational, and personal). The number and acuity of symptoms and degree of functional impairment determine the severity of the depression- or anxiety-related diagnosis (mild, moderate, or severe).

Signs and symptoms of depression include (National Institute of Mental Health [NIMH], 2011):

- Persistent sad, anxious, or "empty" feelings
- Feelings of hopelessness or pessimism
- Feelings of guilt, worthlessness, or helplessness
- Irritability, restlessness
- Loss of interest in activities or hobbies once pleasurable, including sex
- Fatigue and decreased energy
- Difficulty concentrating, remembering details, and making decisions
- Insomnia, early-morning wakefulness, or excessive sleeping
- Overeating or appetite loss
- Thoughts of suicide, suicide attempts
- Aches or pains, headaches, cramps, or digestive problems that do not ease even with treatment

Cognitive, affective, and behavioral anxiety-related symptoms are specific to the particular type of anxiety disorder one is experiencing. Common types of anxiety-related disorders presented at college counseling centers include

TABLE 7.1 *DSM-5* Classifications for Anxiety- and Depression-Related Disorders

Anxiety Disorders
Agoraphobia
Anxiety Disorder Due to Another Medical Condition
Generalized Anxiety Disorder
Other Specified Anxiety Disorder
Panic Disorder
Selective Mutism
Separation Anxiety Disorder
Specific Phobia
Social Anxiety Disorder
Substance/Medication-Induced Anxiety Disorder
Unspecified Anxiety Disorder
Depressive Disorders
Depressive Disorder Due to Another Medical Condition
Disruptive Mood Dysregulation Disorder
Major Depressive Disorder
Other Specified Depressive Disorder
Persistent Depressive Disorder (Dysthymia)
Premenstrual Dysphoric Disorder
Substance/Medication-Induced Depressive Disorder
Unspecified Depressive Disorder
Obsessive-Compulsive and Related Disorders
Body Dysmorphic Disorder
Excoriation
Hoarding Disorder
Obsessive-Compulsive Disorder
Obsessive-Compulsive and Related Disorder Due to Another Medical Condition
Other Specified Obsessive-Compulsive and Related Disorder
Substance/Medication-Induced Obsessive-Compulsive and Related Disorder
Trichotillomania
Unspecified Obsessive-Compulsive and Related Disorder
Adapted from American Psychiatric Association (2013).

generalized anxiety disorder, social anxiety disorder, panic disorder, and specific phobia. In accordance with the *DSM-5* (2000), additional anxiety-related symptoms common on college campuses include PTSD, obsessive-compulsive disorder, and acute stress disorder. Additionally, the high comorbidity between depression and anxiety symptoms (APA, 2013) makes it likely that students will present with a combination of anxiety- and depression-related symptoms.

Common symptoms across anxiety disorders include (APA, 2013):

- Excessive worry and fear
- Avoidant behaviors
- Sleep disturbance (hypersomnia, insomnia, or waking during sleep)
- Physical symptoms (i.e., increased heartbeat, shortness of breath, sweating, dizziness, and muscle tension)
- Restlessness
- Irritability
- Difficulty with concentration and focus
- Racing thoughts

The complex interaction of biological, environmental, psychological, and temperamental factors influence the development, severity, and chronicity of depression and anxiety (APA, 2013; NIMH, 2011). Individuals with a family history of mental illness have an increased risk for developing mental health concerns. Research with monozygotic twins showed an almost 40% concordance rate for depression (Takahashi, 2006). Environmental risk factors for developing depression- or anxiety-related concerns can include growing up in a chaotic and/or abusive environment, experiencing trauma and poverty, and undergoing major life changes (i.e., divorce). Certain temperamental characteristics such as neuroticism, fear of negative evaluation, and behavioral inhibition are associated with the development of depression- and anxiety-related disorders (APA, 2013).

CULTURAL CONSIDERATIONS

Cultural variables impact the prevalence and presentation of symptoms and level of help-seeking behaviors. Women show higher lifetime rates of depression and anxiety disorders and use treatment more often than do their male counterparts (APA, 2013; Kessler et al., 2003). The National Survey on Drug Use and Health (NSDUH; SAMHSA, 2012) showed that 12% of female students reported experiencing a major depressive episode in the past year, whereas only 4.5% of male students reported experiencing an episode. Additionally, college females are more likely to endorse feeling helpless, overwhelmed, sad, anxious, exhausted, lonely, unable to function, anger, and sleep disturbance than their male counterparts (ACHA, 2013).

Investigations exploring the prevalence rates of anxiety and depression by race and ethnicity are somewhat inconsistent, with some studies showing higher prevalence rates for White individuals, while other research shows higher prevalence rates for ethnic minority groups (for a review see Herman et al., 2011). Examining the rates of major depressive episodes in the past year for full-time, traditional-age college students, the 2013 NSDUH showed that rates were highest for multiracial students (17.6%), followed by Hispanic (9.1%), White (8.4%), Black (7.4%), and Asian (6.3%) students (no data were available on Native American and Native Hawaiian or Pacific Islander student groups) (SAMHSA, 2012). According to the National Healthcare Disparities Report (CDC, 2012) lifetime anxiety prevalence rates are greater for White individuals than for other races (Black individuals are 20% less likely, and Hispanic individuals are 30% less likely to experience anxiety than White individuals).

Cultural stigma, mistrust of mental health services, acculturation, and immigration status impact ethnic minorities' use of mental health care and presentation of symptoms. For example, stigma and mistrust related to mental health services serve as barriers for African American and Hispanic groups entering treatment during the early onset of depression or anxiety symptoms. Thus, when they present for treatment, they are likely presenting with higher levels of pathology. When they arrive for treatment, African American and Hispanic groups report higher levels of sadness, hopelessness, feeling worthless, and feeling as if everything is an effort than other cultural groups (CDC, 2012). American Indian/Alaska Natives are twice as likely to experience feelings of nervousness or restlessness as compared to their White peers (CDC, 2012). Ethic minorities' are also more likely to report somatic complaints, than cognitive and affective symptoms of anxiety and depression (Lu, Lim, & Mezzich, 1995). Exacerbated symptoms and levels of acuity may be attributed to the experience of minority stress, bias, and discrimination. Considering this, it is important for counseling centers to avoid overpathologizing ethnic minority students and accurately assess if somatic complaints are related to depression- and anxiety-related disorders.

ROLE OF THE COUNSELING CENTER

Assessment of Depression- and Anxiety-Related Disorders

Multiple methods exist to help clinicians assess for anxiety and depression. This includes asking anxiety- and depression-oriented questions in client intake paperwork and during clinical interviews, and using assessment instruments. Often clients will specifically state that their reason for seeking services is related to feeling depressed or anxious. Counseling centers differ in how initial clinical interviews are structured, with some centers using standardized schedules such as the Structured Clinical Interview for *DSM* Disorders (SCID; First, Williams, Spitzer, & Gibbon, 2007) or center-created interview schedules. Assessing depression and anxiety includes obtaining information regarding (a) symptoms; (b) length of time symptoms have been present; (c) severity of symptoms; (d) degree of functional impairment;

(e) previous diagnosis and treatment; (f) family history of mental illness; (g) health history (to rule out organic causes to anxiety or depression); (h) exacerbating factors (e.g., substance use and risk-taking behavior); and (i) protective factors (e.g., social support).

Numerous assessment instruments are available to help facilitate diagnosis of depression- and anxiety-related disorders; however, the cost, time associated with use of assessment instruments, and educational qualification levels (some instruments require clinicians to have a doctoral degree or have completed extensive training) can be prohibitive to counseling centers. The unfortunate consequence of such barriers is that some centers may refrain from using assessment instruments that could be useful in providing collaborative information to clinical interviews, identifying symptoms, or diagnoses not considered by clinicians, tracking change and progress, and aiding with differential diagnosis.

The Counseling Center Assessment of Psychological Symptoms-62 (CCAPS-62; Locke et al., 2011; and the abbreviated version CCAPS-32) is an assessment instrument designed specifically for college counseling centers. The most recent update of this free instrument assesses eight levels of functioning including depression, generalized anxiety, and social anxiety. This assessment can be used at any point during treatment. For example, some centers will give the CCAPS measure to clients at every session, others may use it at intervals (e.g., every fifth session), or it may be used as a single measure. The Millon College Counseling Inventory (MCCI; Millon, Strack, Millon, & Grossman, 2006) is another multidimensional measure developed specifically for college counseling centers. This personality inventory includes items for assessing depression, and stress and anxiety. Other instruments that measure several areas of psychopathology including depression and anxiety are the Personality Assessment Inventory (PAI; Morey, 2007), Minnesota Multiphasic Personality Inventory (MMPI; Butcher, Dahlstrom, Graham, Tellegen, & Kaemmer, 1989), Brief Symptom Inventory (BSI; Derogatis & Melisaratos, 1983), and Outcome Questionnaire-45 (OQ45; Lambert, Lunnen, Umphress, Hansen, & Burlingame, 1994). Instruments specifically measuring depression include the Beck Depression Inventory-II (BDI-II; Beck, Steer, & Brown, 1996), and Reynolds Depression Screening Inventory (RDSI; Reynolds & Kobak, 1998). The Beck Anxiety Inventory (BAI; Beck & Steer, 1993), Posttraumatic Stress Disorder Checklist (PTSD Checklist; Weathers, Litz, Herman, Huska, & Keane, 1993), State-Trait Anxiety Inventory (STAI; Spielberger, Gorsuch, Lushene, Vagg, & Jacobs, 1983), Liebowitz Social Anxiety Scale (LSAS; Liebowitz, 1987), and Social Interaction Anxiety Scale (SIAS; Mattick & Clarke, 1998) are among the anxiety measures used by counseling centers. The SIAS is presented in the appendix to this chapter. Symptom checklists are another manner for clinicians to ascertain depression and anxiety symptoms. Centers can use instruments such as the Symptom Checklist-90 (SCL-90; Derogatis, 1994) or may develop their own checklists. This discussion is not intended to be exhaustive; to minimize previously mentioned barriers to assessment, counseling centers should determine the specific instruments that would most effectively serve their student population and center needs.

Treatment

Individual Counseling

Individual counseling is an effective means for treatment and relapse prevention of depression- and anxiety-related symptoms (NIMH, 2011) and is a primary treatment modality within college counseling. Individual counseling provides students with psychoeducation and support and can help students identify the causes of depression and anxiety, work to improve mood and stress management, and maintain healthy changes. Coming to terms with a depression- or anxiety-related disorder may be difficult for students who develop anxiety and depression while in college. Individual counseling can provide a safe space to share their reactions and to have their experiences normalized.

A variety of psychotherapy approaches have been found to be efficacious in the treatment of depression and anxiety (Imel & Wampold, 2008). Such models include interpersonal, Adlerian, relational–cultural, psychodynamic and solution-focused therapies. However, cognitive behavioral therapies (CBTs) are most frequently used in treatment for depression and anxiety disorders (SAMHSA, 2015). CBT is an active and goal-directed approach to therapy. CBT focuses on examining the relationship among thoughts, feelings, and behaviors, and modifying patterns of thinking to improve coping and functioning (National Alliance on Mental Illness, 2012). Table 7.2 provides a list of CBT-related interventions.

Group Counseling

Group counseling is another efficacious treatment for depression and anxiety. In addition to learning skills for addressing psychological symptoms, group counseling can normalize feelings and provide emotional support, help students put their issues or symptoms into better perspective, and practice newly found skills. Counseling centers have a variety of options for developing and leading groups for students with anxiety and depression, and, similar to individual counseling, multiple theoretical orientations have produced successful results (Bjornsson et al., 2011). Not surprising, anxiety and depression groups are two of the most common issue-based groups in college counseling (Mistler et al., 2012). Counseling centers simply use the titles Anxiety Group (University of Illinois at Urbana–Champaign, and Michigan State) or Depression and Anxiety Group (Northeastern University Counseling Services); while other counseling centers have titles such as Facing the Fear: Overcoming Anxiety and Panic (Texas State University), and Out of the Blue Group (Cornell University). Other centers may choose to address the needs of students with anxiety and depression in their general interpersonal process groups and general skill-building/psychoeducational groups. These groups hold titles such as General Therapy Group, Interpersonal Process Group, Mindfulness Group, or Women's or Men's Group. The structure of groups is dependent on the needs of students and the center's available group resources. Following is a group case example for Ronald, a graduate student in chemical engineering who is experiencing mild to moderate depression and anxiety.

TABLE 7.2   CBT-Related Interventions

Systematic desensitization	Relaxation training	Problem solving
Disputing irrational beliefs	Relabeling or reframing	Role playing
Socratic questions	Positive self-talk	Affirmations
Teaching the difference between irrational and rational beliefs	Activity scheduling	Journaling
Mental and emotional imagery	Cognitive and covert modeling	Letter writing
Thought stopping	Diversion or distractions	Systematic assessment of alternatives
Assertiveness and communication training	Bibilotherapy	Impulse control
Persuasion	Reinforcement	Stress inoculation training
Flooding	Biofeedback	Token economies
Exposure therapy	Anxiety/fear hierarchy	Natural consequences

Adapted from Seligman (2001).

African American Student Group: Interpersonal Process Group

Initial Stage of Group

Group members introduce themselves and are acclimated to the group process. Members are encouraged to share any fears and anxiety associated with the group process, and Ronald notices that most members have similar anxiety regarding opening up as he does. Members share the reasons they joined the group and process cultural barriers related to sharing problems and seeking help. Ronald shares his desire to improve his mood, another member in the group shares a similar goal. Other members' goals are focused on building healthy relationships, deciding on a major, anxiety, and identity exploration.

Transition Stage

Group sessions begin with a "check-in" in which each member provides a brief update on his or her status, goals, experiences, and can bring up a topic or issue the member wants to address. A member brings up a recent relationship issue. Ronald and other members provide the member with feedback and he shares examples and struggles within his own relationships, in which he in-turn receives feedback. Another member poses the question "Who am I?" which allows all members to discuss issues related to self-discovery. From these conversations Ronald is more aware of how relationship dynamics have positively and negatively influenced his depression symptoms, his desire for more support from his partner, his future aspiration of being a financial provider for his family, and the need to be more communicative with his advisor. This awareness brings significant anxiety for Ronald. His group leaders notice his quietness and encourage Ronald to work through the anxiety and share his feelings with the group.

(continued)

African American Student Group: Interpersonal Process Group (*continued*)

Working Stage

Facilitators lead members through a mask activity in which each member draws a facial mask that represents who he or she is. Ronald shares similar experiences with other members who express difficulty integrating their African American and student identities. He shares that he feels like his true identity is hidden while at school. Other images on his mask represent his feelings of insecurity and inadequacy. The group processes where their ideas regarding emotional expression derived, aspects of emotional expression they want to maintain, and aspects they want to change. They discuss how they can best make changes, which informs Ronald that he can be in more control over his depression symptoms. Ronald feels supported and accepted by his group members. He begins to think that he can allow himself to be more authentic as long as he has a support system to help him address issues of bias or discrimination and setbacks.

Working Stage Continued

Two group members have a conflict regarding feedback that one member interpreted as being judgmental. As well as the two members discussing the issue, other members share how the conflict impacted them. Group facilitators acknowledge the bravery group members have in allowing themselves to work through the conflict. This example reminds Ronald that conflict is not bad and can be helpful to relationships. He shares his desire to have a more supportive and directive relationship with his research advisor. Facilitators discuss communication skills and then Ronald and another group member complete a role play. Several members discuss having made initial progress and are now experiencing set backs. Facilitators discuss how set backs are a natural part of change and present ways to refute self-defeating talk. Each member devises a plan for handling future set backs.

Final Stage

During the later group sessions, Ronald regularly shares improvements (improved sleep, decreased ruminative thoughts, feeling happier, being more accepting of his flaws). He attributes this to "letting it out" at group, enjoying spending time with his partner, and making progress on his research. At the final group Ronald shares his progress and future goals. Ronald explains that he continues to experience moments of depression; however, they are for shorter periods of time and less intense. He stated his gained insight of tying his sense of worth to academics and feeling either an elevated or depressed mood based on his research progress. With this insight he explained that group helped him recognize other markers for self-worth. Ronald noted a general decline in his stress level, which he attributes to the support from group and ideas he received from group members.

Medication

The combination of medication and psychotherapy can effectively treat cognitive, emotional, and physical symptoms of depression and anxiety, and in some cases, is the most effective treatment for achieving remission (March et al., 2007). Although antidepressant and antianxiety medications can assist in addressing depression and anxiety, a number of barriers can prevent counseling center staff from exploring medication with clients. For one, clinicians may feel deficient in their training or expertise to discuss medication with their clients. To avoid potential ethical and legal issues related to scope of competence, clinicians may refrain from initiating medication conversations. Additionally, personal values regarding medication (e.g., belief that medications are overprescribed, thinking some clients are looking for an easy answer, or negative personal or clinical experiences) can deter clinicians from discussing medication with clients.

It is not the clinician's role to prescribe medication (unless they have prescription privileges) or recommend specific medication; however, clinicians play a vital role in helping clients use medication effectively. Use of medication may help facilitate students' meeting their goals, yet they may be unaware that medication is a treatment option or may have misconceptions regarding medication. Clinicians have a responsibility to educate clients regarding treatment options including that of medication (SAMHSA, 2009) and can suggest students meet with a psychiatrist for consultation to answer questions that are beyond the clinician's competency level. Clients can make comments that are adamantly against the use of medication such as, "I don't want to be on medication for the rest of my life," "Medication is a crutch," "I'm not that crazy!" Other students may believe in the falsity of the "miracle pill" and think that medication will absolve any responsibility they have for creating change. Initiating conversations regarding medication can help to dispel misconceptions and minimize the effects of stigma associated with taking medication. The potential for increased suicidality with the use of antidepressants is a serious concern (U.S. Food and Drug Administration [FDA], 2007). Seeing clients weekly (or biweekly), clinicians have front-row seats for observing changes (both positive and negative) and side effects clients are experiencing. Considering that clients meet more frequently for therapy than they do for psychiatric medication management checks, clinicians are in a position to aid in clients' development of strategies for taking medication regularly and effectively, identifying adverse effects, and building communication skills and confidence to help clients communicate more effectively with their physician. Ideally, on a college campus that has psychiatric care, clinicians and psychiatrists or general practitioners are in regular consultation regarding individual students' treatment. A list of medications commonly used to treat depression and anxiety are listed in Table 7.3.

Self-Help Resources

Not all students experiencing depression and anxiety are in need of professional services and may respond well to self-help resources. Self-help resources can be provided online, during outreach presentations, or suggested as a lower level intervention for students who present to the counseling center with mild symptoms and impaired functioning. This can include providing students with educational material, worksheets and brochures detailing coping and healthy living strategies, bibliotherapy, and self-assessments.

Referral

Not all students presenting with depression and anxiety are well-suited for counseling within the university counseling center, and/or staff may not have the resources to see all students entering into the center. As such, students with depression and anxiety may be referred out for services. Common reasons for referral include the likelihood of students' needs being better addressed in long-term therapy (particularly for centers with a session limit), the specificity of students' needs is beyond the competency or scope of center clinicians (i.e., a student with a misophonia diagnosis—a neurological disorder in which negative reactions, such as anger and irritation, are triggered by certain sounds—may be better served by a specialist outside the center), and students needing inpatient, partial hospitalization or entrance into intensive outpatient programs.

TABLE 7.3   Antidepressant and Antianxiety Medications

Trade Name	Generic Name	FDA-Approved Age
Antidepressant Medications (Also Used for Anxiety Disorders)		
Anafranil (tricyclic)	clomipramine	10 and older (for OCD only)
Asendin	amoxapine	18 and older
Aventyl (tricyclic)	nortriptyline	18 and older
Celexa (SSRI)	citalopram	18 and older
Cymbalta (SNRI)	duloxetine	18 and older
Desyrel	trazodone	18 and older
Effexor (SNRI)	venlafaxine	18 and older
Elavil (tricyclic)	amitriptyline	18 and older
Emsam	selegiline	18 and older
Lexapro (SSRI)	escitalopram	18 and older; 12–17 (for major depressive disorder)
Ludiomil (tricyclic)	maprotiline	18 and older
Luvox (SSRI)	fluvoxamine	8 and older (for OCD only)
Marplan (MAOI)	isocarboxazid	18 and older
Nardil (MAOI)	phenelzine	18 and older
Norpramin (tricyclic)	desipramine	18 and older
Pamelor (tricyclic)	nortriptyline	18 and older
Parnate (MAOI)	tranylcypromine	18 and older
Paxil (SSRI)	paroxetine	18 and older
Pexeva (SSRI)	paroxetine mesylate	18 and older
Pristiq (SNRI)	desvenlafaxine	18 and older
Prozac (SSRI)	fluoxetine	8 and older
Remeron	mirtazapine	18 and older

(continued)

TABLE 7.3   Antidepressant and Antianxiety Medications (*continued*)

Trade Name	Generic Name	FDA-Approved Age
Sarafem (SSRI)	fluoxetine	18 and older for premenstrual dysphoric disorder (PMDD)
Sinequan (tricyclic)	doxepin	12 and older
Surmontil (tricyclic)	trimipramine	18 and older
Tofranil (tricyclic)	imipramine	6 and older (for bedwetting)
Tofranil-PM (tricyclic)	imipramine pamoate	18 and older
Vivactil (tricyclic)	protriptyline	18 and older
Wellbutrin	bupropion	18 and older
Zoloft (SSRI)	sertraline	6 and older (for OCD only)
Antianxiety Medications (All of These Antianxiety Medications Are Benzodiazepines, Except BuSpar)		
Ativan	lorazepam	18 and older
BuSpar	buspirone	18 and older
Klonopin	clonazepam	18 and older
Librium	chlordiazepoxide	18 and older
oxazepam (generic only)	oxazepam	18 and older
Tranxene	clorazepate	18 and older
Valium	diazepam	18 and older
Xanax	alprazolam	18 and older

MAOI, monoamine oxidase inhibitor; OCD, obsessive-compulsive disorder; SNRI, serotonin–norepinephrine reuptake inhibitor; SSRI, selective serotonin reuptake inhibitor.

Source: National Institute of Mental Health, U.S. Department of Health and Human Services National Institutes of Health (2012).

With approximately 42% of clients unsuccessfully utilizing referrals (and almost 60% of clients of color) (Owen, Devdas, & Rodolfa, 2007), many centers can attest that referred out students have a high rate of reentrance to the university counseling center. To increase the chances of students with depression and anxiety best utilizing referrals options, centers can develop a strong referral list for accessible providers and organizations with expertise in the treatment of college students and anxiety and depression, work to increase students' motivational levels in engaging in treatment and utilizing the referral, and follow up with students during the referral process. Take, for example, Tamara who is being referred out for treatment of chronic depression and PTSD. After completing an intake at the counseling center the therapist empathizes with Tamara's presenting concerns, compliments her initiative for seeking treatment, educates her on treatment options, and informs her that her needs are best served in longer-term outpatient care, beyond that provided at the counseling center:

> Tamara, this is something you have dealt with for a very long time. I know it wasn't easy for you to come in and share this. I am impressed with the hard work you have done so far. We want to make sure you receive the best treatment for your needs. This includes engaging in longer-term therapy, which we do not provide here at the counseling center. You've come this far already, let's make sure we get you connected with a therapist in the community since your motivation is so high right now. I want to discuss several treatment providers with you and then schedule a follow-up meeting for next week where we can address any issues that may arise with connecting with the referral.

Accessing referrals may prove particularly cumbersome for students whose motivation or energy levels are low as a consequence of depression symptoms and for students who feel anxious or overly stressed about using a referral. Having the student or therapist call the referral while in the therapist's office and having at least one follow-up session with the student can help facilitate successful use of referrals.

Outreach and Consultation

Outreach

Students in Distress

The majority of students who experience anxiety and depression never visit a counseling center or seek other treatment. These students may be unaware that counseling services are available on their campus, refrain from treatment due to stigma, may have time or financial restrictions, or may seek assistance from other people in their lives and community. Considering the high prevalence of anxiety and depression and the fact that approximately 65% to 70% of students with mental health issues do not seek treatment (Eisenberg, Hunt, Speer, & Zivin, 2011; Herman et al., 2011), outreach serves as a vital function in educating the greater campus community and providing services to students who are unlikely to initiate treatment.

Depression and anxiety outreach may be general for the entire university community (classes, groups, and orientations), or specific to target students who are at higher risk for developing mental health concerns. Students and their families may hold the erroneous belief (or hope) that coming to college will end existing mental health issues (Mental Health America, 2016). In reality, stressors associated with college attendance can trigger a return or exacerbation of anxiety and depression symptoms. Students who are at risk for developing anxiety and depression (i.e., family history) may face their first episode while at college. Early intervention can help prevent the development or severity of anxiety and depression symptoms. New students and their parents should be aware of mental health warning signs, treatment options, and how to access treatment. Counseling centers can be present and provide psychoeducation presentations and written information during high school and transfer student campus visits, new student orientations, and parent orientations. Such information can also be distributed in parent newsletters and new student information packages.

Anxiety and depression outreach can be as simple as tabling at events or programs to more formal presentations and projects. Presentations and programs vary in length from several minutes to week-long or month-long programming. Counseling centers can develop and advertise anxiety and depression presentations that can be requested by the university community. Again, considering the high prevalence rates for depression and anxiety, having regular and ongoing outreach targeted to these topics, such as a weekly workshop open to all students, is beneficial. Certain times of the year can cause a spike in depression and anxiety symptoms. Providing increased programming during the beginning of the semester, prior to holiday breaks, and during midterm and finals weeks may catch a wider pool of students who need immediate care.

Although anxiety and depression outreach is likely most effective when programming is designed to best meet the needs of the intended audience, there are certain areas that should be addressed in any anxiety or depression outreach.

Anxiety and depression outreach guidelines:

1. Provide education regarding anxiety and depression. This includes information pertaining to warning signs, potential causes/stressors, and emotive, cognitive, physical, and behavioral reactions to anxiety and depression
2. Address the impact anxiety and depression may have on functioning, specifically academic functioning and other areas of importance for college students
3. Include cultural expressions and experiences of depression and anxiety
4. Present basic tips/tools for coping with symptoms
5. List treatment options that are inclusive of alternative therapies and holistic treatment interventions
6. Offer referral information that includes campus, local, and national resources

Helping a Student in Distress
Before seeking treatment, students may seek assistance from peers, family, and advisors/professors. Albeit caring, peers, family, and university staff can feel underresourced in assisting a student in distress. Assisting a student in

distress also can take a toll on the helper. Without sufficient self-care, lay helpers can be left with feelings of frustration, worry, burnout, and anger. Outreach programs targeted at identifying and helping students in distress can provide peers, family, and faculty/staff with more resources for helping students with anxiety and depression, as well as self-care techniques. These outreach programs include:

1. Educating and dispelling myths about anxiety and depression
2. Knowing the warning signs of anxiety and depression
3. Using communication skills to engage the student in distress
4. Information about how to provide a referral if needed
5. Self-care strategies for the helper

A primary goal of this type of outreach is to empower the helpers to reach out effectively to students in distress and aid these students in seeking help, not to become the students' therapists or to take on the responsibility of solving the students' problems.

Outreach Considerations

Tablings

- Host tablings at orientations, university events and presentations, health fairs, and so on.
- Have written information available for students to take (brochures, pamphlets) that at a minimum describe symptoms, potential causes, and treatment resources. Centers can develop their own pamphlets or can access depression and anxiety pamphlets through the unabridged student counseling virtual pamphlet collection available at www.dr-bob .org/vpc.
- Use table displays (trifolds and posters) to post information regarding anxiety and depression.
- In discussing common concerns, tabling staff provide students with information about anxiety and depression and how to seek treatment.
- Staff are prepared to answer general questions regarding depression and anxiety.

Presentations and Workshops

- Many centers have preconstructed presentations that community groups can request. Titles include Anxiety Management; Assertiveness; Beating Depression; Coping With Depression; Coping With Performance Anxiety; Feeling Better: Finding Your Way Out of Depression; How to Help a Friend in Distress; Mind Over Mood; Stress Management 101; Stressbusters; Stress Management for Ethnic Minorities; Stress Management for International Students; Suicide Awareness; Test Anxiety; Stressed or Distressed?: How to Know, How to Help; Time Management; and Concentration.

National Depression Screening Day

- National Depression Screening Day (NDSD) is held each October during Mental Illness Awareness Week. In October 2012, 40,795 students completed CollegeResponse NDSD (Screening for Mental Health, Inc., n.d.), a brief online or in-person screening for depression, bipolar disorder, generalized anxiety disorder, and PTSD. Campuses can participate and develop events for NDSD and can also offer ongoing screenings online and in-person for students. Screenings can be offered at the counseling center or a centralized location on the campus such as a student center during lunch hours. Students complete the quick screening and then counseling center clinicians score each screening and hold a brief (1–5 minutes) private meeting with each student to provide basic feedback, offer educational material, and refer students who may benefit from more services.

Additional Depression- and Anxiety-Related Dates

- Counseling centers can consider providing depression and anxiety outreach programs during the many mental health awareness calendar events: Mental Health Month (May), PTSD Awareness Month (June), National Minority Mental Health Awareness Month (July), National Recovery Month, (September), National Suicide Prevention Week (September), Mental Illness Awareness Week (October), National Bipolar Awareness Day (October), and OCD Awareness Week (October).

Consultation

Staff members, faculty, advisors, administrators, and parents regularly seek consultation from counseling centers. Given the significant rates of anxiety and depression, it can be assumed that many of these consultations are related to anxiety and depression. During consultations, counseling center clinicians may be sought for help communicating to and referring a student in distress, answering general questions related to anxiety and depression, receiving information regarding a student of concern, or providing resources to a student in distress. Counseling center consultation is also regularly sought in regard to academic dispositions related to anxiety and depression. In the best-case scenario, clinicians can empower students to discuss academic concerns and distress with their professors and work toward devising plans for rectifying the issue. In other scenarios, counseling center clinicians find themselves in consultation with the Dean of Students office and/or professors regarding academic dispositions of their clients. The Dean of Students office may rely on the counseling center for assessment and diagnosis of depression and anxiety disorders, as well as recommendations for academic considerations. Depending on the counseling center's and the university's policies, academic considerations and recommendations can take many forms. This can include writing letters to support students' (a) receiving extensions on papers; (b) delayed exams; (c) obtaining an incomplete grade; (d) dropping or withdrawing from a course(s); and (e) obtaining a medical leave of absence for mental health concerns (Meilman, 2011). As such, counseling centers are a viable resource for students struggling with mental health concerns to address both their mental health issues and academic issues without penalty (Meilman, 2011). To avoid professors feeling compelled to make exceptions for students or asking clinicians questions that invade the student's privacy, Meilman (2011) suggests that counseling centers rely on the Dean of Students office to contact professors and minimize the clinician's direct communication with professors.

When communicating with the dean, it remains important to respect the student's privacy and confidentiality by only reporting information that is pertinent to addressing the student's need. Details regarding the specifics of trauma, abuse, or interpersonal and family issues are likely unnecessary. For example, academic recommendations may be provided without sharing the details of a sexual assault or an embarrassing stress-induced physiological reaction. In most cases, a listing of symptoms, description of functional impairment, provision of a diagnosis, and recommendations suffice in aiding the dean's office in making decisions regarding the student's disposition. It is good practice to review disposition letters with clients prior to releasing any information to the dean. This way the client has the chance to provide feedback, is aware of the information being disclosed, and is informed of any therapist recommendations. An example of a letter for a hardship withdrawal due to depression is presented in the appendix to this chapter.

As well as being sought for consultation, counseling centers can initiate consultation with other university constituents, particularly medical staff. Medical staff frequently see students with anxiety and depression symptoms, yet do not consistently screen for anxiety and depression. The U.S. Preventive Services Task Force (USPSTF) recommends depression screening for all adults by primary care practices (Agency for Healthcare Research and Quality, 2009). Counseling center staff can consult with and provide training to campus medical providers to assist in the development of structured screenings that work within their system. Results from a pilot study on structured depression screening in primary medical centers showed that students felt positive about the screening, the screening identified students who would not have typically been diagnosed with depression, and the time between identifying students with depression and connecting the students with a mental health professional was shortened (Chung et al., 2011).

INNOVATIVE IDEAS FOR HELPING STUDENTS

Innovative interventions to address the high volume of students experiencing depression and anxiety serve the purpose of exposing a greater number of students to depression and anxiety treatment/interventions, preventing the development of or reducing the severity of depression and anxiety, and decreasing the demands placed on already taxed counseling centers.

Use of Technology

Livestreaming Videos and Podcast

Issues related to class time, organization involvement, familial and work commitments, and symptoms related to anxiety and depression (e.g., social anxiety and lack of energy) prevent students from possibly attending outreach workshops and counseling services. Livestreaming and/or posting recorded outreach presentations and podcasts online allow more individuals to access services remotely. A working father of two may be unable to attend an 11 a.m. stress management workshop, but can benefit from viewing the workshop when his schedule allows.

Computer-Based Therapy Interventions

Online self-assessment measures are not new to counseling centers; links to online self-assessments for anxiety and depression are readily available on many counseling center websites. Online self-assessments provide users with anxiety and depression education, help users identify symptoms, and discuss self-help and treatment options. After completing self-assessments counseling centers have the option of engaging with students for further treatment.

Programs such as the Interactive Screening Program (ISP; American Foundation for Suicide Prevention, 2011), a brief online questionnaire that identifies depression and other mental health problems, allow centers to engage with students who may not typically present for counseling. After completing the anonymous questionnaire, the user is contacted by a counseling center clinician typically via the ISP portal. Depending on the student's needs, the user is simply acknowledged for completing the questionnaire, invited to visit the counseling center for further assistance, or provided with referrals. On one campus between August 2012 and July 2013, 411 students completed the ISP of which 52% engaged in one online dialogue with a clinician, and 30% (123 students) presented to the counseling center for at least one session (Endale, personal communication, 2013). Out of the 123 students who attended at least one session, some students became ongoing center clients, 12 students declined services or were referred out, and three students were hospitalized (Endale, personal communication, 2013). Although it is unknown how many of these students would have eventually initiated contact with the counseling center on their own, it can be assumed that use of this tool and similar tools provides centers with greater access to the almost 70% of students who do not present for treatment.

Computerized cognitive behavioral therapy (cCBT) and e-mail cognitive behavioral therapy (eCBT) are newer methods for remotely treating anxiety and depression. Beating the Blues (Proudfoot, 2004), MoodGYM (Christensen, Griffiths, & Groves, 2004), BluePages (Centre for Mental Health Research, 2004), and Overcoming Depression on the Internet (ODIN; Clarke et al., 2002) are among the current online CBT treatment programs. As further research is released, use of cCBT may prove to be a viable treatment option and referral source for counseling centers. A research review of these programs reported three studies showing evidence of effectiveness in treating depression and symptom reduction and one study failing to demonstrate effectiveness (with ODIN) (Kaltenthaler, Parry, Beverley, & Ferriter, 2008). The benefits of cCBT are that it allows students to engage in treatment on their own time and at their own pace, engages students in exercises that can be revisited as needed, may connect well with students who are technologically minded, are cost-effective (i.e., MoodGYM is a free program), and decreases the potential volume of students being seen in therapy at counseling centers (Richards & Timulak, 2013).

Social Media

Use of social media (e.g., Facebook and Twitter) are current and relevant ways for connecting with students. Given that students take to social media to post messages related to anxiety and depression (Moreno et al., 2011), counseling centers can use social media to provide support resources to distressed students and serve as a resource for those aiding students in distress. Counseling center social media posts can include depression and anxiety facts and tips for coping, campus events related to anxiety and depression, ways students can access center services, and national and regional information regarding mental health.

Campus Recreational Center Collaborations

Mental health benefits associated with aerobic exercise include reduced levels of stress, anxiety, depression, and suicidality, and improvements in mood, self-confidence, cognitive functioning, interest in sex, sleep, endurance, energy, and stamina (Sharma, Madaan, & Petty, 2006; Taliaferro, Rienzo, Pigg, Miller, & Dodd, 2008). Engaging in regular exercise can be challenging for students with anxiety and depression. Students who are unfamiliar with exercise and uncertain as to how to use equipment feel intimidated by large recreation centers; those students who are not positively encouraged to work out are unlikely to use such a viable resource. Collaboration with campus recreation centers can minimize barriers associated with physical exercise.

The Georgia Institute of Technology Counseling Center is currently piloting a Healthy Lifestyles for the Mind and Body program to help facilitate counseling center clients' use of the recreational center. Clinicians identify clients who would benefit from supplementing their mental health treatment with exercise, but have identified barriers that prevent them from using the campus recreation center. After signing a release of information form, the student is referred to the recreational center contact liaison. From there, the student is contacted by the health liaison and e-mailed an orientation video. The student then attends an initial consultation appointment with the health liaison, which involves exploring the student's physical and mental health goals and current health status. This assessment allows the health liaison to develop a fitness plan to best accomplish the student's stated goals. Considering the student's needs, activities may involve providing a tour of the facility and instruction on using equipment, matching the student with a workout partner, providing a personal trainer, or suggesting fitness classes. The student attends follow-up consultations with the liaison to assess progress and initiate changes depending on the student's needs. The goals of the program are to enhance mood and anxiety treatment, help students feel more comfortable and supported on campus, provide an additional social outlet, and help students develop self-care options that can help with relapse prevention.

CONCLUSION

Treating depression and anxiety may be considered the primary job of college counseling centers. The high number of students presenting each day with anxiety and depression and an even larger number of students with anxiety and depression symptoms who fail to ever enter a counseling center require college counseling centers to have expertise in assessment and psychotherapy treatment of depression and anxiety and to have a formidable presence on the general campus population. The association between mental health and academic, interpersonal, and intrapersonal success make counseling centers an invaluable resource to the campus community. The inability of counseling centers to see the rising volume of students presenting with depression and anxiety calls for campus administrators to allocate more resources to college counseling centers and for centers to continue to develop innovative ways to reach students in distress and to improve overall campus mental wellness.

REFERENCES

Agency for Healthcare Research and Quality. (2009). Screening for depression in adults: U.S. Preventive Services Task Force recommendation statement. *Annals of Internal Medicine, 151,* 784–792.

American College Health Association. (2013). *American College Health Association–National College Health Assessment II: Reference Group Executive Summary spring 2013.* Hanover, MD: Author.

American Foundation for Suicide Prevention. (2011). *Interactive Screening Program manual 2011–2012 (ISP).* New York, NY: Author.

American Psychiatric Association. (2000). *Diagnostic and statistical manual of mental disorders* (4th ed., text revision). Arlington, VA: Author.

American Psychiatric Association. (2013). *Diagnostic and statistical manual of mental disorders* (5th ed.). Arlington, VA: Author.

Beck, A. T., & Steer, R. A. (1993). *Manual for the Beck Anxiety Inventory (BAI).* San Antonio, TX: Psychological Corporation.

Beck, A. T., Steer, R. A., & Brown, G. K. (1996). *Manual for the Beck Depression Inventory-II (BDI-II).* San Antonio, TX: Psychological Corporation.

Bjornsson, A. S., Bidwell, L. C., Brosse, A. L., Carey, G., Hauser, M., Seghete, K. L. M., . . . Craighead, W. E. (2011). Cognitive–behavioral group therapy versus group psycho-therapy for social anxiety disorder among college students: A randomized controlled trial. *Depression and Anxiety, 28,* 1034–1042.

Butcher, J. N., Dahlstrom, W. G., Graham, J. R., Tellegen, A., & Kaemmer, B. (1989). *Minnesota Multiphasic Personality Inventory-2: Manual for administration and scoring.* Minneapolis: University of Minnesota Press.

Centers for Disease Control and Prevention. (2012). 2010 National Healthcare Disparities Report (NHDR). *Summary Health Statistics for U.S. Adults: National Health Interview Survey, 2010.* Retrieved from http://www.cdc.gov/nchs/data/series/sr_10/sr10_252.pdf

Centers for Disease Control and Prevention. (2013). *Leading causes of death reports, national and regional, 1999–2010.* Retrieved from http://webappa.cdc.gov/sasweb/ncipc/leadcaus10_us.html

Centre for Mental Health Research. (2004). *BluePages.* Australian National University, Canberra, Australia: Author.

Christensen, H., Griffiths, K., & Groves, C. (2004). *MoodGYM training program: Clinician's manual.* Canberra, Australia: Centre for Mental Health Research.

Chung, H., Klein, M. C., Silverman, D., Corson-Rikert J., Davidson, E., Ellis, P., & Kasnakian, C. (2011). A pilot for improving depression care on college campuses: Results of the College Breakthrough Series Depression (CBS-D) project. *Journal of American College Health, 59*(7), 628–639.

Clarke, G., Reid, E., Eubanks, D., O'Connor, E., Debar, L. L., Kelleher, C., . . . Nunley, S. (2002). Overcoming Depression on the Internet (ODIN): A randomized controlled trial of an Internet depression skills intervention program. *Journal of Medical Internet Research, 4*(3), E14.

Derogatis, L. R. (1994). *Symptom Checklist-90-R: Administration, scoring, and procedures manual* (3rd ed.). Minneapolis, MN: National Computer Systems.

Derogatis, L. R., & Melisaratos, N. (1983). The Brief Symptom Inventory: An introduc-tory report. *Psychological Medicine, 13,* 595–605.

Eisenberg, D., Hunt, J. B., Speer, N., & Zivin, K. (2011). Mental health service utiliza-tion among college students in the United States. *Journal of Nervous and Mental Disease, 199*(5), 301–308.

First, M. B., Williams, J. B. W., Spitzer, R. L., & Gibbon, M. (2007). *Structured Clinical Interview for DSM-IV-TR Axis I Disorders: Clinical Trials Version (SCID-CT).* New York, NY: Biometrics Research, New York State Psychiatric Institute.

Herman, S., Archambeau, O. G., Deliramich, A. N., Kim, B. S. K., Chiu, P. H., & Frueh, B. C. (2011). Depressive symptoms and mental health treatment in an ethnoracially diverse college student sample. *Journal of American College Health, 59*(8), 715–720.

Imel, Z., & Wampold, B. (2008). The importance of treatment and the science of common factors in psychotherapy. In S. D. Brown & R. W. Lent (Eds.), *Handbook of counseling psychology* (4th ed., pp. 249–262). Hoboken, NJ: Wiley.

Kaltenthaler, E., Parry, G., Beverley, C., & Ferriter, M. (2008). Computerised CBT for depression: A systematic review. *British Journal of Psychiatry, 193,* 181–184. Retrieved from http://www.ncbi.nlm.nih.gov/pubmed/18757972

Kessler, R. C., Berglund, P., Demler, O., Jin, R., Koretz, D., Merikangas, K. R., . . . Wang, P. S. (2003). The epidemiology of major depressive disorder: Results from the National Comorbidity Survey Replication (NCS-R). *Journal of the American Medical Association, 289*(23), 3095–3105.

Lambert, M. J., Lunnen, K., Umphress, V., Hansen, N., & Burlingame, G. M. (1994). *Administration and scoring manual for the Outcome Questionnaire (OQ-45.1).* Salt Lake City, UT: IHC Center for Behavioral Healthcare Efficacy.

Liebowitz, M. R. (1987). Social anxiety scale. *Modern Problems of Pharmacopsychiatry, 22,* 141–173.

Locke, B. D., Soet Buzolitz, J., Lei P.-W., Boswell, J. F., McAleavey, A. A., Sevig, T. D., . . . Hayes, J. A. (2011). Development of the Counseling Center Assessment of Psychological Symptoms-62 (CCAPS-62). *Journal of Counseling Psychology, 58*(1), 97–109.

Lu, F. G., Lim, R. F., & Mezzich, J. E. (1995). Issues in the assessment and diagnosis of culturally diverse individuals. In J. Oldham & M. Riba (Eds.), *Review of psychiatry* (pp. 477–510). Washington, DC: American Psychiatric Press.

March, J. S., Silva, S., Petrycki, S., Curry, J., Wells, K., Fairbank, J., . . . Severe, J. (2007). The Treatment for Adolescents With Depression Study (TADS): Long-term effectiveness and safety outcomes. *Archives of General Psychiatry, 64*(10), 1132–1143.

Mattick, R. P., & Clarke, J. C. (1998). Development and validation of measures of social phobia scrutiny fear and social interaction anxiety. *Behaviour Research and Therapy, 36*(4), 455–470.

Meilman, P. W. (2011). Academic dispensations and the role for the counseling center. *Journal of College Student Psychotherapy, 25,* 259–268.

Mental Health America. (2016). *What's your plan? College with a mental health disorder.* Retrieved from http://www.mentalhealthamerica.net/whats-your-plan-college-mental-health-disorder

Millon, T., Strack, S. N., Millon, C., & Grossman, S. (2006). *Millon College Counseling Inventory (MCCI®) manual.* Minneapolis, MN: Pearson.

Mistler, B. J., Reetz, D. R., Krylowicz, B., & Barr, V. (2012). *The Association for University and College Counseling Center Directors annual survey: Reporting period: September 1, 2011 through August 31, 2012.* Retrieved from http://www.aucccd.org/support/Monograph_2012_AUCCCD%20Public.pdf

Moreno, M. A., Jelenchick, L. A., Egan, K. G., Cox, E., Young, H., Gannon, K. E., & Becker, T. (2011). Feeling bad on Facebook: Depression disclosure by college students on a social networking site. *Depression & Anxiety, 28*(6), 447–455.

Morey, L. C. (2007). *Personality Assessment Inventory professional manual* (2nd ed.). Lutz, FL: Psychological Assessment Resources.

National Alliance on Mental Illness. (2012). *Cognitive behavioral therapy fact sheet.* Retrieved from www.nami.org/factsheets/CBT_factsheet.pdf

National Institute of Mental Health. (2011). *Depression* (NIH Publication No. 11-3561). Retrieved from http://www.nimh.nih.gov/health/publications/depression/index.shtml

National Institute of Mental Health, U.S. Department of Health and Human Services, National Institutes of Health. (2012). *Mental health medications* (NIH Publication No. 12–3929 revised). Retrieved from http://r.search.yahoo.com/_ylt=A0LEVipMLYFXZUIAc0AnnIlQ;_ylu=X3oDMTEyYjRraGEzBGNvbG8DY mYxBHBvcwMzBHZ0aWQDQjIwOTBfMQRzZWMDc31-/RV=2/RE=1468112332/RO=10/RU=https%3a%2f%2feducation.ucsb.edu%2fsites%2f default%2ffiles%2fhosford_clinic%2fdocs%2fMental_Health_Medications.pdf/RK=0/RS=Vb3NMMCYR2Ws7zVrvLSoU1JATT4-

Owen, J., Devdas, L., & Rodolfa, E. (2007). University counseling center off-campus referrals: An exploratory investigation. *Journal of College Student Psychotherapy, 22*(2), 13–29. doi:10.1300/J035v22n02_03

Proudfoot, J. (2004). Computer-based treatment for anxiety and depression: Is it feasible? Is it effective? *Neuroscience and Biobehavioural Reviews, 28,* 353–363.

Reynolds, W. M., & Kobak, K. A. (1998). *Reynolds Depression Screening Inventory: Professional manual.* Odessa, FL: Psychological Assessment Resources.

Richards, D., & Timulak, L. (2013). Satisfaction with therapist-delivered vs. self-administered online cognitive behavioural treatments for depression symptoms in college students. *British Journal of Guidance and Counseling, 41*(2), 193–207.

Screening for Mental Health, Inc. (n.d.). CollegeResponse. *National Depression Screening Day (NDSD).* Retrieved from https://mentalhealthscreening.org/programs/college/alcohol.aspx

Seligman, L. (2001). *Systems, strategies, and skills of counseling and psychotherapy.* Upper Saddle River, NJ: Prentice-Hall.

Sharma, A., Madaan, V., & Petty, F. D. (2006). Exercise for mental health. *Primary Care Companion to the Journal of Clinical Psychiatry, 8*(2), 106.

Spielberger, C. D., Gorsuch, R. L., Lushene, R., Vagg, P. R., & Jacobs, G. A. (1983). *Manual for the State-Trait Anxiety Inventory.* Palo Alto, CA: Consulting Psychologists Press.

Substance Abuse and Mental Health Services Administration. (2009). *Illness management and recovery: Practitioner guides and handouts* (HHS Publication No. SMA-09-4462). Rockville, MD: Center for Mental Health Services, Substance Abuse and Mental Health Services Administration, U.S. Department of Health and Human Services.

Substance Abuse and Mental Health Services Administration, Center for Behavioral Health Statistics and Quality. (2012). *The NSDUH report: Major depressive episode among full-time college students and other young adults, aged 18 to 22.* Rockville, MD: Author.

Substance Abuse and Mental Health Services Administration. (2015). *Treatments for mental disorders.* Retrieved from http://www.samhsa.gov/treatment/mental-disorders#depressive

Takahashi, L. K. (2006). Neurobiology of schizophrenia, mood disorders, and anxiety disorders. In L. I. McCance & S. E. Huether (Eds.), *Pathophysiology: The biologic basis for disease in adults and children* (pp. 605–622). St. Louis, MO: Elsevier Mosby.

Taliaferro, L. A., Rienzo, B. A., Pigg, R. M., Miller, M. D., & Dodd, V. J. (2008). Associations between physical activity and reduced rates of hopelessness, depression, and suicidal behavior among college students. *Journal of American College Health, 57*(4), 427–435.

U.S. Food and Drug Administration. (2007). *FDA proposes new warnings about suicidal thinking, behavior in young adults who take antidepressant medications.* Retrieved from http://www.fda.gov/NewsEvents/Newsroom/PressAnnouncements/2007/ucm 108905.htm

Weathers, F., Litz, B., Herman, D., Huska, J., & Keane, T. (1993, October). *The PTSD Checklist (PCL): Reliability, validity, and diagnostic utility.* Paper presented at the Annual Convention of the International Society for Traumatic Stress Studies, San Antonio, TX.

APPENDIX

Social Interaction Anxiety Scale

Patient Name: _____   Date: _____

Instructions: For each item, please circle the number to indicate the degree to which you feel the statement is characteristic or true for you. The rating scale is as follows:

0 = **Not at all** characteristic or true of me.
1 = **Slightly** characteristic or true of me.
2 = **Moderately** characteristic or true of me.
3 = **Very** characteristic or true of me.
4 = **Extremely** characteristic or true of me.

CHARACTERISTIC	NOT AT ALL	SLIGHTLY	MODERATELY	VERY	EXTREMELY
1. I get nervous if I have to speak with someone in authority (teacher, boss, etc.).	0	1	2	3	4
2. I have difficulty making eye contact with others.	0	1	2	3	4
3. I become tense if I have to talk about myself or my feelings.	0	1	2	3	4
4. I find it difficult to mix comfortably with the people I work with.	0	1	2	3	4
5. I find it easy to make friends my own age.	0	1	2	3	4
6. I tense up if I meet an acquaintance in the street.	0	1	2	3	4
7. When mixing socially, I am uncomfortable.	0	1	2	3	4
8. I feel tense if I am alone with just one other person.	0	1	2	3	4
9. I am at ease meeting people at parties, etc.	0	1	2	3	4
10. I have difficulty talking with other people.	0	1	2	3	4
11. I find it easy to think of things to talk about.	0	1	2	3	4

(continued)

Social Interaction Anxiety Scale (*continued*)

CHARACTERISTIC	NOT AT ALL	SLIGHTLY	MODERATELY	VERY	EXTREMELY
12. I worry about expressing myself in case I appear awkward.	0	1	2	3	4
13. I find it difficult to disagree with another's point of view.	0	1	2	3	4
14. I have difficulty talking to attractive persons of the opposite sex.	0	1	2	3	4
15. I find myself worrying that I won't know what to say in social situations.	0	1	2	3	4
16. I am nervous mixing with people I don't know well.	0	1	2	3	4
17. I feel I'll say something embarrassing when talking.	0	1	2	3	4
18. When mixing in a group, I find myself worrying I will be ignored.	0	1	2	3	4
19. I am tense mixing in a group.	0	1	2	3	4
20. I am unsure whether to greet someone I know only slightly.	0	1	2	3	4

Source: Mattick and Clarke (1998).

Academic Disposition Letter: Withdrawal Due to Depression

Date

Dean of Students Office
333 University Drive
City, State, Zip

To Whom It May Concern:

I am writing this letter in support of Philip Day's request for a medical hardship withdrawal for the 20XX Fall semester (please see enclosed release of information form). Mr. Day attended individual therapy with this writer from XX/XXXX to XX/XXXX and has been in group counseling from XX/XXXX to present. As such, I feel I have sufficient knowledge of Mr. Day to write this letter.

Symptoms experienced by Mr. Day fit the criteria for Major Depressive Disorder. He has experienced a depressed mood for most of the day, nearly every day for the last 4 weeks, has diminished interest in pleasurable activities and has excessive negative feelings. Mr. Day completed the Beck Depression Inventory-II (BDI-II) and Beck Anxiety Inventory (BAI), self-report instruments that measure depression and anxiety. His BDI-II score was in the severe range and BAI score was in the moderate range. Mr. Day has a history of interpersonal, family of origin, and financial concerns that exacerbate his depression symptoms. Mr. Day was voluntarily hospitalized at Local Psychiatric Hospital XX/XX/XXXX to XX/XX/XXXX for suicidality. Posthospitalization, Mr. Day showed an improved mood and complied with treatment recommendations; however, continued intensive care is needed.

There is clear evidence that Mr. Day's presenting concerns negatively impacted his academic performance. Mr. Day has expressed his interest in graduating from University and recognizes the importance of maintaining his mental health to achieve this goal. He has been provided with therapy and psychiatry referrals to continue his care following the withdrawal. Prior to re-enrolling, it is recommended that Mr. Day provide documentation of his participation in therapy.

Sincerely,

Staff Psychologist, PhD

CHAPTER EIGHT

ADDICTIONS AND SUBSTANCE ABUSE

Kimber Shelton and Geoff Bathje

ALCOHOL AND DRUG USE AND THE COLLEGE CAMPUS

Alcohol and other drugs (AOD)/substance use on college campuses has been an ongoing challenge for campus administrations, health services and health promotion, housing, and counseling centers. New and innovative ways of misusing and abusing substances present a constant challenge for assessment, diagnosis, prevention, and treatment efforts. College campuses struggle to develop and implement policies and procedures that appropriately address AOD issues while also preserving the developmental needs of students and protecting the campus reputation. Yet the impact substance misuse has on the entire campus demands that college communities, including counseling centers, develop and implement effective programs that educate the college community on the effects of substances on users and nonusers, and address the treatment and recovery needs of students.

The misuse of substances by college students has a significant physiological, emotional, economic, and academic cost. By far, the most serious consequence of substance use is the premature death and injury of college students. Alcohol-related incidents are the third leading cause of death for teens and young adults (Center for Young Women's Health, 2013). Annually, approximately 2,000 college students age 18 to 24 die from alcohol-related unintentional injuries, primarily death caused by motor vehicle accidents (Hingson, Zha, & Weitzman, 2009). In 2009, 3,360,000 students between the ages of 18 and 24 reported driving while under the influence of alcohol and each year approximately 600,000 students experience a serious injury while under the influence of alcohol (Hingson et al., 2009). Alcohol contributes to unintentional deaths, but is also linked to suicide. Each year, 1.2% to 1.5% of students attempt suicide while under the influence of drugs or alcohol (Presley, Leichliter, & Meilman, 1998).

The majority of assaults on college campus are AOD-related. Nearly 700,000 AOD-related physical assaults occur each year on college campuses and 100,000 students report alcohol-related sexual assaults (Hingson et al., 2009). Other alcohol-related consequences include the development of health problems, vandalism, property damage, and police involvement (arrests). The consequences of assault may be jail and imprisonment, campus sanctions, or expulsion, and suspension for the assailant. For those assaulted, consequences could include hospitalization, posttraumatic stress disorder symptoms, and academic impairment due to missed class and study time due to the time needed for recovery. The statistics on unprotected sex while under the influence of drugs or alcohol are also alarming. About 400,000 students engage in unprotected sex while under the influence of alcohol or drugs and more than 100,000 reported being too intoxicated to recall if they consented to sex (Hingson, Heeren, Zakocs, Kopstein, & Wechsler, 2002).

Substance misuse negatively impacts the academic achievement and the mental well-being of college students. A study by Wechsler et al. (2002) showed that 25% of college students reported impaired academic functioning (e.g., increased class absences, falling behind, poor performance on exams and papers, lower grades) due to alcohol use.

Use, Misuse, Abuse, Dependence, and Addiction

Counseling center staff members without significant training or experience in working with substance use issues may have difficulty determining whether a client's alcohol or substance use is problematic or not. As a result, staff's reactions to clients' substance use may be based on their own personal experiences or opinions. It is important to recognize that drug or alcohol *use* does not automatically lead to problems. However, when a person experiences negative consequences (e.g., social, academic, job related, health, legal), it can be defined as *misuse* (Fisher & Harrison, 2009). AOD *abuse* has been defined as the continued use despite negative consequences (American Psychiatric Association [APA], 2000). AOD *dependence* can be defined as compulsive use despite consequences (APA, 2000). The categorical distinction between substance abuse and dependence has been removed from the fifth edition of the *Diagnostic and Statistical Manual of Mental Disorders* (*DSM-5*; APA, 2013) and replaced with a continuum of substance abuse disorders with varying severity levels. It is important to note that "addictions" are not defined in the *DSM*, though *DSM-5* moves closer to the definition of addiction by adding criteria for "cravings" and removing criteria related to "trouble with law enforcement," which was biased by racial, class, and gender inequalities in law enforcement related to substance use and possession.

Nature of Substance Misuse and Abuse

Alcohol Use

Alcohol is by far the most misused substance by college students (and the general population). Alcohol is a depressant acting on the central nervous system that in low doses causes euphoria, mild stimulation, and lowered inhibition. In higher doses, alcohol causes drowsiness, slurred speech, motor coordination problems, and sexual dysfunction. Chronic effects of heavy alcohol use by teens and young adults include neuronal atrophy in the brain regions that affect executive functioning and memory, verbal retrieval, attention, visual–spatial functioning, and language skills (see Lisdahl & Tapert, 2012). A list of commonly abused drugs (including alcohol) and the acute effects and health risks are listed in Table 8.1.

TABLE 8.1 Commonly Abused Drugs

Substances: Category and Name	Examples of Commercial and Street Names	DEA Schedule[a]/ How Administered[b]	Acute Effects/Health Risks
Tobacco			
Nicotine	Found in cigarettes, cigars, bidis, and smokeless tobacco (snuff, spit tobacco, chew)	Not scheduled/ smoked, snorted, chewed	Increased blood pressure and heart rate/chronic lung disease; cardiovascular disease; stroke; cancers of the mouth, pharynx, larynx, esophagus, stomach, pancreas, cervix, kidney, bladder, and acute myeloid leukemia; adverse pregnancy outcomes; and addiction
Alcohol			
Alcohol (ethyl alcohol)	Found in liquor, beer, and wine	Not scheduled/ swallowed	In low doses, euphoria, mild stimulation, relaxation, lowered inhibitions; in higher doses, drowsiness, slurred speech, nausea, emotional volatility, loss of coordination, visual distortions, impaired memory, sexual dysfunction, loss of consciousness/ increased risk of injuries, violence, fetal damage (in pregnant women); depression; neurologic deficits; hypertension; liver and heart disease; addiction; and fatal overdose
Cannabinoids			
Marijuana	Blunt, dope, ganja, grass, herb, joint, bud, Mary Jane, pot, reefer, green, trees, smoke, sinsemilla, skunk, weed	I/smoked, swallowed	Euphoria; relaxation; slowed reaction time; distorted sensory perception; impaired balance and coordination; increased heart rate and appetite; impaired learning, memory; anxiety; panic attacks; psychosis/cough; frequent respiratory infections; possible mental health decline; and addiction
Hashish	Boom, gangster, hash, hash oil, hemp	I/smoked, swallowed	
Opioids			
Heroin	*Diacetylmorphine:* smack, horse, brown sugar, dope, H, junk, skag, skunk, white horse, China white, cheese (with OTC cold medicine and antihistamine)	I/injected, smoked, snorted	Euphoria; drowsiness; impaired coordination; dizziness; confusion, nausea; sedation; feeling of heaviness in the body; slowed or arrested breathing/constipation; endocarditis; hepatitis; HIV; addiction; and fatal overdose
Opium	*Laudanum, paregoric:* big O, black stuff, block, gum, hop	II, III, V/ swallowed, smoked	

(*continued*)

TABLE 8.1 Commonly Abused Drugs (*continued*)

Substances: Category and Name	Examples of Commercial and Street Names	DEA Schedule[a]/ How Administered[b]	Acute Effects/Health Risks
Stimulants			
Cocaine	*Cocaine hydrochloride:* blow, bump, C, candy, Charlie, coke, crack, flake, rock, snow, toot	II/snorted, smoked, injected	Increased heart rate, blood pressure, body temperature, metabolism; feelings of exhilaration; increased energy and mental alertness; tremors; reduced appetite; irritability; anxiety; panic; paranoia; violent behavior; psychosis/weight loss; insomnia; cardiac or cardiovascular complications; stroke; seizures; and addiction
Amphetamine	*Biphetamine, Dexedrine:* bennies, black beauties, crosses, hearts, LA turnaround, speed, truck drivers, uppers	II/swallowed, snorted, smoked, injected	Also, for cocaine—nasal damage from snorting Also, for methamphetamine—severe dental problems
Methamphetamine	*Desoxyn:* meth, ice, crank, chalk, crystal, fire, glass, go fast, speed	II/swallowed, snorted, smoked, injected	
Club Drugs			
MDMA	Ecstasy, Adam, clarity, Eve, lover's speed, peace, uppers	I/swallowed, snorted, injected	MDMA—mild hallucinogenic effects; increased tactile sensitivity, empathic feelings; lowered inhibition; anxiety; chills; sweating; teeth clenching; muscle cramping/sleep disturbances; depression; impaired memory; hyperthermia; addiction
Flunitrazepam[c]	*Rohypnol:* forget-me pill, Mexican Valium, R2, roach, Roche, roofies, roofinol, rope, rophies	IV/swallowed, snorted	Flunitrazepam—sedation; muscle relaxation; confusion; memory loss; dizziness; impaired coordination/ addiction
GHB[c]	*Gamma-hydroxybutyrate:* G, Georgia home boy, grievous bodily harm, liquid ecstasy, soap, scoop, goop, liquid X	I/swallowed	GHB—drowsiness; nausea; headache; disorientation; loss of coordination; memory loss/unconsciousness; seizures; coma
Dissociative Drugs			
Ketamine	*Ketalar SV:* cat Valium, K, Special K, vitamin K	III/injected, snorted, smoked	Feelings of being separate from one's body and environment; impaired motor function/anxiety; tremors; numbness; memory loss; nausea
PCP and analogs	*Phencyclidine:* angel dust, boat, hog, love boat, peace pill	I, II/swallowed, smoked, injected	Also, for ketamine—analgesia; impaired memory; delirium; respiratory depression and arrest; death
Salvia divinorum	Salvia, Shepherdess's herb, Maria Pastora, magic mint, Sally-D	Not scheduled/ chewed, swallowed, smoked	Also, for PCP and analogs— analgesia; psychosis; aggression; violence; slurred speech; loss of coordination; hallucinations

(*continued*)

TABLE 8.1 Commonly Abused Drugs (*continued*)

Substances: Category and Name	Examples of Commercial and Street Names	DEA Schedule[a]/ How Administered[b]	Acute Effects/Health Risks
DXM	Found in some cough and cold medications: Robotripping, Robo, Triple C	Not scheduled/ swallowed	Also, for DXM—euphoria; slurred speech; confusion; dizziness; distorted visual perceptions
Hallucinogens			
LSD	*Lysergic acid diethylamide:* acid, blotter, cubes, microdot, yellow sunshine, blue heaven	I/swallowed, absorbed through mouth tissues	Altered states of perception and feeling; hallucinations; nausea Also, for LSD and mescaline—increased body temperature, heart rate, blood pressure; loss of appetite; sweating; sleeplessness; numbness; dizziness; weakness; tremors; impulsive behavior; rapid shifts in emotion Also, for LSD—flashbacks, hallucinogen persisting perception disorder Also, for psilocybin—nervousness; paranoia; panic
Mescaline	Buttons, cactus, mesc, peyote	I/swallowed, smoked	
Psilocybin	Magic mushrooms, purple passion, shrooms, little smoke	I/swallowed	
Other Compounds			
Anabolic steroids	*Anadrol, Oxandrin, Durabolin, Depo-Testosterone, Equipoise:* roids, juice, gym candy, pumpers	III/injected, swallowed, applied to skin	Steroids—no intoxication effects/ hypertension; blood clotting and cholesterol changes; liver cysts; hostility and aggression; acne; in adolescents—premature stoppage of growth; in males—prostate cancer, reduced sperm production, shrunken testicles, breast enlargement; in females—menstrual irregularities, development of beard, and other masculine characteristics Inhalants (varies by chemical)—stimulation; loss of inhibition; headache; nausea or vomiting; slurred speech; loss of motor coordination; wheezing/cramps; muscle weakness; depression; memory impairment; damage to cardiovascular and nervous systems; unconsciousness; sudden death
Inhalants	*Solvents (paint thinners, gasoline, glues); gases (butane, propane, aerosol propellants, nitrous oxide); nitrites (isoamyl, isobutyl, cyclohexyl):* laughing gas, poppers, snappers, whippets	Not scheduled/ inhaled through nose or mouth	
Prescription Medications			
CNS depressants Stimulants Opioid pain relievers	For more information on prescription medications, please visit http://www.nida.nih.gov/DrugPages/PrescripDrugsChart.html		

(*continued*)

TABLE 8.1 Commonly Abused Drugs (*continued*)

CNS, central nervous system; DXM, dextromethorphan; GHB, gamma-hydroxybutyriane; HIV, human immunodeficiency virus; MDMA, methylenedioxymethamphetamine; OTC, over-the-counter; PCP, phencyclidine.

[a]Schedule I and II drugs have a high potential for abuse. They require greater storage security and have a quota on manufacturing, among other restrictions. Schedule I drugs are available for research only and have no approved medical use; Schedule II drugs are available only by prescription (unrefillable) and require a form for ordering. Schedule III and IV drugs are available by prescription, may have five refills in 6 months, and may be ordered orally. Some Schedule V drugs are available over the counter.

[b]Some of the health risks are directly related to the route of drug administration. For example, injection drug use can increase the risk of infection through needle contamination with staphylococci, HIV, hepatitis, and other organisms.

[c]Associated with sexual assaults.

Principles of Drug Addiction Treatment

More than three decades of scientific research show that treatment can help drug-addicted individuals stop drug use, avoid relapse, and successfully recover their lives. Based on this research, 13 fundamental principles that characterize effective drug abuse treatment have been developed. These principles are detailed in the National Institute on Drug Abuse's *Principles of Drug Addiction Treatment: A Research-Based Guide*. The guide also describes different types of science-based treatments and provides answers to commonly asked questions.

1. **Addiction is a complex but treatable disease that affects brain function and behavior.** Drugs alter the brain's structure and how it functions, resulting in changes that persist long after drug use has ceased. This may help explain why abusers are at risk for relapse even after long periods of abstinence.
2. **No single treatment is appropriate for everyone.** Matching treatment settings, interventions, and services to an individual's particular problems and needs is critical to his or her ultimate success.
3. **Treatment needs to be readily available.** Because drug-addicted individuals may be uncertain about entering treatment, taking advantage of available services the moment people are ready for treatment is critical. Potential patients can be lost if treatment is not immediately available or readily accessible.
4. **Effective treatment attends to multiple needs of the individual, not just his or her drug abuse.** To be effective, treatment must address the individual's drug abuse and any associated medical, psychological, social, vocational, and legal problems.
5. **Remaining in treatment for an adequate period of time is critical.** The appropriate duration for an individual depends on the type and degree of his or her problems and needs. Research indicates that most addicted individuals need at least 3 months in treatment to significantly reduce or stop their drug use and that the best outcomes occur with longer durations of treatment.
6. **Counseling—individual and/or group—and other behavioral therapies are the most commonly used forms of drug abuse treatment.** Behavioral therapies vary in their focus and may involve addressing a patient's motivations to change, building skills to resist drug use, replacing drug-using activities with constructive and rewarding activities, improving problem-solving skills, and facilitating better interpersonal relationships.
7. **Medications are an important element of treatment for many patients, especially when combined with counseling and other behavioral therapies.** For example, methadone and buprenorphine are effective in helping individuals addicted to heroin or other opioids stabilize their lives and reduce their illicit drug use. Also, for persons addicted to nicotine, a nicotine replacement product (nicotine patches or gum) or an oral medication (bupropion or varenicline) can be an effective component of treatment when part of a comprehensive behavioral treatment program.

(*continued*)

TABLE 8.1 Commonly Abused Drugs (continued)

8. **An individual's treatment and services plan must be assessed continually and modified as necessary to ensure it meets his or her changing needs.** A patient may require varying combinations of services and treatment components during the course of treatment and recovery. In addition to counseling or psychotherapy, a patient may require medication, medical services, family therapy, parenting instruction, vocational rehabilitation, and/or social and legal services. For many patients, a continuing care approach provides the best results, with treatment intensity varying according to a person's changing needs.

9. **Many drug-addicted individuals also have other mental disorders.** Because drug abuse and addiction—both of which are mental disorders—often co-occur with other mental illnesses, patients presenting with one condition should be assessed for the other(s). And when these problems co-occur, treatment should address both (or all), including the use of medications as appropriate.

10. **Medically assisted detoxification is only the first stage of addiction treatment and by itself does little to change long-term drug abuse.** Although medically assisted detoxification can safely manage the acute physical symptoms of withdrawal, detoxification alone is rarely sufficient to help addicted individuals achieve long-term abstinence. Thus, patients should be encouraged to continue drug treatment following detoxification.

11. **Treatment does not need to be voluntary to be effective.** Sanctions or enticements from family, employment settings, and/or the criminal justice system can significantly increase treatment entry, retention rates, and the ultimate success of drug treatment interventions.

12. **Drug use during treatment must be monitored continuously, as lapses during treatment do occur.** Knowing their drug use is being monitored can be a powerful incentive for patients and can help them withstand urges to use drugs. Monitoring also provides an early indication of a return to drug use, signaling a possible need to adjust an individual's treatment plan to better meet his or her needs.

13. **Treatment programs should assess patients for the presence of HIV/AIDS, hepatitis B and C, tuberculosis, and other infectious diseases, as well as provide targeted risk-reduction counseling to help patients modify or change behaviors that place them at risk of contracting or spreading infectious diseases.** Targeted counseling specifically focused on reducing infectious disease risk can help patients further reduce or avoid substance-related and other high-risk behaviors. Treatment providers should encourage and support HIV screening and inform patients that highly active antiretroviral therapy (HAART) has proven effective in combating HIV, including among drug-abusing populations.

Source: National Institute on Drug Abuse (2009).

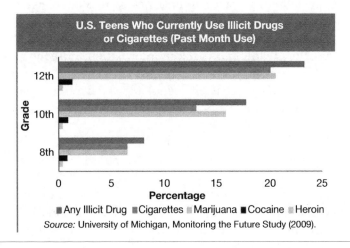

U.S. Teens Who Currently Use Illicit Drugs or Cigarettes (Past Month Use)

Source: University of Michigan, Monitoring the Future Study (2009).

(continued)

TABLE 8.1 Commonly Abused Drugs (*continued*)

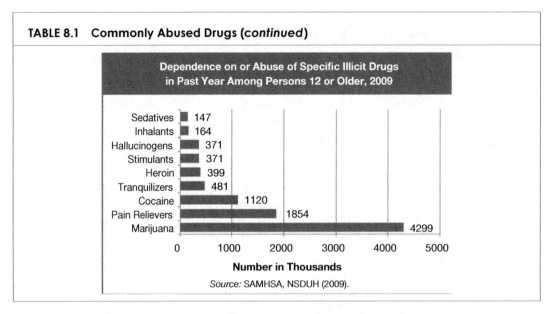

Dependence on or Abuse of Specific Illicit Drugs in Past Year Among Persons 12 or Older, 2009

Drug	Number in Thousands
Sedatives	147
Inhalants	164
Hallucinogens	371
Stimulants	371
Heroin	399
Tranquilizers	481
Cocaine	1120
Pain Relievers	1854
Marijuana	4299

Source: SAMHSA, NSDUH (2009).

The most common substance-related issue on college campuses is binge drinking, with approximately 40% of students reporting engaging in binge drinking (Johnston, O'Malley, Bachman, & Schulenberg, 2012). The National Institute on Alcohol Abuse and Alcoholism (NIAAA) National Advisory Council (2002) defines binge drinking as a "pattern of drinking alcohol that brings blood alcohol concentration (BAC) to 0.08 gram-percent or above, and 'heavy drinking' as five or more binge drinking episodes in a month. For a typical adult, this blood-alcohol level corresponds to consuming five or more drinks (male), or four or more drinks (female) in about 2 hours" (p. 5). For many students, binge drinking begins prior to their attendance at college. A study examining binge drinking from 1975 to 2007 found that 72% of high school seniors had a full alcohol drink, (drank to completion) 26% engaged in binge drinking, and 55% had reported drinking to intoxication (Johnston, O'Malley, Bachman, & Schulenberg, 2007). Upon entrance into college, binge drinking rates increase with approximately 40% of college students reporting binge drinking in the past 2 weeks (NIAAA, 2002).

Students are often unaware of what is considered moderate, binge, and high-risk/heavy drinking. A lack of information, misconceptions held by students, and certain characteristics related to the college environment negatively impact college students' use of alcohol and the likelihood of engaging in high-risk and binge drinking. Table 8.2 provides a summary of moderate, binge, and high-risk drinking behaviors.

Students may hold the erroneous belief that some alcoholic beverages are safer than others or have less potential for abuse. For example, a student may drink beer instead of wine or liquor with the belief that he or she is less likely to become intoxicated or develop problems. This student fails to recognize that the same quantity of alcohol (or more accurately ethanol) in a 12-oz. bottle of beer is present in a standard glass of wine or a standard shot of liquor. Additionally, students may not account for the size or amount of alcohol in their drink. For example, one large glass of high-alcohol beer or one strong

TABLE 8.2 Moderate, Heavy, and Binge Drinking

Moderate or "Low-Risk" Drinking

Research shows that people who drink moderately may be less likely to experience an AUD. These drinking levels, which differ for men and women, are:

For Men: No more than four drinks on any single day AND no more than 14 drinks per week

For Women: No more than three drinks on any single day AND no more than seven drinks per week

To stay low-risk for AUDs, you must keep within both the single day and weekly limits.

Even within these limits, you can have problems if you drink too quickly or have other health issues. To keep your risk for problems low, make sure you:

- Drink slowly
- Eat enough while drinking

Certain people should avoid alcohol completely, including those who:

- Plan to drive a vehicle or operate machinery
- Take medications that interact with alcohol
- Have a medical condition that alcohol can aggravate
- Are pregnant or trying to become pregnant

Heavy or "At-Risk" Drinking

For healthy adults in general, heavy drinking means consuming more than the single day or the weekly amounts listed previously. About one in four people who drink above these levels already has alcohol dependence or alcohol abuse problems.

Binge Drinking

Binge drinking means drinking so much within about 2 hours that BAC levels reach 0.08 g/dL. For women, this usually occurs after about four drinks, and for men, after about five.

Drinking this way can pose health and safety risks, including car crashes and injuries. Over the long term, binge drinking can damage the liver and other organs.

AUD, alcohol use disorder; BAC, blood alcohol concentration.

Adapted from National Institute on Alcohol Abuse and Alcoholism (n.d.).

mixed drink may contain as much alcohol as two or more standard drinks. Assuming that they are drinking less, the student may mistakenly engage in binge drinking. Figure 8.1 provides definitions of what is considered a standard drink.

While some students unknowingly binge drink, other students may actively seek to become intoxicated. The campus environment may support alcohol misuse as a "rite of passage," students may hold the belief that high academic rigor allows for periods of intoxication (i.e., having the mentality of "work hard, party hard"), or hold the belief that alcohol abuse is expected or normative. Research routinely demonstrates that college students overestimate the AOD use of their peers (Perkins, Haines, & Rice, 2005). Holding the false belief that peers are heavy AOD users may lead students to increase or justify their misuse/abuse of alcohol.

Gender presents as a significant risk factor in college student alcohol (and drug) use. With the exception of Vicodin, males out use women in every drug category (Johnston et al., 2012). This is particularly true when it comes to binge drinking. With extreme binge drinking—10 or more drinks in a row in the last 2 weeks—24% of college males report engaging in this behavior versus 7% of college females (Johnston et al., 2012). Where a student resides also impacts the

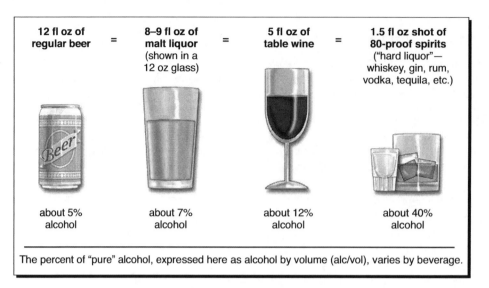

| 12 fl oz of regular beer | = | 8–9 fl oz of malt liquor (shown in a 12 oz glass) | = | 5 fl oz of table wine | = | 1.5 fl oz shot of 80-proof spirits ("hard liquor"— whiskey, gin, rum, vodka, tequila, etc.) |

about 5% alcohol   about 7% alcohol   about 12% alcohol   about 40% alcohol

The percent of "pure" alcohol, expressed here as alcohol by volume (alc/vol), varies by beverage.

Figure 8.1   What is a standard drink?
Adapted from National Institute on Alcohol Abuse and Alcoholism (n.d.).

use of alcohol. As summarized by the NIAAA (2002), students living in fraternity and sorority housing have the highest levels of alcohol use, followed by students living in on-campus dorms. Rates of alcohol use tend to be lower for students who live independently in off-campus housing, are living with their parents, or are attending a community college. Nonetheless, the gap between male and female drug and alcohol use has been narrowing and substance use among women should not be overlooked based on lower average levels of use (Grucza, Norberg, & Bierut, 2009).

Drug and alcohol abuse on college campuses has also been found to vary by race and ethnicity. Specifically, African American and Asian students have been found to have lower levels of substance use than European American students, with European American males having the highest rates of substance abuse (Wechsler & Nelson, 2008). Other demographic factors that have been found to correlate with drinking include age and marital status. Specifically, older students and married students have been found to consume less alcohol and engage in less frequent binge drinking than their younger, unmarried peers. Interestingly, on campuses with more women, racial/ethnic minority students, and older students, drinking was lower overall, but also for European American males (Wechsler & Kuo, 2003). This suggests that problematic drinking is reduced for all demographic groups as the campus norms shift toward more moderate use of alcohol.

Additional campus factors that influence college drinking are extracurricular organizations and geographical location as universities with prominent Greek life and athletic teams and schools in the Northeast reporting higher incidents of alcohol use by students (NIAAA, 2002). Considering the proclivity of alcohol use on college campuses, it is not surprising that self-reports show that 19% to 36% of students meet the criteria for alcohol abuse in the past 12 months (Knight et al., 2002).

Illicit Drug Use

Drug use is highest among people in their late teens and 20s. In 2011, 23.8% of 18- to 20-year olds reported using an illicit drug in the past month (National Institutes of Health [NIH], 2012). The most common "illicit" (in some states marijuana use is not illegal) drug used by college students is marijuana. Granted, although concrete causal data do not yet exist, there is correlational, self-report, and recent neuropsychological data on the physiological effects of marijuana use. Acute use of marijuana impairs judgment and motor coordination and slows reaction time (NIH, 2012). For marijuana users who began using during adolescence (prior to age 17) chronic effects of marijuana have been associated with processing speed, attention, memory, and executive functioning deficits (NIH, 2012; National Institute on Drug Abuse [NIDA], 2012).

Students are frequently unaware of the impact marijuana use may have on academic performance and motivation. Take, for example, the 19-year-old male student presenting for counseling as his grades, attention span, and motivational level have decreased. When asked about his substance use, he reports smoking a bowl three to five times weekly since the beginning of the school year. Delta-9-tetrahydrocannabinol (THC) impacts the areas of the brain that are responsible for pleasure, memory, thinking, concentration, motivation, coordination, and sensory and time perception (NIH, 2012). After use, THC continues to affect the brain for days or weeks, or, among regular, daily users, for months. This student is likely unaware that his marijuana use may be the cause of his changed academic performance, or if not the cause, greatly impacts his ability to improve his performance. Any effective intervention with this student would have to include addressing his ongoing marijuana use, including assessing his knowledge on the impact of marijuana, awareness of any consequences he has experienced, and providing psychoeducational information and counseling as needed. Other commonly used drugs by college students include inhalants, cocaine (including crack cocaine), hallucinogens, and methamphetamine (Substance Abuse and Mental Health Services Administration [SAMHSA], 2005).

Prescription Drug Misuse

Misuse of prescription drugs, including sedatives, stimulants, and pain relievers (opioids), is an ever-increasing problem on college campuses, with rates of prescription drug abuse being highest among those age 18 to 25 (SAMHSA, 2009). Prescription misuse is defined as taking the medication in a manner differently than prescribed, at a higher dose than recommended, or self-medicating with someone else's medication (U.S. Food and Drug Administration [FDA], 2010). In three studies of college students who were prescribed to stimulate medication for attention deficit/hyperactivity disorder (ADHD), 27% to 40% of students reported misuse of their stimulant medication (i.e., taking a higher dose and taking more frequent doses) (Arria, 2008; Sepulveda et al., 2011), and in two studies, 10% to 25% of students reported taking the stimulant medication with the intent to get high

(Sepulveda et al., 2011; Upadhyaya et al., 2005). As a group, students are most likely to misuse their own medications and will then obtain prescription medications from peers (McCabe & Boyd, 2005). Rates of obtaining medication from drug dealers are not on the Internet but are relatively low for college students.

National studies show that college students have the highest rates of nonprescription opioid use (McCabe, Teter, Boyd, Knight, & Wechsler, 2005), which is the second most common drug after marijuana (SAMHSA, 2009). Unlike other prescription drugs, which are obtained from a personal prescription or friends, women are more likely to obtain sedatives and pain medications from family members (McCabe & Boyd, 2005).

College students misuse prescription drugs for a number of reasons including self-medication of mental health-related concerns or emotional pain, to stay up studying (stimulants), and as a means for socializing. Despite perceptions that prescription medications are safe compared to street drugs, misuse of prescription drugs can cause increased blood pressure or heart rate, organ damage, addiction, difficulty in breathing, seizures, overdose, heart attack, stroke, and death. Additionally, abuse of prescription drugs places students at an increased risk for polysubstance use and dependence (SAMHSA, 2009), further complicating treatment and recovery. Table 8.3 provides a summary of commonly misused or abused prescription drugs by college students.

TABLE 8.3   Drugs of Choice—The Most Highly Abused Prescription Drugs Among College Students

	Used to Treat	How They Work in Body	Potential Problems if Misused or Abused
Stimulants (e.g., Ritalin, Concerta, Adderall)	Narcolepsy, ADHD, and other conditions	Speed up brain activity causing increased alertness, attention, and energy that come with elevated blood pressure, increased heart rate and breathing	Can lead to dangerous increases in blood pressure, which places added strain on the heart. Dangerous increases in heart rate and respiration are also possible
Sedatives/tranquilizers (e.g., Valium, Xanax, Ativan, Klonopin, Ambien)	Anxiety, tension, panic attacks, and sleep disorders	Slow down or "depress" the function of the brain and central nervous system	Can cause withdrawal seizures
Opioid analgesics (e.g., Vicodin, OxyContin, Percocet, methadone)	Moderate to severe pain, may be prescribed after surgery	Block pain message from reaching the brain	Can cause respiratory depression, slow and shallow breathing

ADHD, attention deficit/hyperactivity disorder.

Source: National Council on Patient Information and Education (2010). Reprinted with permission.

INTERVENTIONS AND TREATMENT OPTIONS FOR COLLEGE AND UNIVERSITY COUNSELING CENTERS

In 2002, the Task Force of the National Advisory Council on Alcohol Abuse and Alcoholism produced a landmark report, "A Call to Action: Changing the Culture of Drinking at U.S. Colleges," with a 2007 updated report (NIAAA, 2007). The report reviewed a range of evidence-based treatment and intervention practices aimed at reducing alcohol use and minimizing consequences. Evidence showed that simple alcohol education alone had minimal effectiveness in reducing alcohol use or in creating ongoing change. Best results came from treatment and intervention programs that were multimodal, combining individual and group programs that incorporate educational or awareness components, cognitive behavioral interventions (i.e., providing skills for moderating and reducing alcohol use), goal clarification, life skills training, and motivational enhancement techniques (Larimer & Cronce, 2002). While most college and university counseling centers do not have the resources to treat more severe substance use disorders, many offer some form of substance abuse services. These may include prevention and health promotion, screening, comprehensive assessment, early intervention, referral, or maintenance for students in recovery.

Screening, Brief Intervention, Referral to Treatment

Brief intervention (BI) and treatment have been shown to be effective treatment modalities at reducing high-risk substance abuse behaviors (SAMHSA, 2009). SAMHSA provides an assessment and treatment framework that can help college counseling centers offer services to students with substance use issues—screening, brief intervention, referral to treatment (SBIRT). SBIRT is designed to provide early intervention for individuals with risky AOD use, and the timely referral to more intensive substance abuse treatment for individuals with a substance abuse disorder. Appropriate to the college counseling center where resources are limited and the majority of students are presenting with substance misuse and abuse, the goal of BIs is to reduce the harm that could result from continued or increased substance use (National Highway Traffic Safety Administration, 2007). Figure 8.2 provides an outline of the SBIRT model.

Screening and Assessment of Substance Use Disorders

Despite the prevalence of substance use on college campuses, clinicians often fail to adequately assess, or even screen for, alcohol and other drug use. In one study, only half of college counselors mentioned alcohol use with their clients even when the clients' level of alcohol use merited concern (Matthews, Schmidt, Conclaves, & Bursley, 1998). Counselors may also overestimate the degree to which they assess substance use. In another study, 92.7% of counselors reported that they regularly ask about substance use, but only 38.5% asked a question about substance use in response to vignettes (Freimuth, 2008). Additionally, counselors were substantially more likely to ask a question about substance use

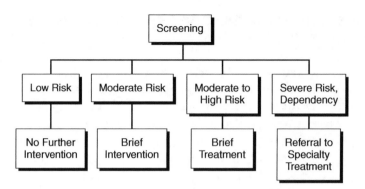

Figure 8.2 Screening brief intervention/treatment, referral to treatment (SBIRT).
Source: Substance Abuse and Mental Health Services Administration (2011).

when clients explicitly mentioned their substance use than when unprompted. Reasons for not screening included a lack of confidence in the counselor's ability to assess substance use problems, a belief that clients do not tell the truth about substance use, worry about questioning clients' integrity, and fear of frightening or angering clients.

Some college counseling centers provide mandated assessments to students who violate campus code of conduct policies regarding substance use. Targeting this population is important as it poses a higher risk for problematic alcohol involvement and are disproportionately heavier alcohol users (Caldwell, 2002). Considering that mandated referrals for treatment benefit students as much as those who are self-referred (Sia, Dansereau, & Czuchry, 2000), a mandated status does not have to be a barrier to screening and intervention.

In accordance with the SBIRT model, screening for substance use should be universal. While not every counselor may feel qualified to assess and treat substance use disorders, it is essential that all counselors develop a level of skill and comfort to screen each client for substance use disorders (similar to universal screening for risk of harm), and make appropriate referrals. Counseling center directors would be well advised to consider including AOD screening questions in intake paperwork, while also emphasizing to staff counselors the importance of following up on these questions during the intake session. Several brief screening instruments are available for free use. The Michigan Alcohol Screening Test (MAST; Selzer, 1971) is a 25-item inventory to assess problematic drinking. The Drug Abuse Screening Test (DAST; Skinner, 1982) was adapted from the MAST to assess for problematic use of other drugs, and is available in 10-, 20-, and 28-item versions. A briefer instrument, which is commonly used by primary care physicians to screen for alcohol use disorders (AUDs), is the four-item CAGE (Ewing, 1984). The CAGE-AID is an expanded version of the CAGE designed to capture both alcohol and substance abuse (Brown & Rounds, 1995). The 10-item Alcohol Use Disorders Identification Test (AUDIT) is another popular measure for screening for alcohol use problems (Babor, Higgins-Biddle, Saunders, & Monteiro, 2001). Several brief versions of the AUDIT are available, including the four-item Fast Alcohol Screening Test (FAST), the three-item AUDIT-C, and the three-item AUDIT-3. Each of these scales correlates highly to the full AUDIT measure and has similar specificity and sensitivity (Laux, Perera-Diltz, & Calmes, 2012).

While screening instruments do not provide enough information to make a diagnosis, they are sensitive to problematic substance use and can help clinicians identify the need for further assessment or referral. Screening is also the first step in the process of substance use disorder assessment. SAMHSA (1998) recommends that if screening is positive, the clinician should implement crisis intervention if necessary, followed by an assessment plan. The assessment plan should include gathering past assessment information, current findings, and family, school, and medical collateral information to inform diagnosis and intervention planning. Comprehensive substance abuse assessment tools can be helpful in gathering current findings. One of the most popular and thorough instruments is the semistructured Addiction Severity Index (ASI; McLellan, Luborsky, O'Brien, & Woody, 1980), which is useful in many different settings. The ASI assesses demographic data, medical status, employment status, support status, legal status, family history, social relationships, psychiatric status, and past 30 days use, lifetime use, and route of administration for 12 categories of drugs. Another instrument that is popular in college and university counseling centers is the Substance Abuse Subtle Screening Inventory-3 (SASSI-3; Miller, 1997). The SASSI inquires about negative consequences of use, loss of control, and using to change thoughts or feelings. While it is as effective as other measures at identifying substance use disorders, it does not appear to achieve the goal of overcoming client denial or dishonesty according to a meta-analysis (Feldstein & Miller, 2007).

Screening and assessment instruments as well as clinical interviews are instrumental to determining the level of care needed by students. Consider two students: James is a PhD student mandated for an AOD assessment after violating the campus ordinance of no alcohol on campus. During the clinical interview, James reports a recent break up, buying a bottle of wine during lunch, and the intent to take the wine home to drink that evening. He reports typically drinking one to two times a month having three to four drinks in a sitting (low-risk drinking) and denies ever experiencing any consequences for his past use. He acknowledges the intent to drink today was to help cope with feelings of rejections. He states that the bottle of wine accidently fell out of his bag during a class. His AUDIT score is six, with the recommendation of Alcohol Advice, and SASSI results suggest no evidence of substance dependence. Given his limited risk factors, James can likely benefit from brief alcohol education and coping, and possible short-term counseling to transition from his relationship.

Now let's look at Amanda, an 18-year-old college freshman mandated after being transported to the hospital for alcohol poisoning. She began drinking at age 15, experiences blackouts approximately four to five times yearly, and drinks two times a week having four to six drinks per sitting (high-risk drinking). Her AUDIT score is 19, with the recommendation Simple Advice, plus Brief Counseling and Continued Monitoring, and her SASSI results suggest evidence of substance dependence. With her high number of risk factors (i.e., early onset of alcohol use, experience of negative consequences, history of blackouts, binge drinking) and assessment results, Amanda requires a higher level of specific substance abuse treatment that may or may not be within the scope of her college counseling center.

These two examples highlight the importance of completing a brief screening, therefore make sure that the appropriate therapeutic intervention is provided.

Brief Intervention and/or Brief Treatment

For most campuses, the number of students presenting with substance dependence will be much lower than the number of students presenting with low- to moderate-risk substance use and no signs of substance dependence. At the counseling center of one of the authors where universal screening is done, AUDIT scores reveal that 96.3% of counseling clients scored within the Alcohol Education and Simple Advice ranges, whereas only 3.3% scored in the Advice-Counseling and Continued Monitoring and Specialist Evaluation ranges. Thus, the majority of students are well suited for BI and/or BI models.

SAMHSA defines BI as one to five sessions lasting from 5 minutes to 1 hour (2011). The goal of the BI is to provide education regarding students' AOD use and to enhance their motivation in reducing risky behavior. Counseling centers can access an endless supply of free brief treatment intervention programs, modules, and protocols available through SAMHSA, NIH, and NIAAA. Brief treatment is intended to address both the immediate and long-standing issues that have developed from AOD misuse and to help students obtain long-term care (SAMHSA, 2011). Brief treatment usually occurs in five to 12 sessions. A number of brief treatments exist for AOD use including brief cognitive behavioral therapy, brief strategic/interactional therapies, brief humanistic and existential therapies, brief psychodynamic therapy, brief family therapy, and time-limited group therapy.

Referral to Treatment (RT)

A referral for more intensive treatment is necessary for students who meet the criteria for substance dependence (as defined by *the Diagnostic and Statistical Manual of Mental Disorders,* fourth edition, text revision [American Psychiatric Association, 2000]) or substance-related disorder in the moderate to severe range (*DSM-5*) or for students detoxing from alcohol or benzodiazepines (withdrawal can lead to death). The importance of creating the conditions that increase the likelihood of a client following through with referral cannot be overstated. As high as 80% of individuals with problematic substance use are in the precontemplation or contemplation stages of change (Center for Substance Abuse Treatment, 1999). The precontemplation stage of change is characterized by lack of insight into the problem or little desire or confidence in ability to change. The contemplation stage is characterized by ambivalence about change. Neither of these stages of change is conducive to referral, particularly if clients are simply given treatment recommendations without adequate time to process the need for the referral or follow-up.

Counseling centers may consider allowing for at least one session (if not more) of motivational interviewing to increase the likelihood of clients following through on referrals to comprehensive substance use assessment, self-help groups, or treatment. While counseling centers may be reluctant about the liabilities of continuing a relationship with clients who appear to have serious substance use issues, even a single session of motivational interviewing has been shown to substantially increase the likelihood of follow-through in taking a referral and completing treatment (Center for Substance Abuse Treatment, 1999). Furthermore, failing to help students with substance abuse problems may be the greater liability. For example, two universities (the University of Miami and the Massachusetts Institute of Technology) were ordered to pay $14 million and $6 million, respectively, for substance-related student deaths (National Center on Addiction and Substance Abuse [CASA], 2007).

Counseling centers should maintain a comprehensive list of substance abuse referral information, including referrals to inpatient and outpatient treatment centers, addiction specialists, self-help groups, and mandated treatment providers (e.g., DUI classes). Addiction specialists and comprehensive treatment centers will provide a comprehensive assessment before recommending a level of care, so the referring clinician does not need to be responsible for identifying the appropriate level of care. However, it may be helpful to be familiar with the American Society of Addiction Medicine (ASAM, 2013) level of care guidelines, as they are standard in the field for placement. The levels of care include early intervention, outpatient services, intensive outpatient services, partial hospitalization services, inpatient/residential services, and medically managed intensive inpatient services.

If referring clients to a self-help group, it is important to first prepare clients for the experience. The clinician should have a list of days and times of local meetings, along with the name of a contact affiliated with the group. This information can be readily found online. A regular complaint by students is feeling as if they do not fit into self-help groups (e.g., students are younger than other group members, other members have extensive years of using, socioeconomic differences). If possible, students would be referred to self-help groups that are student focused or regularly attended by college-age students. Of particular importance is discussing the client's spiritual beliefs prior to referral, as spirituality is a major component of 12-step meetings (e.g., Alcoholics Anonymous [AA], Narcotics Anonymous [NA]). Nonreligious clients may prefer a secular organization, such as SMART Recovery or Alcoholics Anonymous for Atheists and Agnostics. It is also important to note that the 12-step model includes a disease conceptualization of addiction and takes an abstinence view toward drugs and alcohol. Clients with a more moderate usage history may find this approach to be off-putting or unnecessary. SMART recovery is based on cognitive behavior and solution-focused principles, does not require abstinence, and can accommodate both substance addictions and behavioral process addictions (e.g., sexual addictions, pathological gambling). When referring a client to self-help groups, it may also be beneficial to ask the client to commit to attending several different meetings to find the one that is the best fit, as each group can have its own personality.

SBIRT Guidelines

Counseling center staff, even those with limited AOD treatment experience, can feel empowered to use the SBIRT model. Following simple guidelines can help clinicians service students in the counseling center or quickly connect them with community referrals. The following are two commonly used SBIRT guidelines.

FRAMES (Miller & Sanchez, 1994):

- Feedback is given to the individual about personal risk or impairment.
- Responsibility of the individual for change.
- Advice about ways to create change is provided by the clinician.
- Menu of alternative self-help and treatment options are provided.
- Empathic style is used by clinician.
- Self-efficacy or optimistic empowerment is engendered in the participant.

5As (adapted from Fiore et al., 2008):

1. Ask about substance use.
2. Advise to quit through clear personalized messages.
3. Assess willingness to reduce use or quit.
4. Assist to moderate or quit.
5. Arrange follow-up and support.

An example of 5As approach: Roger is a 19-year Korean American male presenting with family of origin stressors and is looking for advice on how to cope during summer break, which begins in 2 weeks. As part of the universal screening process, his clinician has checked initial paperwork that included his AUDIT score and then queries information regarding his AOD use during the clinical interview (Ask). Roger reports alcohol use two times monthly, having two to four drinks per sitting, but finds that he drinks more than he intends to (5–7 drinks) prior to breaks, which leads to intoxication. He denies experiencing any academic, social, or legal consequences. Assessment of his use and AUDIT score lead his clinician to determine that Roger can benefit from a BI. His clinician empathizes with his presenting concerns and provides feedback on how alcohol use impacts his mood and level of stress and serves as a coping mechanism (Advise). She advises Roger to continue to utilize low-risk drinking behaviors prior to break and informs him that increasing his level of drinking will place him at increased risk for developing alcohol-related problems. Roger expresses his understanding and desire to obtain additional coping strategies (Assess). She then assists him with improving his coping skills suggesting that he write down his feelings before drinking and spending time with sober or low-risk drinking friends prior to break. The dyad schedules a follow-up meeting for when he returns to campus after the break (Arrange). This BI could reasonably be completed within 10 minutes.

Additional Treatment Options

Outreach, Prevention, and Promotion

Multimodal outreach and prevention programs are necessary to fully meet the needs of college campuses. Counseling centers engage in primary prevention (targeted toward young people who have not yet tried substances), secondary prevention (targeted toward those who have used substances without major consequences, and aimed at avoiding high risk use or use of riskier substances), and tertiary prevention (which can include treatment and relapse prevention). Developed by the NIDA (1997) an alternative model of prevention exists that is applicable to college campuses. This model includes universal prevention (programs geared toward an entire population; e.g., a college campus), selective prevention (programs designed for select groups within a population deemed to be at high risk; e.g., students in fraternities or sororities), and indicated prevention (targeting individuals who show signs of developing a problem with substance use; e.g., students arrested for alcohol violations). Similarly, the NIAAA (2002) recommended a three-in-one approach to alcohol intervention on campuses, which includes targeting individual students, the entire student body, and the greater college community.

A variety of programs have been attempted to reduce substance use on college campuses, including cognitive, affective, behavioral, and social norming approaches. When developing programs, it is important for counseling centers to consider goals and usefulness of the intended program. Some types of outreach have been shown to be more effective than others; in fact, some AOD treatment programs have shown to be ineffective or even harmful. For example, knowledge-based programs that simply provide objective information about drugs have been shown to be ineffective on their own (Swisher, Warner, & Herr, 1972). Furthermore, affective campaigns that attempt to frighten users away from drugs by portraying the most negative consequences may actually serve to increase, rather than decrease, experimentation with drugs (van Wormer & Davis, 2003). Instead of these tactics, evidence shows that adolescents and college students respond well to interventions that provide values clarification (e.g., identifying natural conflicts between a client's values and drug use), teaching alternatives to drugs (e.g., identifying ways to relax and be social without drinking), promotion of personal effectiveness, and social skills (to enhance self-esteem and positive social experiences), providing accurate norms about AOD, and drug refusal skills (Hart & Ksir, 2012). Correcting mistaken norms may be particularly effective, as one study of 76,130 college students found the gap between perceived and actual norms to be the strongest predictor of personal alcohol consumption (Perkins et al., 2005).

Notably, prevention programs have increasingly included harm reduction components, as opposed to a focus on abstinence from substances or complete elimination of underage drinking. The harm reduction perspective recognizes that it is not possible to have a drug-free society, and therefore societies should work to reduce the harmful consequences of drug use (MacCoun, 1998). Examples of harm reduction include media campaigns such as the "Friends don't let friends drive drunk" campaign, or late hour bus services on campus to reduce sexual assault, robbery, or other violence toward people under the influence of alcohol. One of the authors once implemented an outreach program that included a "pour test" where students would pour water into cups to measure out a typical drink they would pour for themselves, and then measure the contents to determine whether it was more than one standard drink. Note that these programs attempt to mitigate harmful effects of substance use (e.g., drinking and driving, assault, and drinking more than intended), rather than attempting to eliminate substance use.

Lastly, the culture of the campus cannot be overlooked as part of a prevention strategy. CASA (2007) made recommendations for reducing drug and alcohol abuse on campus:

- There are clear policies banning drugs on campus (including in campus housing).
- Smoking should be banned on campus.
- Recreational events (including sporting events) should be drug and alcohol free.
- Universities should not accept endorsements from the tobacco or alcohol industry.
- Substance abuse prevention should be included in the curriculum.
- Classes and exams should be scheduled on Fridays and Saturdays.
- Efforts should be made to identify students at highest risk of substance abuse.
- Adequate resources should be allocated to mental health, wellness, and prevention services.
- Assessment and intervention services should be provided to the extent that it is possible.

Students can also engage in a number of self-directed screening tools and psychoeducation courses, most of which can be made readily available through the counseling center website. Developed by San Diego State University Research Foundation, the Echeckup To Go Marijuana and Alcohol are personalized psychoeducational and behavioral change motivated computerized programs. The reports can be used independently by students or incorporated into therapy. Another self-directed tool is Marijuana 101 (developed by 3rd Millennium Classrooms), an individualized online course that uses psychoeducation and motivational strategies to engage students in building awareness of the physical, social, and health effects that marijuana has, and the legal consequences associated with its use, and provides students with tools for making changes. Additional counseling centers can provide students with MyStudentBody (www.mystudentbody.com), a program developed to reduce risks on campus including AOD risks.

Group Interventions

Group therapy is one of the most widely used treatment modalities for substance use (Center for Substance Abuse Treatment, 2005). Group interventions can take the form of providing support, therapy, and psychoeducation.

Support Groups and Group Therapy

Many college campuses can support students in substance abuse recovery and treatment by offering on campus AA, NA, other affiliate 12-step groups, or "anonymous" alternatives like SMART Recovery. On-campus self-help groups provide different functions. First, attending a self-help group on campus is likely convenient for many students as they are already on campus. Second, traditional-age college students may feel disconnected from community self-help groups that may have an older population or a population with a more chronic-use history. On-campus self-help groups provide students with a greater peer reference and may increase their participation in their own treatment. When a campus group is not available, self-help group websites (e.g., www.aa.org or www.smartrecovery.org), provide a comprehensive list of local AA meetings to which clinicians can refer students. It would benefit the counseling center to have a list of self-help meetings close to campus that are readily available to students.

Counseling centers can also provide students with group psychotherapy housed in the counseling center. Attendance in group counseling can be in conjunction with ongoing individual therapy, or only group therapy depending on the student's level of need. Group therapy is not only beneficial in addressing substance use issues, but can also help students address issues impacted by substance use such as self-esteem, relationship issues, and trauma. Centers can decide if group therapy will be provided for a specific level or type of use, or if groups are open to students who are questioning or exploring AOD use to students who are in abstinence and recovery. College counseling centers have a variety of different titles for these groups such as Understanding the Impact of Substances on Our Lives (Georgia Institute of Technology), Finding Balance: Alcohol and Drug Harm Reduction (Ithaca College), and Alcohol and Other Drug Abuse Group (AODA) (North Dakota State University).

Group Psychoeducation

As previously mentioned, psychoeducation alone has been shown to be less effective in producing cognitive or behavioral changes regarding AOD use. However, in conjunction with other interventions, such as values clarification, motivational enhancement techniques, and cognitive behavioral therapy (CBT) skill building, psychoeducation becomes another tool in harm reduction. Prime-for-Life is a psychoeducational program aimed at producing attitudinal and behavioral changes to AOD use. It uses a three-unit persuasion-based teaching process focused on preventing high-risk behavior through exploring personal perceptions of risks, reflecting on those progressing toward the development of AOD dependence, and protecting students from the development of dependence by identifying choices that are protective versus detrimental to their lives. Cultivating Healthy Opportunities in College Environments (CHOICES) is another psychoeducation program aimed at college students. CHOICES is a 90-minute program focused on providing current information on substance use and helping them identify healthy lifestyle alternatives to help them better meet academic and personal goals.

Integrated Treatment Options

Collegiate Recovery Communities

College campuses have extremely varied ranges in the amount and type of AOD services available to students. A select few universities demonstrate innovative and comprehensive recovery and treatment programs aimed at responding fully to students with AOD-related concerns. The Center for the Study of Addiction and Recovery at Texas Tech University is an excellent model for creating a collegiate recovery program. Their program notes that a lack of peer support is a primary barrier faced by college students in recovery. With this information and the fact that individuals are most likely to maintain sobriety with long-term interventions, it makes sense to provide students with collegiate recovery communities. The collegiate recovery program offers students the opportunity to continue in their recovery while also continuing to pursue academic educational endeavors. Students in the collegiate recovery program register for a mandatory 1-hour credit seminar in addiction/recovery, and attend any of the 12-step meetings that run Monday through Friday on the Texas Tech campus. The program has developed a peer tutorial program where students obtain tutoring from others peers in recovery, has an Association of Students About Service (ASAS) that involves engaging in service projects to the larger community, and provides scholarships to all participants. Based on Texas Tech's program, there are collegiate recovery communities or programs replicated at 12 other universities.

AOD Treatment Teams

Counseling centers that may not have the resources for full collegiate recovery communities can enhance treatment provided to students with substance abuse concerns through utilization of an AOD treatment team. AOD treatment teams are multidisciplinary teams comprised of counselors/psychologists, trainees, psychiatrists, and other mental health professionals. The AOD treatment team can take a team approach in determining the level of care individuals need, staffing cases, and developing campus programs. Members of the treatment team will also have increased specialization in working with AOD-related issues, thus are able to see mandated AOD cases or clients with more acute substance-related issues. Inclusion of trainees on the AOD treatment team can also enhance the center's training program. Trainees are provided with education, practical experience, and supervision with AOD issues and the college population. Finally, given the systemic nature of substance abuse on college campuses, an AOD treatment team would be well advised to build relationships with other departments and offices on campus that have a stake in campus drug and alcohol use, such as campus health centers, student affairs, Greek life, campus police, and campus leadership, to name just a few.

CONCLUSION

The misuse and abuse of substances on campuses present an issue for the entire campus community. It is imperative for counseling centers to address the needs of individual students struggling with substance issues and to take responsive steps to the impact substances have on the greater community.

REFERENCES

American Psychiatric Association. (2000). *Diagnostic and statistical manual of mental disorders* (4th ed., text revision). Washington, DC: Author.

American Psychiatric Association. (2013). *Diagnostic and statistical manual of mental disorders* (5th ed.). Washington, DC: Author.

American Society of Addiction Medicine. (2013). *The ASAM criteria: Treatment criteria for addictive, substance-related, and co-occurring conditions* (3rd ed.). Chevy Chase, MD: Author.

Arria, A. M. (2008). Underage drinking and alcohol dependence among college students: An update from the College Life Study. *Maryland Alcohol and Drug Abuse Administration: Compass, 2,* 1–2.

Babor, T. F., Biddle-Higgins, J. C., Saunders, J. B., & Monteiro, M. G. (2001). AUDIT: *The Alcohol Use Disorders Identification Test: Guidelines for use in primary health care.* Geneva, Switzerland: World Health Organization. Retrieved from http://apps.who .int/iris/handle/10665/67205

Brown, R. L., & Rounds, L. A. (1995). Conjoint screening questionnaires for alcohol and drug abuse. *Wisconsin Medical Journal, 94,* 135–140.

Caldwell, P. E. (2002). Drinking levels, related problems and readiness to change in a college sample. *Alcoholism Treatment Quarterly, 20*(2), 1–15.

Center for Substance Abuse Treatment. (1999). *Enhancing motivation for change in substance abuse treatment* (Treatment Improvement Protocol series No. 35 [TIP 35]). Rockville, MD: Substance Abuse and Mental Health Services Administration.

Center for Substance Abuse Treatment. (2005). *Substance abuse treatment: Group therapy* (Treatment Improvement Protocol series No. 41 [TIP 41]). DHHS Publication No. (SMA) 05-3991. Rockville, MD: Substance Abuse and Mental Health Services Administration. Retrieved from http://www.ncbi.nlm.nih.gov/books/NBK64223

Center for Young Women's Health. (2013). *College health: Alcohol and drugs.* Retrieved from http://www.youngwomenshealth.org

Ewing, J. A. (1984). Detecting alcoholism: The CAGE questionnaire. *Journal of the American Medical Association, 252,* 1905–1907.

Feldstein, S. W., & Miller, W. R. (2007). Does subtle screening for substance abuse work? A review of the Substance Abuse Subtle Screening Inventory (SASSI). *Addiction, 102,* 41–50.

Fiore, M. C., Jaén, C. R., Baker, T. B., Bailey, W. C., Benowitz, N. L., Curry, S. J., … Wewers, M. E. (2008). *Treating tobacco use and dependence: 2008 update.* Clinical Practice Guideline. Rockville, MD: U.S. Department of Health and Human Services.

Fisher, G. L., & Harrison, T. C. (2009). *Substance abuse: Information for school counselors, social workers, therapists, and counselors* (4th ed.). Boston, MA: Pearson.

Freimuth, M. (2008). Another missed opportunity? Recognition of alcohol use problems by mental health professionals. *Psychotherapy Research, Practice, and Training, 45,* 405–409.

Grucza, R. A., Norberg, K. E., & Bierut, L. A. J. (2009). Binge drinking among youths and young adults in the United States: 1979–2006. *American Academy of Child and Adolescent Psychiatry, 48,* 692–702.

Hart, C. L., & Ksir, C. (2012). *Drugs, society, and human behavior* (15th ed.). New York, NY: McGraw-Hill.

Hingson, R. W., Heeren, T., Zakocs, R. C., Kopstein, A., & Wechsler, H. (2002). Magnitude of alcohol-related mortality and morbidity among U.S. college students ages 18–24. *Journal of Studies on Alcohol, 63*(2), 136–144.

Hingson, R. W., Zha, W., & Weitzman, E. R. (2009). Magnitude of and trends in alcohol-related mortality and morbidity among U.S. college students ages 18–24, 1998–2005. *Journal of Studies on Alcohol and Drugs, 16*, 12–20.

Johnston, L. D., O'Malley, P. M., Bachman, J. G., & Schulenberg, J. E. (2007). *Monitoring the Future: National survey results on drug use, 1975–2006: Volume I, Secondary school students* (NIH Publication No. 07-6205). Bethesda, MD: National Institute on Drug Abuse.

Johnston, L. D., O'Malley, P. M., Bachman, J. G., & Schulenberg, J. E. (2012). *Monitoring the Future: National results on adolescent drug use: Overview of key findings, 2011.* Ann Arbor: Institute for Social Research, The University of Michigan.

Knight, J. R., Wechsler, H., Kuo, M., Seibring, M., Weitzman, E. R., & Schuckit, M. (2002). Alcohol abuse and dependence among U.S. college students. *Journal of Studies on Alcohol, 63*(3), 263–270.

Larimer, M. E., & Cronce, J. M. (2002). Identification, prevention and treatment: A review of individual focused strategies to reduce problematic alcohol consumption by college students. *Journal of Studies on Alcohol, 14*, 148–163.

Laux, J. M., Perera-Diltz, D. M., & Calmes, S. A. (2012). Assessment and diagnosis of addictions. In D. Capuzzi & M. D. Stauffer (Eds.), *Foundations of addictions counseling* (2nd ed., pp. 101–126). Upper Saddle River, NJ: Pearson.

Lisdahl, K. M., & Tapert, S. (2012). Chronic effects of heavy alcohol and marijuana use on the brain and cognition in adolescents and young adults. In H. R. White & D. L. Rabiner (Eds.), *College drinking and drug use* (pp. 63–82). New York, NY: Guilford Press.

MacCoun, R. J. (1998). Toward a psychology of harm reduction. *American Psychologist, 53*, 1199–1208.

Matthews, C. R., Schmid, L. A., Conclaves, A. A., & Bursley, K. H. (1998). Assessing problem drinking in college students: Are counseling centers doing enough? *Journal of College Counseling, 12*, 3–9.

McCabe, S. E., & Boyd, C. J. (2005). Sources of prescription drugs for illicit use. *Addictive Behaviors, 30*(7), 1342–5130.

McCabe, S. E., Teter, C. J., Boyd, C. J., Knight, J. R., & Wechsler, H. (2005). Nonmedical use of prescription opioids among U.S. college students: Prevalence and correlates from a national survey. *Addictive Behavior, 30*(4), 789–805.

McLellan, A. T., Luborsky, L., O'Brien, C. P., & Woody, G. E. (1980). An improved diagnostic instrument for substance abuse patients. The Addiction Severity Index. *Journal of Nervous and Mental Diseases, 168*, 26–33.

Miller, G. A. (1997). *The Substance Abuse Subtle Screening Inventory-3 manual.* Spencer, IN: Spencer Evening World.

Miller, W. R., & Sanchez, V. C. (1994). Motivating young adults for treatment and lifestyle change. In G. S. Howard & P. E. Nathan (Eds.), *Alcohol use and misuse by young adults* (pp. 55–82). Notre Dame, IN: University of Notre Dame Press.

National Center on Addiction and Substance Abuse. (2007). *Wasting the best and the brightest: Substance abuse at America's colleges and universities.* New York, NY: Author.

National Council on Patient Information and Education. (2010). *Taking action to prevent and address prescription drug abuse: "Get the Facts" prescription drug abuse on college campuses.* Retrieved from http://www.talkaboutrx.org/documents/GetTheFacts.pdf

National Highway Traffic Safety Administration. (2007). *Screening and brief intervention tool kit for college and university campuses.* Retrieved from http://www.nhtsa .gov/links/sid/3672toolkit

National Institute on Alcohol Abuse and Alcoholism. (n.d.). *Overview of alcohol consumption.* Retrieved from http://niaaa.nih.gov/alcohol-health/overview-alcohol -consumption

National Institute on Alcohol Abuse and Alcoholism. (2002). *A call to action: Changing the culture of drinking at U.S. colleges.* Final Report of the Task Force on College Drinking. NIH Publication No. 02–5010. Rockville, MD: Author.

National Institute on Drug Abuse. (2009). *Commonly abused drugs.* Retrieved from http://www.drugabuse.gov/sites/default/files/cadchart_2.pdf

National Institute on Drug Abuse. (2012). *Marijuana abuse.* NIDA Research Report Series 1-12, 2012. Retrieved from http://www.drugabuse.gov/sites/default/files/ rrmarijuana.pdf

National Institutes of Health. (2012). *Drugfacts: Nationwide trends.* Retrieved from http://www.drugabuse.gov

Perkins, H. W., Haines, M. P., & Rice, R. (2005). Misperceiving the college drinking norm and related problems: A nationwide study of exposure to prevention information, perceived norms and student alcohol misuse. *Journal of Studies on Alcohol and Drugs, 66,* 470–478.

Presley, C. A., Leichliter, M. A., & Meilman, P. W. (1998). *Alcohol and drugs on American college campuses: A report to college presidents: Third in a series, 1995, 1996, 1997.* Carbondale, IL: Core Institute, Southern Illinois University.

Selzer, M. L. (1971). The Michigan Alcoholism Screening Test: The quest for a new diagnostic instrument. *American Journal of Psychiatry, 127,* 1653–1658.

Sepulveda, D. R., Thomas, L. M., McCabe, S. E., Cranford, J. A., Boyd, C. A., & Teter, C. J. (2011). Misuse of prescribed stimulant medication for ADHD and associated patterns of substance use: Preliminary analysis among college students. *Journal of Pharmacy Practice, 24*(6), 551–560.

Sia, T. L., Dansereau, D. F., & Czuchry, M. L. (2000). Treatment readiness training and probationers' evaluation of substance abuse treatment in a criminal justice setting. *Journal of Substance Abuse Treatment, 19,* 459–467.

Skinner, H. (1982). The drug abuse screening test. *Addictive Behaviors, 7,* 363–371.

Substance Abuse and Mental Health Services Administration. (1998). *Screening and assessing adolescents for substance use disorders.* CSAT Treatment Improvement Protocol (TIP), 31. Rockville, MD: Author.

Substance Abuse and Mental Health Services Administration. (2005). *SAMHSA, 2002, 2003, and 2004 NSDUH: College enrollment status and past year illicit drug use among young adults: 2002, 2003, and 2004.* Retrieved from http://www.samhsa.gov/ data/2k5/college/college.pdf

Substance Abuse and Mental Health Services Administration. (2009). Screening, brief intervention, and referral to treatment: New populations, new effectiveness data. *SAMHSA News, 17*(6), 1–20.

Substance Abuse and Mental Health Services Administration. (2011). *Screening, brief intervention and referral to treatment (SBIRT) in behavioral healthcare.* Retrieved from http://www.samhsa.gov/prevention/SBIRT/SBIRTwhitepaper.pdf

Swisher, J. D., Warner, R. W., & Herr, E. L. (1972). Experimental comparison of four approaches to drug abuse prevention among ninth and eleventh graders. *Journal of Counseling Psychology, 19*(4), 328–332. doi:10.1037/h0033084

Upadhyaya, H. P., Rose, K., Wang, W., O'Rourke, K., Sullivan, B., Deas, D., & Brady, K. T. (2005). Attention-deficit/hyperactivity disorder, medication treatment, and substance use patterns among adolescents and young adults. *Journal of Child and Adolescent Psychopharmacology, 15*(5), 799–809.

U.S. Food and Drug Administration. (2010). *Combating misuse and abuse of prescription drugs: Q&A with Michael Klein, Ph.D.* FDA Consumer Health Information. Retrieved from www.fda.gov

van Wormer, K., & Davis, D. (2003). *Addiction treatment: A strength perspective.* Pacific Grove, CA: Brooks/Cole.

Wechsler, H., Lee, J. E., Kuo, M., Seibring, M., Nelson, T. F., & Lee, H. (2002). Trends in college binge drinking during a period of increased prevention efforts: Findings from 4 Harvard School of Public Health college alcohol student surveys: 1993–2001. *Journal of American College Health, 50*, 203–217.

Wechsler, H., & Kuo, M. (2003). Watering down the drinks: The moderating effect of college demographics on alcohol use of high-risk groups. *American Journal of Public Health, 93*(11), 1929–1933.

Wechsler, H., & Nelson, T. F. (2008). What we have learned from the Harvard School of Public Health college alcohol study: Focusing attention on college student alcohol consumption and the environmental conditions that promote it. *Journal of Studies on Alcohol and Drugs, 69*, 481–490.

CHAPTER NINE

COMPLEX MENTAL HEALTH ISSUES ON THE COLLEGE CAMPUS

Shannon J. Hodges

Research on college student mental health concerns during this past decade has documented significantly increasing numbers of students diagnosed with or who will experience a severe mental disorder (Benton, Robertson, Tseng, Newton, & Benton, 2003; Gallagher, 2014; Grayson, 2006). College counseling center staff are faced with a seemingly increasing pathologized student population (Grayson, 2006), a far cry from previous eras. Incidence rates of depression, anxiety, and suicide attempts have increased exponentially (Benton et al., 2003; Gallagher, 2014; Grayson, 2006). This much-discussed and well-documented increase in mental disorders among the college student population has occasionally left college faculty, student affairs staff, and even college counselors feeling overwhelmed with regard to the serious and persistent student mental health needs (Gallagher, 2014; Grayson, 2006; Kay, 2011). One almost gets the sense that college campuses have become like the psychiatric hospitals of previous eras, with well-manicured lawns, gothic buildings, and a population teeming with psychoses, addictions, and dangerous behaviors. Although this last statement clearly is an exaggeration, practically everyone seemingly agrees that more college students than ever are besieged with serious mental health issues.

When I began my doctoral study in the late 1980s, college counseling services, though certainly serving some students with serious and persistent mental disorders, were still viewed as quaint centers where students could work on self-esteem issues, homesickness, deal with romantic breakups, get career advice, and address issues of sexuality. Naturally, students continue to grapple with these traditional developmental issues, though much of the recent college counseling focus has been on addressing more serious pathology (Gallagher, 2014; Grayson, 2006; Kay, 2011).

In addition to the documented rise in severe mental disorders on college campuses, high-profile tragedies such as those at Virginia Tech, Northern Illinois University, and others, have caused the college counseling profession to rethink the types of services they provide (Nolan, Ford, Kress, Anderson, & Novak, 2005). The National Survey of Counseling Center Directors (Gallagher, 2014) has for several years reflected heightened concern by college counseling center directors regarding the increase in prevalence and severity of students with mental disorders. The most recent findings by Gallagher (2014) showed that a total of 286,700 students sought campus mental health services:

- 94% of directors reported significant trends of more severe student psychopathology. Specifically:
- 89% anxiety disorders
- 69% crisis requiring immediate response (e.g., suicide threats and attempts)
- 60% psychiatric medication issues
- 58% clinical depression
- 47% learning disabilities
- 43% campus sexual assault
- 35% self-injurious behaviors (e.g., cutting, burning, etc.)
- 34% issues related to early sexual abuse

We can see from these statistics reported by college counseling center directors that today's college students are very stressed, which is manifested in a variety of potential mental health disorders. There is much debate regarding the reasons for increases in serious mental disorders among the college population, though there is little disagreement that severe psychotic disorders are more common among today's college student population. The diagnostic criteria for mental disorders are published in the *Diagnostic and Statistical Manual of Mental Disorders*, fifth edition (*DSM-5*; American Psychiatric Association [APA], 2013). The diagnostic categories comprising these disorders are schizophrenia and other psychotic disorders, personality disorders (most especially borderline personality disorder [BPD] and narcissistic personality disorder), affective disorders such as major depression and bipolar disorder, anxiety disorders like posttraumatic stress disorder (PTSD) and many that are seen in college counseling centers (Lippincott, 2007). The demands that students suffering from major mental disorders place upon college counseling centers can place significant stress on the students in question, to say nothing of the stress on counseling center staff. Gilbert opined, "When confronted with severe pathology, some clinicians, I fear, are either naïve about the magnitude of the task or grandiose about their abilities accomplish it in a university setting" (1992, p. 699). It should be stated, of course, that the college counseling center's ability to respond to major mental illness depends on the availability of inpatient or outpatient psychiatric assistance, the training and experience of staff, and an understanding of the limits of an outpatient mental health counseling center.

The typical age of onset for many severe psychotic disorders is late adolescence through early adulthood (Becker, Martin, Wajeeh, Ward, & Shern, 2002; Collins & Mowbray, 2005), an age range coinciding with the college population. Unlike previous eras in collegiate history, the Americans with Disabilities Act (ADA) of 1988 prohibits colleges from denying admission on the basis of a mental disorder (Wheeler & Bertram, 2012). Consequently, many students arrive at college with preexisting mental disorders. These same students often are on antipsychotic medication and periodically experience severe symptoms throughout their collegiate careers (Gilbert, 1992; Kitzrow, 2003). Furthermore, many students suffering from a serious and pervasive mental disorder will choose to cease taking their medication, resulting in serious, often disturbing, behavior that impacts numerous people on campus including roommates, resident advisor's, classmates, faculty, and counseling center staff (Hodges, 2001; Kitzrow, 2003; Nolan et al., 2005). The question for college administrators and counseling center staff then becomes, "Now that we have these students, how do we serve their needs?"

With the ADA, psychotropic medications with fewer debilitating side effects, and a college counseling center staff more aware and better trained to address mental disorders, students with psychiatric disorders have a chance to complete their degrees, albeit realizing it may take them more than 4 years to graduate. Some research has indicated poor academic and retention outcomes for college students with severe mental disorders, with some 80% dropping out without completing a degree (Collins & Mowbray, 2005). The silver lining, however, is that for students with severe mental disorders who receive counseling services, the retention rate is 14% higher (Kitzrow, 2003). This latter statistic should be instructive for faculty, administrators, parents, and students with severe mental disorders. Clearly, college counseling centers can play an important role in retention of students with severe mental disorders. A critical factor is a well-trained staff prepared to treat students with, say, schizophrenia, bipolar disorder, and other significant mental disorders. Counseling centers must also be adequately staffed to address severe mental health needs, in addition to the typical student population they counsel for developmental issues (e.g., homesickness, relationship breakups, career indecision, roommate conflicts). Timely referrals to the counseling center by friends, faculty, administrators, campus religious leaders, and so forth also is an important link in the ability to identify and get high-needs students into the counseling center.

IDENTIFYING HIGH-NEEDS STUDENTS WITH SEVERE MENTAL DISORDERS

Based on my 30 years of experience in higher education as student, graduate student, student affairs administrator (counseling center, residence director, Greek life, etc.), counselor, and professor, the weakest link in the process of serving students with mental disorders is in getting them to the counseling center. Someone—resident advisor, roommate, faculty advisor, minister, coach, parent, custodian, or friend—has to make the effort to encourage the student to seek counseling. In my near decade of providing counseling in colleges, I have witnessed numerous people walk a student down to the counseling center as a means of support. Many students, particularly those who have never been in counseling, will likely need encouragement to seek counseling. It is also likely that many students, even those with severe mental disorders, do not see their behavior as unusual or problematic. In the Stages of Change model discussed in Chapter 4 (Prochaska, DiClemente, & Norcross, 1992), in the initial stage (i.e., precontemplation) individuals are unaware that they have a problem even though it may be obvious to those around them as they may be exhibiting psychotic symptoms (auditory, visual, tactile hallucinations, etc.). In the Prochaska et al. (1992) conceptual model, it isn't until students reach the second stage, contemplation, that they begin to entertain they have a problem and need help. This second step, when students are open to feedback, is where referrals become timely. The Stages of Change model is somewhat reminiscent of Alcoholics Anonymous (AA) where the first step of admitting there is a problem is the most significant admission of all (Alcoholics Anonymous, 2013). Prior to this admission, even extreme problematic behavior is not seen as problematic.

MAKING THE REFERRAL

Because many readers of this book may not be college counseling professionals, it is important to specifically cite how referrals can be made for students with severe mental disorders. The following case example provides an example of how to make such a referral.

The Case of Tom

Tom is a college sophomore at Traditional State University studying mechanical engineering. He has been a very good student and even on the academic honor roll, but recently he has been exhibiting unusual behavior. His roommate has observed Tom having whispering conversations with himself. The "self-talk" seems to have become louder and more disturbing of late and his roommate is concerned about Tom's behavior. He tries to speak with Tom about his concerns, but Tom gets angry saying, "You're just like them!" Concerned, the roommate speaks with their resident advisor, who meets with Tom and his roommate. Tom becomes very upset and paranoid, accusing the resident advisor and roommate of being in league with his parents, faculty advisor, and even the college president. He states, "I know you're out to get me!" and then storms out of the room. The next day, his calculus professor reprimands Tom for his self-talk, whereupon Tom begins screaming obscenities at the professor and various students.

The next day the dean of students contacts Tom and mandates he go to the counseling center for assessment and counseling, else he will be suspended for disrupting the campus learning environment as stated in the campus behavior code. Tom is also required to allow the counselor to release that he has sought counseling and that the counselor can provide a prognosis to the dean of students. Tom reluctantly meets with Tomasina, who completes a clinical intake and schedules Tom to take the Minnesota Multiphasic Personality Inventory– Second Edition (MMPI-2), a comprehensive clinical assessment that provides proscriptive information on the mental health of the test taker. Tom completes the MMPI-2, which indicated elevation on the clinical scales of paranoia, schizophrenia, and social inversion. Tom also admits that he has been under the care of a psychiatrist for the past year who had given him a diagnosis of schizoaffective disorder, but recently stopped taking his medications (Risperdal) because it makes him sleepy and inhibits his ability to study long hours.

Tomasina develops a treatment plan for Tom that includes 10 counseling sessions. Tom agrees to meet with the campus psychiatrist for an evaluation the following day, and to take the medication the doctor prescribes at the recommended dosage. Tomasina will work with Tom to recognize symptoms of his disease and how to manage it. She loans him a workbook with self-help exercises, with the requirement that he complete one exercise each week, then discuss the exercise with her the following session. Tom refuses to allow Tomasina to contact his parents. She informs Tom if his behavior continues to decompensate, she likely will be required to do that for his and other students' best interests. She also warns Tom if he becomes disruptive in class again, he faces disciplinary action and dismissal.

In this case example, Tom is a student in good academic standing at the university. He also has a major mental disorder and likely could be on medication for his entire adult life. The positive note here is that Tom has been a good student when he is on medication and attending class. Like many clients diagnosed with a major mental disorder, cessation of medication results in decompensating behavior that can be concerning to the individual and those around him. While "strange" behavior is no crime, and students cannot legally be removed from college simply for outlier behaviors such as talking to themselves, tics, odd clothing, and such, disruption of the learning environment and the health and safety of students and others are serious concerns.

Mandated Withdrawals

Colleges must also be aware of how to deal with students such as Tom suffering from mental disorders. Because colleges cannot legally discriminate against students with mental disorders (May, 2006; Wheeler & Bertram, 2012), Tom simply cannot be dismissed from the institution due to his diagnoses. But the college can hold Tom accountable to the same student behavior code to which all other students are held accountable. In point of fact, should a university deviate from the behavior code and treat a student like Tom differently, it may be open to litigation and violations of the ADA (May, 2006; Remley & Herlihy, 2010). Colleges must provide Tom, and all students, due process prior to mandating a withdrawal from the institution.

Mandated withdrawals have become the "sticky wicket" in collegiate mental health circles. During previous eras in higher education, colleges could simply screen out anyone who appeared to have a mental disorder (or any other disability) and if a student developed a mental disorder while at college, said student could simply be dismissed. With federal laws such as Section 504 and the ADA, students with disabilities who likely would have been dismissed in previous eras cannot be discriminated against and must be given fair accommodations. Two recent challenges to mandated withdrawals provide food for thought. In *Doe v. Hunter College* (Bower & Schwartz, 2010), a student with depression voluntarily admitted herself to a hospital after swallowing a large number of Tylenol pills. After spending a few days in the hospital, she returned to her dormitory room to find she had been banned from the residence hall for one semester and required to be evaluated by someone at the counseling center prior to returning. The college's policy required all students engaging in self-injurious thoughts and behaviors were to be suspended for one semester. Doe sued and won in district court, with the court handing down a verdict that Hunter College had discriminated against Ms. Doe due to having suspended her prior to an evaluation and without a disciplinary hearing (denied due process). The court also ruled that if given the opportunity, Doe might have been able to prove she could live safely within the residence hall. The case was settled for a large amount of money and Hunter College withdrew its automatic dismissal policy (Bower & Schwartz, 2010).

In *Nott v. George Washington University*, Jordan Nott sought treatment for depression at the university counseling center. Still very depressed, he voluntarily admitted himself to the university hospital for suicidal ideation. Soon after his admission to the hospital, his residence hall director sent him a letter stating he could not return until he had been cleared to do so by the counseling center. The next day, the Student Judicial Services sent him a letter charging him with the George Washington University code of conduct prohibiting "endangering behavior." Jordan was suspended from the university pending a disciplinary hearing, barred from his dorm room, and threatened with arrest for trespassing if he returned to campus. Rather than face the hearing, Nott withdrew from George Washington University and sued the school alleging violation of the ADA, Section 504, and the Fair Housing Act, among other laws (Bower & Schwartz, 2010). Nott challenged the mandated withdrawal policy and, based on the advice of legal counsel, George Washington University settled out of court with Mr. Nott and revised the mandated leave policy.

The U.S. Department of Education Office of Civil Rights (OCR) has found ADA violations in several cases similar to *Doe* and *Nott* at Mariatta College, DeSales University, Bluffton University, and others (Bower & Schwartz, 2010). In these cases, and others, colleges were found to have violated the ADA and their own student behavior policy by not providing due process to students dismissed due to mental health issues. The court decisions of *Doe* and *Nott*, along with the U.S. Department of Civil Rights, have illustrated that colleges must tread lightly regarding mandated withdrawals. The OCR ruled that a mandated withdrawal should be used only in cases where a student cannot remain safely in school even with accommodations, and also if a student poses a "direct threat" to the health and safety of others (Bower & Schwartz, 2010). In the complaint against DeSales University involving a student evicted from his dormitory after posting information about suicide on his dorm room door and engaging in self-injurious cutting, the Department of Education OCR stated that:

> In a direct threat situation, a college needs to make an individualized determination of the student's ability to safely participate in the college's program based on reasonable medical judgment relying on the most current medical knowledge or the best available objective evidence. (Bower & Schwartz, 2010, p. 131)

Determining whether a student constitutes a direct threat requires a thorough evaluation that must address the duration of the risk, nature and severity of potential harm, probability that actual harm will occur, the imminence of potential harm, and whether reasonable policies, practices, or procedures will sufficiently reduce potential risk to an acceptable level (Bower & Schwartz, 2010). Institutions must consider less restrictive alternatives to mandated withdrawals (e.g., move the student to a different dorm, require an evaluation, require the student to take antipsychotic medication) that would provide the student an opportunity to remain in college.

Mandatory Counseling and Evaluation

Due to the high-profile tragedies at Virginia Tech and other campuses, college counselors are under pressure to share concerns regarding students and to provide mandated counseling and assessment (Gallagher, 2014). Generally, mandated counseling has traditionally involved abuse of alcohol and drugs, suicide ideation or attempts, and most recently, threats to others (Grayson & Meilman, 2006; Lippincott, 2007). Administrators often require such students to attend a certain number of counseling sessions to remain enrolled in college. The weak link in this mandatory model often is the lack of specifics. Administrators want problems to go away while counselors are charged with the task of trying to determine what success is in mandatory referrals. Does success mean the student won't use alcohol or drugs again? If so, this likely is unrealistic. Does success mean the student won't threaten suicide again? But if the student doesn't inform others of suicidal impulses, he or she may not receive timely help and this could have dire consequences for the student and potentially the institution.

Success, then, will likely look more like timely intervention that helps mandated students alter their behaviors, particularly in the manner of identifying stressors and voluntarily seeking mental health services prior to a suicide attempt. Success with students with major mental disorders will realistically mean students taking prescribed medications and checking into the counseling center when they are tempted to reduce or cease medication altogether. College counselors, then, are all about promoting behavioral change in students regardless of the theoretical orientation from which the counselors operate. Counselors must of necessity coach administrators that students with major mental illnesses may continue to dress and act bizarrely and that such behavior does not constitute a threat to themselves or others.

When a student is mandated for an evaluation, counseling should always be part of the follow-up beyond the evaluation. After all, any student mandated for a mental health evaluation likely could benefit from counseling. College counseling centers I have worked in all required counseling after the assessment was completed, and while there is debate about counseling people who don't want it, my own experience is it may be beneficial. Nevertheless, the specifics of a mandated assessment should be made clear to the student. The counselor providing the assessment should explain during informed consent that he or she represents the university, that the student will be required to sign a release of information to provide essential information from the assessment to the designated administrator (e.g., vice president for student services, dean of students, assistant dean of students). The college counselor must also explain what assessments he or she will use (clinical interview, MMPI-2 or other standard assessment, review of previous counseling or psychiatric records should they have them available, etc.). The counselor must also explain if he or she will be making a recommendation that the student take a leave from school. Finally, the counselor must make it clear that the student has the right for an independent mental health consultation should the student wish to challenge the results of the assessment.

After the evaluation has been completed, the counselor should schedule the first counseling session as soon as possible to focus on the themes raised in the assessment. Naturally, the mandated student is likely to be less than an enthusiastic partner in this process. But part of the counselor's "teachable" moment lies in illustrating how and why the session might be helpful. Initially, the student's main motivation is likely to be getting out of treatment as quickly as possible. An astute counselor must learn how to engage and redirect the student client without taking offense at any "baiting" behavior. The following fictional narrative between college counselor and client provides an example of this:

> *Counselor*: "Okay, we've completed the assessment phase. Before we start, I'm curious how you feel about being here for treatment."
>
> *Student*: "Curious, huh? Look, I don't fucking want to be here, alright! I don't have a fucking problem, you're the fucking problem! You and the hall director and my RA and that Kangaroo court of a discipline committee!"
>
> *Counselor*: "So, given all that what would you like from me?"
>
> *Student*: "I'd like you to just tell them I don't need to come talk to a quack like you! That's what I'd like."
>
> *Counselor*: "You know, I've dealt with the dean and the discipline committee for a lot of years and they won't just take my signature. We have to show them evidence you've changed."
>
> *Student*: "Just like I thought! You're as bad as them!"
>
> *Counselor*: "Look, you want out of here, right?"
>
> *Student*: "Yeah." (Wary)
>
> *Counselor*: "Alright then, help me get you out of here."
>
> *Student*: "How?" (affect has now shifted)
>
> *Counselor*: "We need to figure out how to write a treatment plan that works. And it's going to have to take a few sessions, maybe six. Then, you have to help me write the letter to the student conduct committee the dean of students chairs."
>
> *Student*: "Why can't you just write it now?"
>
> *Counselor*: "Like I said, I've dealt with them before and they will want to see change over several sessions. They will also want to see a letter explaining how you have changed your behavior."

Student: "What other options do I have?" (exhales audibly)

Counselor: (Shrugs) "The Student Conduct Committee seems serious. It's possible you could be expelled from college if you don't comply. Now look, that's your decision too." (hands are open and voice is even)

Student: (Student pauses momentarily) "Gotta stay in school . . . nothing at home for me." (Brief pause) "Okay, where do we start?"

The previous scenario is fictional but one that gets played out often in college counseling centers across the country. Initially, the student is profane and noncompliant, but because the counselor does not react in anger, the student's behavior deescalates. Then the counselor is able to show the mandated client there is something in counseling for him or her, namely the opportunity to remain in school. The counselor also lets the student know that the student has choices, one of which is to discontinue counseling, which likely would mean being expelled from school. In this case, the student elects to get engaged in counseling with the expectation of remaining in college. The fictitious student initially comes in very hostile and likely is in the precontemplation stage. The Stages of Change model is one particularly applicable for college counseling centers. The model is outlined in the following.

Prochaska et al. (1992) developed the Stages of Change theory to address the potential for change in clients. The stages are:

1. *Precontemplation*: The client is unaware there is a problem, despite the fact it is clear to those around him or her.
2. *Contemplation*: The client begins to entertain the possibility he or she has a problem, yet is not ready to do anything about it.
3. *Preparation*: The client begins to make small changes for short periods of time (say, 1 month).
4. *Action*: The client becomes more serious about changing his or her behavior and makes changes that can last as long as 3 months.
5. *Maintenance*: The client becomes more serious about change and makes changes lasting 6 months or longer.

The Stages of Change is a conceptual framework that naturally fits with mandated populations. Mandated clients often present for evaluation or counseling angry and convinced they have no problem, despite ample evidence to the contrary. The aforementioned fictional client comes into counseling in the precontemplative stage (or phase). Through an encounter with a savvy counselor, he moves into contemplation and finally into preparation. Granted, this is the initial session and regression would be expected at some point, but this client has entertained the possibility of change.

A useful assessment regarding client change is Miller and Brown's *What I Want From Treatment* (1999), an assessment that measures client change on 69 items related to alcohol use, stress, abuse, and so on This handy 69-item assessment has a range of 0 to 207, mean = 103, with higher scores being consistent with greater motivation for change. Conversely, lower scores (below the mean) are consistent with less motivation for change. Because awareness of a problem likely is the first stage toward getting help, this assessment by Miller and Brown (1999) can be very timely for college counselors as it suggests client motivation at the onset of counseling. College counselors could then assess a client's increasing motivation for change after a few sessions by readministering the test. Clearly, motivation is a key indicator of future therapeutic success. The motivation level can change for the better provided the counselor can create the therapeutic attachment. To create this attachment, the counselor must illustrate to the client that the client has something to gain (e.g., remain in school, stay on athletic scholarship, remain in the residence hall). Naturally, creating the therapeutic attachment with a hostile, mandated client can be much easier to write about than to do in person!

The challenge for college counselors is that most of the students mandated for counseling pose no threat to anyone, yet they are required to continue in treatment perhaps after the crisis has passed. Legally, the state can mandate an individual to inpatient or outpatient treatment only if that individual presents an imminent threat to self or others (Bower & Schwartz, 2010). Individuals who do not pose an imminent threat can choose whether or not they wish to seek counseling or other mental health services. Colleges, however, may as part of their disciplinary require students to continue with a few sessions of counseling after an alcohol or serious behavioral incident (suicide threat or attempt, campus violence, etc.). But the critical factor for the college, once again, lies in providing the mandated student due process. Without due process, colleges have violated the student's rights and run the risk of inviting litigation. The recommendation here is for the college to have clear guidelines in its code of conduct. The college's code of conduct must focus on behavior and not on mental disorder. Thus, should a student be cited in violation of the code of conduct, the appropriate official and judicial board must focus on errant behavior that deviates from the code. When using counseling services as part of the disciplinary sanctions, a suggestion would be to require the student to change the troublesome behavior (e.g., drug and alcohol abuse, fighting) and meet a set number of sessions (e.g., 6–8), and for the counselor to write a letter addressing how well the student has met the required goals.

HIGH-RISK DISORDERS IN COLLEGIATE MENTAL HEALTH SETTINGS

Naturally, there are many issues of concern for college and university counseling staff. It's likely that a "high-risk" disorder may be debatable depending on the specific client, level of support, and available resources the client and/or the counseling center have at their disposal. Nevertheless, "high risk" for our purposes will be those resistant to therapeutic intervention and potentially higher lethality.

Eating Disorders

The treatment of eating disorders continues to be very challenging for college counseling centers. Identifying students who have eating disorders, getting them to access the counseling center and then attaining successful outcomes pose major challenges (Sheehy & Commerford, 2006). Feeding and Eating Disorders are defined in the *DSM-5* as an ongoing disturbance of eating or eating-related behavior that results in the altered consumption or absorption of food and that significantly impairs physical health or psychosocial functioning (APA, 2013, p. 329). Anorexia nervosa (AN), bulimia nervosa (BN), and binge eating disorder (BED) all are major health disorders college students, particularly college women, struggle with. It has become difficult to clearly distinguish among the three categories as students with AN may not have experienced severe weight loss and their menses may continue despite alarmingly low body weight (Sheehy & Commerford, 2006).

AN (binge eating/purging) is characterized by severe food restriction resulting in below normal body weight (less than 85% of expected weight), extreme fear of weight gain, body image distortion, and amenorrhea for at least 3 months (APA, 2013). For a more complete description, see the "Feeding and Eating Disorders" section of the *DSM-5* (APA, 2013, pp. 329–354).

BN (purging or nonpurging type) is characterized by recurrent episodes of binging, recurrent and inappropriate compensatory behavior to prevent weight gain, for example, fasting, use of laxatives, diet pills, vomiting, and so on (purging subtype), or excessive exercise (nonpurging subtype; APA, 2013). Criteria for the diagnosis are that binging and compensatory behaviors must occur at least twice weekly for 3 months.

BED refers to recurrent episodes of binging that produce significant distress for the individual. The binging episodes occur at least twice weekly for 6 months with no inappropriate compensatory behaviors.

Otherwise Specified Feeding or Eating Disorder is a category that refers to any difficulties that closely approximates the criteria for AN, BN, and BED but where the clinician determines the diagnostic features do not meet criteria for any other specific feeding and eating disorder (APA, 2013).

Prevalence

It is very challenging to accurately estimate the prevalence of eating disorders on the college campus due to the large number of eating disordered students who refuse to seek help. Around 0.4% of young women meet criteria for AN, the prevalence of BN in young females is 1% to 1.5%, and 1.6% of young women meet criteria for BED (APA, 2013). One study suggests that as many as 50% of college women have experienced some form of an eating disorder (*U.S. News & World Report*, 2012). Athletes, particularly in sports that emphasize a trim body, such as gymnastics, cross country, track, and wrestling, can promote eating disorders. Female athletes commonly struggle with eating disorders, including the "athletic triad" of amenorrhea, disordered eating, and osteoporosis (Johnson et al., 2004).

Etiology

There are many theories regarding the cause of eating disorders: genetic, personality, family dynamics, societal pressure, and so on (Striegal-Moore & Smolak, 2001). Clearly images presented in the media such as magazine covers, films, commercials, and so forth present an ideal for women that is both unhealthy and unrealistic for the majority of women. People prone to develop eating disorders are more likely to accept standards of beauty presented by the media (Frank & Thomas, 2003). Many college women with eating disorders are highly competitive regarding academic performance, physical attraction, body image, and social popularity. Such women are very self-critical regarding their own appearance and may have a self-image that bears little resemblance to reality.

Family factors include depression or over-controlling parents. Burch (1978) considered that AN originated from the dysfunction in the mother–child dyad. Crisp (1980), a cognitive behavioral therapy (CBT) therapist, preferred to enlist the person with an eating disorder into an active collaboration in treatment. Motivation to change must be assessed and reinforced. Cognitive techniques such as reframing and addressing unrealistic fears and goals are targeted along with normalizing healthy eating as well as weight gains. Eating disorders sufferers may have received and internalized the message of "You're not good enough" from parentally sources and striving for perfection in their body may be an effort to win attention from parents (Frank & Thomas, 2003). Histories of trauma, particularly sexual abuse, have been shown to be related to eating disorders (Jacobi, Hayward, de Zwann, Kraemer, & Argas, 2004). People with eating disorders often feel misunderstood and that they are never good enough and frequently strive to measure up to some unrealistic mark.

For women, the unrealistic and often unhealthy images of "attractive" women on the covers of magazines, in ads, on TV, in the movies, and so forth depict an ideal few women can measure up to. In many instances, what the media portrays is patently false. For example, film executives for the popular movie *Pretty Woman*, starring Julia Roberts, considered Roberts's legs not attractive enough and cropped legs from a model onto Roberts's upper body to create the desired image for the film's poster! The attempt to match up to unrealistic and, in many cases, false, media standards creates pressure on women, particularly young college women (Fredrickson & Roberts, 1997). As a means of illustration, compare Marilyn Monroe's figure in movies and photos to that of contemporary female models gracing the covers of magazines. Oddly, the woman many consider the sexiest woman of all time likely would not make the cut as a cover girl today!

Treatment Approach

Students with eating disorders present multidimensional syndromes requiring a team approach with professionals from multiple professions such as counselors, nutritionists, medical professionals, and peer support groups. Professionals involved in treating eating disorders need to establish regular lines of communication in order to provide unified and consistent treatment. Functioning as a team also helps to counter the dynamics of denial, manipulation, and splitting that so often characterize students with eating disorders. For the more severe sufferers, residential treatment may be a realistic option, as many college counseling centers will lack the resources needed to effectively combat ingrained psychopathology comorbid with eating disorders. College counselors and collegiate health services will need to make arrangements with parents when their adult child with an eating disorder needs to withdraw from college to address this illness. College counselors must also be prepared to meet resistance from parents who understandably may have difficulty accepting the gravity of the situation.

Counselors should use a variety of assessments in treating students with eating disorders: the Beck Depression Inventory-II to monitor depression and potential for suicide ideology, the Eating Disorders Inventory for severity of the eating disorder, and What I Want From Therapy change form (Miller & Brown, 1999) to assess attitudinal change and drug use, as both indicators are very important in treating students with eating disorders. Physicians and other health care professionals will want to monitor physical changes with the patient. A referral to a nutritionist could be valuable for developing a healthier diet. Some students may benefit from a support group when they are healthy enough to be involved in such an after-care endeavor.

Self-Injurious Behaviors

College counselors have reported an increase in students presenting with self-injurious behaviors (SIBs) for some length of time (Kress, 2003). The topic has received increased attention in the professional literature, on college counseling Listservs, mailing lists, at conferences, and in professional training. Yet, there has been limited research in the area of SIBs in the collegiate population (White, Trepal-Wollenzier, & Nolan, 2002). While SIBs have not garnered the attention needed in the college counseling research, it's likely many college counselors would cite them as an area of major concern as well as an unhealthy practice comorbid with sexual abuse, eating disorders, addiction, depression, and anxiety, to name a few.

Overview of SIBs

SIBs refer to intentional self-abuse to one's body without the intention of suicide. It can range from cutting skin, burns, biting, scratching skin, and punching walls or other hard, immovable surface. Perhaps the most common of these involves students cutting some part of the body, or "cutters" as such individuals are often called in college. It is very important to understand the distinction between SIBs and suicidal intention. Many researchers have asserted that SIBs are not suicidal gestures but rather function as a form of self-revulsion and even coping behavior (Schwartz, Cohen, Hoffman, & Meeks, 1989; Sonneborn & Vanstraelen, 1992). SIBs can then be defined as an intentional act with the aim to do harm to the body without any intention to die (Simon & Favazza, 2001).

SIBs are most commonly seen in college women who struggle with one or more of the aforementioned issues (e.g., sexual assault, eating disorders, depression).

According to Briere and Gil (1998), roughly 1% to 4% of the general population engages in SIBs. Mid to late adolescence seems a particularly risky time regarding SIBs with some 14% to 40% engaging in SIBs (Favazza & Conterio, 1988; Suyemoto & MacDonald, 1995). Though females far more than males admit to SIBs, it is important to remember that females are more willing than males to seek treatment and the college population likely is no different. Men—college males and older—tend to hide their SIBs and are less likely to seek treatment.

Why People Engage in SIBs

There are numerous reasons that students engage in SIBs. Some research suggests self-injury serves as a form of autonomic reinforcement (i.e., emotional regulation) or is a means of obtaining support from others (Nock & Prinstein, 2004). Further research indicates people self-injure as a means of diminishing dissociation, depersonalization, and derealization and to relieve feelings of numbness (Simon & Favazza, 2001). Many self-injurers state self-harm assists them in gaining a sense of management over their own emotional pain and disappointment (Kress, 2003). Feeling pain may be preferable to numbness and pain may serve as a constructive way to release tension (and many popular songs have suggested this). Unfortunately, self-abuse is a maladaptive method of dealing with emotional distress and intervention is necessary to break this cycle. Yet clients who regularly commit SIBs often are resistant to treatment. Medical model theories have proposed that self-injurers have genetic predispositions or chemical imbalances (e.g., serotonin imbalance), or may experience a rush of endorphins when self-injuring, all of which could in part explain why they continue to engage in self-abusive behavior. SIB clients often do express a sense of "letting off steam" when they self-injure, which may be related to all these medical model theories regarding SIBs.

According to Deiter, Nicholls, and Pearlman (2000), domestic violence and sexual abuse are two of the best predictors of SIB's. Students who self-injure are likely to have grown up in families where divorce or parental neglect was evident (Carroll, Schaffer, Spensley, & Abromowitz, 1980; Patterson & Kahan, 1983). While divorce is very common among the families of college students, sexual abuse is far less common, leaving one to consider abuse may be the more significant predictive variable. Regardless, SIB among college students seems to have steadily increased over the last two decades.

People who have been subjected to abuse frequently experience emotional dysregulation as they are victims of circumstances they may neither control nor escape. Dysregulation, or internalizing their emotional pain, retards the personal growth process leaving sufferers unable to articulate their discomfort for fear of further abuse. Self-injury may then be a predictable form of unhealthy coping, given that the victims cannot address the root of their behavior (e.g., violence).

According to Fong (2003), individuals with a lack of impulse control may be more likely to engage in SIBs. Fong theorized that SIBs share two qualities with impulse control disorders (e.g., gambling or theft): (a) an inability to resist impulses or urges to engage in a particular behavior, and (b) an increase in autonomic nervous system activity before the act is followed by a sense of relief after the act. Fong also noted SIBs tend to become quickly reinforced. Thus, timeliness in identifying and referring students engaged in SIBs is crucial for successful treatment.

Treatment Options

Counselors working with students who self-injure must adopt a nonjudgmental attitude and demonstrate empathy for the student. According to Nock and Prinstein (2004), a primary goal for the counselor is to establish a safe, focused counseling relationship exemplified by respect for the student's dignity and well-being. Naturally, establishing such a constructivist relationship may prove very difficult for the counselor given that the self-injurious student may have been abused by an authority figure and other significant people in her or his life. A challenge is for the counselor to be able to move beyond the role of authority figure.

Many college counselors have begun to use CBT as the treatment of choice for students who self-injure. But, eye movement desensitization and reprocessing (EMDR) has become very popular in many parts of the country and dialectic behavior therapy (DBT) has recently been adopted as a treatment of choice for clients who self-injure. CBT and DBT focus on eliminating cognitive distortions, addressing autonomic thoughts, and altering patterns of faulty thinking that support SIBs by utilizing homework exercises, role-plays, reframing, desensitization, and conditioning. DBT has more recently received attention as a helpful approach to managing SIBs in clients with BPD. DBT includes both behavioral and eastern Zen-type techniques into a cognitive approach that emphasizes a type of radical acceptance of the client's pain (Carey, 2011). DBT has been shown to have been successful in reducing symptoms of SIBs in a 1-year follow-up study (Linehan, Armstrong, Suarez, Allon, & Heard, 1991). Still, another 1-year follow-up study found that DBT did not significantly reduce feelings of hopelessness among clients diagnosed with BPD who engage in SIBs (Raj, Kumaraiah, & Bhide, 2001).

But it's likely that any approach—EMDR, CBT, DBT, and so on—should involve a team of professionals. SIBs are multidimensional in nature involving numerous factors in the client's life. In addition to personal counseling, college counselors likely will be engaged in a consultant role, referring to physicians for medication, a support group for extended social connection, body work approaches such as yoga, massage, or acupuncture, in addition to other referral resources. Homework, such as utilizing a workbook on reducing self-injury and healing whatever abuse occurred is also likely to be a staple of any treatment of SIBs.

Students With Autism and Asperger's Syndrome

It has only been recently that college officials began to acknowledge students with autism and Asperger's syndrome. High-profile individuals such as Temple

Grandin, a professor of agriculture, writer, inventor, and national spokesperson for autism spectrum disorder (ASD) spectrum have changed society's perception of the disorder. Estimates regarding the number of persons that are diagnosed with ASD have been revised dramatically. For decades the prevalence of ASDs had been estimated at 4 or 5 per 10,000 births (Wing, 1976). More recently, those estimates had been revised to 6 per 1,000 persons (Strock, 2004). That figure has also been significantly revised to approximately 1 in 88 (Centers for Disease Control and Prevention [CDC], 2013). These new figures strongly suggest that students with ASD are enrolled in colleges across the country and have been for some period of time.

Autism was originally diagnosed by Kanner in 1943 and ASD is a diagnostic category in the *DSM-5* (2013). According to the *DSM-5* the diagnostic criteria for ASD are based on persistent difficulties in social communication and social interaction across multiple contexts, and restrictive, repetitive patterns of behavior, activities, or interests (APA, 2013, p. 50). The *DSM-5* lists specific criteria and also outlines severity including with and without intellectual impairment (APA, 2013). Behavioral symptomology in the diagnosis of any of the ASD disorders can range from mild to severe. Many persons diagnosed on the spectrum will also be diagnosed as "developmentally delayed," though recent research has established that ASD clients may be of normal to above-average intelligence.

The most recent edition of the *DSM* attempts to unify pervasive developmental disorders (e.g., autism and Asperger's) under the category ASD. Previously, in the fourth edition, text revision of the *DSM* (*DSM-IV-TR*; APA, 2000), Asperger's was a separate though related diagnostic category. Regardless of the debate around similarities and differences on the ASD spectrum, all involve social, cognitive, behavioral, occupational, and educational challenges for ASD students, their families, roommates, and professors.

Assessing ASD Students in the Counseling Center

Students on the ASD spectrum are likely to seek assistance or be referred to the counseling center for issues such as depression, anxiety, academics, and interpersonal conflicts (Browning & Miron, 2007). Many ASD students presenting at the counseling center, especially those who are on the higher functioning end of the spectrum, may not have been diagnosed with ASD, thus necessitating an evaluation. College counselors should be attuned to difficulties in language, cognition, social functioning, and responses to sensory stimuli. Sensory processing difficulties may include being hypersensitive or hyposensitive to tactile, auditory, visual, olfactory, proprioceptive, and vestibular sensory information (Bogdashina, 2003; Strock, 2004).

Assessing a student for ASD should involve a clinical interview, use of a standardized assessment targeting ASD, and document review of previous assessment records (from other clinicians such as neurologists, psychiatrists, etc.). The Autism Quotient (AQ), a 50-item survey instrument, was developed by Baron-Cohen, Wheelwright, Skinner, Martin, and Clubley (2001). There are also many additional assessments that screen for ASD, though the AQ is currently the most popular.

The Case of Jonathan

Jonathan is an example of a college student on the high functioning level of the ASD spectrum. Jonathan is an 18-year-old freshman who has been referred to the counseling center by his resident advisor. Jonathan has had three different roommates since fall, all of whom have requested a move due to Jonathan's "odd" behavior. Though potentially a good student, Jonathan has started to skip classes and is in danger of getting into academic difficulty. Jonathan was initially reluctant to go to the counseling center as he had negative experiences with counselors and psychologists in high school. He finally agrees to seek counseling after his resident advisor walks him over for support. The counselor, Maria, recognized Jonathan's unusual behavior, speech, and affect during the interview. Jonathan tends to perseverate on topics to an extreme degree and while knowledgeable on many topics, he seems unaware of how his message is being received by others, who often tune him out.

Maria decides to administer the AQ, which indicated Jonathan is a candidate for further ASD screening. One of the items, "I know how to tell if someone listening to me is getting bored," motivated Jonathan to ask how one would know such a thing. Maria then initiated a discussion of how Jonathan might know that others were bored with him. Jonathan is puzzled at how to answer this question. After further discussion, Maria refers Jonathan to a local neurologist who specializes in ASD. She also commits to work with him using a standard behavioral approach that includes a weekly workbook that educates Jonathan on recognizing behavioral cues of peers.

Counseling approaches for ASD students should involve skill building targeting reading social cues in other people. For example, how to know when classmates are tuning them out, peer relations with roommates, and how to function in a classroom environment are all important in any treatment plan involving ASD students. The counselor must also be realistic regarding social improvement of ASD students as many behaviors are deeply ingrained. Counselors should also be aware that standard approaches to conducting counseling such as direct eye contact may leave the ASD students feeling uncomfortable (Browning & Miron, 2007). A soft, comfortable tone of voice conveying empathy is essential, as is the willingness of the counselor to repeat themes of counseling for consistency.

Counselors should also inquire about the ASD student's high school experience. This demonstrates respect for the client and also may provide the counselor with insight into strategies that can help the ASD student function in college. Counselors must also remain vigilant regarding changes in the ASD student's demeanor regarding increased anxiety, depression, social isolation, and SIBs. Involving significant people in the ASD student's life will also be a necessity. A release to speak to parents or guardians, roommates, a resident advisor, and so on in order to get a wide-angle view of challenges the ASD student is facing can be crucial for treatment. Counselors should furthermore check to see if the ASD student needs an academic accommodation (e.g., longer time for exams, or taking tests in a quiet room). It may be advisable at some point to bring a roommate, spouse, or parent into a session of counseling in order to help coach both the ASD student and significant person on how to address behavior.

It is also fair to understand that students on the ASD spectrum may be targets for bullying (Hamilton, 2012). While bullying may be more common in P–12 education, it also occurs in college, though there is surprisingly little in the literature on this phenomenon. But, as a long-time college counselor, former director of a college counseling center, and supervisor of collegiate living groups for 10 years, bullying does occur and likely is more serious than many college officials would like to admit. ASD students also are going to stand out both due to their unusual behavior and because they may present with an affect that would seem inappropriate in many circumstances. Students on the ASD spectrum should understand the social challenges college will place upon them, as in college most students will not be living with a supportive family and will have to build new relationships (usually a challenge to students on the ASD spectrum), live in an unfamiliar environment, and negotiate an entirely different set of academic expectations and social norms.

Teaching Coping Skills

Psychoeducational groups have become popular on virtually all college campuses. A perusal of any college counseling center's website is likely to turn up information on support groups for managing anxiety and depression, eating disorders, 12-step programs, time management, and so forth. Colleges should work to offer similar groups for students with ASD. Such support groups likely prove more challenging for small, liberal arts colleges with full-time equivalent enrollments under 3,000, but efforts should nevertheless be made. Support groups for students with ASD should include orientation to the university (its academic and student services) and strategies for adapting to college classes, residence halls, and social situations such as dances, concerts, and athletic events. It is vital to assist students with ASD to understand and reinforce norms regarding expected behavior, nonverbal communication, tone of voice, hand gestures, and so forth (Browning & Miron, 2007).

There are numerous additional topics that could be covered in ASD student support groups. Role-playing various academic and social situations related to the topic of discussion should be incorporated into the design of the groups as this increases the likelihood students will begin to put pro-social skills into action. Students in the groups should also discuss successes and successful failures (meaning they tried the new behavior even if they were not successful) and receive coaching and support from the group facilitator and group members. Counselors serving as facilitators should anticipate the need to actively recruit students with ASD from the residence halls through academic advisors, coaches, and other sections of the campus as many students will be reluctant to seek out the counseling center on their own.

A final suggestion regarding students with ASD is the use of video role-play and feedback with a counselor. The concept outlined by Shore (2003, in Browning & Miron, 2007) is to assist students with ASD in learning appropriate social interaction through role-play and video replay with critique and coaching. Counselors can role-play common student interactions such as roommate conflict scenarios, meeting with professors, classroom protocol, cafeteria etiquette, and so on. The video may be reviewed as many times as necessary to increase the student's awareness of her or his behavior and the effect on others. The counselor should coach the student to understand and then role-play more appropriate behavior in such interactions. Shore (2003) suggests counselors may replay the video many times for the student, focusing initially on, say, eye contact, then tone of voice, interpersonal distance, and so forth. Each review of the video is an attempt to help the student (a) understand the reasons behind the other person's behavior; (b) recognize any misunderstandings that occurred in the role-play; (c) understand the unwritten rules of social engagement; (d) learn what information she or he is misunderstanding; and (e) understand what impact the student's behavior has on the other party (Browning & Miron, 2007). Counselors should also be realistic in the timeframe it can take for students with ASD regarding understanding social cues (Grandin, 2006). Furthermore, students on the ASD spectrum will vary in their ability and willingness to engage in psychoeducational groups, just as with students with other mental health and learning disability issues.

FUTURE TRENDS

Though trends may change in this dynamic 21st century, the established pattern is that students with complex mental health issues are likely to continue to matriculate to college campuses. Federal legislation such as the ADA and other landmark acts of Congress have provided access to educational venues that were closed in previous eras. College counselors likely will continue to have to stretch their skills and services in order to serve students with major mental disorders. There are naturally some limits regarding serving high-needs students with major mental disorders such as schizophrenia, bipolar disorder, and students on the ASD spectrum. College counselors will also need to be resource professionals, connecting students with mental disorders with community support groups and teaching many of these students how to succeed in social interactions. Though the Internet age could mean more students with major disorders elect to take classes online to avoid social stigma, many are likely to continue to choose traditional residential education. College counselors will need to be prepared to continue to address these needs.

REFERENCES

Alcoholics Anonymous. (2013). *Alcoholics Anonymous: Big book* (4th ed.). New York, NY: Author. Retrieved from www.aa.org/bigbookonline

American Psychiatric Association. (2000). *The diagnostic and statistical manual of mental disorders* (4th ed., text revision). Washington, DC: Author.

American Psychiatric Association. (2013). *The diagnostic and statistical manual of mental disorders* (5th ed.). Washington, DC: Author.

Baron-Cohen, S., Wheelwright, S., Skinner, R., Martin, J., & Clubley, C. (2001). The autism-spectrum quotient (AQ): Evidence from Asperger syndrome/high functioning autism, males and females, scientists nand mathematicians. *Journal of Autism and Developmental Disabilities, 31*(1), 5–13.

Becker, M., Martin, L., Wajeeh, E., Ward, J., & Shern, D. (2002). Students with mental illness in a university setting: Faculty and student attitudes, beliefs, and experiences. *Psychiatric Rehabilitation Journal, 25*, 359–368.

Benton, S. A., Robertson, J. M., Tseng, W., Newton, F. B., & Benton, S. L. (2003). Changes in counseling center client problems across 13 years. *Professional Psychology Research and Practice, 34*, 66–72.

Bogdashina, O. (2003). *Severe perceptual issues in autism: Different sensory experiences, different perceptual worlds.* Philadelphia, PA: Jessica Kingsley.

Bower, K., & Schwartz, V. (2010). Legal and ethical issues in college mental health. In J. Kay & V. Schwartz (Eds.), *Mental health care in the college community* (pp. 133–142). Hoboken, NJ: Wiley.

Briere, J., & Gil, E. (1998). Self-mutilation in clinical and general population samples: Prevalence, correlates, and functions. *American Journal of Orthopsychiatry, 68*, 609–620.

Browning, S., & Miron, P. (2007). Counseling students with autism and Asperger's for success: A primer for success as a social being and a student. In J. Lippincott & R. Lippincott (Eds.), *Special populations in college counseling.* Alexandria, VA: American Counseling Association.

Burch, H. (1978). *The golden cage: The enigma of anorexia nervosa.* Cambridge, MA: Harvard University Press.

Carey, B. (2011, June 23). Expert on mental illness reveals her own fight. *New York Times.* Retrieved from www.nytimes.com/2011/06/23/health/23lives.html

Carroll, J., Schaffer, C., Spensley, J., & Abramowitz, S. I. (1980). Family experiences in self-mutilating patients. *American Journal of Psychiatry, 137*, 852–853.

Centers for Disease Control and Prevention. (2013, March). *CDC estimates 1 in 88 children in United States has been identified as having an autism spectrum disorder.* CDC Report 65. Atlanta, GA: Author. Retrieved from http://www.cdc.gov/media/releases/2012/p0329_autism_disorder.html

Collins, M. E., & Mowbray, C. T. (2005). Higher education and psychiatric disabilities: National survey of campus disability services. *American Journal of Orthopsychiatry, 75*, 304–315.

Crisp, A. (1980). *Anorexia nervosa: Let me be.* London, UK: Academic Press.

Deiter, P. J., Nicholls, S. S., & Pearlman, L. A. (2000). Self-Injury and self-capacities: Assisting an individual in crisis. *Journal of Clinical Psychology, 56*, 1173–1191.

Favazza, A. R., & Conterio, K. (1988). The plight of chronic self-mutilators. *Community Mental Health Journal, 24*, 22–30.

Fong, T. (2003). Self-mutilation: Impulsive traits suggest new drug therapies. *Current Psychiatry, 2*(2), 144–152.

Frank, J. B., & Thomas, C. D. (2003). Externalizing self-perceptions, self-silencing, and the prediction of eating pathology. *Canadian Journal of Behavioral Science, 35*, 219–228.

Fredrickson, B. L., & Roberts, T. A. (1997). Objectification theory: Toward understanding women's lived experiences and mental health risks. *Psychology of Women, 21*, 173–206.

Gallagher, R. P. (2014). *National survey of college counseling centers*. Alexandria, VA: International Association of Counseling Services, Inc.

Gilbert, S. P. (1992). Ethical issues in the treatment of severe psychopathology in university and college counseling students. *Journal of Counseling & Development, 70*, 695–699.

Grandin, T. (2006). *Thinking in pictures: Using the mysteries of autism*. New York, NY: Vintage Books.

Grayson, P. A. (2006). Overview. In P. A. Grayson & P. W. Meilman (Eds.), *College mental health practice* (pp. 1–20). New York, NY: Routledge.

Hamilton, J. (2012, April 23). Children with autism are often targeted by bullies. *NPR Blog*. Retrieved from http://www.npr.org/blogs/health/2012/04/23/151037898/children-with-autism-are-often-targeted-by-bullies

Hodges, S. (2001). University counseling centers in the twenty-first century: Looking forward, looking back. *Journal of College Counseling, 14*, 65–77.

Jacobi, C., Hayward, C., deZwann, M., Kraemer, H. C., & Agras, W. S. (2004). Coming to terms with risk factors for eating disorders: Application of risk terminology and suggestions for a general taxonomy. *Psychological Bulletin, 130*, 19–65.

Johnson, C., Crosby, R., Engel, S., Mitchell, J., Powers, P., Whittrock, D., & Wonderlich, S. (2004). Gender, ethnicity, self-esteem, and disordered eating among college athletes. *Eating Behaviors, 5*, 147–156.

Kanner, L. (1943). Autistic disturbances of affective contact. *Nervous Child, 2*, 217–250.

Kay, J. (2011). The rising prominence of college and university mental health issues. In J. Kay & V. Schwartz (Eds.), *Mental health care in the college community*. London, UK: Wiley-Blackwell.

Kitzrow, M. A. (2003). The mental health needs of today's college students: Challenges and recommendations. *National Association of Student Personnel Administrators, 41*, 167–181.

Kress, V. E. (2003). Self-injurious behaviors: Assessment and diagnosis. *Journal of Counseling and Development, 81*(4). doi:1556-6678.2003.tb00276.X

Linehan, M. M., Armstrong, H. E., Suarez, A., Allmon, D., & Heard, H. L. (1991). Cognitive behavioral treatment of chronically parasuicidal borderline patients. *Archives of General Psychiatry, 48*, 1060–1064.

Lippincott, J. A. (2007). When psychopathology challenges education: Counseling students with severe psychiatric disorders. In J. A. Lippincott & R. B. Lippincott (Eds.), *Special populations in college counseling: A handbook for mental health professionals*. Alexandria, VA: American Counseling Association.

May, R. (2006). Legal and ethical issues. In P. A. Grayson & P. W. Meilman (Eds.), *College mental health practice*. New York, NY: Routledge.

Miller, W. R., & Brown, J. M. (1999). *Enhancing motivation for change in substance abuse treatment*. In Substance Abuse and Mental Health Services Administration, Treatment Improvement Protocol (TIP) Series 35. Center for Substance Abuse Treatment (DHHS Publication No. SMA 99-3354). Rockville, MD: Substance Abuse and Mental Health Services Administration.

Nock, M. K., & Prinstein, M. J. (2004). A functional approach to the assessment of self-mutilating behavior. *Journal of Consulting and Clinical Psychology, 72*, 885–890.

Nolan, J. M., Ford, S. J. W., Kress, V. E., Anderson, R. I., & Novak, T. C. (2005). A comprehensive model for addressing severe and persistent mental illness on campus: The new diversity initiative. *Journal of College Counseling, 8*, 172–179.

Patterson, E. M., & Kahan, J. (1983). The deliberate self-harm syndrome. *American Journal of Psychiatry, 140*, 867–872.

Prochaska, J. O., DiClemente, C. C., & Norcross, J. C. (1992). In search of how people change: Applications to addictive behaviors. *American Psychologist, 47*, 1102–1114.

Raj, M. A. J., Kumaraiah, V., & Bhide, A. V. (2001). Cognitive-behavioural intervention in deliberate self-harm. *Acta Psychiatrica Scandinavica, 104*, 340–345.

Remley, T., & Herlihy, B. (2010). *Ethical, legal, and professional issues in counseling* (3rd ed.). Upper Saddle River, NJ: Pearson.

Schwartz, R. H., Cohen, P., Hoffman, N. G., & Meeks, J. E. (1989). Self-harm behaviors (carving) in female adolescent drug abusers. *Clinical Pediatrics, 28*, 340–346.

Sheehy, J., & Commerford, M. (2006). Eating disorders. In P. A. Grayson and P. W. Meilman (Eds.), *College mental health practice* (pp. 261–280). New York, NY: Routledge.

Shore, S. (2003). *Beyond the wall: Personal experiences with autism and Asperger syndrome*. Shawnee Mission, KS: Autism Asperger Publishing.

Simon, D., & Favazza, A. R. (2001). Self-injurious behaviors: Phenomenology and assessment. In D. Simon & E. Hollander (Eds.), *Self-injurious behaviors: Assessment and treatment* (pp. 1–28). Washington, DC: American Psychiatric Press.

Sonneborn, C. K., & Vanstraelen, P. M. (1992). A retrospective study of self-inflicted burns. *General Hospital Psychiatry, 14*, 404–407.

Striegal-Moore, R. H., & Smolak, L. (2001). *Eating disorders: Innovative directions for research and practice*. Washington, DC: American Psychological Association.

Strock, M. (2004). *Autism spectrum syndromes (pervasive developmental syndrome)*. NIH Publication No. NIH 04-5511. Bethesda, MD: National Institute of Mental Health.

Suyemoto, K. I., & MacDonald, M. L. (1995). Self-cutting in female adolescents. *Psychotherapy, 32*, 162–171.

U.S. News & World Report. (2012). Eating disorders. New York, NY: Author. Retrieved from http://health.usnews.com/health-conditions/mental-health/eating-disorders/overview

Wheeler, A. N. W., & Bertram, B. (2012). *The counselor and the law: A guide to legal and ethical practice* (6th ed.). Alexandria, VA: American Counseling Association.

White, V. E., Trepal-Wollenzier, H., & Nolan, J. (2002). College students and self-injury: Intervention strategies for counselors. *Journal of College Counseling, 5,* 105–113.

Wing, L. (1976). *Early childhood autism: Clinical, educational, and social aspects* (2nd ed.). Oxford, UK: Pergamon Press.

CHAPTER TEN

CRISIS AND TRAUMA COUNSELING

Shannon J. Hodges

AUTHOR'S NOTE

Crisis and trauma are terms that have become alarmingly common in the United States. It seems that on a regular basis the media reports a high profile incident at a P–12 school, college, or in the workplace. For the purposes of this chapter, crisis and trauma interventions involve those of both an individual nature—students who do harm to themselves—and of a mass nature—students who do harm to multiple students or perpetuate events that threaten the safety of many students. Other forms of individual crisis and trauma such as those involving sexual assault are covered in another chapter.

THE TRAUMA OF SUICIDE

Suicide is the second leading cause of death among college students (National Institute of Mental Health [NIMH], 2009). This sobering statistic is something college counselors and student affairs professionals have known for decades. Sadly, many college students will contemplate ending their lives and some will make actual attempts at suicide. An unfortunate few will actually "succeed" and die. Suicides call into question the stability, safety, and security of higher education (Silverman, 2005a).

Decades ago, when I (Hodges) was an undergraduate working freshman orientation, a parent approached me and asked, "Is my son going to be safe here?" As a green, eager, impressionable student having just completed my freshman year of college, I was puzzled. I had lived in a small, quiet, residence hall normally reserved for upper classmen and graduate students and had been sheltered from a lot of distractions and dangers. I stated the campus seemed safe and inquired further as to what she meant. She replied that she had heard so much about college suicides and campus stress that she was very worried about her son and only child. Following up on the conversation I was put in touch with a staff counselor at the university counseling center. He listened patiently to me as I related the story. "I just want to be able to tell this woman her son will be safe here," I explained. The middle-aged man nodded sagely and said while there was an excellent chance her son would be safe and secure, guarantees were impossible. He related that driving to work was routine for most people and virtually all the time people arrive to work safely. But, he went on to say, some people get into auto accidents and are injured and even killed.

Suicide prevention is a bit like the driving scenario in the patient–counselor scenario mentioned earlier. Most students will be safe and secure from suicide during their collegiate years and will graduate, or transfer, or withdraw and be physically and psychologically safe. Some unfortunate students, however, will attempt and a few will even succeed at suicide. In the driving scenario, there are precautions one can take: wear a seat belt, obey traffic laws, drive a car with air bags, don't drink and drive, and so forth. But, the unexpected can still occur both out on the road and on the college campus. To adapt the driving scenario to the college mental health field, "safe" students, if such isn't an oxymoron, likely limit their alcohol consumption, refrain from drug use, regularly attend classes, get to know their academic advisor, utilize health and career services, and most importantly seek counseling services when stressed. They will make friends and join clubs and organizations and in doing so, help create healthy alliances that provide a buffer against suicide. Still, like the driving scenario, there are no guarantees a given student will reach her or his destination safely. Naturally, in living a life utilizing the aforementioned resources, the odds are in the student's favor.

But like the concerned parent mentioned earlier, there is significantly greater awareness regarding college student suicides than in my previous four decades in higher education. A heightened sense of awareness regarding the threat of suicide has elevated the focus on prevention and treatment (Kitzrow, 2003). Still, regardless of the long-term threat, college student suicide is a poorly understood phenomenon among the general public and even among many college administrators. Though the literature on college student suicides and prevention is quite extensive, any attempt to synthesize the findings is marred by inconsistencies in definitions, methodologies, and reported results (Maris, Berman, & Silverman, 2000; Silverman, 2005b). The one thing no one debates is that college student suicide is a persistent and serious threat for a small portion of the campus (Gallagher, 2014).

While research literature on the risk factors for suicide (environmental, psychological, genetic, etc.) is increasing, far more attention has been focused on the rates of completed suicides than on the greater number that are prevented. In fact, one of the challenges of college counselors is they often are invisible to the public until there is a suicide. In my own experience, college counselors are often an afterthought to many administrators and faculty until a crisis emerges. To understand suicide requires an exploration of the factors that precipitate suicide attempts.

Suicide Rates

The numbers can vary considerably. The American College Health Association's (ACHA) 2012 results suggest 7.5% of every 100,000 students commit suicide. One in 12 has made a suicide plan and 1.5 out of every 100 have actually made an attempt (ACHA, 2012). ACHA's 2008 study indicated 26% of male college students and 32% of female college students report being depressed enough to consider suicide (ACHA, 2008). The National Survey of Counseling Center Directors in 2011 reported 87 suicides in the past calendar year. Of these 87, 73% were males, 80% undergraduates, 86% Caucasian, and 65% had no known previous psychiatric history.

Clearly, suicide, suicide attempts, and threats of suicide are serious issues for college counselors and administrators. Naturally, anyone concerned will likely ask, "Why is suicide such a problem for college students?" There are many reasons for why suicide is such an insidious problem for college students, and we examine some of them in the following.

Risk Factors and Warning Signs

Clearly, college is a stressful time in the lives of many students, especially those of traditional age. Traditional-age students are transitioning from a home environment where they may have had strong social connections (friends, classmates, athletic teammates, parents, etc.) into one where they must establish new connections. Occasionally, students are housed with roommates with different values and lifestyles and conflict is created. Some students from a rural area may be overwhelmed, and others from urban regions may attend a rural campus and feel out of place due to cultural and ethnic differences. Some students may never have spent significant amounts of time away from home while others may have been popular in their home town and feel anonymous at the university. Beyond these typical transitional issues, several common risk factors have been noted:

> Risk factors for suicide include traumatic or stressful life events, prior attempts, isolation and lack of emotional support, and access to a suicide method. (ACHA, 2012)

> Warning signs may include academic difficulties, depression, mood swings, social withdrawal, feelings of hopelessness, substance abuse, and obsession with death. (ACHA, 2012)

> Additional signs of concern include depression, drug and alcohol abuse, hopelessness, family history of suicide, lack of social connections, impulsivity, trauma history, and availability of firearms. (Granello & Granello, 2007)

Warning Signs

Counselors and student affairs professionals should learn to recognize warning signs of potential suicide and intervene with them. In residential college settings, resident advisors (RAs), sorority or fraternity sisters and brothers, coaches, academic advisors, campus ministers, and faculty likely will be the first line of defense in suicide prevention. College counseling centers must cultivate a strong working relationship with these and other campus professionals in order to quickly identify and intervene with troubled students. Warning signs may be verbal: "I'm thinking of ending things," "I'd be better off dead," "Life sucks and isn't worth it," or "I just can't go on much longer," and similar refrains are the type to be sensitive to regarding suicide prevention. Behavioral warning signs may consist of social withdrawal and isolation, alcohol and drug abuse, absenteeism from class and declining academic performance, and poor grooming and hygiene when previously the student was neat and presentable. Psychiatric signs could be increased manic or depressive behaviors, self-injurious behaviors (e.g., self-mutilation by cutting, burning), panic attacks, and impulsivity, to name a few. Perhaps the most significant predictor is that of hopelessness (Minkoff, Bergman, Beck, & Beck, 2006; Seligman, 2011) as hopeless people see little reason to continue taking their medications, attending class, grooming, exercise, and maintaining previous resilience.

Prevention Factors

In this era of increased accountability it is critical that college counselors not only intervene in mental health issues, but also work on preventive care. In the case of suicide, this means establishing strong systems for emotional and social support. Support groups run through the counseling center can be an effective means of prosocial support. Common support groups at the collegiate level often target stress management, gay and lesbian issues, soldiers returning to college, grief recovery groups, trauma recovery groups, and so forth. One way support groups assist is in the way of peers who have experienced similar issues and who provide emotional support and accountability to one another. Support groups differ from therapy groups—while support groups promote good mental health, the primary focus is emotional support. The advantage is that if a student in the group needs more care than the group can provide, group members can encourage the individual to seek counseling.

Another factor in promoting resilience is that of the RA in collegiate living communities. While RAs are usually not professional counselors, they serve an important role as the first line of defense for students in campus residential living groups. Part of the role of an RA is overseeing the health and welfare of the students on their floor or in their living group. RAs usually get basic "first aid" type mental health training in listening skills, noticing behavioral changes and alcohol and drug abuse, and so forth. RAs also are trained in how to approach and talk about sensitive issues related to alcohol, sex, and suicide among others. Having served nearly a decade as an RA myself (Hodges) and having worked many years in university counseling centers, the RA counseling center relationship is very important on residential campuses, and counseling services should cultivate a strong relationship with this important group of student leaders.

Regardless of how athletics are perceived by faculty and staff, coaches can also serve as an important link for college counseling centers. College athletes are a select student population in higher education and at small colleges (5,000 full-time equivalent enrollments or less), where a high percentage of the general student population participates in intercollegiate sports. Because there is much performance and time pressure on student athletes, they may be more susceptible to anxiety, depression, alcohol and drug abuse, eating disorders, and academic-related stress (Thompson & Sherman, 2005). Increased stress levels likely predispose athletes to thoughts of suicide. Coaches will notice when student athletes' performance decline and prudent coaches will assess the emotional and mental health angle by a timely referral to the counseling center. College counseling centers will need to develop a good referral resource with administrators, coaches, and athletic trainers at their institution. Larger National Collegiate Athletic Association (NCAA) Division I sports programs may have their own counseling services, though some athletes may still prefer to come to the university counseling center as it may provide more autonomy and anonymity than an "in-house" operation.

Campus ministers serve the spiritual needs of many college students. At most universities, ministers, rabbis, imams, priests, and so forth can be evidenced working through separate campus religious organizations and interfaith organizations. The majority of campus religious leaders have little mental health training, though they often will provide spiritual-based counsel to students. Most campus religious leaders will make use of the counseling center when they have reached the parameters of their expertise. College counseling center staff can generate a number of referrals through the campus ministry. Certainly there may be times when the counselor and the campus religious leader may disagree and relations may be sensitive, but campus religious leaders will encounter a lot of student psychopathology, and good relations between counseling and the ministry are essential. Campus religious leaders may also be very helpful in encouraging students to seek out and continue with counseling services. Perhaps the most sensitive issue for many counselors and religious leaders remains sexual orientation, though not all religious organizations view gays and lesbians as aberrant. Still, while there will be issues of disagreement, counseling centers should be encouraged to reach out to campus religious leaders.

Another important contact for college counseling centers is veterans' services (note that veterans' services will be identified by many different titles on college campuses). Given the noted large numbers of military veterans matriculating to college campuses and the trauma many have experienced, the counseling center needs to be an active participant with this student population. American military veterans are far more likely to entertain thoughts of suicide than fellow students (Mozes, 2011). Because ex-servicewomen and -servicemen may have received a mixed message regarding seeking mental health while on active duty, the counseling center may need to make a concerted effort to establish a relationship with ex-soldiers. Examples of how counseling services might build rapport are by offering support groups and meeting with campus military liaisons (the campus Veterans Office, Reserve Officers' Training Corps [ROTC] leaders, student veterans' organizations, etc.). Counseling staff with military backgrounds or who come from a military family may have an easier time establishing a relationship as veterans tend to trust other veterans or at least those they perceive as understanding veterans' issues.

A student group that should not be forgotten when it comes to suicide prevention is gay, lesbian, and transgender students. Sexual minorities have a significantly higher rate of suicide (American Association of Suicidology, n.d.;

Bagley & Tremblay, 2000) than the general student population. Though most campuses now provide more visible means of support for sexual minorities (e.g., safe havens, peer support groups, campus organizations with office space, nondiscrimination status), research clearly indicates sexual minorities feel more stress, anxiety, and isolation, experience more bullying, and so forth than any other student population. Negative images as portrayed in conservative media and evangelical religious organizations also have helped continue a hostile environment for sexual minorities. In fact, 76 countries have made homosexuality illegal and seven have made it a capital offense (Deathpenaltynews, 2011). It is little wonder then that sexual minorities experience fear and anxiety in higher education. The counseling center should take an active role in promoting equal rights for sexual minorities and participate in safe haven training, offer support groups and other similar means of support. Counseling centers should also cultivate an ongoing relationship with leaders of gay, lesbian, and transgender student organizations as such students will be in need of emotional and psychological support. Support is especially important for students preparing to come out to their parents.

Assessment of Suicide

There are many operational methods for assessing suicide. Many, if not most, college counseling services will assess for suicide potential in the intake portion of the assessment. Intake questionnaires commonly ask if the student is or recently has contemplated suicide. The Beck Depression Inventory, second edition (BDI-II) (Beck, Steer, & Brown, 2003) contains an item on suicide and another on hopelessness. Other simple assessments such as the SAD PERSONS checklist (Patterson, Dohn, Bird, & Patterson, 1983) offers simple and quick assessments to assess the possibility of suicide. More informal methods of assessment are simply asking the client, "Are you considering suicide?" This questions should be followed by, "Do you have a plan for suicide?" Fortunately, most students who have considered suicide have not formulated a plan for suicide. In the event a student has made a plan, the counselor should ask, "What does the plan involve?" and "On a scale of 1 to 10, with 1 being totally unlikely and 10 almost certainly, how likely is it you will carry out this plan?" The most important factor in assessing and preventing suicide is the rapport between the client and the counselor (Granello & Granello, 2007); counselors must establish a supportive, nonjudgmental approach that invites the client to disclose his or her thoughts and intentions regarding suicide. Still, there are a number of questions to cover:

- What is the client's sense of hope? Does the client believe the stress or issues in his or her life will lessen and improve? (The counselor might ask this as a scaling question: "On a scale of 1 to 10, with 1 being 'things won't improve' to 10 being 'things will definitely improve,' what would your score be at present?")
- Have the client list positive attributes for living: "What are some reasons for continuing to go on living? List as many as you can."

- Some counselors use a variation of the "miracle question" (deShazer, 1985) to potential suicide victims: "Imagine that at some point in the future the problems that have led you to contemplate suicide are no longer a stress in your life. What would be different about your life?" After the client answers, say "Okay, in the meantime, what can we do to make life more meaningful until this day comes?"
- "Who are you closest to?" If the client has someone, ask, "Would you be able to call on this person in an emergency?" If the client answers, "No one," then ask, "Okay, we need to work on making friends. How can we start this process?"
- Because many students will have some spiritual beliefs, it's important to investigate this angle. "Do you have a spiritual faith or practice that has helped you in the past? Is that belief system or practice helpful now?"
- Many suicidal students will be using alcohol or other drugs as a coping mechanism. Ask about this: "What role does alcohol or other drugs play in your life?" (Ask about cigarettes and overreliance on caffeine as well.)
- Fitness can be a buffer against depression, anxiety, and other mental health issues. Investigate the client's exercise regimen: "Do you work out? How often during the week do you work out?"
- Lack of sleep can exacerbate depression and anxiety. Investigate the client's sleep patterns: "How well do you sleep at night? How many hours of sleep do you get each night (on average)?"

It is likely that anyone reading this book already knows that many clients are reluctant to openly discuss their thoughts or plans for suicide until they feel they can trust their counselor. Again, a nonjudgmental approach illustrated by a calm, supportive tone of voice and appropriate body language (e.g., open, relaxed posture, appropriate head nodding, appropriate eye contact) is necessary. These types of dispositions convey to the client that the counselor is competent and interested in addressing the issues of suicide. After all, if the client senses the counselor is anxious regarding disclosure of suicide, the client is likely to cease disclosing important information to the counselor. A strong therapeutic alliance is critical to successful outcomes in all types of counseling and especially in crisis situations (Granello & Granello, 2007).

Should the college student acknowledge some level of suicidal intent the counselor needs to follow up with specific questions. For example, "Do you have a plan for suicide?" "What's the likelihood you would follow through on this plan?" "How long have you had a plan for suicide?" "What has kept you from following through on this plan?" The student's answers to these types of questions provide the counselor with concrete information regarding the student's intent to attempt suicide.

Crisis Intervention and Treatment

Fortunately, the crisis phase of suicide intervention tends to be brief. The counselor's plan during this time is simple: Keep the student safe. Safety usually involves a battery of activities: notifying parents or guardians, possible hospitalization, posthospitalization plan, medication, ongoing counseling, spiritual support for many, continued assessment, possible group counseling, support group, and so forth (Silverman, 2006; Silverman & Glick, 2010). Basically, there is a long list of possible interventions for students in crisis. The important point is timely intervention followed by extensive support services such as those previously outlined.

Hospitalization

Given the reality of managed care, there are very few psychiatric beds available to college students. For students who are hospitalized, psychiatric stays likely will be brief (generally 1–3 days) and the student will return to campus and the care of the college or university counseling center.

Hospitalizing a student involves a thorough clinical assessment involving risk factors: Will the student commit to safety? Has the student had previous suicide attempts? Has the student been hospitalized previously for psychiatric issues or a suicide threat or attempt? The counselor needs to assess the rewards of hospitalization (e.g., more secure environment, provide a respite from collegiate pressures, access to a psychiatric team, possible rediagnosis) with the risks (many psychiatric centers are overcrowded and understaffed, psychiatric hospitalization may harm student's future career). It also must be noted that the insurance company will likely decide if the student is to be hospitalized. If the decision is made to hospitalize the student, she or he must be completely informed of this decision and why it is being made. The counselor must also address confidentiality and why it needs to be broken in order to inform parents or guardians, roommates, and significant others.

When the student returns from the hospital the aftercare plan should involve the college counseling center. The student released from the hospital likely has a prescription for a psychoactive medication (often a selective serotonin reuptake inhibitors [SSRI] for depression) and her or his plan is to continue in counseling. Most research evidence consistently illustrates a combination of counseling plus medication is more efficacious than either alone (Grayson & Cooper, 2006). The treatment plan should address the root causes of what led to the student becoming suicidal. In addition to standard counseling and medication, self-instructional systems such as workbooks are highly recommended in order for the student to monitor treatment progress. Workbooks targeting depression, anxiety, cognitive change, social phobia, eating disorders, and so forth are inexpensive and readily available through major book retailers. After the student has met treatment goals, it may be advisable to refer the student to a campus-based or off-campus support group.

The following case studies exemplify possible student suicide crisis scenarios.

The Case of Dave

Dave, a 22-year-old, Caucasian pre-med student who has wanted to be a doctor since junior high, received the disappointment that he was denied admission to all 10 medical schools to which he had applied. The last rejection, a medical school he was certain he'd get into, was crushing. That evening, he got drunk and, upon returning to his apartment, began threatening to jump from the fifth story window and had to be talked out of it by his two roommates. The roommates contacted campus police who contacted the on-call staff from the counseling center. The counselor, Jen, assessed Dave at the campus police station. Dave had calmed down considerably by this time, was sober, and was ready to talk. He filled Jen in on what had happened regarding medical school. He denied that he would have jumped though admitted he had threatened to do just that. He also denied any specific plan to attempt suicide and agreed to come in at 8:30 the following morning when the counseling center opened. Jen, therefore, made the decision not to hospitalize him. She wrote down his appointment on a card with her name on it (the card also included the 24-hour crisis line).

The Case of Yen-Song

Yen-Song is a 22-year-old Korean American student majoring in engineering. She has struggled with the challenging mechanical engineering curriculum since matriculating to the university. Yen-Song has had a troubled week: First she was informed she did not get the summer internship she had wanted. Then, her girlfriend broke up with her the following day. Yen-Song, an introvert by nature, has no close friends to call on. After a few days, she began to despair regarding her chosen career and more significantly whether life is really worth living. She mentions to a fellow engineering student that she's "Not sure life's worth living." The student is alarmed and informs the RA who talks to Yen-Song. Yen-Song admits that she's very upset and sees little reason to believe her life will improve. With the RA's encouragement, the RA and Yen-Song walk to the counseling center. Yen-Song is assessed by Fahad, a counseling center staff. She admits to being very depressed and wondering if she can go on given all the bad news received this week. She admits to considering suicide. Her plan would be to purchase a bottle of aspirin, swallow the bottle, and chase it down with beer. Fahad administers the BDI-II and Yen-Song scores 33 (very high), indicating that she feels hopeless and suicidal based on the BDI-II indicators. After consulting with Yen-Song and then the counseling center director, Fahad makes the decision to hospitalize Yen-Song.

Yen-Song spends two nights in the psychiatric wing of the local hospital, where she is diagnosed with major depression, given a prescription for Wellbutrin, and entered into group therapy. Upon release, she is linked up with the university counseling center for extended treatment and medication monitoring with the counseling center's psychiatrist. After a couple of sessions, Yen-Song confesses to Fahad she needs to withdraw from the university for the remainder of the term. She plans to return home and assess her career plans.

In both of the aforementioned cases, students were in crisis precipitated by life changes and disappointments. In Dave's case, he was more able to self-regulate his emotions and behavior and was amenable to immediate treatment on campus. Yen-Song, on the other hand, was more isolated and seemed less hopeful regarding her life when in crisis. Based on Yen-Song's BDI-II results, especially on construct of hopelessness, the counselor decided to hospitalize her. In both cases, the staff counselor or the hospital wanted to get the students back to campus and in counseling. Both students were given a medication and in each case followed through with counseling. Yen-Song was elected to withdraw from college and rethink her occupational plans.

Medications to Help Prevent Suicide

There are numerous medications for the treatment of depression, which is likely the primary mental health diagnosis related to suicide ideology and gestures. Some studies suggest that the use of antidepressants in therapy has lowered suicide rates in clinical populations (Isacsson, Holmgren, Druid, & Bergman, 1997), but there are some arguments regarding the methodology of these studies (Silverman, 2006). Meanwhile, there is much controversy as to whether certain classes of antidepressants can be linked to mood deterioration and increased suicide risk in clients who have recently begun medication (Mann & Kapur, 1991).

SSRIs are the most common type of antidepressant used in the treatment of depression. But some research seems to indicate SSRIs have the potential to exacerbate symptoms of anxiety leading to an increased risk for suicide (Isacsson et al., 1997; Montgomery, 1997). When medications are prescribed to suicidal students, careful monitoring of dosage levels and subsequent behavioral changes is essential. In my own experience (Hodges), many clients will cease taking their medications when they feel slightly better, thus reducing or eliminating any therapeutic advantage the medication may have provided. Counselors and medical professionals must carefully monitor the client for any decrease in behavioral functioning, irritability, agitation, or unwanted side effects (Shaffer & Pfeffer, 2001).

When the primary counselor works with a prescribing physician or health care professional, keeping direct lines of communication open between the counselor and medical professional is critical to client care. The counselor should inquire of the client about mood and behavior to address any positive or detrimental change. Such information must then be reported to the medical professional. Basically, though medication, and in particular SSRIs can play an important role in the mental health treatment of college students, medications must be carefully monitored and even changed based upon their impact on the client.

Primary Treatment Approaches

Any perusal of the literature will turn up numerous approaches to counseling. All counselors will have their favorite approach, or as is more common, "approaches" as most counselors integrate multiple approaches in their practice (Corey, 2012). Some common theoretical approaches to counseling are cognitive behavioral therapy (CBT; Beck, 1976), psychodynamic therapy (Kernberg, 1976), existential/humanistic therapy (Rogers, 1951; Yalom, 1980), and lately dialectical behavioral therapy (DBT; Linehan, 1993).

Psychodynamic therapy is essentially a neo-Freudian approach adapted to a managed care world. Psychodynamic approaches tend to emphasize past family treatment emanating from early childhood years and how that early socialization impacts the client in the present. "Healing" is more about understanding the powerful role parental figures played in the client's life. There is little argument that psychodynamic approaches have much to offer with regard to understanding past and present personal and familial dynamics. Research regarding psychodynamic approaches and evidence of change, however, has generally been inconclusive (Sharf, 2008).

Humanistic and existential approaches were very popular in previous decades and remain so even today. Many college counselors will continue to practice from a humanistic or existential framework. Key techniques such as empathy, genuineness, acceptance, and reflecting feeling are common in this approach. Existential approaches are characterized by addressing meaning or a lack of meaning in the client's life (Frankl, 1978). Once again, however, the efficacy of humanistic and existential approaches is not robust (Corey, 2009).

CBT has been shown to be very effective at reducing depressive symptoms (Beck, 2005). Cognitive therapy addresses maladaptations in thinking and behavior. Beck (1976) believes thinking errors are at the root of suicidal thoughts. Thus, before anything else, the CBT counselor must address the client's schemas, or patterns of cognitions. CBT directly addresses issues of suicidal thoughts and behaviors and, consequently, may be part of the reason for the approach's success. Many college counselors are now utilizing CBT as a primary approach to treatment of suicidal students.

DBT (Linehan, 1993) is an evidence-based approach for chronically "parasuicidal" clients diagnosed with borderline personality disorder. Parasuicide is defined here as acute, deliberate, nonfatal, self-injurious behaviors (Linehan, 1993). DBT treatment focuses on validation and empowerment of the client. The counselor strives to assist clients in moderating their behavior and emotional reactions, checking outside reality, and regulating their own behavioral response (Linehan, 1993). Other key DBT skills are mindfulness, interpersonal effectiveness training, and techniques to address acute distress. DBT is growing in popularity as an approach to clients struggling with ongoing depression and self-injurious behaviors.

THE ROLE OF MEANING IN COLLEGE COUNSELING

Regardless of what theoretical approach the college counselor is using, it is strongly advisable at some point to address the important constructs of hope and meaning. Hope likely is the most critical issue; if the client is absent any significant hope, the client is less likely to remain in therapy and more likely to attempt suicide (Beck, 1976, 2005). Likewise, meaning in life is another very important construct for the counselor to assess and address with each client (Frankl, 1978). As most college students are under a good deal of pressure (e.g., grades, work, family pressures, college debt, anxieties about future job), meaning in life is likely a question everyone in counseling should entertain. It is likely that as hope and life meaning begin to lessen, the client is most likely to become more depressed and pessimistic about the future. Seligman (2011) promotes learned optimism as a method of increasing the client's hopefulness and optimism. He also expresses that optimism can be easily learned and that optimistic people are happier, more productive, and even live longer (Seligman, 2011).

Counseling essentially is built on the foundation of the power of choice as a key ingredient in client success and fulfillment (Glasser, 2001). This may be especially true in college and university settings where people are pursuing their educational and career dreams. The majority of the collegiate population likely is very optimistic, otherwise they very likely would not be in college. Naturally, variations are to be found within a subset of any population. While this generation of college students seems more anxious and depressed and is increasingly medicated, my own sense is that most still are excited about their future. The very fact that students are willing to seek counseling illustrates they wish to regain their sense of meaning, hope, and optimism. The recommendation here, especially with clients in crisis, is to help them reestablish life meaning and hope, and to help teach them to become more optimistic. Naturally, this is much easier to write than to instill in clients.

GENERAL RECOMMENDATIONS FOR COUNSELING SUICIDAL CLIENTS

This chapter contains a lot of information and resources for counseling college students who are suicidal. The chapter has explored reasons for suicidal ideation, counseling approaches, psychopharmacological interventions, and important constructs to address with college students (e.g., hope, optimism, life meaning). In addition, college counselors should remember to keep their approach with suicidal students simple, as students in crisis are typically overwhelmed and may be unable to process complex information given their stress level. Here are basic considerations:

1. Use standard assessments such as the BDI-II to help assess potential for suicide and hopelessness. Remember, hopelessness is a better predictor of suicide than the question on suicide (Beck, 1976). Readministering the BDI-II after two sessions also provides a sense of whether the client is improving.
2. Naturally, get the student to contract for immediate counseling (say six–eight sessions) and refer the student for medication.
3. With the student's permission, involve relevant members of the student's immediate family (make sure this would be therapeutically helpful).
4. With the student's permission, involve pertinent people in the student's life such as an RA, coach, close friend, academic advisor, spiritual advisor, and so forth.
5. Encourage the student to develop healthy activities such as exercise, social engagements, and healthier diet (lower in fat, sugar, caffeine, alcohol, etc.). Collaborate with and refer the client to appropriate referrals.
6. Assess whether the student has close friendships. Isolated people are more likely to consider and attempt suicide. If necessary, teach the

student how to make healthy friendships. In point of fact, many students may not know how to create close friendships and Facebook, Twitter, e-mail, and so forth likely may be detrimental in this regard.

7. During each session, evaluate the client's sense of optimism and life meaning. You might use a scaling question for this:

"On a scale of 1 to 10, with 1 representing 'feeling hopeless' and 10 representing 'feeling very hopeful,' where are you on this scale at present? How can we improve 1 point during this session?" (If the student answers "One," ask "What can we do to get you to a 2 during this session?" If the student says "4," ask, "What can we do to help get you to a 5?" and so forth).

8. Homework can be an important way of extending therapy beyond the session. Numerous workbooks that address depression and anxiety are available at a low cost (many college counseling centers will already have these for student use). Counselors can also devise their own homework and tailor it to the client's needs. But get the clients doing something therapeutic.

9. Does the student have creative hobbies? Developing interests outside of classes can have a positive impact. Are there clubs and organizations the student would be interested in joining?

10. There is much research indicating clients who consider and attempt suicide report having less meaning in their lives. Ask the student, "What brings meaning to your life?" Then expand upon whatever it is that brings the student meaning. If the student doesn't know, then make exploration of and developing meaning part of the ongoing process.

CAMPUS-WIDE CRISES

In the last 10 years in higher education we have witnessed tragic events such as mass killings at Northern Illinois University and Virginia Tech. Tragedy certainly is nothing new to the college campus, as automobile accidents have long held tragic consequences regarding college mortality, to say nothing of campus suicides, and the occasional homicide. But, mass spree murders such as at the University of Texas in 1966 and Virginia Tech represent an entirely different type of crisis. It is also worthy of mention that homicides, auto accidents, and suicides are but some of the crises that challenge colleges. Hurricane Katrina devastated colleges from the Florida Gulf Coast all the way to the Texas Gulf Coast with New Orleans colleges hit the hardest (almost 2,000 people died in the New Orleans area). These various tragedies highlight a need for college campuses to have organized, developed emergency procedures in place to address the aftermath of a crisis. In some cases such as suicide and auto accidents, colleges have had quite a bit of practice (sadly) in dealing with the emotional fallout in the wake of such tragedies. But in circumstances involving more complex trauma (e.g., murders at Virginia Tech), few if any would have been prepared for this level of tragedy.

What Is a Crisis?

The aforementioned examples of campus crises are examples of how a crisis can have a devastating impact on a college campus. Having mentioned this, many of the previously noted campus tragedies were of significant variation. The shootings at Kent State University were significantly different than, say, the sniper killings at the University of Texas. No one would seriously argue Kent State, the University of Texas, Hurricane Katrina, and so forth were not crises. But they were different types of crises, each requiring different types of responses. In the post-Katrina period, many colleges in New Orleans had to close for extended periods, or in the case of Tulane, they moved operations to another location. Thus, a crisis will vary depending on the type, severity, duration, and the institutional and or governmental response.

While many definitions of the word "crisis" exist and are used, depending on the nature of crisis, for our purposes a crisis is defined as follows:

A crisis is a major unpredictable event that has potentially negative results. The event and its aftermath may significantly damage an organization and its employees, products, services, financial condition, and reputation. (Barton, 1993)

Perception of a Crisis

Most people likely would describe a crisis as a traumatic experience or event with personal, psychological, or financial consequences. Regarding higher education, the tragic shootings at Virginia Tech touched the lives of thousands of people, and an entire nation was shocked and then mourned in the aftermath. High-profile tragedies such as Katrina can threaten an institution's mission, employees, students, financial reputation, and in some cases its very survival. In such examples of overwhelming crisis, the perception likely is initial panic. Later, after the imminent crisis has passed, the aftermath likely will be complex.

Finks (1986) has argued that a crisis can be both a negative as well as a positive event. He notes that the Chinese symbol for crisis is a combination of two words, danger and opportunity. There clearly is an element of danger in a crisis, whatever the crisis may be (e.g., shooting, natural disaster, suicide). But the "positive" aspect may be a deeper recognition of a need to adapt and address potential challenges. The "opportunity" perhaps lies in a campus's recognition of and future planning to deal with and address potential campus crises. For example, let's take the violent trauma that occurred at Virginia Tech where 33 people were killed by an enraged student. Naturally, for the families of the victims, opportunity is unlikely to be in their lexicon when referring to the incident. But the opportunity is to create a critical response team to anticipate and address both tragic incidents and their aftermath. It must also be admitted that there is no precise manner of anticipating when a crisis may occur. But a critical response plan with major players identified that can prepare for and be ready to respond to a crisis is a reality all campuses must address. This would be a campus plan where administration, faculty, student affairs, staff, and students are aware of the plan and have access to that plan (Zdziarski, Dunkel, Rollo, & Associates, 2007).

SCHOOL SHOOTINGS: HIGH-PROFILE TRAGEDIES IN P–12 AND COLLEGE SETTINGS

Perhaps the most notable aspect of school violence lies in the numerous tragic incidents occurring since the late 1990s in high schools and on college campuses—tragedies such as at Columbine and recently at Aurora, Colorado (off campus but a University of Colorado student), Virginia Tech, Northern Illinois University, and several others. Naturally, threat assessment by trained mental health professionals (e.g., psychologists, counselors, social workers) and law enforcement experts has become a major focal point in the United States. The Federal Bureau of Investigation (FBI) has spent several decades crafting a profile of the type of individual likely to attempt mass killings using weapons. In 1999, the FBI released their comprehensive study *The School Shooter: A Threat Assessment*. The FBI was quick to state their model was not a "profile of the school shooter or a checklist of danger signs" (1999, p. 7). Rather, the FBI touted the model as a "rational, and standardized method of evaluating and responding to threats" (p. 7). The FBI model mentions assessors of school violence as psychologists, counselors, and other professionals (1999).

In the beginning of the document, the FBI is simply explaining what mental health professionals already know—predicting violence is very difficult to do with any degree of reliability (FBI, 1999). The FBI model does outline different levels of threats: low level, medium level, and high level, with differentiation being the level of specificity of the threat and the perpetrator's experience with weapons (FBI, 1999). The FBI model created a four-pronged assessment (1999):

1. Student personality
2. Family dynamics
3. School dynamics
4. Social dynamics

The FBI outlines that in the four-pronged assessment there is no precise cut-off score that would determine violence. Rather, the profile assesses how much mastery or disappointment the troubled student has had during his or her formative years. One of the difficulties mentioned in *The School Shooter* is the difficulty in bringing troubled youth to the attention of mental health professionals. Naturally, the problem in many instances of high-profile tragedies is that the perpetrator of mass violence either was not brought to the attention of legal or mental health professionals or, as in the tragedy in Aurora, Colorado, various people in contact with the shooter did not have the full picture of the shooter. *The School Shooter: A Threat Assessment* underscores the challenges in gathering pertinent information and in making valid predictions of high-profile tragedies

(FBI, 1999). There is also the reality that successful interventions will result in no accolades for mental health professionals while examples of high-profile violence will bring scorn and indignation upon counselors, psychologists, and law enforcement professionals. For college and university counselors, the most prudent advice one could glean from the FBI model is to have some type of systematic assessment for identifying and then addressing potentially violent students while realizing that no threat assessment approach has been shown to be particularly valid or reliable (FBI, 1999). Still, it behooves colleges and universities to train their counseling staff and campus police in threat assessment, response, and an approach that addresses how to respond to the aftermath of a tragedy.

FORMING A CAMPUS CRISIS MANAGEMENT TEAM

Crisis management is a general term encompassing any activities when a campus prepares for and responds to a trauma. Before forming the team, administrators, counselors, campus police, and so forth should develop the mission and scope of the crisis management team (CMT). A critical component of the crisis management plan is the creation of a team of people charged with addressing crisis situations. The CMT should be a diverse group of people made up from components of the campus including, though not limited to, central administration, campus police, physical plant, faculty, health center, and counseling services. It is imperative that the CMT be able to work as a coordinated unit both in times of noncrisis planning and during crises and should have delineated responsibilities and authority (Zdziarski et al., 2007). Blyth (2001) asserts that it is the CMT's role to protect core assets—people, finances, and reputation—during crisis times. The CMT must also communicate with campus administration, faculty, students, and legal authorities during crisis times.

Who Should be on the CMT?

There is no exact "playbook" for determining team members, though clearly counseling services, campus police, faculty, administration, students, and perhaps campus clergy should be represented. The team should be large enough to represent various walks of the campus yet small enough so that it can act quickly without becoming mired in bureaucracy. The CMT should report to the institution's president. A suggestion for CMT members is given in the following

> Counseling services
> Campus police
> Campus medical center
> Faculty member (one or two)
> Campus clergy
> Administrator (dean of students or designee)
> Student (upperclassmen or graduate student)
> Community safety member (from police, emergency services, etc.)

Scope and Mission of the CMT

College campuses have various names and designs for their CMTs. After numerous campus tragedies, CMTs have developed a focus on threat assessment. Naturally, threat assessment is very difficult to discern with any degree of accuracy (FBI, 1999; Van Brunt, 2012). Regardless of the difficulty and inherent problems in violence prediction (e.g., identification, legal rights, poor reliability, and validity of rating instruments), some type of threat assessment likely is better than no assessment. Certainly this chapter is not a comprehensive statement regarding identifying, managing, and preventing campus tragedies. Additional resources are listed at the conclusion of this chapter.

The Mission of the CMT

Mission statements should be brief paragraphs that delineate the basic purpose and responsibilities of the CMT. Here is an example of Cornell University's Alert Team.

Cornell University Alert Team

Mission

The mission of Cornell University's Alert Team is to promote: (a) the health and safety of the campus community and (b) community member health, well-being, and successful experiences by coordinating information and developing support plans for people of concern.

Purpose

The purpose of the Alert Team is to serve as the coordinating hub of existing resources, focused on prevention and early intervention in community situations involving members experiencing distress or engaging in harmful or disruptive behaviors. The team will develop intervention and support strategies and offer case coordination. This team will regularly review and assess these situations and recommend actions in accord with university policies.

Responsibilities

- Receive, review, and catalog information about community concerns regarding member behavior.
- Perform initial assessment of risk and refer cases to officials as needed for additional assessment.
- Develop specific strategies to manage potentially harmful or disruptive behavior to protect the safety and rights of both the individual and the university community.
- Make recommendations to university officials on appropriate actions consistent with university policies and procedures.

- Engage in ongoing refinement of team procedures and protocols to foster optimal team functioning and interface with the university community.
- Identify university policy and procedural issues warranting further examination and refer such matters to appropriate entities including the Mental Health Policy Group. (Jed Foundation, n.d., p. 5; reprinted with permission)

Cornell University's Alert Team illustrates the general concept of a CMT mission, procedures, purposes, and responsibilities. A sample mission statement might look like the following.

Sample Mission Statement for CMTs

The CMT is committed to improving campus safety through a proactive, collaborative, coordinated, objective, thoughtful, and educational approach to the prevention, identification, assessment, intervention, and management of crisis situations that pose or may reasonable pose, a threat to the health, safety, and well-being of the campus community.

(Jed Foundation, n.d., p. 5; reprinted with permission)

Key considerations regarding CMTs' mission statements lie in ensuring the basic purposes for which the CMTs have been established. Though CMTs likely focus on students, faculty, staff, and visitors may also be impacted by campus trauma thus mission statements should be broad in scope though brief in nature.

Zdziarski et al. (2007) have set forth several criteria for CMTs as follows.

Skills and Competencies for CMTs

CMT members need particular skills and competencies.

1. Availability: Team members must be available to respond to a crisis in a timely manner. Some institutions designate alternates to the CMT as part of the training and planning process.
2. Knowledge of resources: Team members must understand the institutional supports available and how to tap into them. For example, a campus police officer may have contacts with the municipal police department, a nurse or physician may have connections with the local hospital, a campus counselor may have connections with the local mental health provider, and so forth.
3. Team player mind-set: CMT members will need to work on consensus in order to function before, during, and after a crisis. Team members must build strong relationships with each other.
4. Trainability: The CMT must dedicate quality time to orientation and ongoing training. The institution must recognize participation on the CMT as a vital part of campus safety and create rewards for serving on the CMT.

5. Diversity of communication skills: Good communication policy and practice will help accomplish the following goals:

> Assist in the actual management of a crisis
> Provide direction to faculty, staff, and students
> Reduce rumors and uncertainty
> Ensure that clear and accurate information is disseminated to interested constituencies and the public at large
> Maintain the institution's credibility and minimize damage to its reputation (Zdziarski et al., 2007, pp. 59–60).

6. Assessment skills: CMT members must be able to assess crisis situations and develop a strategic response. Team members representing different areas of expertise will have a diverse set of skills. This diverse approach can be critical in crafting a response to whatever crisis has occurred. After the imminent crisis has passed, assessment skills play a valuable role in addressing the aftermath of the crisis (i.e., mental health response, public relations, reassuring the campus and community and families of students) and in assessing the performance of the CMT.

7. Team leadership: Perhaps the most important part of the CMT lies in selecting the chair of the CMT. Likely, the institution's president or another high-ranking administrator will select the chair of the CMT. The CMT chair's relationship to the college's president is a key ingredient to the success of the committee (Zdziarski et al., 2007), particularly given that when a crisis occurs communication with the president can largely determine the success or failure of the CMT. In researching CMT-type committees, leadership often falls to the chief student affairs officer (Zdziarski et al., 2007). Other chairs could be faculty or professional staff with significant experience in critical incident trauma resolution teams. Some faculty or staff may have gained such experience in the military, police, or firefighter professions, and the medical or mental health field. Regardless of what profession the chair represents, she or he must be able to communicate effectively between the administration and the CMT committee, be calm and focused in the face of a crisis, and be facile at coordinating services during crisis periods.

Power (2001), suggests the CMT leader must balance three key demands in order to help the team operate effectively.

1. **Team needs:** What does the CMT need to function as a cohesive unit?
2. **Task needs:** What is the nature of the crisis?
3. **Individual team needs:** What does each team member require to perform at maximum effectiveness?

Power goes on to state, "I guess it's all about CMT Leadership, which, like swimming, cannot be learned just by reading about it. It is best done with good advice and actually trying it out—before you are thrown into the deep end."

Taking a cue from Power's aforementioned quote, CMT chairs need to drill their team on a regular basis in order to ensure team members know their roles and can function as a cohesive unit should a crisis occur. The reality is, of course, that no one can predict with any degree of accuracy when a crisis may happen. But given the dynamic nature of life, particularly on college campuses, the potential for crisis is always present. With risks such as suicide, shooting sprees, natural disasters (e.g., floods, hurricanes, earthquakes, tornados), terrorist threats, fires that kill numerous students, and so forth, CMT teams are a shrewd idea for any institution.

CMT Training

Proper training is critical for developing an effective, efficient, well-functioning CMT (Blyth, 2001). CMT training should consist of drilling for natural and terrorist crises and involve ongoing education for members of the CMT. As it is likely that members of the team will change due to retirement, people taking other jobs, new assignments, and so forth, continuous education will be a necessity. Training should involve mental health, law enforcement, and health care professionals among others.

CMT First Response

The following are examples of CMT functions during a crisis:

- The CMT will coordinate services with campus and community police and first responders.
- The CMT will set up a command center to better coordinate operations. The command center will operate on a 24/7 basis.
- The CMT will arrange communications with the college president and coordinate communications to the media, parents, and families.
- The CMT will arrange for relocation of students.
- After the immediate crisis is over, the CMT will arrange for counseling, debriefing, memorials, or other services deemed appropriate.
- The CMT chair will meet with the CMT to critique the CMT's performance during the crisis. (The institution's president may suggest an outside reviewer in some cases.)

Debriefing

Debriefing has been a common practice among the military and first responders. Although popular in many first responder trainings, there is no documented research to support the efficacy of critical incident stress debriefing (CISD; Bledsoe, 2002). In fact, some research indicates CISD may be harmful to participants (National Institute of Mental Health, 2002). The NIMH, in conjunction with the U.S. Department of Health and Human Services, Department of Defense, Department of Veterans Affairs, Department of Justice, and the American Red Cross, held a meeting to reach consensus on best practices in evidence-based early psychological intervention for survivors of mass trauma. In their report, based on a comprehensive review of the literature, the panel did not recommend CISD or critical incident stress management (CISM; NIMH, 2002). Given the questionable efficacy of debriefing, it is not recommended for professional practice.

CONCLUSION

This chapter has focused on campus crises. A crisis can be individual (student suicide) or collective (e.g., Virginia Tech shootings, Hurricane Katrina). The reality is that crises of varying sizes and impacts will occur on college campuses and campuses must be prepared to address them in a proactive manner by creating CMTs. CMTs will not be able to avoid a crisis or trauma, but its collective expertise and training provide a college the opportunity to better address a crisis when it does emerge.

A detailed campus crisis plan extends well beyond the available pages in this chapter and book. The recommendation here is for all college campuses to create CMTs and prepare them to address various and sundry possible crises. Naturally, no CMT, regardless of how experienced or skilled can anticipate all potential traumatic scenarios. But, a well-organized, prepared CMT team can help an institution function during and in the aftermath of a crisis. Perhaps one of the biggest lessons learned from tragedies as varied as Hurricane Katrina and the mass shooting deaths at Virginia Tech is that a well-prepared CMT can indeed help make a difference in effective response to a crisis. In both Katrina and Virginia Tech, crisis units were disorganized, had inefficient leadership initially, and were unable to effectively address the needs presented.

Because this is a text on college and university counseling the recommendation is to have at least one member of the counseling center staff be a regular member of the CMT. Given that emotional and psychological effects will be paramount in a major trauma, having a trained counselor on the crisis team is a critical necessity. A further recommendation is that all college counseling centers, from large universities to small colleges and community colleges, should identify at least one counseling center staff (or several given the size of the staff) to receive additional training in trauma response. The staff counselor (or counselors) should regularly update the director of the counseling center and the center staff. It is further recommended that the trained staff hold in-service training for the remainder of the counseling center staff. CMT members should also offer ongoing campus-wide training for faculty, staff, and students as a means of providing skill building and to ensure the campus has a well-trained team in place.

SOME CAMPUS CRISIS RESOURCES FOR COUNSELORS

Desinger, G., Randazzo, M., O'Neill, D., & Savage, J. (2008). *The handbook for campus threat assessment and management teams*. Boston, MA: Applied Risk Management.

Dunkle, J. (2010). *Dealing with the behavioral and psychological problems of students: A contemporary update: New directions for student services.* New York, NY: Wiley.

Jed Foundation. (n.d.). *Balancing safety and support on campus: A guide for campus teams.* New York, NY: Author.

Lake, P. F. (2011). *Foundations of higher education law and policy: Basic legal rules, concepts and principles for student affairs.* Washington, DC: National Association of Student Personnel Administrators.

Van Brunt, B. (2012). *Ending campus violence: New approaches to treatment.* New York, NY: Routledge.

Zdziarski, E. L., II, Dunkel, N. W., Rollo, J. M., & Associates. (2007). *Campus crisis management: A comprehensive guide to planning, prevention, response, and recovery.* San Francisco, CA: Jossey-Bass.

REFERENCES

American Association of Suicidology. (n.d.). *Suicidal behavior among lesbian, gay, bisexual, and transgender youth fact sheet.* Washington, DC: Author. Retrieved from www.suicidology.org/c/document_library/get_file?folderld=232&name=DLFE-334 .pdf

American College Health Association. (2008). Reference group executive survey, Fall 2008. In J. Burrell (Ed.), *College and teen suicides: The grim numbers behind suicides and attempts.* Retrieved from http://www.youngadults.about.com/od/ healthandsafety/qt/suicide.htm

American College Health Association. (2012). *National college health assessment: Fall 2012 reference group executive summary.* Hanover, MD: Author. Retrieved from www .acha-ncha.org/docs/acha-ncha-ii_referencegroup_executivesummary_fall2012.pdf

Bagley, C., & Tremblay, R. (2000). Elevated rates of suicidal behavior in gay, lesbian, and bisexual youth. *Crisis: The Journal of Crisis Intervention and Suicide Prevention,* 21(3), 111–117.

Barton, L. (1993). *Crisis in organizations: Managing and communicating in the heat of chaos.* Cincinnati, OH: South-Western Publishing.

Beck, A. E. (1976). *Cognitive therapy and emotional disorders.* New York, NY: International Universities Press.

Beck, A. T., Steer, R. A., & Brown, G. K. (2003). *Beck Depression Inventory-II manual.* San Antonio, TX: Psychological Corporation.

Beck, J. S. (2005). *Cognitive therapy: Basics and beyond.* New York, NY: Guilford Press.

Bledsoe, B. E. (2002). CISM: Possible liability for EMS services? *Best Practices in Emergency Services,* 5(6), 66–67.

Blyth, B. T. (2001, July). Creating your school's crisis management team. *School Business Affairs,* 67, 16–18.

Corey, G. (2009). *Theory and practice of counseling and psychotherapy* (8th ed.). Belmont, CA: Thompson-Brooks/Cole.

Corey, G. (2012). *Theory and practice of counseling and psychotherapy* (9th ed.). Boston, MA: Cengage.

Deathpenaltynews. (2011, September 2). *Executed for being gay*. Retrieved from http://www.deathpenaltynews.blogsport.com

deShazer, S. (1985). *Keys to solutions in brief therapy*. Boston, MA: W. W. Norton.

Federal Bureau of Investigation. (1999). *The school shooter: A threat assessment*. Quantico, VA: FBI.

Finks, S. (1986). *Crisis management: Planning for the inevitable*. New York, NY: American Management Association.

Frankl, V. E. (1978). *The unheard cry for meaning*. New York, NY: Simon & Schuster.

Gallagher, R. P. (2014). *National survey of college counseling centers*. Alexandria, VA: International Association of Counseling Services, Inc.

Glasser, W. H. (2001). *Counseling with choice theory: The new reality therapy*. New York, NY: Harper-Collins.

Granello, D. H., & Granello, P. F. (2007). *Suicide: An essential guide for helping professionals and educators*. Boston, MA: Allyn & Bacon.

Grayson, P. A., & Cooper, S. (2006). Depression and anxiety. In P. Grayson & P. A. Meilman (Eds.), *College mental health practice*. New York, NY: Routledge.

Isacsson, G., Holmgren, P., Druid, H., & Bergman, U. (1997). The utilization of antidepressants: A key issue in the prevention of suicide. An analysis of 5281 suicides in Sweden during the period 1992–1994. *Acta Psychiatrica Scandinavica, 96*, 94–100.

Jed Foundation. (n.d.). *Balancing safety and support on campus: A guide for campus teams*. New York, NY: Author.

Kernberg, O. F. (1976). *Objective-relations theory and clinical psychoanalysis*. New York, NY: Aronson.

Kitzrow, M. A. (2003). The mental health needs of today's college students: Challenges and recommendations. *NASPA Journal, 41*, 165–179.

Linehan, M. M. (1993). *Cognitive behavioral therapy of borderline personality disorder*. New York, NY: Guilford Press.

Mann, J. J., & Kapur, S. (1991). The emergence of suicidal ideation and behavior during antidepressant psychopharmacology. *Archives of General Psychiatry, 48*, 1027–1033.

Maris, R. W., Berman, A. L., & Silverman, M. M. (2000). *Comprehensive textbook of suicidology*. New York, NY: Guilford Press.

Minkoff, K., Bergman, E., Beck, A. T., & Beck, R. (2006). Hopelessness, depression, and attempted suicide. *American Journal of Psychiatry, 130*(4), 455–459.

Montgomery, S. A. (1997). Suicide and antidepressants. *Annals of the New York Academy of Sciences, 149*, 329–338.

Mozes, A. (2011, August 4). Many military vets in college plagued by thoughts of suicide. *U.S. News & World Report*. Retrieved from www.usnews.com/health

National Institute of Mental Health. (2002). *Mental health and mass violence: Evidence-based early psychological intervention for victims/survivors of mass violence.*

A workshop to reach consensus on best practices (NIH Publication No. 02-5138). Washington, DC: U.S. Government Printing Office.

National Institute of Mental Health. (2009). *Evidence-based prevention is goal of largest ever study of suicide in the military.* Press Release. Washington, DC: Author. Retrieved from http://www.nimh.nih.gov/news/science-news/2009/evidence-based -prevention-is-goal-of-largest-ever-study-of-suicide-in-the-military.shtml

Patterson, W. M., Dohn, H. H., Bird, J., & Patterson, G. A. (1983). Evaluation of suicidal patients. The SAD PERSONS scale. *Psychosomatics, 24*(4), 343–349.

Power, P. (2001). *Crisis management teams: Who needs them?* Retrieved from http:// www.experts.com/Articles/Crisis-Management-Teams-Who-Needs-Them-By -Peter-G-Power

Rogers, C. R. (1951). *Client-centered therapy.* Boston, MA: Houghton-Mifflin.

Seligman, M. E. P. (2011). *Learned optimism: How to change your mind and your life.* New York, NY: Vintage Books.

Shaffer, D., & Pfeffer, C. (2001). Practice parameter for the assessment and treatment of children and adolescents with suicidal behavior. *Journal of the American Academy of Child and Adolescent Psychiatry, 40*(Suppl.), 24S–51S.

Sharf, R. S. (2008). *Theories of psychotherapy and counseling: Concepts and cases* (4th ed.). Belmont, CA: Brooks/Cole.

Silverman, M. M. (2005a). Helping college students cope with suicidal impulses. In R. I. Yuft & D. Lester (Eds.), *Assessment, treatment, and prevention of suicidal behavior* (pp. 379–429). Hoboken, NJ: Wiley.

Silverman, M. M. (2005b). *The Big 10 Universities Suicide Study . . . and beyond.* SAMHSA suicide prevention grantee orientation meeting, December 13, 2005, Washington, DC. Retrieved from http://www.sprc.org/grantees/pdf/SP_Campus_ Silverman.pdf

Silverman, M. M. (2006). Suicide and suicidal behaviors. In P. A. Grayson & P. W. Meilman (Eds.), *College mental health practice.* New York, NY: Routledge.

Silverman, M. M., & Glick, R. L. (2010). Crisis and crisis intervention on college campuses. In J. Kay & V. Schwartz (Eds.), *Mental health care in the college community* (pp. 157–178). West Sussex, UK: Wiley-Blackwell.

Thompson, R. A., & Sherman, R. T. (2005). *Managing student-athletes' mental health issues.* Bloomington Center for Counseling and Human Development. Retrieved from http://www.princeton.edu

Van Brunt, B. (2012). *Ending campus violence: New approaches to treatment.* New York, NY: Routledge.

Yalom, I. D. (1980). *Existential psychotherapy.* New York, NY: Basic Books.

Zdziarski, E. L., II, Dunkel, N. W., Rollo, J. M., & Associates. (2007). *Campus crisis management: A comprehensive guide to planning, prevention, response, and recovery.* San Francisco, CA: Jossey-Bass.

CHAPTER ELEVEN

SEXUAL ASSAULT AND HARASSMENT

Kimber Shelton

SEXUAL VIOLENCE ON THE COLLEGE CAMPUS

Joanna, a sophomore, is a star volleyball player at a small liberal arts college. She selected her college for its high political science ranking as she aspires to enter law school after college. After a weekend tournament, Joanna and several of her volleyball teammates decide to attend a party thrown by other athletes. That night Joanna is sexually assaulted by a male on the football team. In the following weeks, her coach notices a decline in her athletic performance and that she appears withdrawn. Her coach suggests she visit the counseling center. Joanna tells her therapist about the assault and expresses her concern because she does not want to get the male in trouble and fears being ostracized by other athletes.

Winten is a 26-year-old graduate student. During his intake session he reports feeling hypervigilant, having difficulty connecting with others, particularly males, trouble asserting himself, easily irritated, and has frequent sexual performance issues, which have not gone unnoticed by his partner. He discloses that at age 18, he was sexually assaulted by his roommate's cousin. He denies ever sharing these details with anyone before today.

Nydia has been working with her therapist for 2 months and has improved her self-esteem, decreased symptoms of depression, and improved her relationships. In passing, she describes her annoyance with her male lab partner who sits too close, somehow finds ways to inappropriately brush up against her, "always" makes comments about her shape, and routinely asks her out on dates. She comments that he is really smart and that they have gotten As on all their assignments so far. She then goes on to describe a weekend trip with her parents.

The Centers for Disease Control and Prevention (CDC, 2014) defines sexual violence as "any sexual act that is perpetrated against someone's will." This definition encompasses completed and attempted sexual acts and abusive sexual contact and noncontact sexual abuse. This broad definition of sexual violence is inclusive of sexual assault and rape, stalking, and sexual harassment. Campuses face an ongoing struggle in preventing sexual violence, creating policies for responding to incidents of sexual violence, providing services for survivors of sexual violence, and creating a culture of nonviolence in which sexual violence is not tolerated. This chapter outlines sexual violence on college campuses as well as implication for counseling centers.

Sexual Assault and Rape

The terms *sexual assault* and *rape* are often used interchangeably when describing a range of nonconsensual sexual acts, and are used interchangeably throughout this chapter. Sexual assault is considered to be any type of nonconsensual sexual activity including inappropriate touching; vaginal, anal, or oral penetration; and attempted rape. Sexual assaults occur by verbal, visual, or any other means that forces a person to join in unwanted or nonconsensual sexual contact or attention (Office of Women's Health, 2012). Nonconsensual sex acts occur when the victim is unable to grant consent (e.g., age, intellectual disability, incapacitation due to drug or alcohol use or being asleep), or is compelled to engage in the sex act through coercion, intimidation, threats, or physical force (Attorney General's Sexual Assault Task Force, 2006; Krebs, Lindquist, Warner, Martin, & Fisher, 2007). Rape is typically reserved for nonconsensual sexual acts that involve penetration (Bureau of Justice Statistics, 2016; Koss, 1992).

One in five women and one in 71 men will experience a sexual assault in their lifetime (Black et al., 2011). In comparison to their same-aged female peers, college females are at an increased risk of experiencing a sexual assault (DeKeseredy & Schwartz, 1998; Koss, Dinero, Seibel, & Cox, 1988). The National College Women Sexual Victimization (NCWSV; Fisher, Cullen, & Turner, 2000) found that 20% to 25% of college women experience a sexual assault. Rates of sexual assault for men also tend to be higher for the college population. Approximately 15% of men are victims of sexual assault while in college (Fisher et al., 2000), in comparison to the estimates of 3% to 10% of adult men in the general population who experience rape (Black et al., 2011; Kassing & Prieto, 2003; Pino & Meier, 1999). Although research is relatively sparse in this area, findings in one study showed that gay and bisexual male college students were more susceptible to sexual assault than their heterosexual counterparts (Hines, Armstrong, Palm Reed, & Cameron, 2012).

Risk Factors

Use of alcohol is directly related to the majority of sexual assaults on college campuses, with both the victim of sexual assault and perpetrator of sexual assault being under the influence of alcohol. The 2007 Campus Sexual Assault Study (Krebs et al., 2007) found that 89% of female victims reported drinking alcohol and 82% reported being drunk before their victimization. In the same study, male perpetrators of sexual assault reported that 86% of victims were drinking before the incident and 81% of perpetrators were drinking prior to the incident. Alcohol is also involved in the sexual assault experiences of men.

Approximately 70% of college men were drinking and/or using drugs at the time that they experienced forced sexual touching, and 86% of college men were drinking when they experienced sexual assault/rape (Reed, Amaro, Matsumoto, & Kaysen, 2009). Unfortunately, education and awareness regarding alcohol use and sexual assault brought little change to sexual assault statistics in the past two decades. In a college population sample over 20 years ago, Koss et al. (1988) found that 74% of rape perpetrators and 55% of rape victims had been drinking alcohol.

Students with less college experience are also more susceptible to sexual assault. In comparison to juniors and seniors, the rates of sexual assault are higher for freshman and sophomore college students (Krebs et al., 2007). Other risk factors for sexual assault include use of substances other than alcohol (e.g., marijuana), prior sexual victimization, lifestyle activities (e.g., attending fraternity parties, number of sexual partners), being unknowingly drugged, and prior or current intimate partner violence (Krebs et al., 2007).

Reporting Sexual Assault

Sexual assault is the most common crime on college campuses, yet it continues to have serious rates of underreporting. An alarming 90% to 95% of women who experience a sexual assault on campus never report the incident to law enforcement and the reporting rates are estimated to be even less for male victims (Fisher et al., 2000). A host of reasons are responsible for the failure to report incidents of sexual assault. Women victims list shame, guilt, embarrassment, not wanting friends and family to know, concerns about confidentiality, and fear of not being believed as reasons for not reporting (Sable, Danis, Mauzy, & Gallagher, 2006). Female victims must also contend with rape myths before moving forward (e.g., it is the woman's fault). Not only are these same barriers even more intense for male victims (Sable et al., 2006), men face additional barriers that discourage reporting. Men are prevented from coming forward after a sexual assault due to a perceived fear of being judged as gay (Sable et al., 2006) and must also contend with myths related to masculinity that disallow men from being victims of rape and celebrate male sexual conquest (e.g., men should want to have sex, men cannot be physically overpowered by female sex partners).

As well as emotional barriers, stigma, and myths preventing men and women from reporting sexual assault, perception (and possibly the normalization) of sexual violence limit the reporting of sexual assault. Survivors fail to report rape because they do not consider the acts of sexual assault against them to be rape or do not believe the incident is significant enough to warrant reporting. In one study, approximately half of the women who reported criteria that met the legal definition of rape did not consider the incident to be rape (Fisher et al., 2000). In another study, 56% of women who were forcibly sexually assaulted and 67% of women who were incapacitated (by drugs or alcohol) sexual assault victims failed to report because they did not consider the situation serious enough to report (Krebs et al., 2007). The relationship between the perpetrator and victim also discourages reporting. Nine out of 10 sexual assault victims will know their perpetrator (e.g., boyfriend, ex-boyfriend, classmate, friend, acquaintance, or coworker) and their assault will occur while on a date or at a party (Fisher et al., 2000; Krebs et al., 2007). Having continued contact with the perpetrator, dependence on the perpetrator, and fear of retaliation stand in the way of making a sexual assault report. Some sexual assault victims will not report the sexual assault because they are unaware of treatment options or the importance of treatment, have distrust in the legal system or have cultural and language barriers that make it difficult to seek help (Sable et al., 2006). For example, international students who experience a sexual assault may be unfamiliar with laws and on- and off-campus resources to successfully obtain assistance after an assault. Many of the aforementioned barriers are present in the case of Joanna. She has not reported her sexual assault as she continues to interact with the perpetrator and those who know the perpetrator, fears being alienated by other athletes, has taken some responsibility for the incident (not wanting to get the male in trouble) and, prior to her coach's suggestion, Joanna may have been unaware that services were available to her.

Stalking

Stalking is "a course of conduct directed at a specific person that would cause a reasonable person to feel fear" (Stalking Resource Center, 2012). These behaviors include making unwanted phone calls, sending unsolicited or unwanted letters or e-mails, following or spying on the victim, showing up at places without a legitimate reason, waiting at places for the victim, and leaving unwanted items or presents, posting information, or spreading rumors about the victim on the Internet or by word of mouth (Baum, Catalano, Rand, & Rose, 2009; Stalking Resource Center, 2012). According to the National Violence Against Women (NVAW) Survey (Tjaden & Thoennes, 2000), more than 1 million women and almost 400,000 men had been stalked each year. Rates of stalking are high within college campuses, with approximately 21% of male and female college students reporting being stalked (13%–52.4% of female students and 11%–23.2% of male students) (Buhi, Clayton, & Surrency, 2008; Fisher et al., 2000; McNamara & Marsil, 2012). Stalking behaviors are typically perpetrated by someone the victim knows, most likely a former dating partner (intimate partner stalking) (Haugaard & Seri, 2004; Modandie, Reid Meloy, McGowan, & Williams, 2006).

Similar to experiences of sexual assault, those who experience stalking do not always consider stalking behaviors to be stalking. In one study, 42.5% of participants met the behavioral criteria for experiencing stalking (e.g., unwanted calls/hang-ups, unwanted messages, unwanted gifts/e-mails, and perpetrator waited, drove by, followed, showed up); however, only 12% expressed the belief that they had been a victim of stalking (McNamara & Marsil, 2012). Victims of stalking and campus administration are mistaken to underestimate the seriousness of stalking. Stalkers can threaten, attack, sexually assault, or kill victims, making it imperative to appropriately assess and intervene with any stalking occurring on- and off-campus (Stalking Resources Center, 2008).

Sexual Harassment

Sexual harassment, a form of sex discrimination, is comprised of a host of unlawful actions that harass a person based on his or her sex (U.S. Equal Employment Opportunity Commission, n.d.). This can include unwelcome sexual advances, requests for sexual favors, and other verbal or physical harassment of a sexual nature. As with other forms of sexual violence, sexual harassment has a strong prevalence on college campuses. Approximately two thirds of college students experience some form of sexual harassment (Hill & Silva, 2005). Also similar with other forms of sexual violence is the consistent underreporting of sexual harassment on college campuses. When sexual harassment occurs on the college campus, less than 10% of victims report the offense to campus officials (Hill & Silva, 2005) and are unlikely to label these acts as sexual harassment (Magley & Shupe, 2005).

College students can experience sexual harassment from peers, coworkers, faculty, and staff. Considering that college students are around their peers more than other university constitutents, they are more likely to experience sexual harassment from peers; however, students are less likely to endorse their peers' acts as sexual harassment and are more likely to label acts by those with greater power (e.g., faculty, staff, university administration) as sexual harassment (Bursik & Gefter, 2011). Take Nydia for example. The behaviors of her lab partner demonstrated unwanted sexual attention, unwelcome advances, inappropriate touching, and an invasion of her physical space, yet she does not identify such behaviors as sexual harassment. She only shares such information as a mundane report on recent experiences since her last therapy session. Yet, if such behaviors were demonstrated by a graduate assistant or professor, she might share such information with a greater cause for concern, which fails to recognize the actions of her peer as sexual harassment.

Reports of sexual harassment are greater for women; however, there is more information available regarding the sexual harassment experiences of male college students. In a recent study exploring sexual harassment of Mexican American and Caucasian American college students, researchers found that the majority of Mexican American (73.7%) and Caucasian (84.4%) college men reported experiencing at least one harassing behavior (Kearney & Rochlen, 2012). Similar to their female counterparts, the majority of harassment came from males (52.7%) and men were unlikely to label such acts as sexual harassment (Kearney & Rochlen, 2012).

IMPLICATIONS FOR COLLEGE COUNSELING CENTERS

Physical and Mental Health Issues

Sexual violence takes a toll on the physical and mental well-being of survivors. Physical costs of sexual assault include possible contraction of a sexually transmitted infection (STI) (approximately 40% of rape survivors receive a sexually transmitted disease [STD]; Holmes, Resnick, Kirkpatrick, & Best, 1996), unplanned pregnancy, and physical trauma to genital and nongenital areas (Holmes et al., 1996). As stalking progresses, the threat of violence toward the individual being stalked advances. Victims of stalking can suffer from physical injuries caused by their attacker and potential death (Stalking Resources, 2012).

In addition to coping with physiological trauma, sexual violence survivors can experience immediate and chronic psychological and emotional consequences. It is estimated that 49% of rape survivors and 24% of other sexual assault survivors develop posttraumatic stress disorder (PTSD) (Sidran Foundation, 2009). Other common reactions to sexual assault include feeling anxiety, confusion, fear, anger, grief, panic, concentration difficulty, guilt and self-blame, withdrawing, relationship disruptions, preoccupation with the crime, and an increased risk of substance use. Additionally, sexual violence survivors are at a greater risk for developing suicidality. Rape victims have been found to be 13 times more likely to attempt suicide than individuals who have not been victimized (National Center for PTSD, 2008).

Male and female victims of stalking feel vulnerable and fearful of what their stalker may do, may feel helpless and believe that their freedom is restricted, or may feel humiliated and ashamed by their actions or the actions of their stalker (Abrams & Robinson, 2008). They are more likely to experience depression, impaired health, and injury, and engage in substance abuse than their peers who have not been stalked (Davis, Coker, & Sanderson, 2002). Sexual harassment victims may feel unsafe in their workplace, labs, dorms, and classrooms and have a general sense that the campus environment is intimidating, hostile, or offensive. Victims of sexual violence share the experience of intrusive memories and nightmares, appetite and sleep disturbances, anxiety, and hypervigilance. Considering the physical and psychological impact of sexual assault, academic and functioning impairment can occur. Students may be distracted from their work due to flashbacks and hypervigilance, could be fatigued throughout the day caused by appetite changes and disrupted sleep, and may miss class time or deadlines as a result of treatment and judicial responsibilities.

Treatment

Unwanted sexual attention and sexual assault are among the top traumas college students report experiencing (Frazier et al., 2009), making it highly likely that college counseling centers will see students who report experiencing such traumas. Treatment of trauma begins with regular assessment of trauma. Although a high number of students experience behaviors consistent with sexual violence, most students do not acknowledge such experiences as sexual violence. Centers cannot rely solely on clients' admission to experiences of sexual violence and instead should routinely assess for experiences of trauma with all clients (i.e., asking trauma-related questions on initial paperwork and during intake appointments).

According to the National Survey of Counseling Center Directors (Mistler, Reetz, Krylowicz, & Barr, 2012), approximately 11% of students seek treatment for the presenting concerns of sexual/physical assault/acquaintance rape and stalking. However, considering the significant underreporting of sexual violence, students who have a history of sexual violence may likely present to treatment with other identified mental health concerns. There is no single best treatment for trauma and a diverse number of counseling theories and methods are available to assist trauma survivors. Cognitive behavioral therapy, including techniques such as cognitive restructuring, exposure therapy, and eye movement desensitization and reprocessing (EMDR), are among the most frequently cited models (Hamblen, 2008). A number of treatment approaches operate via a three-stage model for treating individuals who have experienced trauma. Early stages of trauma focus on establishing safety and stabilization prior to exploring the traumatic experience, and end with building the client's ability to maintain improved health and functioning (see Courtois & Ford, 2009; Herman, 1997). The gradual progression into trauma exploration is based on the premise of establishing an environment that empowers exploration and reestablishes a client's sense of control, whereas moving too quickly into trauma exploration may serve to retraumatize individuals who do not have adequate coping skills for processing the trauma. Depending on the severity of the trauma and the client's level of readiness, trauma work with clients may extend beyond session limits set by counseling centers. As such, work done within the center may focus on immediate and early interventions that are crisis oriented, such as improving coping and functioning, reducing emotional distress, reducing the development of significant symptoms, educating about effects of trauma, and building a support system (Kress, Trippany, & Nolan, 2003).

A staged model approach would be appropriate for Winten. Prior to processing his previous sexual assault, Winten and his therapist would work to establish a strong working alliance, build Winten's coping skills so that he is better prepared to handle any emotional reactions he may have from exploring trauma, educate Winten on the psychological, emotional, and physical consequences of sexual trauma to help normalize any reactions he may have, and build his support system. His therapist would provide Winten with general psychoeducation on trauma work, which would explain that trauma work may be lengthy and that Winten should not get discouraged if he feels his progress is moving too slowly. Psychoeducation can also help to build trust and safety for Winten as he would be aware of the work his trauma therapy would entail upfront. His therapist would attend to gender and cultural issues related to trauma by focusing on examining and dispelling myths regarding men, masculinity, and trauma. Depending on Winten's readiness for change, it could take as few as three sessions to 10 or more sessions just to engage in the beginning phase of trauma exploration.

With their high comorbidity, therapy models have also been constructed to address issues related to substance use and sexual trauma. One such model developed by a National Institute on Drug Abuse (NIDA) grant, Seeking Safety, is a 12-week manualized program that is adaptable to a variety of clinical settings and populations (Najavits, 2002). Seeking Safety is adaptable to different clinical settings and populations and is appropriate for both individual and group formats that respond to the trauma and substance abuse needs of women who have these needs. Seeking Safety is based on five central ideas: (a) safety as the priority; (b) integrated treatment of PTSD and substance abuse disorder; (c) a focus on ideals; (d) four content areas: cognitive, behavioral, interpersonal, and case management; and (e) attention to therapist processes.

Counseling centers may also provide specific groups for survivors of sexual violence. There are advantages to treating sexual violence trauma in specific groups rather than in general interpersonal process groups. For one, as with individual counseling, group exploration of trauma also requires clients to build safety and coping skills prior to trauma exploration. Within a general interpersonal process group, trauma survivors may feel pressured to share experiences about their trauma before they are ready and other group members may unknowingly express the expectation for greater sharing before safety is established. Second, experiences expressed in group may trigger a traumatic reaction in the sexual violence survivor. Such a trigger response can inadvertently disrupt the group experience or place unwanted focus on the sexual violence survivor. For example, hearing another group member's experience of getting drunk and engaging in sex at a party may cause another group member to remember her experience of being assaulted. The sexual assault survivor begins crying and leaves the room. The group is disrupted as the group leader leaves the room to check on the individual, the member who shared the experience may feel regret or confusion for sharing, and upon returning, the sexual assault survivor may feel compelled to share the experience to explain the reaction. Addressing sexual violence in a specific group can help normalize emotional experiences and triggers, can provide a feeling of increased safety and understanding, and provide the opportunity of increased attention on trauma-specific work. Trauma and sexual assault groups have many different names within the university counseling center community: Sexual Assault Support Group (Towson University Counseling Center), Survivors of Sexual Assault (Indiana University Counseling and Psychological Service), Journey to Healing Group (Florida State University Counseling Center), and Voices of Recovery: Healing From Sexual Abuse and Sexual Assault (Texas Woman's College Counseling Center).

Approximately 30% of female stalking victims and 20% of male stalking victims seek counseling (Tjaden & Thoennes, 1998). According to Abrams and Robinson (2008), goals for treating stalking victims include: (a) alleviating the emotional and physical symptoms of depression, anxiety, and PTSD; (b) rebuilding confidence and trust in others; (c) improving safety; and (d) discouraging the stalking behaviors if at all possible. Counseling goals for individuals who have experienced sexual harassment are educating such clients on sexual harassment and the possible effects of sexual harassment, addressing any emotional and psychological concerns caused by the sexual harassment, empowering clients with education and tools for addressing sexual harassment and supporting clients' decisions regarding addressing the sexual harassment.

Advocacy

Counseling centers can advocate for victims of sexual violence on and off the college campus. On campus, advocacy efforts by counseling centers can include establishing protocols for addressing safety on campus and the campus's response to sexual violence. In the best case, sexual violence survivors are able to come forward regarding their victimization and obtain resources; however, due to frequent underreporting and barriers to reporting, campuses should have a means for confidential and anonymous reporting. Confidential reporting can allow campuses to have a more accurate picture of sexual violence on their campuses, and thus can more systematically focus resources and attention. Confidential reporting varies from university to university, however, and may include demographic information about the victim and assailant (sex, academic standing), the victim's relationship to the assailant, information on where the offense occurred (on-campus or off-campus), type of incident (e.g., sexual assault, attempted rape), and substance use. Confidential means for reporting include Oregon's Guidelines for Comprehensive Sexual Assault Response and Prevention on Campus (Attorney General's Sexual Assault Task Force, 2006), which defines sexual assault and provides number of guidelines for responding to and preventing campus sexual assault. The guidelines are inclusive of medical and counseling response. Guidelines specific to college counseling centers are presented in the appendix to this chapter.

Counseling centers can also work with survivors to enhance their ability to advocate for themselves. Such efforts include educating and supporting clients in obtaining protective and restraining orders, seeking legal recourse, and encouraging individual students and student groups to speak up regarding sexual violence on their campus.

Outreach and Consultation

Sexual violence outreach efforts have been targeted at perpetrators and victims and all genders. Counseling centers can participate in outreach initiatives that increase the campus's awareness of sexual violence, prevention (risk reduction for both potential victims and perpetrators), dismantle myths that perpetuate a culture of violence, and encourage victims of sexual violence to seek treatment. Prevention programming provided by the counseling center can ensure that sensitivity for sexual assault survivors is included in all outreach programming, education of the public on the victims' experience of sexual assault and the aftereffects of trauma, and can serve to increase a feeling of safety that encourages victims to seek assistance (Lee, Caruso, Goins, & Southerland, 2003).

A shocking 42% of college female rape survivors never report the incident to anyone (Koss, Gidycz, & Wisniewski, 1987; Krebs et al., 2007). Student victims of sexual assault who do share their experience of assault are more likely to report the assault to a friend than they are to a family member, and are even less likely to report the incident to a mental health professional or law enforcement agency (Fisher et al., 2000). This makes it extremely important for counseling centers to participate in outreach efforts targeted at identifying and assisting peers who are victims of sexual assault. Outreach targeted at peers can focus on dispelling myths regarding sexual assault (e.g., men cannot be victimized), discourage victim blaming (e.g., avoiding asking questions such as, "Why did you go there?" or "Why did you get so drunk?"), encourage support, and provide referral resources.

As well as developing programs, counseling center staff can have a presence at campus programs offered by other organizations. General outreach programs related to substance use, relationships, and assertiveness can also serve as a means of raising sexual violence awareness. There are also numerous national sexual violence programs in which the counseling center can participate: Take Back the Night programs, Sexual Assault Awareness Month (SAAM, April), National Day to End Sexual Violence (April), and National Stalking Awareness Month (January). The National Sexual Violence Resource Center (2013) provides a number of outreach initiatives that counseling centers can sponsor or participate in through other campus organizations, such as setting up an awareness booth, sponsoring a movie screening, hosting an open house, and participating in a march.

Finally, providing adequate services to victims of sexual violence means having strong consultative relationships with a number of other university and local organizations that include:

- *Dean of Students Office.* Counseling center staff may be asked to consult with or seek out consultation with the Dean of Students office. Clients who are victims of sexual assault can experience a number of academic and judiciary issues. Counseling centers can advocate for victims to obtain academic dispositions related to the sexual assault, which may include excusing missed classes, receiving time to make up missed assignments or exams, withdrawing from a course, or withdrawing from the institution. Navigating through academic judiciary issues can be a challenging and exhausting process for students. The counseling center can serve as a support, and advocate for students as they move through campus due process.
- *Victim Support Resources, Women's Resource Center, and Sexual Assault Awareness Teams.* For campuses with victim support, resources are a valuable support to center staff. Center staff may not have specific training or education regarding completing a rape examination, criminal charges, prosecuting perpetrators, or specific university resources (e.g., temporary housing or emergency loans). Additionally, depending on the therapeutic working relationship and needs of the client, clients may want to separate legal/judicial issues from counseling and may not want to disclose to others that they are obtaining mental health services. Campus victim support can help students traverse legal and judicial issues without compromising confidentiality when working with center clinicians.
- *Campus Police.* Although reporting rates are low, campus (or local) police may be contacted after a sexual assault has occurred. As first responders

to victims of sexual violence, campus police are charged with having knowledge of the law, procedures, and resources regarding sexual violence. Consultation and training provided by the counseling center can aid police in developing a rapport and responding empathically to the immediate emotional needs of sexual violence victims. Depending on the counseling center's crisis and emergency policies, police departments may contact the counseling center for consultation or to speak directly with the victim of sexual assault. The police department and counseling center can work together to develop protocols and guidelines that encourage increased collaboration.

- *Student Organizations.* Student organizations, including Greek life, athletics, men's and women's specific groups, and social and academic clubs, may seek consultation from the counseling center. Consultation can range from general questions regarding sexual assault, requests for presentations, specific questions regarding supporting a peer who was victimized, to providing crisis incident services.

- *Campus Administration.* Counseling center clinicians can play an important role in policy development regarding sexual violence on campus. The counseling center should be sought out for (or can seek out) placement on sexual violence committees. Centers can also advocate establishing policies, programs, and resources for campuses that do not yet have such supports in place.

- *Campus Health Center.* The campus health center and counseling center can be a referral source for one another in terms of sexual assault victims. Counseling centers can encourage clients to obtain STI screenings, emergency contraception, and reproductive health needs from the health center. In turn, health centers can encourage students to seek counseling to process the emotional ramifications resulting from sexual assault.

- *Local Community Groups.* Some students may prefer to receive services off-campus. They may not want to be reminded or triggered while on campus, may desire services from organizations addressing issues specific to their cultural background, or may require services that are not available on campus. Building strong working relationships with community groups such as hospitals, therapists, shelters, and advocacy groups allows for a smoother referral process and more immediate access to care. Additionally, all counseling centers should be equipped with contact information for rape and crisis hotlines, and crime victims' assistance programs.

REFERENCES

Abrams, K. M., & Robinson, G. E. (2008). Comprehensive treatment of stalking victims: Practical steps that help ensure safety. *Psychiatric Times*, 43–51.

Attorney General's Sexual Assault Task Force. (2006). *Campus response committee general guidelines for comprehensive sexual assault response and prevention on campus: Version I.* Retrieved from http://r.search.yahoo.com/_ylt=A0LEViZGPYFXV0kAdAAnnIlQ:_ylu=X3oDMTEyM2ZqY3NsBGNvbG8DYmYxBHBvcwMxBHZ0aWQDQjlwOTBfMQ

RzZWMDc3I-/RV=2/RE=1468116423/RO=10/RU=http%3a%2f%2foregonsatf
.org%2fwp-content%2fuploads%2f2011%2f02%2fCampus-Guidelines-for-Sexual-
Assault-Response-Prev_Lina-.pdf/RK=0/RS=T0W2zyZ.jvjO0vGWfuOP9BlJm88-

Baum, K., Catalano, S., Rand, M., & Rose, K. (2009). *Stalking victimization in the United States: National Crime Victimization Survey.* Washington, DC: The Bureau of Justice Statistics, NCJ 224527.

Black, M. C., Basile, K. C., Breiding, M. J., Smith, S. G., Walters, M. L., Merrick, M. T., & Stevens, M. R. (2011). *The National Intimate Partner and Sexual Violence Survey (NISVS): 2010 summary report.* Retrieved from http://www.cdc.gov/ViolencePrevention/pdf/NISVS_Report2010-a.pdf

Buhi, E. R., Clayton, H., & Surrency, H. H. (2008). Stalking victimization among college women and subsequent help-seeking behaviors. *Journal of American College Health, 57,* 419–425.

Bureau of Justice Statistics. (2016). *Rape and sexual assault.* Retrieved from http://www.bjs.gov/index.cfm?ty=tp&tid=317

Bursik, K., & Gefter, J. (2011). Still stable after all these years: Perceptions of sexual harassment in academic contexts. *Journal of Social Psychology, 151*(3), 331–349.

Centers for Disease Control and Prevention. (2014). *Sexual violence definitions.* Retrieved from http://www.cdc.gov/violenceprevention/sexualviolence/definitions.html

Courtois, C. A., & Ford, J. D. (2009). *Treating complex traumatic stress disorders: An evidence-based guide.* New York, NY: Guilford Press.

Davis, K. E., Coker, A. L., & Sanderson, M. (2002). Physical and mental health effects of being stalked for men and women. *Violence and Victims, 17,* 429–443.

DeKeseredy, W. S., & Schwartz, M. D. (1998). *Woman abuse on campus: Results from the Canadian national survey.* Thousand Oaks, CA: Sage.

Fisher, B. S., Cullen F. T., & Turner M. G. (2000). *The sexual victimization of college women.* NCJRS Publication No. 182369. Washington, DC: National Criminal Justice Reference Service, U.S. Department of Justice. Retrieved from https://www.ncjrs.gov/pdffiles1/nij/182369.pdf

Frazier, P., Anders, S., Perera, S., Tomich, P., Tennen, H., Park, C., & Tashiro, T. (2009). Traumatic events among undergraduate students: Prevalence and associated symptoms. *Journal of Counseling Psychology, 56*(3), 450–460.

Hamblen, J. (2008). *"What is PTSD?"* National Center for PTSD. U.S. Department of Veterans Affairs. Retrieved from http://www.ncptsd.va.gov/ncmain/ncdocs/handouts/handout_What%20is%20PTSD.pdf

Haugaard, J. J., & Seri, L. G. (2004). Stalking and other forms of intrusive contact after the dissolution of intimate or romantic relationships. *Violence and Victims, 18*(3), 279–297.

Herman, J. (1997). *Trauma and recovery: The aftermath of violence: From domestic abuse to political terror.* New York, NY: Basic Books.

Hill, C., & Silva, E. (2005). *Drawing the line: Sexual harassment on campus.* Retrieved from http://www.aauw.org/learn/research/upload/DTLFinal.pdf

Hines, D., Armstrong, J. L., Reed K. P., & Cameron, A. (2012). Gender differences in sexual assault victimization among college students. *Violence and Victims, 27,* 922–940.

Holmes, M., Resnick, H. A., Kirkpatrick, D. G., & Best, C. L. (1996). Rape-related pregnancy: Estimates and descriptive characteristics from a national sample of women. *American Journal of Obstetrics and Gynecology, 175*(2), 320–325.

Kassing, I. R., & Prieto, L. R. (2003). The rape myth and blame-based beliefs of counselors-in-training toward male victims of rape. *Journal of Counseling and Development, 81,* 453–461.

Kearney, L. K., & Rochlen, A. B. (2012). Mexican-American and Caucasian university men's experience of sexual harassment: A preliminary report. *Psychology of Men & Masculinity, 13*(3), 264–269.

Kress, V. E. W., Trippany, R. L., & Nolan, J. M. (2003). Responding to sexual assault victims: Considerations for college counselors. *Journal of College Counseling, 6,* 124–133.

Koss, M. P. (1992). Rape on campus: Facts and measures. *Planning for Higher Education, 20*(3), 21–28.

Koss, M. P., Dinero, T. E., Seibel, C., & Cox, S. (1988). Stranger, acquaintance, and date rape: Are there differences in the victim's experience? *Psychology of Women Quarterly, 12,* 1–24.

Koss, M. P., Gidycz, C. A., & Wisniewski, N. (1987). The scope of rape: Incidence and prevalence of sexual aggression and victimization in a national sample of higher education students. *Journal of Consulting and Clinical Psychology, 55*(2), 162–170.

Krebs, C. P., Lindquist, C., Warner, T., Martin, S., & Fisher, B. (2007). *The Campus Sexual Assault (CSA) study. Performance period: January 2005 through December 2007.* Washington, DC: National Institute of Justice. Retrieved from https://www.ncjrs.gov/pdffiles1/nij/grants/221153.pdf

Lee, R. W., Caruso, M. E., Goins, S. E., & Southerland, J. P. (2003). Addressing sexual assault on college campuses: Guidelines for a prevention/awareness week. *Journal of College Counseling, 6,* 14–23.

Magley, V. J., & Shupe, E. I. (2005). Self-labeling sexual harassment. *Sex Roles, 53,* 173–189.

McNamara, C. L., & Marsil, D. F. (2012). The prevalence of stalking among college students: The disparity between researcher and self-identified victimization. *Journal of American College Health, 60*(2), 168–174.

Mistler, B. J., Reetz, D. R., Krylowicz, B., & Barr, V. (2012). *The Association for University and College Counseling Center Directors annual survey reporting period: September 1, 2011 through August 31, 2012.* Retrieved from http://www.aucccd.org/support/Monograph_2012_AUCCCD%20Public.pdf

Modandie, K., Meloy, J. R., McGowan, M. G., & Williams, J. (2006). The RECON typology of stalking: Reliability and validity based upon a large sample of North American stalkers. *Journal of Forensic Sciences, 51,* 152.

Najavits, L. M. (2002). Seeking Safety: A new psychotherapy for posttraumatic stress disorder and substance abuse. In P. Ouimette & P. Brown (Eds.), *Trauma and substance abuse: Causes, consequences, and treatment of comorbid disorders.* Washington, DC: American Psychological Association.

National Center for PTSD. (2008). *Sexual assault against females.* Washington, DC: U.S. Department of Veterans Affairs. Retrieved from http://www.ptsd.va.gov/public/PTSD-overview/women/sexual-assault-females.asp

National Sexual Violence Resource Center. (2013). *Sexual Assault Awareness Month.* Retrieved from http://www.nsvrc.org

Office of Women's Health. (2012). *Sexual assault fact sheet.* Retrieved from http://www.womenshealth.gov

Pino, N. W., Meier, R. K. (1999). Gender differences in rape reporting. *Sex Roles, 40,* 979–990.

Reed, E., Amaro, H., Matsumoto, A., & Kaysen, D. (2009). The relation between interpersonal violence and substance use among a sample of university students: Examination of the role of victim and perpetrator substance use. *Addictive Behaviors, 34,* 316–318.

Sable, M. R., Danis, F., Mauzy, D. L., & Gallagher, S. K. (2006). Barriers to reporting sexual assault for women and men: Perspectives of college students. *Journal of American College Health, 55*(3), 157–162.

Sidran Foundation. (2009). *Posttraumatic stress disorder fact sheet.* Towson, MD: Sidran Foundation. Retrieved from www.tema.ca/lib/PTSD%20Fact%20Sheet.pdf

Stalking Resources Center. (2008). *Violence against women.* Retrieved from www.ovw.usdoj.gov

Stalking Resources Center. (2012). *Stalking information.* Retrieved from www.ovw.usdoj.gov

Tjaden, P. & Thoennes, N. (1998). *Stalking in America: Findings from the National Violence Against Women Survey.* NCJ 169592. Washington, DC: U.S. Department of Justice, National Institute of Justice.

Tjaden, P., & Thoennes, N. (2000). *The full report on the prevalence, incidence, and consequences of violence against women: Findings from the National Violence Against Women Survey.* Washington, DC: National Institute of Justice and Centers for Disease Control and Prevention. U.S. Department of Justice.

U.S. Equal Employment Opportunity Commission. (n.d.). *Facts about sexual harassment.* Retrieved from http://www.eeoc.gov

APPENDIX

Campus Response Committee General Guidelines for Comprehensive Sexual Assault Response and Prevention on Campus: Counseling-Specific Response

1. Publishing the location, hours, and available medical services, including counseling, in response to sexual assault.
2. Providing access to 24-hour medical or emergency mental health services in response to sexual assault, or contract with local community providers for a 24-hour (or after-hours) response.
3. Providing victims/survivors with access to the full range of sexual assault medical services, including forensic evidence collection conducted by a Sexual Assault Nurse Examiner (SANE), or collaborate with local community providers for the full range of services.
4. Providing access to female and male medical/counseling providers so that victims/survivors may select a specific gender if desired.
5. Providing free or affordable, quality, and professional medical and counseling services in the aftermath of sexual assault and low-cost follow-up care, and/or collaborate with a local community provider for these services.
6. Designating at least one campus medical and counseling professional to participate on the campus and/or community SART.
7. Requiring and facilitating sexual assault specific training for all medical and counseling professionals.
8. Establishing medical professionals and health services staff as reporters for anonymous reporting to ensure that records and documentation of sexual assault are captured, even when the victim/survivor does not wish to disclose to campus or criminal justice system officials.
9. Providing mental health professionals on campus who specialize in counseling sexual assault survivors, or collaborate with local community providers for counseling services.
10. Providing information on crime victim's compensation to all patients and victim/survivors seeking medical or mental health services

Adapted from Attorney General's Sexual Assault Task Force (2006).

CHAPTER TWELVE

SPECIFIC POPULATIONS

Kimber Shelton

INTERNATIONAL STUDENTS

Fernando, a 27-year-old graduate student from Chile, presents to the college counseling center with suicidal ideation. Like the majority of international students, Fernando relies on family financial contribution and a graduate assistantship stipend for his income. He experiences significant academic pressure from his family and also applies a great deal of pressure on himself to succeed. Fernando fears he may earn a C in a course, which as a graduate student could jeopardize his academic tenure and embarrass his family.

Lin, a Taiwanese undergraduate student, will be graduating in the spring. For the last 5 years, she has been in a long-distance relationship with her partner who resides in Taiwan. Her family and partner expect her to return to Taiwan after she graduates and marry her partner within the next 2 years. Lin is considering graduate school in the United States, feels apprehensive about marrying, and is unsure of how she could possibly transition back to living with her parents after living on her own for 5 years.

For the 2012 to 2013 academic year, a record high of 819,644 international students were enrolled in U.S. colleges and universities (Institute of International Education [IIE], 2013). The top 10 countries of origin for international students is presented in Table 12.1. There is a mutually beneficial relationship between international students and the United States. The reputation of U.S. colleges and universities, opportunity to obtain specializations not available in their home country, increased ability to acquire employment in the international workforce, independence, and freedom to pursue personal and professional development are among the many reasons international students seek higher education in the United States (Obst & Forster, 2005). From the U.S. standpoint, financial, creativity, and diplomacy contributions are welcomed attributes brought by international students. Summarized in a joint hearing presented to subcommittees in the U.S. House of Representatives, international students and scholars spend approximately

TABLE 12.1   Top Places of Origin for International Students: 2012/2013

Rank	Place of Origin	Number of Students
1.	China	235,587
2.	India	96,754
3.	South Korea	70,627
4.	Saudi Arabia	44,566
5.	Canada	27,357
6.	Taiwan	21,867
7.	Japan	19,568
8.	Vietnam	16,098
9.	Mexico	14,199
10.	Turkey	11,278

Source: Institute of International Education (2013).

$13.5 billion annually in the United States, bring a level of ingenuity that has been particularly beneficial to advances in science and medicine, and obtain skills to support economic growth in their home countries and confront global social issues (House of Representatives, 2007).

Issues and Policies That Impact International Students

Although there is a positive relationship between the United States and international students, international students face many challenges while pursuing their degree in the United States. Similar to their domestic student peers, transitioning to college, increased academic rigor, and developmental issues pose potential obstacles for international students. Dissimilar to their domestic peers, international student status may serve to complicate transitional issues as international students must quickly adapt to the U.S. educational system and culture to achieve academic success and avoid any immediate negative academic consequences. Adjustment can be further complicated by acculturation issues, language barriers, and political unrest in their home country (Mori, 2000; Olivas & Li, 2006). During the time this chapter was written, social media alerted the world to the great civil unrest in Turkey, which may have emotional consequences for the 11,000 Turkish students studying in the United States (IIE, 2013). Concern for the safety of family members or changes to the political climate of their home country can cause emotional and psychological distress that can interfere with academic success. While studying in the United States, international students may experience acts of discrimination and xenophobia, which undermine feelings of safety and create a host of psychologically challenging dilemmas.

> . . . in the days and even weeks following September 11, 2001, many South Asian students including myself had to wake up the middle of the night to shop at our 24-hour grocery store. Growing xenophobia during daytime by some ignorant people who mistook us as radical Muslim terrorists held us back from shopping in the daytime. (p. 100)

International students can also experience issues related to visa, financial aid, familial stress, and policies related to their home country. With over 50% of international students reporting experiencing some issue related to their visa status (Obst & Forster, 2005), visa documentation and procedures present a unique challenge. The time allocated for rectifying visa-related issues is time taken away for academics, research, or campus involvement, which can negatively affect the emotional functioning of international students. International students are not eligible for U.S. financial aid (with the exception of federally funded exchange programs); thus, the majority of international students pay tuition through family and personal funds and campus employment (IIE, 2013). Financial stressors can seriously impair the mental health of international students and potentially their partners. International scholars may arrive in the United States with partners or spouses who are unable to work (without proper visas). Having worked in their home country, the change in employment identity and income can have deleterious impact on international students and their families. Additionally, some countries, such as South Korea, have mandatory military requirements or other national policies that can impact international students' studies or their desire to return or remain in the United States.

IMPLICATIONS FOR COLLEGE COUNSELING CENTERS

Mental Health Concerns and Barriers to Treatment

Given the added stressors experienced by international students, it is no surprise that international students present to college counseling centers with a variety of concerns. Yi, Giseala, and Kishimoto (2003) identified academic, physical health, financial, vocational, and personal issues as five distinct domains impacting the mental well-being of international students. Academic concerns and depression symptoms are top presenting concerns for graduate international students (Nilsson, Berkel, Flores, & Lucas, 2004; Yi et al., 2003). Take the experience of Fernando, the graduate student from Chile who presented to his college counseling center with suicidal ideation. For domestic students, a C may not seem like the end of the world, but for Fernando, earning a C has major financial, geographical, and social implications for him and his family. It is likely that he receives financial support from family members, which intensifies his feeling of academic pressure. He fears his failure will disappoint and embarrass his family should he be removed from his graduate program. Prolonged anguish and humiliation seems unbearable, thus his development of suicidal ideation.

Additional presenting concerns for international students include anxiety, assertiveness issues, academic major selection, vocational issues, relationship issues, isolation, loneliness, and self-esteem issues (Nilsson et al., 2004; Yi et al., 2003). One study showed that 44% of international graduate students reported emotional or stress-related problems significantly affecting their well-being or academic performance that year (Hyun, Quinn, Moadon, & Lustig, 2007).

Despite the additional stressors international students experience, they underutilize college counseling services. Studies on two campuses showed that approximately 2% of international students obtain treatment at counseling centers (Nilsson et al., 2004; Yakushko, Davidson, & Sanford-Martens, 2008). Furthermore, arrival to the counseling center does not mean that international students are reaping the full benefits of therapy. One third of international students drop out of therapy after the initial session (Nilsson et al., 2004) and 60% of international students attend five or fewer sessions (Yakushko et al., 2008). There are a number of reasons international students fail to enter treatment or prematurely drop out of counseling. Cultural stigma presents as a real barrier to treatment utilization. Western therapy models tend to focus on ideals such as individualization, emotional expression, and assets therapy as a useful tool. Students coming from countries that value collectivism, conformity, and emotional restraint may hold negative views of or be uncomfortable with communication styles influenced by Western therapy. International students may also feel that therapy is a violation of cultural norms regarding privacy (individual and family) and that sharing problems with others is a sign of weakness. Additionally, culturally insensitive models can cause international students to feel as if their culture is not well respected in treatment considerations, which may cause limited session attendance. Take Lin, for example; should her therapist minimize cultural norms regarding marriage and collectivism, the dyad could experience a therapeutic rupture, which could hamper Lin's openness in therapy, cause her to feel misunderstood, and lead to premature dropout.

Some international students may fail to show for counseling because they are uncertain of what counseling means or the benefits of therapy (Pope, Singaravelu, Chang, Sullivan, & Murray, 2007). Other international students may present to the counseling center after exhausting other resources, thus arriving to the counseling center in crisis. After the crisis is contained, international students may no longer recognize the significance of ongoing therapy, again leading to early termination. Finally, international students may be unaware that their college has a counseling center. In a study with 551 international graduate students, 39% of the students reported being unaware that their college even had a counseling center (Hyun et al., 2007).

Although international students' utilization rates are low, for students who do appear and engage in therapy, the effects are beneficial (Yakushko et al., 2008). Therefore, centers must demonstrate a commitment to educate international students of counseling center services, destigmatize mental health care, and provide easy access to services.

Culturally Appropriate Therapy and Outreach

Therapy

When working with international students, counselors must demonstrate multicultural competence that shows self-awareness, knowledge of the cultural background of students, and skills in developing and implementing culturally appropriate interventions. Lin and Pedersen (2007) offer guidelines for multinational competence for work with international students:

Individual Level of Awareness in the Process of Psychotherapy

1. Be aware of the concept of psychotherapy in different cultures
2. Be aware of the cultural values of a "good client" in traditional psychotherapy
3. There is no counselor with magical multicultural knowledge, but be a counselor who is multiculturally competent and will keep an open mind

Sociocultural and Sociopolitical Level of Awareness for the Life of International Students

Sociocultural

1. Social cultural adjustment distress
2. Friendliness is not equal to friendship in U.S. culture
3. Oppression, prejudice, and ignorance

Sociopolitical

1. Awareness of language/accent barriers
2. Awareness of the different nationalities/ethnicity among the category of international students
3. Awareness of immigration stress
4. Power differential and the null environment in academia ("an environment that neither encourages nor discourages individuals"; Freeman 1979, cited in Pope, 2007, p. 294)

Additional recommendations for therapy with international students are providing services in a location that minimizes potential stigma that students may face; the counseling center comprised staff that are ethnically and linguistically diverse, able to provide therapy in student's native tongue; implementing peer mentoring or education programs as peers may be more accessible to international students; and continued staff multicultural competence training in working with international students (Mori, 2000).

Group therapy may also be a means for assisting international student groups. An international student group can provide a supportive, structured environment, assist in decreasing acculturative stress, and address other emotional or behavioral issues international students may face. In developing a group, it is important to consider the acculturation status of potential group clients, communication styles (i.e., direct vs. indirect communication), cultural and ethnic backgrounds, and the relationship between group values and the values of each individual member (Walker & Conyne, 2007).

Outreach and Consultation

The on-campus Office of International Education/International Student Resource Center should be a strong liaison to the counseling center. Clinicians may never receive specific training on the unique issues or polices faced by international students. One way to build competence is by providing trainings and having a positive relationship with the Office of International Student Education/International Student Services. The Office of International Student Education holds information on visa requirements, financial aid, and other issues that uniquely impact international students, and also has direct contact with the campus's international study body. The Office of International Education can act as a liaison for international students and the counseling center and as a consultant for counselors working with international students who are addressing issues related to international student status.

International students are likely to engage with and learn about counseling center services from a number of constituents before presenting at the counseling center, including university doctors and nurses, friends, family, and faculty members (Yakushko et al., 2008). Stigma associated with therapy and the manifestation of physical symptoms may have international students presenting more frequently for health services. Therefore, medical professionals and counseling center staff can work together as allies in connecting international students to mental health treatment. It is imperative that health center staff are familiar with mental health concerns, particularly somatic complaints, are aware of counseling center services, and are able to refer students to the counseling center.

International graduate students who have positive relationships with their advisor tend to experience less stress and emotion-related issues (Hyun et al., 2007). When stress- and emotion-related issues occur, international students may first turn to advisors or peers. Advising faculty and students on identifying students in distress, destigmatizing counseling, and how to make referrals to the counseling center can increase international students' access to counseling center services. In addition to external means, international students learn of counseling centers from center websites, flyers, and orientations (Hyun et al., 2007; Yi et al., 2003). Center websites and advertising in places frequented by international students (housing, campus transportation, English as a second language [ESL] office, international clubs, and organizations) are other mechanisms for alerting international students to counseling services.

Cultural Considerations

To best attract and assist international students, counseling centers must be aware of the specific needs of international students on their campuses. There is great diversity among international students and as such there is great diversity in the needs of international students. International students' experience differences in relation to their socioeconomic status, cultural values and customs, ethnic identities, native language, geographical location, and educational experiences. Their reactions, adjustment, and acculturation to the United States and their needs can be impacted by the cultural and political landscape of their home country. Using international students' home country as a marker, one study found that students' needs differed based on the region of the world from which students originated (Tidwell & Hanassab, 2007). In total, most international students reported their greatest needs being related to immigration and visa requirements, career information, and acquiring academic skills. After immigration and visa requirements, and career and academic needs, international students showed great diversity. African students had the most needs out of all students and their needs were greatest for culture and discrimination concerns. Southeast Asian students experienced communication, cultural, and personal needs. International students from the Americas, Asia, and European Union experienced communication and cultural needs; Middle Eastern students experienced communication and personal needs; and Oceania students experienced personal and cultural needs (Tidwell & Hanassab, 2007).

Intersecting identities also impact international students' transition, functioning level, and need for counseling services. Oba and Pope (2013) noted several challenges faced by lesbian, gay, bisexual, and transgender (LGBT) international students, one challenge being that some come from cultures in which sexual and gender identity are affirmed, others in which sexual and gender diversity are marginalized. Thus, when entering the United States, LGBT international students may feel as if they are limited by U.S. social norms, which can lead to isolation and loneliness, while other students may feel more liberated in identity exploration and expression. Therefore, therapists best respond to students needs when they are able to address transitional needs, as well as needs related to intersecting identities. Gender is another identity that can impact international students and their needs. In measuring needs, international women reported having more needs (e.g., immigration, culture, and personal needs) than reported by international men (Tidwell & Hanassab, 2007).

There is a direct relationship between acculturation and utilization of counseling center services. Students who have been in the United States for longer periods of time and have attended more semesters of college are more likely to be aware of and use college counseling resources and have a more positive view of therapy than students with a lower acculturation status (Yakushko et al., 2008; Zhang & Dixon, 2003). Berry (1980) defined four acculturation strategies: (a) assimilation; (b) separation; (c) integration; and (d) marginalization. Assessment, conceptualization, and treatment interventions will vary based on international students' levels of acculturation. Depending on where students are in their acculturation process they will have different demands. A summary of acculturation stages is presented in Table 12.2.

TABLE 12.2 Acculturation Stages

Assimilation

International students are excited about their arrival in the United States and emersion into U.S. culture. They are focused on adapting to U.S. cultural norms and may experience disengagement from the cultural norms from their original country.

- Possible Emotive Reactions: Excitement, surprise, optimism, inhibition, confusion, fear
- Possible Needs: Assistance adjusting to U.S. norms related to laws and policies, academics, and relationship building

    Ugo is the first person in his family to study outside of his home country of Nigeria. Arriving in the United States he is excited about trying new foods, visiting new cities, meeting new people and obtaining his degree. Individuals he has met in the United States have been helpful and kind.

Separation Stage

Enthusiasm and idealization regarding the United States fade and international students begin to reject U.S. culture and experience a reemersion into the customs and culture of their home country. This shift could result in experiences of discrimination or prejudice; cultural value conflict; feeling misunderstood; and academic, relationship, or identity difficulties. During this stage, international students may seek connection with students from a similar ethnic background or with other international students.

- Possible Emotive Reactions: Anger, frustration, fear, disappointment, pessimism, sadness, regret, exhaustion, loneliness, isolation
- Potential Needs: Validation and normalizing of emotions, identification of systemic and internal barriers that may be impeding on international students' success, assistance connecting with peers and building relationships, developing skills for coping with emotional reactions related to transitioning, and advocacy for resolving issues related to discrimination or bias

    Once considered helpful and friendly, Ugo begins to feel as if peers and professors are speaking to him in a condescending manner and doubt his abilities to be academically successful. Many of the professors insist on students calling the professor by their first name, which is contrary to Ugo's cultural values associated with respect and reverence. There have been times when students have laughed at his accent, made comments that demonstrate a lack of awareness about Lagos, the metropolitan city he grew up in, and he is routinely asked questions that feel demeaning such as, "Do you grow up around lions?" He feels misunderstood by his U.S. peers and seeks to connect with other African students and has befriended a Caribbean international student that lives in his dorm.

Integration or Biculturalism

International students value and appreciate their dual cultural experience. They both adapt to U.S. cultural norms and maintain a sense of identity and pride in their culture of origin. They may seek or have relationships with both U.S. students and other international students, have developed tools and skills for navigating in the United States, and feel connected to their cultural identity and strengths.

- Potential Emotive Reactions: Content, happy, realistic, supported, capable, interdependent
- Potential Needs: Resolving cultural value conflicts that may emerge, having a space to discuss transition and progress, and responding to disillusionment around U.S. culture or the culture of the home country

(continued)

TABLE 12.2 Acculturation Stages (*continued*)
Ugo has built relationships with other international students who have introduced him to their friendly group of U.S. students. He feels more comfortable in class and has formed relationships with several students from his class. Instead of seeing things as "right or wrong," he has identified cultural values that are most important to him, which has allowed him flexibility and openness to try new experiences. Ugo also understands the importance of feeling supported and makes weekly calls to his family in Nigeria where he speaks in Yoruba.
Marginalization
International students both reject (or are rejected by) U.S. culture and also their own culture. They find themselves unable to adapt to the United States and either never felt connected with their home culture or have felt extreme difficulty connecting to others who share their cultural identity in the United States. In their home country, students may have experienced bias due marginalized identities (socioeconomic status, gender, ethnic background) and may continue to have such experiences upon arrival in the United States. ● Potential Emotive Reactions: Isolation, loneliness, inferiority/superiority, lost, disenfranchised ● Potential Needs: Validation of emotive reactions, connectivity with others (those within or outside of their culture), identity exploration, coping, and responding to marginalized identities   *Ugo's father is a doctor in Lagos, his mother was a stay-at-home mother, and his family regularly employs others to clean and cook in the home. In part, Ugo decided to study in the United States to distance himself from the extreme disparity between wealth and poverty in his home country. Arriving in the United States Ugo was immediately exposed to capitalism, materialism, and wealth disparity that mirrored that of his home country. He also had the added experience of individuals in the United States assuming he came from an economically impoverished background, thus had difficulty connecting with others of a similarly socioeconomic background and also not been accepted by those from a lower socioeconomic background who view him as privileged and trying too hard to fit in.*
Adapted from Berry (1980).

STUDENTS WITH DISABILITIES

Ira is a 34-year-old undergraduate student with a visual disability. She is legally blind and is assisted by a seeing-eye dog. Ira has made significant progress in therapy but her session limit is fast approaching, Ira and her therapist are aware that her presenting concerns are better addressed with ongoing therapy. Time constraints have made seeking services off campus difficult for Ira in the past. She relies on disability-assisted public transportation, has financial constrictions, and utilizes disability resource services that require significant time (e.g., enlarging notes and other assistive technologies). Additionally, she and her therapist have a strong working alliance, which neither want to interrupt. Her therapist must make the decision to extend Ira's therapy or refer her to a community provider.

Dennis has been diagnosed with panic disorder. His panic attacks are triggered by situational events, such as stress or conflict with others, but can also occur without any provocation. Dennis has found the fear of having a panic attack and actually having panic attacks during class to be a barrier to academic and exam success. He is seeking accommodations through the campus disability office. The disability office is seeking assessment and accommodation recommendations from the counseling center.

Background

According to the Americans with Disabilities Act Amendments Act (ADA, 2008), a disability is defined as "(a) a physical or mental impairment that substantially limits one or more major life activities of such individual; (b) a record of such an impairment; or (c) being regarded as having such an impairment." Major life activities include tasks such as caring for oneself, seeing, hearing, eating, sleeping, standing, breathing, learning, reading, and concentrating. This includes, but is not limited to physical disorders such as epilepsy, multiple sclerosis, HIV, loss of a limb(s), cancer, diabetes, and addiction. The definition of disability also applies to mental disorders including intellectual disabilities, mental illness, emotional issues, learning disorders, organic brain syndrome (Corrigan, 1998), and other *Diagnostic and Statistical Manual of Mental Disorders*, fifth edition (*DSM-5*; American Psychiatric Association [APA], 2013).

Important legislation has increased the college enrollment rates of students with disabilities. The Rehabilitation Act of 1973, the "first comprehensive disability law" (Corrigan 1998, p. 181), expressed nondiscrimination under federal grants and programs (i.e., colleges and universities) and the ADA (1990) provided protection against discrimination in employment, public service, public accommodations, and telecommunications. Individuals with Disabilities Education Act (IDEA) of 1997 provided students with free and appropriate K–12 education. With the implementation of Individualized Educational Plans (IEPs) and advances in psychotropic medication, more individuals were able to successfully complete high school and enroll into college. The most recent amendment, ADA Amendments Act of 2008, broadened the definition of disability and changed the interpretation of the ADA and federal disabilities laws that were limiting to individuals with disabilities. Increased enrollment status in postsecondary education can also be attributed to assistance and instructive technological advancements, disability support services, and increased public awareness (Prentice, 2002).

During the 2007 to 2008 academic year, 11% of undergraduate college students reported a disability (U.S. Department of Education, 2012). A survey conducted by National Center for Education Statistics found that of reported disabilities, 31% were specific learning disabilities (LD), 18% were attention deficit hyperactivity disorder (ADHD), 15% were mental illness/psychological or psychiatric conditions, and 11% were health impairment/conditions (Raue & Lewis, 2011). These findings are consistent with other research that demonstrates the higher prevalence of counseling centers seeing more students with LD rather than physical disabilities (HEATH Resource Center, 1998).

IMPLICATIONS FOR COUNSELING CENTERS

College counseling centers provide two very important services to students with disabilities: (a) assessment and documentation of disability, and (b) counseling and advocacy (Collins & Mowbray, 2005).

Assessment, Documentation, and Accommodations

Although 11% of students report a disability, the figures are likely much higher, considering that many students do not report their disability or seek accommodations. Student may be unaware that accommodations exist or that their particular disability(ies) is covered under the accommodations policy and ADA law. Some students with a disability neither desire nor need accommodations to achieve academic goals. Other students may be unaware of the potential benefits of obtaining academic accommodations or the process as to how to acquire accommodations. The benefit of a documented disability is that it allows college students to obtain accommodations that may advance their ability to perform academically well. In order to obtain academic accommodations, most universities mandate that students provide evidence of a documented disability. Some counseling centers are able to provide disability assessment, while other universities may require student to seek outside services. Universities differ in their requirements; however, in general, university accommodation requirements include (a) diagnostic evaluation by a licensed psychologist or psychiatrist; (b) *DSM* diagnosis; and (c) history of impairment documentation of specific functional or educational impairments (Gibson, 2000). College counseling centers can support students with disabilities by providing accommodations recommendations.

With the majority of disabilities on college campuses being learning and psychological disabilities, it would seem appropriate for counseling centers to be a primary diagnostic resource. Clinicians can provide documentation and diagnosis of mental illness and psychiatric conditions, which can assist students' abilities to obtain proper accommodations. As well as completing a clinical interview, a number of personality assessment instruments can aid in the diagnosis of mental illness. However, counseling centers may be severely limited in their ability to provide assessment and documentation of LD and ADHD. Standardized testing batteries for LD and ADHD are costly, time-consuming, and require a particular skill level. For example, the upfront cost of purchasing assessment instruments are beyond what many centers can afford (thousands of dollars); the assessment batteries take hours to administer, interpret, and write-up; and many assessments require specialized training/licensure, thus limiting the number of clinicians available to provide LD and ADHD assessments. For these reasons providing assessment, documentation, and accommodation recommendations may fall outside of the scope of the counseling center.

Considering that counseling centers are likely to see students presenting with LD- and ADHD-related issues, having a strong referral list for testing is a necessity. Some university systems offer centralized LD and ADHD assessments for students within the university system. This testing may be more affordable, but high demands for services can lead to long wait times for assessment. Depending on the region and doctoral training programs, referral to doctoral training clinics may be a viable and cost-efficient means for completing testing. Under the supervision of licensed psychologists, doctoral trainees provide psychological testing at a reduced fee. Again, the high demand for testing and the training component of testing can lead to extended wait times for students seeking accommodations. Referral to private practitioners is another testing resource for students. Students may be able to obtain an assessment much more quickly from a private practitioner; however, the cost tends to be much greater than that provided by university-related facilities.

Counseling and Advocacy

Attitudes and Stereotypes

Persons with disabilities—physical, cognitive, or psychological—have been subjugated to oppressive experiences in employment, housing, and recreational environments (Sue & Sue, 2015; Wendell, 1996). Misinformation about disability (perceived), limited exposure to individuals with disability, and operating from stereotypes serve as relationship-building barriers for college students with disabilities. Their disability status is seen as a central characteristic that trumps other personality characteristics, and the specific disability(ies) is perceived to be more severe and negative than it actually is (Seo & Chen, 2009). Therefore, individuals interacting with persons with disabilities fail to attend to other personality characteristics and attributes, instead focusing only on preconceived ideas of the person's ability status.

In addition to viewing the disability as the primary characteristic, a number of stereotypes negatively affect the manner in which individuals view and interact with persons with disabilities. Individuals with disabilities have been stereotyped as evil and to be feared, brave for having overcome barriers related to their disability, superheros, or possessing extraordinary and gifted talents that compensate for their disability, helpless and dependent, having a chip on their shoulder, incompetent, and asexual (Sutherland, 1981; Wolfson & Norden, 2000). Being male and having a disability often results in the stereotypes of being considered angry, inferior, and lazy (Nario-Redmond & Michelle, 2010). Persons with disabilities can face further challenges related to multiple marginalized identity status. For instance, women with disabilities are often stereotyped as being childlike, dependent, asexual, poor, unfit mothers, and incapable of living a fulfilling life (Asch, Rousso, & Jefferies, 2001; Nario-Redmond & Michelle, 2010; Sue & Sue, 2015).

In the mental health profession, a disability identity often trumps other identities, including other marginalized identities. In a study of the intersection of disability and ethnicity in psychological testing, the majority of professionals (62.7%) reported selecting testing instruments with consideration of the client's disability status, while only 28.7% reported selecting testing instruments with consideration to the client's race or ethnicity (Horin, Hernandez, & Donoso, 2012).

Therefore, there is a lack of consideration for providing ethnoculturally normed instruments or consideration for the implications associated with the intersection of ability and ethnic minority status.

On the college campus, students with disabilities receive a mixed message from their peers. College students generally express positive societal views regarding individuals with physical and mental disabilities; support services for individuals with mental disabilities; and express accepting and tolerant views of individuals with disabilities (Al-Naggar, 2013). However, in terms of personal relationships and connections, college students express difficulty communicating with individuals with mental illness, fearing those with mental illness will act violently and desiring social distance between themselves and individuals with mental illness (Al-Naggar, 2013). Individuals report a level of comfort working with and dating someone with a disability; however, they report that they would not marry someone with a disability (Hergenrather & Rhodes, 2007; Miller, Chen, Glover-Graf, & Kranz, 2009).

Academic and Career Issues

The transition from high school to college can present unique challenges to students with disabilities. Wolanin and Steele (2004) note, "In higher education, the student is protected against discrimination and provided an equal opportunity, but there is no process aimed at achieving success" (p. viii). Students who obtained accommodations under IDEA may expect to have similar accommodations in college, but do not have the same access (Beecher, Rabe, & Wilder, 2004). As such, student may not feel as supported and struggle when facing new challenges with less support (Beecher et al., 2004). Beecher notes the example of a high school student having previously obtained detailed notes and outlines from teachers. Upon entrance into college, the student must visit the disability resource center, provide or obtain documentation of his or her disability, provide professors with appropriate information regarding accommodations, and possibly advocate to receive accommodation. Revisiting the case of Dennis, visiting the Office of Disability Services, the counseling center, and communicating with professors may prove challenging and actually trigger the panic attacks he has been trying to avoid. Yet, all these steps are necessary for Dennis to obtain appropriate academic accommodations.

Although a college degree can significantly improve the ability of persons with disabilities to gain employment, students with disabilities face barriers that can negatively impact their ability to graduate from college. The rates for drop out with psychiatric disability are twice as high as the general population (86% with psychiatric disability vs. 30%–40% for the general population; Hartley, 2010). In one longitudinal study, 25% of students with disabilities left college after their first year and 51% of students with disabilities left without return after their third year (Mamiseishvili & Koch, 2012). Students with orthopedic or physical conditions were at an increased risk for dropping out sometime within the first 3 years of college. Of all students, students with depression were most likely to fail to persist to their second year than other students with disabilities (Mamiseishvili & Koch, 2012).

The impact of a college education for individuals with disabilities cannot be minimized. Individuals with disabilities face rates of underemployed, unemployed, or living on a low income that surpass that of the general population; this is particularly true for women with disabilities and individuals with visible disabilities. Women with disabilities make less than women without disabilities and earn approximately $700 less monthly than men with disabilities (Berkeley Planning Association, 1996), and persons with visible disabilities earn less than counterparts with invisible disabilities (Yin, Shaewitz, & Megra, 2014). Higher education produces a level of economic freedom for students with disabilities. College graduates with disabilities are 63% more likely to gain employment than individuals with disabilities who do not obtain a college degree (Dutta, Kundu, & Schiro-Geist, 2009). As such, it is particularly important for college counseling centers to act as advocates for and appropriately respond to academic and career needs of student with disabilities.

Student Mental Health and Emotional Needs

Given the social oppression, exposure to negative attitudes and stereotypes, changes to accommodations, and other transitional issues experienced by students with disability, students with disabilities may present with emotional, behavioral, and psychological concerns that negatively impact their academics. Students with disabilities could face experiences of isolation; have difficulty building a community with other students with disability; and receive mixed messages from their peers without disabilities. Connecting with other students with disabilities could present a challenge, as students with disabilities are underrepresented on college campuses and many students may not openly share their disability. Additionally, there is great diversity in disability; therefore, a shared disability status does not necessarily produce a shared relationship bond.

Students with disabilities are not immune from internalizing negative societal messages regarding persons with disabilities (Megivern, Pellerito, & Mowbray, 2003). Decreased self-confidence and stereotype threat can hamper academic success and identity exploration. Other students can feel isolated because they feel embarrassed sharing their disability status with other students (Salzer, Wick, & Rogers, 2008). External barriers related to disability, discrimination, issues related to obtaining and utilizing accommodation, campus accessibility and inclusivity issues, and career-related concerns can all negatively impact the ability of students with disabilities to be academically successful and their overall mental and physical health. Students may come to college ill-equipped for navigating the collegiate accommodations process and have difficulty coping with external academic and career barriers; thus, they are in need of advocacy and responsiveness to discriminatory obstacles they can face.

Center Needs and Competence

The role of the counseling center cannot be underestimated with regard to assisting students with disabilities. Clinicians can serve as a lifeline for students with disabilities, particularly for students with psychiatric disabilities. Weiner and Weiner (1996) found that a close relationship with a counselor was an anchor in helping students with psychiatric disabilities remain in college. Clinicians (working at universities that receive federal funding) also have a legal responsibility to provide services to students with disabilities. Under ADA legislation, clinicians working in the college setting are required to provide services to students with disabilities that are comparable to the services offered to the general student body (Goad & Robertson, 2000).

Although there are moral and legal imperatives for service provision to students with disabilities, counseling center staff may struggle in providing effective services to students on their campuses who have disabilities, and in training practicum and intern clinicians. Professionals with disabilities are underrepresented at counseling centers, clinicians lack training in addressing issues unique to students with disabilities or effectively counseling students with disabilities, are deficient in their knowledge of ADA legislation or requirements, and report needing more understanding of issues related to disability to work effectively (Goad & Robertson, 2000; Gordon, Lewandowski, Murphy, & Dempsey, 2002). Therefore, clinicians may struggle with assisting a student such as Ira or with making a decision regarding extending her treatment past the center's session policy. Strategies for improving services for students with disabilities are listed in the following.

Strategies for Improving Services for Students With Disabilities

1. Ensure that the center and staff are compliant with ADA legislation.
2. Implement ongoing training for effectively working with students with disabilities. This includes all center staff—clinicians, trainees, and administrative staff.
3. Ensure that intake paperwork is inclusive of disability identity status markers.
4. Administer psychological and testing assessments that have been normed and are culturally appropriate for students with disabilities.
5. Ensure that the counseling center is accessible to students with disabilities. This includes accessible doors, waiting rooms, offices, and restrooms; accommodations for sign language interpreters; alternate formats for paperwork (i.e., Braille, audio, electronic format, or large print; and effective emergency evacuation plans.
6. Use appropriate language and first-person language (e.g., students with disabilities, mobility impaired vs. disabled people, wheelchair-bound).
7. Ask direct questions regarding a disability and do not make assumptions about a student's disability.

8. Develop a staff liaison to the Office of Disability Services. This position can help the counseling center remain connected to students with disability and provide ongoing consultation regarding providing students with appropriate accommodations.
9. Provide campus-wide outreach and educational experiences regarding disability and include issues related to disability in general outreach programming.
10. Educate clients with mental and physical disabilities regarding policies and procedures for pursuing and utilizing academic accommodations, and provide assistance with obtainment of academic accommodations.

STUDENT VETERANS

Faith joined the military to "see the world." Next thing she knew she was stationed outside of Kabul, Afghanistan. Now, age 28 and discharged, Faith is enrolled as a full-time student at a 4-year college. She finds it difficult to relate to her younger peers and doesn't fit in with the male-dominated veterans group on campus. Used to a specific schedule and now having blocks of free time, she has trouble with time management. She also is uncertain of her class standing, as she has taken numerous courses over the years, and is unclear as to what credits will actually count toward her degree. Faith has seen burned down schools, injured comrades, and grave injustices so she knows that others' circumstances are much worse than hers; therefore, she dares not complain about the difficulties she is having right now.

People have come up to Hassan and have literally said his identity "blows their mind." They cannot believe someone of Middle Eastern descent was in the military. He gets other comments and questions such as, "You were like a covert op?" "Did you feel like a traitor?" "Did you kill people?" . . . He gets so many questions, but no one ever asks him, "Do you miss your friend who died?" "When do you think you will sleep all the way through the night?" "Why does it take drinking more and more to quiet your mind?" or "How can I help you?"

Introduction

Not since World War II have so many servicemen and women entered or reentered college (Cook & Kim, 2009). Thanks to the post 9/11 Government Issued (GI) Bill, higher education is more accessible to many returning veterans. Primarily utilized by those serving in Afghanistan (Operation Enduring Freedom [OEF]) and Iraq (Operation Iraqi Freedom [OIF]), the GI Bill offers tuition benefits, housing, and monies for books. According to the U.S. Department of Veterans Affairs (VA, 2012a), at present there are over 660,000 undergraduate veteran students, comprising approximately 3% of the undergraduate student population. For some student veterans, a college degree is sought to increase chances of employability. Unemployment rates are higher for post-September 2001 veterans than for civilian peers (Kleykamp, 2013); thus, if employment is unavailable, education may be sought to gain skills or tools for career advancement. Other student veterans may have enlisted in the military specifically to receive the educational benefits, later entering or reentering college to complete educational goals.

Servicemen and women, Reserve Officers' Training Corps (ROTC) students, and veterans on campus provide numerous benefits to the overall campus community. They bring unique experiences based on having had deployments all over the world, working with people from diverse backgrounds, being placed in leadership roles, and having received specialized training. With time spent serving in the military, student veterans are more likely to identify as nontraditional students who are older (15% are age 18–23, 31.4% age 24–29, 28.2% age 30–39, 34.9% age 40 or older; U.S. Department of Veterans Affairs, 2012), may have different family makeups, and greater maturity than those of their traditional-age peers (Livingston, Havice, Cawthon, & Fleming, 2011). Of student veterans, 73% are male and 27% are female (Steele, Salcedo, & Coley, 2010). Within the overall military 10% to 12% are female, thus female student veterans are overrepresented in postsecondary education. As such, female veteran students likely have unique experiences that can contribute to the campus environment.

Transitioning from Military to College

Scholars have commented on the difficulties of veterans returning to civilian life postmilitary service (Hoge, 2010). This can include engaging in high-risk injurious behaviors (driving without a seatbelt, not wearing a motorcycle helmet), readjusting to U.S. laws and customs, increased alcohol use, somatic issues, and reorientation to social life (family, friends, peers). Such transitional difficulties also present themselves on the college campus. Navigating through financial aid, establishing peer support, and addressing physical and mental health concerns present as potential challenges for veteran students.

University Preparedness

The increasing numbers of servicemen and women on college campuses have shifted many universities to develop a "veteran-friendly campus." A veteran-friendly campus is defined as "an institution where programs and people are in place to assist with the transitions between college and the military" (Griffin & Gilbert, 2012, p. 5). A study on the current state of campus programs and services offered to student veterans offers a glimpse into universities preparedness in responding to the increasing number of student veterans (Cook & Kim, 2009). The study reports that college campuses are doing more to meet the academic needs of veteran students. For example, of the 723 institutions surveyed, 90% offered alternative curriculum delivery formats (i.e., online, evening, weekend), which benefit military students whose military career or personal life demands greater flexibility.

Despite a shift toward veteran-friendly campuses, most college campuses are underprepared to appropriately provide adequate services to returning student veterans (Diramio & Jarvis, 2011) and academic-related issues continue to exist for veteran and active military students. Deployment for military services automatically removes students from the campus environment and is outside of the military students' control. Regardless of academic standing prior to deployment, students face the obstacle of reenrolling when they return. Of institutions surveyed, 62% require military students to reenroll after deployment (Cook & Kim, 2009). Student veterans may also experience difficulty getting credit for previous courses or work experiences. During deployment, veterans may have attended a number of different schools and had a number of educational experiences that admissions counselors may not be trained to understand or the university is unwilling or unable to accept for academic credit (DiRamio & Jarvis, 2011).

As well as addressing academic-related issues, colleges and universities are attempting to respond to the social and psychological needs of military students and veterans. Fifty-seven percent of universities reported improving programs and services offered to service members and veteran students and approximately 60% included increased services to veteran students in long-term strategic planning (Cook & Kim, 2009). One way in which institutions respond to the needs of veteran students is through the development of an office specific to veteran issues. Forty-nine percent of institutions reported having a dedicated office for veteran and military students. Institutions of higher education show an increased investment in mental and psychological health of student veterans as 50% of institutions have increased on-campus counseling services and off-campus referral procedures (Cook & Kim, 2009). Although, institutions are providing increased counseling services, surprisingly only 42.8% of institutions reported providing counseling staff with training to assist students with posttraumatic stress disorder (PTSD), brain injuries, and other health issues that may impact student veterans. Furthermore, the National Survey of Counseling Center Directors (Gallagher, 2010) found that 56% of colleges have campus psychiatric services available, yet of campuses with psychiatric services only 20 hours of weekly appointments were provided. As stated by Rudd, Goudling, and Bryan (2011), there are no present data to suggest any counseling centers are fully ready to meet the unique demands of student veterans.

Social Support

A lack of resources and campus support has not gone unnoticed by student veterans. The 2010 National Survey of Student Engagement (Indiana University Center for Postsecondary Research, 2010) reported that in comparison to nonveteran peers, veteran students experienced inadequate support on campus. Political and philosophical issues related to age, life experiences, and military service have been expressed as barriers to veteran students' abilities to connect with nonveteran students (DiRamio, Ackerman, & Mitchell, 2008; Livingston, Havice, Cawthon, & Fleming, 2011). Considering the correlation between emotional support with positive mental health and academic adjustment (Whiteman, Barry, Mroczek, & Wadsworth, 2013), student veterans are at great risk of academic and psychological issues without having comparable support. As such, veteran students report a desire to associate and socialize with other veterans (Strickley, 2009). Some veteran students may have difficulty finding a community of veteran students on campus, as only 32% of campuses in the American Council on Education (ACE) study reported having campus veteran or military clubs (Kim & Cook, 2010) such as Student Veterans of America (SVA). However, it must be noted that social support alone does not completely remove the potential development of mental and physical health concerns. Whiteman et al. (2013) found that social support led to little change in veterans who were experiencing psychological distress, pointing to the fact that veterans need greater assistance, potentially provided by college counseling centers.

Mental Health and Disability

It is estimated that one in three veterans from OEF and OIF will develop PTSD (Tanielian & Jaycox, 2008). While in combat, military persons are exposed to multiple traumatic events (Hoge et al., 2004). According to the National Center for PTSD (2010), military persons serving in OEF and OIF report being attacked/ambushed, receiving incoming fire, seeing dead bodies or remains, and knowing someone who has been seriously injured or killed. In a longitudinal study, it was found that student service members and veterans exposed to combat had significant higher rates of PTSD symptoms than those not serving in combat (Barry, Whiteman, & Wadsworth, 2012). Common PTSD symptoms reported by veterans include physiological symptoms (i.e., headaches, nightmares), mental and emotional disturbances (i.e., memory and concentration issues, mood lability), and behavioral issues (i.e., avoiding situations and reckless behavior) (National Center for PTSD, 2010). Exposure to combat is also correlated with poorer health status and lower life expectancy (MacLean & Elder, 2007), including higher rates of alcohol use, cigarette smoking, and depression (Ames & Cunradi, 2004; Jacobson et al., 2008). In comparison to their college peers who primarily reported drinking for social purposes, service members and veterans were more likely to report alcohol use as a means for coping (Whiteman et al., 2012).

Sexual assault poses a very real threat for service and veteran women. The VA estimates that approximately 22% of women veterans report "military sexual trauma" (MST), which includes sexual assault or severe and threatening sexual harassment during their military service (VA, 2011). Service women are also at a greater risk for sustained substance abuse. Service women reported less perceived social support than their male veteran counterparts, yet service women are drastically less likely to receive substance abuse treatment (16.3% vs. 71.2%) (VA, 2012b).

It is also estimated that 40% of veterans from OEF and OIF could have a disability (Grossman, 2009) and are two times as likely to report a disability in comparison to civilian peers (National Survey of Student Engagement, 2010). This includes mental and cognitive disabilities related to PTSD, traumatic brain injury, and depression, as well as physical disabilities such as hearing and vision-related injuries, substantial mobility limitations, disfigurement, burns, and exposure to toxic chemicals (Church, 2009). Veterans with a history of PTSD are also at an increased risk for suicidal ideation and suicide attempt (Brenner et al., 2011; Jakupcak et al., 2009). One study found that veterans with PTSD were almost three times more likely than those without PTSD to make a suicide attempt and veterans with PTSD and a traumatic brain injury were 3.3 times more likely to have made a suicide attempt than veterans with traumatic brain injury alone.

Implications for Counseling Centers

Therapy Services

College counseling centers likely do not see high numbers of veteran students voluntarily seeking treatment. Cultural stigma associated with mental health treatment is also pervasive in military and veteran communities. Presenting to counseling can appear to be a sign of weakness that is inconsistent with a military persona that is strong and protective of others. Veteran students may refrain from therapy services as an avoidant strategy believing that exploring past traumatic experiences to be too difficult. Additionally, some student veterans may obtain mental health services from the local VA hospital and thus not feel a need to utilize campus services.

Although there are a number of treatment barriers, obtaining mental health treatment can be a psychological and academic advantage to student veterans. Counseling can be used as an avenue for exploration and skill-building for addressing academic concerns, relationships concerns, career assistance, and overall readjustment. Counseling centers can also provide specific treatment of PTSD and other psychological concerns, particularly for student veterans who are quick to initiate treatment. Early intervention of PTSD symptoms reduces the severity and acuity of symptoms and decreases the chronicity symptoms (Lapieer, Schwegler, & LaBauve, 2007). There are also secondary psychological benefits associated with higher education. DiRamio and Spires (2009) found that education goals helped with the psychological healing of severely wounded soldiers.

As well as training all staff, counseling centers can also establish a counselor coordinator for student-veterans position specifically designed to provide therapeutic services to veteran and military students and provide community-wide training on veteran issues. Considering the importance of social support, some college counseling centers address the needs of veteran students by offering group counseling for veteran students. For example, University of California, Los Angeles Counseling Center offers students a Student Veteran Group and A&M University Student Counseling Service (SCS) provides a Group for Returning Veterans. The VA is also working with college campuses to be more responsive to the mental health needs of veteran students. Through the VetSuccess on Campus (VSOC) program, the VA places a VA counselor on college campuses to provide vocational testing, career and academic counseling, and adjustment counseling to veteran students as well as referral for more intensive treatment (VA, 2013). In 2013, the VSOC program expanded to an additional 62 campuses in 16 states (VA, 2013).

As previously mentioned, counseling center staff are often undertrained in providing services specific to veteran students. Fortunately, a number of resources are available to help increase counseling centers staff knowledge base and ability to treat veteran students. Table 12.3 provides a list of resources available to college counseling centers.

Consultation and Outreach

Counseling center staff have much to offer the greater campus community through consultation and outreach. Psychiatric disorders such as PTSD and mood disorders can impair veteran students' abilities to fully participate in

---

TABLE 12.3   Student Veterans Resources

Student Groups

Student Veterans of America
SVA is a coalition of student veterans groups on college campuses across the globe. These member chapters are the "boots on the ground" that help veterans reintegrate into campus life and succeed academically.

Training Resources

American Council on Education Veteran-Friendly Institution Counseling Center Program
This program provides free training to college and university mental health counseling centers throughout the country on how to better address issues such as PTSD and suicide prevention in their work treating students.

The Jed Foundation
This organization focuses on college and university suicide prevention. Among resources for the general student body, they provide the free online training, Helping Our Student Veterans Succeed: Understanding and Supporting the Emotional Health of Student Veterans.

U.S. Department of Veterans Affairs
The VA Campus Toolkit, created by the National Center for PTSD, is a collection of free handouts and resources for training and presentations specific to college campuses.

Substance Abuse and Mental Health Services Administration (SAMHSA)
SAMHSA provides extensive resources regarding mental health and substance abuse including the veteran-specific treatment models for veterans and service members with co-occurring disorders—Co-Occurring Disorders in Veterans and Military Service Members

Center for Deployment Psychology (CDP)
CDP's University Counseling Center Core Competency UC4 program is designed to provide valuable and engaging training in an in-person full-day presentation to all clinical staff working in a university or college community and also provides access to online training resources.

PTSD, posttraumatic stress disorder; SVA, Student Veterans of America; VA, Veterans Affairs.

educational endeavors; however, with treatment and appropriate academic accommodations, veteran students with a psychiatric disorder are able to enhance their ability to be academically successful. Consulting and collaborating with the campus Office of Disability Services, the counseling center can provide documentation of psychiatric disabilities to assist veteran students in obtaining appropriate disability accommodations.

For campuses with an Office of Veteran Services, counseling centers can establish a consultative relationship to learn more about the needs of veteran students on their campus and ways to improve the clinical services provided to them. The campus Office of Veteran Services and the local VA can also assist counseling centers in providing in-house and university-wide trainings. Counseling center outreach programs should be inclusive of veteran students and the center should be present at veteran-specific orientations. Furthermore, counseling centers can also support the establishment and maintenance of veteran student groups. Acting as the group advisor or consulting with students attempting to initiate a SVA group, counseling centers help form and maintain the group's viability and can also advocate for space on campus for the group to meet.

STUDENT ATHLETES

Rolland is a 19-year-old soccer recruit from Trinidad. He recently injured his knee and is told that he will have to have surgery. Rolland is fearful that if he does not have a speedy recovery he will lose his scholarship and return to Trinidad, where it will be difficult for him to afford college.

Adela has played basketball since she was 5 years old. She is now a National Collegiate Athletic Association (NCAA) Division I athlete and has enjoyed 4 successful years. Adela will be graduating in May with a sociology degree. She is having trouble dealing with this changing identity, as she will soon no longer be a student athlete and has no idea what the career options are for a sociology major.

Jeremiah is one of the few collegiate athletes who will actually participate in professional athletics. He knows that scouts are coming to his games and feels increased pressure to perform and experiences increased self-doubt. He seeks counseling to rebuild his self-confidence and desires to take his game to the next level physically and psychologically.

Introduction

There are over 450,000 students participating in the NCAA (2013a), more than 60,000 students in the National Association of Intercollegiate Athletes (NAIA, n.d.), and thousands more participating in smaller athletic associations (e.g., United States Collegiate Athletic Association, The National Christian College Athletic Association). Student athletes add to the diversity of college campuses as they represent diverse geographical locations and nationalities, bring athletic gifts and talents to the institution, bring a level of prestige to the university, and instill camaraderie in students and alumni. Additionally, collegiate athletics is a major source of revenue for college campuses. In 2008, the Entertainment and Sports Programming Network (ESPN, 2008) reported the University of Alabama having the largest athletic revenue bringing in $123,769,841 in the fiscal year. NCAA Division I sports teams may produce revenue in the multimillion dollar range; however, it must be noted that such high revenue is uncommon among most universities.

As much as student athletes help to support universities, they are not without controversy. There are those who hold the negative opinions that student athletes received preferential treatment on campus, are not held to the same academic standards as the general student body, receive extra academic accommodations, and have a built-in support system through the athletics department and thus do not warrant use of resources outside of the athletics department. There is some basis for these opinions. The NCAA allows for students who do not meet the minimum entrance requirements to be admitted to colleges under "special admission programs"; however, the same opportunities must also be available for all students (Associated Press, 2009). There are also opinions that value the presence of student athletes and demonstrate respect for the integrity and academic dedication of university athletic programs. Overall, student athletes show great academic success on their campuses and participation in sports has been shown to provide a number of benefits. With the exception of having higher rates of binge drinking 8 years after their senior year of high school, high school athletes were more likely to have a postsecondary education, obtain full-time employment, have higher incomes, greater fitness levels, and smoke less than their nonathlete peers (National Center for Education Statistics, 2005). There was an 82% graduation rate for Division I student athletes who enrolled in 2006 (Hosick, 2013), 35% of NCAA student athletes earn post-graduate degrees, and two thirds of former student athletes feel that that participation in collegiate athletics helped prepare them for life after graduation and reported having a positive overall college experience (NCAA, 2013a; Potuto & O'Hanlon, 2007).

Challenges Faced by Student Athletes

Academic and Athletic Demands

Who student athletes are and their needs are as diverse as the athletic abilities they have. Student athletes encounter similar issues and developmental milestones as nonstudent athletes, but also face a host of physical, mental, and academic challenges specific to their student athlete identity. For one, student athletes face both real and imagined academic and athletic pressures. The competitive nature of sports and the desire to succeed can cause student athletes to set unrealistically high academic and athletic expectations for themselves or cause others to place high demands on them. High-profile student athletes are praised and criticized in the media, are expected to be role models, and idealized by their peers, which can add to their pressure to succeed.

Student athletes may also have difficulty balancing their student identity and athletic identity. To remain eligible to compete, student athletes must maintain a certain grade point average. Regimented practice, travel, and game schedules place added pressure to an already limited time schedule. Student athletes may also have to contend with stereotypes. College students hold stereotypes that the student athlete is the "Big Man on Campus" and that being a student athlete is great (Lawrence, Harrison, & Stone, 2009). However, they also hold many negative stereotypes labeling student athletes as "dumb jocks," lazy, failing to studying, partying a lot, and believing that student athletes only are in college to play sports (Lawrence et al., 2009). Student athletes perceive that professors hold more negative views of them than positive views and hear comments suggesting that student athletes have low intelligence, are not academically motivated, and receive unfair privileges beyond what they earn (Simons, Bosworth, Fujta, & Jensen, 2007). If internalized, such messages can limit student athletes' ability to be academically successful.

Mental Health Concerns

Ten to 15% of college student athletes are estimated to experience psychological and emotional issues that are appropriate for counseling services (Hinkle, 1994). This includes depression, anxiety, relationship concerns, trauma, ADHD, learning disorders, and personality concerns. Suicide is the third leading cause of death of student athletes (Harmon, Asif, Klossner, & Drezner, 2011). In comparison to nonstudent athletes, student athletes report lower wellness scores (with the exception of the exercise factor) on coping-self, physical-self, creative-self, essential-self, and social-self variables (Watson & Kissinger, 2007). These findings suggest that student athletes can benefit from counseling interventions that promote wellness regarding interpersonal relationships, friendship, and love (Watson & Kissinger, 2007). These finding also suggest the importance of initiating campus community interventions to minimize isolation of student athletes and connect student athletes to the campus (outside of athletics) (Watson & Kissinger, 2007).

Athletic participation is not necessarily a buffer against heavy alcohol use; student athletes have been identified as a high-risk group for heavy drinking and for having higher levels of alcohol consumption and greater alcohol-related consequences than nonathletes (Doumas, Turrisi, Coll, & Haralson, 2007; Shields, 1998). High rates of alcohol use may be associated with coping with stress related to athletic performance, time constraints, performance conditions, feelings of isolation, and being less likely to seek help for problems (Doumas et al., 2007). Student athletes are also at greater risk for engaging in multiple high-risk activities such as driving without a seat belt, engaging in unprotected sex, and physical fights, all of which could interfere with athletic and academic performance (Nattiv, Puffer, & Green, 1997).

Student athletes may also experience difficulty obtaining medication for diagnosed ADHD. Prescribing stimulants is the most common pharmacological treatment of ADHD. Athletic associations such as NCAA have strict rules regarding the use of performance enhancement supplements and drugs. NCAA bans drugs and supplements that may produce an unfair performance advantage, which includes the use of stimulant medications used to treat ADHD. Students with ADHD who are taking stimulation medication must meet the specific requirements set by NCAA (2009) or may entirely refrain from seeking pharmacological treatment.

Female student athletes face unique challenges on their college campuses. Female student athletics generally have fewer scholarships, less media exposure, and smaller athletic budgets (Fletcher, Benshoff, & Richburg, 2003). In the case of Adela, she may have been valued for her contribution to the basketball team, but may not have obtained mentoring and guidance regarding postgraduation plans. As she is facing graduation, she likely feels underprepared for a life where basketball is not her primary focus. Female athletes are also more likely to struggle with disordered eating and weight management issues than do their male counterparts (Fletcher et al., 2003). Furthermore, they face contradictory social role norms associated with femininity. Societal standards value femininity markers such as submissiveness and beauty, which differ from athletic attributes related to success such as aggression, strength, power, and competiveness (Miller & Heinrich, 2001; Steinfeldt, Zakrajsek, Carter, & Steinfeldt, 2011).

Barriers to Treatment

A student athlete status can serve as a barrier to help-seeking and counseling. In comparison to their peers, student athletes have a less positive attitude toward help-seeking and underutilize counseling services (Watson, 2005). Student athletes are considered to be strong, well, fit (emotionally and physically), and competent. Stigma associated with counseling and mental health concerns may lead student athletes to feel as if they are weak or inadequate should they seek services. High-profile student athletes may be even more susceptible to scrutiny (or hold the impression that they will be under greater scrutiny) for seeking mental health services. Take the case of Jeremiah for example. He already doubts his self-confidence; what happens when others see him in the waiting room of the counseling center? Would this make them also doubt Jeremiah or question his readiness to play sports professionally? Such questions may prolong the time it takes for Jeremiah to seek help, or he could possibly decide to never visit the counseling center.

Another very real barrier to treatment obtainment is time. Take, for example, the athlete who has weight training in the morning, goes to mandatory tutoring at 11 a.m., attends classes until 3 p.m., practice from 3:30 to 5:30 p.m., and has 2 to 3 hours of homework. During breaks this student athlete eats meals and by the time practice is over, the counseling center is closed. For those athletes who are able to arrange appointments, counselor competence can negatively impact treatment. Most counselors are not trained to work with student athletes and may hold biased views regarding athletes, may not understand the amount of pressure experienced by athletes, or appreciate the culture of the athletic environment. In the case of Rolland, it is imperative for his clinician to recognize the significance an injury can have on his international student status, scholarship, and matriculation through college. Feeling misunderstood by his clinician could result in Rolland feeling more hopeless about his situation.

The relationship between the counseling center and athletics department can either encourage or deter student athletes from obtaining treatment. Counseling centers and athletics departments have separate roles and can feel as if they have separate agendas for student athletes. Hopefully, the primary goal is ensuring the well-being of the student; however, each department may have different approaches for caring for the student. Consider the student athlete who presents with chronic depression, is experiencing frequent suicidal ideation, and has made quasi-suicidal attempts (e.g., drinking half a bottle of Nyquil). The student reveals to the counselor that the ideation is growing stronger and that the student cannot ensure his or her safety. As such, the counselor facilitates the student going to a psychiatric hospital for assessment and intensive care. The student signs a consent for the coach to be contacted regarding being transferred to the hospital; however, the student does not want details regarding sessions released. The coach, who is not privy to the detailed account provided to the counselor, may hold the belief that the student may be better served being surrounded by teammates and traveling during the weekend so the student is not alone. Like others who feel a responsibility to provide care and assistance to the student, the coach may feel frustrated and believe that the counseling center is not cooperating, as no or limited information is released. Although the clinician is acting within ethical and legal codes of his or her jurisdiction, this experience could dampen the relationship between the center and the athletics department.

Role of College Counseling Center

Student athletes may present to counseling centers for issues directly related to their status as a student athlete, or may present with concerns that are unrelated to their student-athlete identity. Student athletes have needs in four primary areas: (a) academic advising; (b) life skill development; (c) clinical counseling; and (d) performance enhancement. College counseling centers can play peripheral or essential roles in all these areas.

Academic Advising and Life Skill Development

As a former student athlete, I remember meeting with an academic advisor during freshman year. I played volleyball and ran track and was scheduled to take 15 credit hours. My academic advisor suggested I take no more than 12 credit hours. I went against his advice and later realized that taking 12 credit hours would have extended my undergraduate tenure for at least one semester, during which time I would no longer have had an athletic scholarship.

Although it is not the role of the counseling centers to serve as an academic advisor, counseling centers are equipped to help students explore their majors, career choices, and the possible intersection of their athletic identity so that students are aware of how their academic and athletic decisions will impact them.

Clinicians cannot assume that student athletes are aware of the unlikelihood that they will become professional athletes (only about 1% of collegiate athletes go on to play sports professionally; NCAA, 2013b). Clinicians can help student athletes explore other employment options that are aligned with their interests, values, strengths, and abilities. Additionally, clinicians can assist student athletes in building coping strategies to effectively handle pressure associated with balancing academic and athletic responsibilities and in improving their communication skills so that students feel empowered when speaking to their academic advisor or coaches.

Counseling centers have much to offer in regard to life skill development. Individual and group counseling and outreach programming are means for educating student athletes on decision making and goal setting, drug and alcohol use, interpersonal communication, time management, and career development, and sexual relationships (Broughton & Neyer, 2001). Centers can collaborate with the athletics department to make life skill development a part of student athletes' annual overall health and prevention assessment. For years, student athletes at Georgia State University completed a preseason half day wellness assessment. During that time, student athletes rotated through different sectors where they received a physical, met with an academic advisor, and completed a mental health screening. Student athletes were typically screened for mood and anxiety disorders, eating disorders, and substance use. Student athletes who scored positive on the screeners met briefly with a clinician and were encouraged to visit the counseling center. The preseason screenings provided students athletes with a viable connection to the counseling center, served to norm mental health care and successfully identified students at risk for developing or experiencing an exacerbation in mental health concerns that had the potential to impede on academic or athletic functioning.

Clinical Counseling

Student athletes' physical health is frequently seen as a priority over mental health, when in reality physical and mental well-being are directly related, with one affecting the other (Thompson & Sherman, 2007). As are other students, collegiate student athletes are at risk for experiencing transitioning and developmental milestone issues, dealing with grief and loss, and may be at an age where mental health concerns tend to present for the first time (i.e., first psychotic break). Their intersecting student and athlete identities can complicate issues they face. A student athlete who is depressed is more susceptible to injury, and conversely, a student athlete who experiences an injury may be more prone to developing depression. Counseling centers that are knowledgeable about the unique stressors related to a student athlete identity can help students traverse through anxiety, depression, relationship issues, disordered eating, substance abuse, or other mental health concerns they present with.

It is important for student athletes to be aware of the services provided at the counseling center and that the services are made attractive to athletes. Many centers such as the University of Houston Counseling Center, explicate or advertise services to student athletes on its counseling center website. Other campuses offer specific programming and groups for students such as the University of Southern California Student-Athlete Injury Group.

Liaison to the Athletics Department

Particularly at universities with larger athletic budgets, the athletics department and culture can feel like a different world from the rest of the campus. To better connect the counseling and athletics worlds, some centers designate an athletics department liaison. A liaison to the athletics department is beneficial in many ways. The liaison is involved in relationship building and development of a referral process; provides coaches, athletic trainers, teammates, and administrative staff with training on identifying and assisting athletes in distress (Neal et al., 2013); engages in crisis management and consultation; and provides education regarding confidentiality to minimize miscommunication. The National Athletic Trainers' Association recommends a team approach to recognizing and referring student athletes with psychological concerns. This includes developing a care and referral plan that involves coaches, trainers, the counseling center, and administrators, team physicians, and community-based mental health care professionals (Neal et al., 2013).

The liaison position is also valuable from a student perspective. Student athletes feel more favorable about counseling if they feel they have a therapist who is well versed in the athletic culture (López & Levy, 2012; Maniar, Curry, Sommers-Flanagan, & Walsh, 2001). This requires the liaison to have familiarity or expertise with university and athletic association's policies and procedures, philosophies for student athletes at their institution, dueling priorities, specific issues related to the culture of their individual team, as well as how they navigate in the total culture, and with time limitations and injuries (Fletcher et al., 2003). The athletics liaison is an identified clinician with whom student athletes may feel more comfortable seeking services. In addition to seeing student athletes in the counseling center, the liaison to athletics may also hold consultation or appointment hours in the athletics department, which can help limit the time pressure athletes face. Depending on the university size, the responsibility of counseling student athletes may be too great for one person. Therefore the entire clinical staff should have training for providing services to student athletes.

Performance Enhancement and Sports Psychology

Finally, athletes may seek counseling services or receive a referral for counseling services directly related to their athlete status. The goal of performance enhancement, sports psychology, exercise psychology, and athletic counseling is to help student athletes achieve optimal performance, perform consistently in training and competition, increase adherence to exercise programs, and help individuals realize their potential. The Association of Applied Sports Psychology (2013) identified eight goals or common psychological skills in the field of applied sport and exercise psychology, most of which are suitable within the college counseling center:

1. Anxiety or energy management—Arousal levels that are too high or too low can negatively impact student athletes' performance. Anxiety and energy management focus on assisting athletes in reaching an arousal level that is appropriate for optimum performance. Common treatments include: (a) breathing exercises; (b) progressive relaxation; (c) meditation; (d) imagery or visualization; and (e) cognitive techniques.

2. Attention and concentration control (focusing)—Developing skills to help maintain focus and intensity in a situation. Common techniques include: (a) attention control training, and (b) techniques to expand awareness.

3. Communication—Enhancing student athletes' ability to improve group cohesiveness and communication with individuals, including team-mates, coaches, parents, and professors. Techniques used with this skill include: (a) teaching active listening and communicating skills; (b) helping individuals create a free and open environment; and (c) assertiveness training.

4. Goal setting—Developing specific goals for enhancing performance or facilitating recovery from an injury. Goal setting includes: (a) emphasis on skill development; (b) identifying target dates for attaining goals; (c) identifying goal achievement strategies; and (d) providing regular goal evaluation.

5. Imagery, visualization, mental practice—Developing sensory and mental skills to assist (a) mental preparation; (b) anxiety control; (c) attention; (d) building self-confidence; (e) learning new skills; and (f) rehabilitation.

6. Self-talk—Building student athletes' skill in providing positive self-talk for optimal performance. Self-talk is used for (a) prompting a specific behavior; (b) improving self-confidence; (c) attention control; (d) motivation; and (e) arousal control.

7. Team building—This is the process of helping the members of a group enhance their ability to work cohesively through the improvement of communication, group objectives, trust, and respect. Team building strategies are often used at the beginning of a season to help group members become more familiar with and trusting of each other. Common techniques include group introductions of each other, ropes courses, and individual and team goal setting.

8. Time management/organization—Time management and organizational skill improvement to reduce stress level. Techniques include: (a) teaching how to use a planner; (b) learning about the demands of a task; (c) setting legitimate goals for tasks; (d) understanding the demands of one's life; and (e) developing preperformance routines.

SEXUAL AND GENDER MINORITY STUDENTS

Riley is an 18-year-old transsexual female. She is excited to be in college, as being away from her conservative hometown allows her to actively pursue transitioning. She is ready to start hormone replacement therapy, legally change her name, and is interested in scheduling a consultation appointment in the future to learn more about surgical options. She is seeking a letter of support to provide to her endocrinologist and wants to know the steps for completing a legal name change. Other than this, she doubts she will have any issues transitioning.

Leland feels like he has living in two worlds. He spends half his time being in a fraternity and is popular, smart, and athletic. The second half of his life is spent wrestling with his same-sex attraction feelings and talking to men online. He grew up with the association of "gay" being abnormal and wrong and has internalized these messages. He also worries that his fraternity brothers may treat him differently if they knew his inside feelings. He is struggling with his identity and wondering if his two selves can ever integrate.

Sexual and Gender Diversity on Campus

Sexual and gender minority students include, but are not limited to, students who identify as lesbian, gay, bisexual (LGB), pansexual, omnisexual, queer, transgender (T), gender nonconforming, genderqueer, transsexual, two spirit, asexual, intersex, and questioning. Determining the number of sexual and gender minority students on college campuses is difficult. For one, universities are not uniform in the manner in which they collect data regarding sexual and gender identity. Second, students may not disclose their sexual or gender identity for fear of possible discrimination or prejudice. Additionally, there is not a consensus on terminology or definitions, thus labels provided for students may or may not capture their sexual or gender identities. However, within the larger society it is estimated that 3.5% to 15% of the U.S. population are lesbian women, gay men, or bisexual individuals (Gates & Newport, 2013; Gelberg & Chojnacki, 1995). There is even less known about the number of individuals who identify with a transgender identity; however, as reported in the National Transgender Discrimination Survey of 2011, approximately 27% of trans individuals hold an undergraduate or graduate degree (Grant et al., 2011). Despite the limitations in recognizing the accurate number of sexual and gender minority students, college campuses and counseling centers are responsible for fostering a welcoming and inclusive environment in which sexual and gender minority students can prosper.

Harassment, Victimization, and Discrimination

Sexual and gender minority students do not always encounter a welcoming and inclusive environment on the college campus or in society in general. Unlike other minority groups who enjoy legal protection against discrimination, federal and state laws and campus policies do not always provide the same protections to sexual and gender minority individuals. At present there are only 17 states and the District of Columbia that issue marriage licenses to same-sex couples (Human Rights Campaign, 2014). Limited legal protections can interfere or prohibit sexual and gender minority individuals' ability to obtaining housing and employment, receive hospital visitations rights, or pursue adoption or child custody.

On the college campus, sexual and gender minority students (and staff and faculty) may experience discriminatory or bias practices in regard to obtainment of on-campus medical treatment, housing opportunities, being recognized by his or her chosen name, and accessibility of insurance with same-sex benefits. Other, more subtle forms of discrimination may include taking courses in which the experiences of sexual and gender minority individuals are excluded and receiving messages regarding the superiority of heterosexual and cisgender[1] experiences and identities.

In the opening case, Leland has legitimate concerns regarding potential detrimental consequences he could face if he shared his same-sex attraction with others. A recent study by Campus Pride (2010) evaluated the campus climate for sexual and gender minority individuals. Results from the 5,149 participants showed that sexual and gender minority students are subjected to harassing and discriminatory behaviors and held negative views of the campuses' climates at rates that substantially exceeded that of their heterosexual and cisgender peers. In comparison to 12% of heterosexual individuals, 23% of sexual identity minority individuals reported experiencing harassment on campus. Sexual identity minorities reported being targets of derogatory remarks, stares, and being singled out as the authority on LGBT issues. In comparison to the 20% of cisgender men and 24% of cisgender women who reported experiencing harassment, an astounding 87% of transmasculine and 82% of transfeminine individuals reported experiencing harassment on campus (Campus Pride, 2010). They identified feeling ignored or excluded, isolated, stared at, and singled out. These findings are consistent with other studies that report high rates of transphobic harassment and victimization, abuse, physical violence or threat of physical violence, sexual violence, and threatening behavior against transgender individuals (Chesir-Teran & Hughes, 2009; Effrig, Bieschke, & Locke, 2011). Sexual and gender minorities of color often fare worse, with reports of harassment and discrimination being 10 times more likely than their White peers (Campus Pride, 2010). Experiences of verbal, physical, and sexual harassment, discrimination, and isolation can interfere with sexual and gender minority students' ability to succeed in college and negatively impact their overall life experience.

---

[1] Cisgender—Term used to describe individuals whose biological sex and gender identity are aligned with societal norms and expectations regarding gender and identity; for example, being born male and identifying with masculine gender role expectations. Transgender individuals experience incongruence between their birth sex and sense of gendered self; for example, being biologically female and identifying with a male sense of gender.

Implications for the Counseling Centers

Presenting Concerns

Like heterosexual and cisgender peers, sexual and gender minority students present to college counseling for a host of concerns, but are more likely to pursue mental health treatment than their heterosexual peers (McAleavey, Castonguay, & Locke, 2011). Higher mental health utilization rates have been attributed to sexual and gender minorities' view of therapy and societal experiences. Sexual and gender minority individuals hold a more positive view of therapy than their counterparts (Liddle, 1996) and also experience higher rates of harassment, victimization, abuse, and minority stress, which place them at a greater risk for developing mental health issues. Minority stress theory asserts that stress associated with a marginalized identity leads to experiences of increased distress, decreased functioning, and greater susceptibility to mental health–related concerns (Meyer, 1995). The experience of minority stress is particularly harmful when the individual's coping resources are unavailable or underdeveloped (Meyer, 1995).

Sexual and gender minority students may seek counseling services for issues directly related to sexual and gender identity or may present with issues that have little direct bearing on their sexual or gender identity status. Overall studies on quality of life, lifestyle, and health indicators show no statically significant differences between LGB and heterosexual individuals (Bronn, 2001; Ketz & Israel, 2002). For those who do experience mental health issues, common psychological concerns identified by sexual and gender minority individuals include depression, anxiety, substance abuse, identity development and management, relationship concerns, career and vocation concerns, spirituality, family of origin, and children and parenting issues (Cochran, Sullivan, & Mays, 2003; Kerr, Santurri, & Peters, 2013; Page, 2004; Schuck & Liddle, 2001). Using Counseling Center Assessment of Psychological Symptoms (CCAPS) data, McAleavey et al. (2011) found that depression and eating concerns subscale scores were significantly higher for college students who identified as either gay or questioning in comparison to the scores of heterosexual peers. They also found that for all sexual minority groups (gay, lesbian, bisexual, questioning, asexual, and queer), scores on the Family Distress scale were significantly elevated as compared to heterosexual students.

Sexual and gender minority students are also at a higher risk for suicidal ideation, planning, and attempts than their heterosexual and cisgender peers (Hass et al., 2011). Suicide ideation and attempts are reported to be three to six times higher than that of heterosexual individuals (Kerr, 2013, Murphy, 2007). The rate of suicidality among transgender individuals is abhorrent. Approximately 30% of transgender individuals and 45% of transgender youth attempt suicide (Clements-Nolle, Marx, & Katz, 2006; Grossman & D'Augelli, 2007; Kenagy, 2005). Issues related to gender identity are the most commonly reported reason for making an attempt. Effrig et al. (2011) explored the suicide rates of transgender college students who were in counseling and who were not in treatment. They found that 62.2% of transgender individuals obtaining mental health treatment at their college counseling center reported seriously considering suicide. This is in comparison to 24.7% of cisgender men and women in treatment who reported seriously considering suicide. In the nonclinical sample, 42.6% of transgender students reported seriously considering suicide in comparison to 16.2% of cisgender men and women. As revealed in these results, the rates of suicide ideation are higher for transgender individual in both clinical and nonclinical samples as compared to cisgender peers. Higher risks for suicide are not evidence of greater psychopathology, but have been contributed to by the harassment, victimization, and marginalization that sexual and gender minorities frequently experience (Russell & Joyner, 2001). Higher substance use has also been attributed to minority stressors related to gender and/or sexual identity. High rates of substance use have been associated with self-medication because of feelings of gender dysphoria, internalized heterosexism, and to cope with experiences of harassment and discrimination (Stevens, 2012).

Clinician Considerations

Clinicians at college counseling centers may find themselves underprepared in providing affirmative services to sexual and gender minority students. Many therapists report receiving no or little training on working with sexual and gender minority clients during their graduate training (Murphy, Rawlings, & Howe, 2002). This is probably even truer for gender minority clients. Consider the case of Riley. Her therapist may be in full support of her transitioning, but may be unfamiliar with the legal issues related to transitioning such as how to change the name on a birth certificate, license, social security card, or passport. Her therapists may be unaware that (in many states) individuals must undergo partial sex/gender affirming surgery (sex change surgery) to have the sex changed on their state driver's license. Her therapist may also collude with Riley's belief that she will experience no issues related to her transition. Therefore, they may fail to explore the transitioning process her family will undergo, build coping resources for potential experiences of harassment, biased, or abusive treatment, or identify the positive and negative issues surrounding being perceived as female (e.g., positives: being affirmed by others and feeling more self-accepting; negatives: being at greater risk for experiencing sexual assault and gender salary disparities).

Furthermore, even therapists who are good natured and value diversity are not immune from internalizing societal homophobia and heterosexism, which could inadvertently interfere with the assessment, conceptualization, or intervention process with sexual and gender minority students. Bias and prejudice can be unintentionally communicated in the form of sexual orientation microaggressions or gender identity microaggressions. Microaggressions are discussed in greater detail in Chapter 2. The most common sexual and gender identity microaggressions therapists make are pathologizing and minimizing sexual orientation and gender identity. Clinicians run the risk of pathologizing sexual orientation with the belief that sexual identity and gender minority status are causes for all presenting concerns (Shelton & Delgado-Romero, 2013), when, in actuality, presenting concerns may have little or no direct relation to sexual or gender identity. Conversely, clinicians equally run the risk of ignoring or minimizing important variables related to sexual and gender minority status. Given the impact of intersecting identities, although sexual or gender identity may not be a client's presenting concern, within holistic treatment it is important for therapists to recognize how cultural identities (including sexual and gender identities) influence worldview, sense of self, and social experiences. Additional sexual orientation microaggressions include: (a) attempts to overidentify with LGBT clients; (b) making stereotypical assumptions about LGBT clients; (c) expressions of heteronormative bias; (d) assumption that LGBT individuals need psychotherapeutic treatment; and (e) warnings about the dangers of identifying as LGBT (Shelton & Delgado-Romero, 2013).

Transgender students may experience the microaggression of denial of bodily privacy (Nadal, 2013). For example, transgender students are frequently asked very personal and detailed questions about their body, specifically sex characteristics that cisgender individuals would be rarely asked (e.g., "Have you had surgery?" "Do you have a penis/vagina?" "Are those your real breasts?"). On the surface, such questions may come across as an attempt to learn more about transgender individuals. However, knowing the specifics of a person's body composition does not necessarily educate someone on transgender individuals or issues, and the accumulative nature of this microaggression communicates that transgender individuals are oddities and perpetually different, and leaves transgender individuals feeling invalid, belittled, and dehumanized (Nadal, 2013).

Affirmative Clinical, Advocacy, and Outreach Services

Affirmative therapy includes utilizing a therapeutic style that is understanding and sensitive to the experiences, identities, and worldview of sexual and gender minorities, celebrates and advocates the sexual and gender minorities' experiences, is a strength-based exploring of contextual and system influences, and is ethically guided (Rutter, 2012). The following section outlines interventions counseling centers can use to advance the affirmative services provided to sexual and gender minority students on their campus and Table 12.4, The College Counseling Center Ally Development Checklist, can be used to assist counseling centers in enhancing their services to sexual- and gender-minority clients.

Counseling Center

Ethical Compliance

Considering that most therapists will work with at least one sexual minority patient during their careers (Liszcz & Yarhouse, 2005) and that sexual minority clients utilize counseling services at rates two to four times greater that do their heterosexual peers (McAleavey et al., 2011), ethical service

TABLE 12.4 Counseling Center Sexual and Gender Minority Ally Checklist

Center

- ☐ The center's diversity statement is inclusive of sexual and gender minority status
- ☐ The center actively recruits and retains staff and trainees with sexual and gender minority status
- ☐ Center paperwork provides multiple identity labels that encompass diverse sexual and gender identity status and/or allow for clients to self-identify
- ☐ Gender neutral pronouns are used on paperwork and during clinical interviews
- ☐ The building that the counseling center is housed in has gender neutral restrooms
- ☐ Specific sexual and gender diversity-related literature is available in the counseling center
- ☐ Center decorum is respectful and celebratory of sexual and gender diversity
- ☐ Center visually displays its ally status (i.e., safe space posters, rainbow flag)
- ☐ Center has a sexual and gender diversity therapy group
- ☐ Center engages in ongoing assessment of the counseling center climate in regard to sexual and gender diversity
- ☐ Center provides affirming individual and group therapy for sexual and gender minority students

Staff

- ☐ As well as adherence to professional ethics codes, center staff adhere to guidelines specific to sexual and gender diversity
- ☐ All staff engage in ongoing training on sexual and gender diversity issues.
- ☐ Center staff have expertise in working with issues commonly experienced by sexual and gender minority students.
- ☐ Staff regularly attend campus-wide sexual and gender diversity focused events and have regular contact with sexual and gender minority student groups
- ☐ Staff have membership in sexual and gender diversity-related professional organizations
- ☐ At least one staff member is able to provide support documentation for transgender students to obtain hormone replace therapy and surgery

Resources and Advocacy

- ☐ Center advocates for queer and trans affirming services on the campus including HRT on campus, same-sex benefits, gender neutral housing, LGBTQ resource center, inclusion of sexual and gender diversity in campus conversations
- ☐ Center provides specific psychoeducation outreaches on sexual and gender diversity issues and is inclusive of sexual and gender diversity in general outreach programming
- ☐ Center has a comprehensive sexual and gender diversity referral list of sexual and gender minority therapists, community support groups, medical professional, mentors, and crisis services.
- ☐ Center actively addresses homophobia, transphobia, biphobia, and heterosexist incidents on campus and advocates for students who have experienced discrimination or abuse

Note: Developed by Kimber Shelton.

HRT, hormone replacement therapy; LGBTQ, lesbian, gay, bisexual, trans, and queer.

delivery is a must. Ethical compliance is delivered through adherence to general professional standards and ethics codes. Ethical compliance is also demonstrated through adherence to sexual- and gender minority-specific guidelines. The American Psychological Association (2012) established 21 guidelines for psychological practice with lesbian, gay, and bisexual clients that provide "(1) a frame of reference for the treatment of lesbian, gay, and bisexual clients and

(2) basic information and further references in the areas of assessment, intervention, identity, relationships, diversity, education, training, and research" (p. 10). Articulated in 16 guidelines, the American Psychological Association's Guidelines for Psychological Practice With Transgender and Gender Nonconforming People (2015) provide a rationale for trans-affirmative practice and guidance for how guidelines may be applied in psychological practice. The American Counseling Association's Competencies for Counseling with Transgender Clients (Burnes et al., 2010) establishes counselor competencies in the areas of (a) human growth and development; (b) social and cultural foundations; (c) helping relationships; (d) group work; (e) professional orientation; (f) career and lifestyle development competencies; (g) appraisal; and (h) research. The World Professional Association for Transgender Health (WPATH, 2012) Standards of Care for the Health of Transsexual, Transgender, and Gender Nonconforming People provide clinical guidance for mental and medical health providers providing services to transgender, transsexual, and gender nonconforming individuals. They include (a) a set of competencies for mental health professionals working with adults who present with gender dysphoria, and (b) tasks related to psychotherapy and recommendations for referral for feminizing/masculinizing hormone therapy and surgery.

Training and Education

Many campus communities have Safe Space or Safe Zone training, and educational training on sexual and gender minority individuals and issues. This training can vary in length and in the subject matter covered. The Safe Space training at my institute is a two-part module that is 4 hours in length. The first module, Safe Space I, focuses on awareness of sexual and gender minority issues and enlists a panel of sexual and gender minority students for a question-and-answer period. The second module, Safe Space II, focuses on ally development and advocacy. Additionally, there is a 2-hour Train-the-Trainers program. All clinical staff and trainees are encouraged to participate in the campus Safe Space training or other training offered on campus.

Centers can make use of seminars, case conference meetings and staff meetings, and informal means for training and education on sexual and gender diversity issues. These can include staff- or trainee-led training, presentations from local and regional experts on sexual and gender minority issues, and panel discussions with sexual and gender minority individuals. Administrators can encourage staff to attend workshops and conferences focused on sexual and gender diversity and informal education can be sought through peer consultation and journal and book readings (i.e., *Psychology of Sexual Orientation and Gender Diversity*, *Journal of Gay and Lesbian Issues in Education*, and *Journal of LGBT Issues in Counseling*).

Diversity

Sexual and gender minorities are not a monolithic group. Intersecting identities will affect the lived experiences of individuals within the community. Although it is important to have a broad understanding of issues impacting sexual and gender minority communities, it is also important to be aware of group and individual differences. For instance, "gay" is frequently associated with White, middle-class, able-bodied men. This association of gay does not account for the experiences of ethnic minorities, individuals with disabilities, women, or the impact of relationship status, geographical location, and political view on one's experience. As well as holding broad knowledge, clinicians must also recognize individual differences and the specific needs of their clients.

Counseling centers can also demonstrate their valuing of diversity by recruiting and retaining sexual and gender minority staff. In no way minimizing the therapeutic effectiveness of affirming ally clinicians, some students may seek or desire to work with a therapist with a sexual or gender minority status. Additionally, sexual and gender minority staff may provide a perspective and contribution that enhances the counseling center's overall culture.

Campus Community

Outreach

Sexual and gender minority students report a general dissatisfaction with the inadequate and insufficient sexual identity and trans-related programming, resources, and counseling services on campuses (Campus Pride, 2010; McKinney, 2005). Providing outreach and educational training to the larger campus community can improve the experiences of sexual and gender minority students, staff, and faculty. This could be through participating in Safe Space trainings or developing a Safe Space program for campuses that do not currently have a program. Other outreach initiatives include providing specific services to sexual and minority student groups (i.e., Pride and/or Lambda Alliance student groups), Greek life, athletics, and student government, or hosting guest speakers in classes. This can also include providing training for medical professions and collaborating with health promotions. Topics may include providing affirmative health care to gender and sexual minorities; targeting high-risk drinking behaviors, depression and anxiety; and transition and name change issues.

Advocacy

Counseling centers can play a vital role in advocating for change in discriminatory or bias polices. A research and mental wellness knowledge base places center staff in a position to initiate or coconstruct sexual orientation and trans-affirming policies and build a community of sexual and gender minority allies (Singh, Meng, & Hansen, 2013). This may include developing zero tolerance policies for sexual and gender identity-related harassment, violence, and abuse; addressing same-sex partner benefits; ensuring equal employment policies; completing campus climate surveys; ensuring gender neutral restrooms; and providing medical treatment (i.e., HRT).

REFERENCES

Al-Naggar, R. A. (2013). Attitudes towards persons with mental illness among university students. *ASEAN Journal of Psychiatry, 14*(1), 1–10.

Americans with Disabilities Act Amendments Act of 2008, S. 3406; Pub L. No. 110–325 (2008, September 25).

Americans with Disabilities Act of 1990, As Amended. Sec. 12102.

American Psychiatric Association. (2013). *Diagnostic and statistical manual of mental disorders* (5th ed.). Arlington, VA: Author.

American Psychological Association. (2012). Guidelines for psychological practice with lesbian, gay, and bisexual clients. *American Psychologist, 67*(1), 10–42.

American Psychological Association. (2015). *Guidelines for psychological practice with transgender and gender nonconforming people.* Retrieved from http://www.apa.org/practice/guidelines/transgender.pdf

Ames, G., & Cunradi, C. (2004). Alcohol use and preventing alcohol-related problems among young adults in the military. *Alcohol Research & Health, 28,* 252–257.

Asch, A., Rousso, H., & Jefferies, T. (2001). Beyond pedestals: The lives of girls and women with disabilities. In H. Rousso (Ed.), *Double jeopardy: Addressing gender equity in special education supports and services* (pp. 13–41). New York, NY: State University of New York Press.

Associated Press. (2009). *Report: Exemptions benefit athletes.* Retrieved from http://sports.espn.go.com/ncf/news/story?id=4781264

Association of Applied Sports Psychology. (2013). *About applied sport and exercise psychology.* Retrieved from http://www.appliedsportpsych.org

Barry, A. E., Whiteman, S. D., & Wadsworth, S. M. (2012). Implications of posttraumatic stress among military-affiliated and civilian students. *Journal of American College Health, 60*(8), 562–573.

Beecher, M. E., Rabe, R. A., & Wilder, L. K. (2004). Practical guidelines for counseling students with disabilities. *Journal of College Counseling, 7,* 83–89.

Berkeley Planning Associates. (1996). *Priorities for future research: Results of BPA's Delphi survey of disabled women.* Oakland, CA: Author.

Berry, J. W. (1980). Acculturation as varieties of adaptation. In A. Padilla (Ed.), *Acculturation: Theory, models, and findings* (pp. 9–25). Boulder, CO: Westview.

Brenner, L. A., Betthauser, L. M., Homaifar, B. Y., Villarreal, G., Harwood, J. E. F., Staves, P. J., & Huggins, J. A. (2011). Posttraumatic stress disorder, traumatic brain injury, and suicide attempt history among veterans receiving mental health services. *Suicide and Life-Threatening Behavior, 41*(4), 416–423.

Bronn, C. D. (2001). Attitudes and self-images of male and female bisexuals. *Journal of Bisexuality, 1,* 5–29.

Broughton, E., & Neyer, M. (2001). Advising and counseling student athletes. *New Directions for Student Services, 93,* 47–53.

Burnes, T. R., Singh, A. A., Harper, A. J., Harper, B., Maxon-Kann, W., Pickering, D. L., . . . Hosea, J. (2010). American Counseling Association: Competencies for counseling with transgender clients. *Journal of LGBT Issues in Counseling, 4*(3–4), 135–159.

Campus Pride. (2010). *State of higher education for LGBT people: Campus Pride 2010 National College Climate Survey.* Charlotte, NC: Author.

Chesir-Teran, D., & Hughes, D. (2009). Heterosexism in high school and victimization among lesbian, gay, bisexual, and questioning students. *Journal of Youth and Adolescence, 38,* 963–975.

Church, T. E. (2009). Returning veterans on campus with war related injuries. *Journal of Postsecondary Education and Disability. Special Issue: Veterans with Disabilities, 22*(1), 43–52.

Clements-Nolle, K., Marx, R., & Katz, M. (2006). Attempted suicide among transgender persons: The influence of gender-based discrimination and victimization. *Journal of Homosexuality, 51,* 53–69.

Cochran, S. D., Sullivan, J. G., & Mays, V. M. (2003). Prevalence of mental disorders, psychological distress, and mental health services use among lesbian, gay and bisexual individuals in the United States. *Journal of Counseling and Clinical Psychology, 71,* 53–61.

Collins, M. E., & Mowbray, C. T. (2005). Higher education and psychiatric disabilities: National survey of campus disability services. *American Journal of Orthopsychiatry, 75*(2), 304–315.

Cook, B. J., & Kim, Y. (2009). *From solider to student: Easing the transition of service members on campus.* Washington, DC: American Council of Education.

Corrigan, M. J. (1998). Counseling college students with disabilities: Legal, ethical, and clinical issues. *Journal of College Counseling, 1*(2), 181–189.

DiRamio, D., Ackerman, R., & Mitchell, R. L. (2008). From combat to campus: Voices of student veterans. *NASPA Journal, 45*(1), 73–102.

DiRamio, D., & Jarvis, K. (2011). Veterans in higher education: When Johnny and Jane come marching to campus. *ASHE Higher Education Report, 37,* 1–144.

DiRamio, D., & Spires, M. (2009). Partnering to assist disabled veterans in transition. *New Direction for Student Services, 126,* 81–88.

Doumas, D. M., Turrisi, R., Coll, K. M., & Haralson, K. (2007). High-risk drinking in college athletes and nonathletes across the academic year. *Journal of College Counseling, 10*(2), 163–174.

Dutta, A., Kundu, M. M., & Schiro-Geist, C. (2009). Coordination of postsecondary transition services for students with disabilities. *Journal of Rehabilitation, 75*(1), 10–17.

Effrig, J. C., Bieschke, K. J., & Locke, B. D. (2011). Examining victimization and psychological distress in transgender college students. *Journal of College Counseling, 14,* 143–157.

Entertainment and Sports Programming Network (ESPN). (2008). *College athletics revenues and expenses—2008.* Retrieved from http://espn.go.com/ncaa/revenue

Fletcher, T. B., Benshoff, J. M., & Richburg, M. J. (2003). A systems approach to understanding and counseling college student athletes. *Journal of College Counseling, 6*, 35–45.

Gallagher, R. P. (2010). *National Survey of Counseling Center Directors.* Alexandria, VA: International Association of Counseling Services, Inc.

Gates, G. J., & Newport, F. (2013). *State of states.* Retrieved from http://www.gallup.com/poll/160517/lgbt-percentage-highest-lowest-north-dakota.aspx

Gelberg, S., & Chojnacki, J. T. (1995). Developmental transitions of gay/lesbian/bisexual-affirmative, heterosexual career counselors. *The Career Development Quarterly, 43*, 267–273.

Gibson, J. M. (2000). Documentation of emotional and mental disabilities: The role of college counseling centers. *Journal of College Counseling, 3*, 63–73.

Goad, C. J., & Robertson, J. M. (2000). How university counseling centers serve students with disabilities: A status report. *Journal of College Student Psychotherapy, 14*(3), 13–21.

Gordon, M., Lewandowski, L., Murphy, K., & Dempsey, K. (2002). ADA-based accommodations in higher education: A survey of clinicians about documentation requirements and diagnostic standards. *Journal of Learning Disabilities, 35*(4), 357–363.

Grant, J. M., Mottet, L. A., Tanis, J., Harrision, J., Herman, J. L., & Keisling, M. (2011). *Injustice at every turn: A report of the National Transgender Discrimination Survey.* Washington, DC: National Center for Transgender Equality and National Gay and Lesbian Task Force.

Griffin, K., & Gilbert, C. (2012). *Easing the transition from combat to classroom: Preserving American's investment in higher education for military veterans through the institutional assessment.* Retrieved from www.americanprogress.org

Grossman, A. H., & D'Augelli, A. R. (2007). Transgender youth and life-threatening behaviors. *Suicide & Life-Threatening Behavior, 37*(5), 527–537.

Grossman, P. D. (2009). Foreword with a challenge: Leading our campuses away for the perfect storm. *Journal of Postsecondary Education and Disability, 22*(1), 4–9.

Harmon, K. G., Asif, I. M., Klossner, D., & Drezner, J. A. (2011). Incidence of sudden cardiac death in National Collegiate Athletic Association athletes. *Circulation, 123*, 1594–1600.

Hartley, M. T. (2010). Increasing resilience: Strategies for reducing dropout rates for college students with psychiatric disabilities. *American Journal of Psychiatric Rehabilitation, 13*, 295–315.

Hass, A. P., Eliason, M., Mays, V. M., Mathy, R. M., Cochran, S. D., D'Augelli, A. R., . . . Clayton, P. J. (2011). Suicide and suicide risk in lesbian, gay, bisexual, and transgender populations: Review and recommendations. *Journal of Homosexuality, 58*(1), 10–51.

Hawkins, B. J., Lawrence, S. M., Harrison, L., Jr., & Mintah, J. (2007). *University students' perceptions of collegiate athletic reform.* Paper presented at the meeting of the American Educational Research Association, Chicago, IL.

HEATH Resource Center. (1998). *Profile of 1996 college freshman with disabilities.* Washington, DC: American Council on Education.

Hergenrather, K., & Rhodes, S. (2007). Exploring undergraduate student attitudes toward persons with disabilities: Application of the disability social relationship scale. *Rehabilitation Counseling Bulletin, 50*(2), 66–75.

Hinkle, J. S. (1994). Practitioners and cross-cultural assessment: A practical guide to information and training. *Measurement and Evaluation in Counseling and Development, 27*, 103–115.

Hoge, C. W. (2010). *Once a warrior always a warrior: Navigating the transition from combat to home.* Guilford, CT: Globe Pequot Press.

Hoge, C. W., Castro, C. A., Messer, S. C., McGurk, D., Cotting, D. L., & Koffman, R. L. (2004). Combat duty in Iraq and Afghanistan, mental health problems and barriers to care. *New England Journal of Medicine, 351*, 13–22.

Horin, E. V., Hernandez, B., & Donoso, O. A. (2012). Behind closed doors: Assessing individuals from diverse backgrounds. *Journal of Vocational Rehabilitation, 37*(2), 87–97.

Hosick, M. B. (2013). *Division I student-athletes make the grade.* Retrieved from http://www.ncaa.org/wps/wcm/connect/public/ncaa/resources/latest+news/2013/october/division+i+student-athletes+make+the+grade

House of Representatives. (2007). *International students and visiting scholars: Trends, barriers, and implication for American universities and U.S. foreign policy. Joint Hearing before the Subcommittee on Internal Organizations, Human Rights, and Oversight of the Committee on Foreign Affairs and the Subcommittee on Higher Education, Lifelong Learning and Competitiveness of the Committee on Education and Labor.* Retrieved from http://www.immagic.com/eLibrary/ARCHIVES/GENERAL/CONGRESS/H0706291.pdf

Human Rights Campaign. (2014). *Marriage center: Marriage recognition.* Retrieved from http://www.hrc.org/campaigns/marriage-center

Hyun, J., Quinn, B., Madon, T., & Lustig, S. (2007). Mental health need, awareness, and use of counseling services among international graduate students. *Journal of American College Health, 56*(2), 109–118.

Indiana University Center for Postsecondary Research. (2010). *The engagement of student veterans: National Survey of Student Engagement.* Bloomington, IN: Indiana University Center for Postsecondary Research.

Individuals with Disabilities Education Act Amendments of 1997 Regulations, 34 C.E.R. 300 ct seq. (1997).

Institute of International Education. (2013). *Top 25 places of origin of international students, 2011/12–2012/13. Open Doors Report on International Educational Exchange.* Retrieved from http://www.iie.org/opendoors

Jacobson, I. G., Ryan, M. A. K., Hooper, T. I., Smith, T. C., Amoroso, P. J., Boyko, E. J., . . . Bell, N. S. (2008). Alcohol use and alcohol-related problems before and after military combat deployment. *JAMA, 300*(6), 663–675.

Jakupcak, M., Cook, J., Imel, Z., Fontana, A., Rosenheck, R., & McFall, M. (2009). Posttraumatic stress disorder as a risk factor for suicidal ideation in Iraq and Afghanistan war veterans. *Journal of Traumatic Stress, 22*(4), 303–306.

Kenagy, G. P. (2005). Transgender health: Findings from two needs assessment studies in Philadelphia. *Health & Social Work, 30*(1), 19–26.

Kerr, D. L., Santurri, L., & Peters, P. (2013). A comparison of lesbian, bisexual, and heterosexual college undergraduate women on selected mental health issues. *Journal of American College Health, 61*(4), 185–194.

Ketz, K., & Israel, T. (2002). The relationship between women's sexual identity and perceived wellness. In D. Atkins (Ed.), *Bisexual women in the twenty-first century* (pp. 227–242). New York, NY: Harrington Park Press.

Kleykamp, M. (2013). Unemployment, earnings and enrollment among post 9/11 veterans. *Social Science Research, 42*(3), 836–851.

Lapieer, C. B., Schwegler, A. F., & LaBauve, B. J. (2007). Posttraumatic stress and depression symptoms in soldiers returning from combat operations in Iraq and Afghanistan. *Journal of Traumatic Stress, 20*(6), 933–943.

Lawrence, S. M., Harrison, C. K., & Stone, J. (2009). A day in the life of a male college athlete: A public perception and qualitative campus investigation. *Journal of Sport Management, 23*(5), 591–614.

Liddle, B. J. (1996). Therapist sexual orientation, gender, and counseling practices as they relate to ratings of helpfulness by gay and lesbian clients. *Journal of Counseling Psychology, 43*, 394–401.

Lin, S., & Pedersen, P. (2007). Multinational competencies of international student service providers. In H. D. Singaravelu & M. Pope (Eds.), *A handbook for counseling international students in the United States* (pp. 285–298). Alexandria, VA: American Counseling Association.

Liszcz, A. M., & Yarhouse, M. A. (2005). Same-sex attraction: A survey regarding client-directed treatment goals. *Psychotherapy: Theory, Research, Practice, Training, 42*, 111–115.

Livingston, W. G., Havice, P. A., Cawthon, T. W., & Fleming, D. S. (2011). Coming home: Student veterans' articulation of college re-enrollment. *Journal of Student Affairs: Research and Practice, 48*(3), 315–331.

López, R. L., & Levy, J. J. (2013). Student athletes' perceived barriers to and preferences for seeking counseling. *Journal of College Counseling, 16*(1), 19–31.

MacLean, A., & Elder, G. H. (2007). Military service in the life course. *Annual Review of Sociology, 33*. Retrieved from http://ssrn.com/abstract=1077638

Mamiseishvili, K., & Koch, L. C. (2012). Students with disabilities at 2-year institutions in the United States: Factors related to success. *Community College Review, 40*(4), 320–339.

Maniar, S. D., Curry, L. A., Sommers-Flanagan, J., & Walsh, J. A. (2001). Student athlete preferences in seeking help when confronted with sport performance problems. *Sport Psychology, 15*(2), 205–223.

McAleavey, A. A., Castonguay, L. G., & Locke, B. D. (2011). Sexual orientation minorities in college counseling: Prevalence, distress, and symptom profiles. *Journal of College Counseling, 14*, 127–142.

McKinney, J. S. (2005). On the margins: A study of the experiences of transgender college students. *Journal of Gay & Lesbian Issues in Education, 3*, 63–75.

Megivern, D., Pellerito, S., & Mowbray, C. (2003). Barriers to higher education for individuals with psychiatric disabilities. *Psychiatric Rehabilitation Journal, 26*(3), 217–231.

Meyer, I. H. (1995). Minority stress and mental health in gay men. *Journal of Health and Social Behavior, 36*, 38–56.

Miller, E., Chen, R., Glover-Graf, N. M., & Kranz, P. (2009). Willingness to engage in personal relationships with persons with disabilities. *Rehabilitation Counseling Bulletin, 52*(4), 211–224.

Miller, J. L., & Heinrich, J. (2001). Gender role conflict in middle school and college female athletes and non-athletes. *Physical Educator, 58*, 124–133.

Mori, S. (2000). Addressing the mental health concerns of international students. *Journal of Counseling & Development, 78*(2), 137–144.

Murphy, H. E. (2007). Suicide risk among gay, lesbian, and bisexual college youth. *Dissertation Abstracts International Section A: Humanities and Social Sciences, 68*(5-A), 1831.

Murphy, J. A., Rawlings, E. I., & Howe, S. R. (2002). A survey of clinical psychologists on treating lesbian, gay and bisexual clients. *Professional Psychology: Research and Practice, 33*, 183–189.

Nadal, K. L. (2013). *That's so gay! Microaggressions and the lesbian, gay, bisexual, and transgender community.* Washington, DC: American Psychological Association.

Nario-Redmond, M. R. 2010. Cultural stereotypes of disabled and non-disabled men and women: Consensus for global category representations and diagnostic domains. *British Journal of Social Psychology, 49*(3), 471–488.

National Association of Intercollegiate Athletes. (n.d.). *About the NAIA.* Retrieved from http://www.naia.org

National Center for Education Statistics. (2005). *What is the status of high school athletes eight years after their senior year?* NCES 2005-303. Atlanta, GA: Author.

National Center for PTSD. (2010). *Returning from the war zone: A guide for military personnel.* U.S. Department of Veteran Affairs. Retrieved from www.ptsd.va.gov

National Collegiate Athletic Association. (2009). *NCAA banned drugs and medical exceptions policy guidelines regarding medical reporting for student-athletes with attention deficit hyperactivity disorder (ADHD) taking prescribed stimulants.* Retrieved from http://cms-athletics.pittstate.edu/dotAsset/218470.pdf

National Collegiate Athletic Association. (2013a). *Student athletes: Current.* Retrieved from http://www.ncaa.org/student-athletes/current

National Collegiate Athletic Association. (2013b). *Estimated probability in competing in athletics beyond the high school interscholastic level.* Retrieved from http://ncaastg.prod.acquia-sites.com/sites/default/files/Probability-of-going-pro-methodology_Update2013.pdf

National Survey of Student Engagement. (2010). *Major differences: Examining student engagement by field of study—annual results 2010.* Bloomington, IN: Indiana University Center for Postsecondary Research.

Nattiv, A., Puffer, J. C., & Green, G. A. (1997). Lifestyles and health risks of collegiate athletes: A multi-center study. *Clinical Journal Sport Medicine, 7*(4), 262–272.

Neal, T. L., Diamond, A. B., Goldman, S., Klossner, D., Morse, E. D., Pajak, . . . Welzant, V. (2013). *Inter-association recommendations for developing a plan to recognize and refer student-athletes with psychological concerns at the collegiate level: An executive summary of a consensus statement.* Retrieved from www.nata.org

Nilsson, J. E., Berkel, L. A., Flores, L. Y., & Lucas, M., S. (2004). Utilization rate and presenting concerns of international students at a university counseling center: Implications for outreach programming. *Journal of College Student Psychotherapy, 19*(2), 49–58.

Oba, Y., & Pope, M. (2013). Counseling and advocacy with LGBT international students, *Journal of LGBT Issues in Counseling, 7*(2), 185–193.

Obst, D., & Forster, J. (2005). Perceptions of European higher education countries: USA. In Academic Cooperation Association Secretariat (Ed.), *Perceptions of European higher education in third countries.* Retrieved from http://r.search.yahoo.com/_ylt=A0LEVr5LHoBXYLkAhdsnnIlQ;_ylu=X3oDMTEyM2ZqY3NsBGNvbG8DYmY xBHBvcwMxBHZ0aWQQDQjlwOTBfMQRzZWMDc3l-/RV=2/RE=1468042956/RO=10/RU=http%3a%2f%2fwww.iie.org%2f~%2fmedia%2fFiles%2fCorporate%2f Publications%2fInternational-Students-in-the-US.pdf/RK=0/RS=DyUwUghh4YNT N53Q7tTXlrIvYis-

Olivas, M., & Li, C. (2006). Understanding stressors of international students in higher education: What college counselors and personnel need to know. *Journal of Instructional Psychology, 33*(3), 217–222.

Page, E. (2004). Mental health services experiences of bisexual women and bisexual men: An empirical study. *Journal of Bisexuality, 4*, 137–160.

Pope, M., Singaravelu, H. D., Chang, A., Sullivan, C., & Murray, S. (2007). Counseling gay, lesbian, bisexual and questioning international students. In H. D. Singaravelu & M. Pope (Eds.), *Handbook for counseling international students in the United States* (pp. 57–86). Alexandria, VA: American Counseling Association.

Potuto, J. R., & O'Hanlon, J. (2007). National study of student-athletes regarding their experiences as college students. *College Student Journal, 41*(4), 947–966.

Prentice, M. (2002). *Serving students with disabilities at the community college.* Los Angeles, CA: ERIC Clearinghouse for Community Colleges.

Raue, K., & Lewis, L. (2011). *Students with disabilities at degree-granting postsecondary institutions* (NCES 2011–018). U.S. Department of Education, National Center for Education Statistics. Washington, DC: U.S. Government Printing Office.

Rudd, M. D., Goudling, J., & Bryan, C. J. (2011). Student veterans: A national survey exploring psychological symptoms and suicide risks. *Professional Psychology, Research and Practice, 42*, 354–360.

Russell, S. T., & Joyner, K. (2001). Adolescent sexual orientation and suicide risk: Evidence from a national study. *American Journal of Public Health, 9*, 1276–1281.

Rutter, P. A. (2012). Sex therapy with gay male couples using affirmative therapy. *Sexual & Relationship Therapy, 27*(1), 35–45.

Salzer, M. S., Wick, L., & Rogers, J. (2008). Familiarity and use of accommodations and supports among postsecondary students with mental illnesses: Results from a national survey. *Psychiatric Services, 59*, 370–375.

Schuck, K. D., & Liddle, B. J. (2001). Religious conflicts experienced by lesbian, gay, and bisexual individuals. *Journal of Gay & Lesbian Psychotherapy, 5*, 63–82.

Seo, W., & Chen, R. K. (2009). Attitudes of college students toward people with disabilities. *Journal of Applied Rehabilitation Counseling, 40*(4), 3–8.

Shelton, K., & Delgado-Romero, E. A. (2013, reprint). Sexual orientation microaggressions: The experience of lesbian, gay, bisexual and queer psychotherapy clients. *Psychology of Sexual Orientation and Gender Diversity, 1*(S), 59–70.

Shields, E. W. (1998). Relative likelihood of in-season and off-season use of alcohol by high school athletes in North Carolina: Trends and current status. *Journal of Alcohol and Drug Education, 43*, 48–63.

Simons, H. D., Bosworth, C., Fujta, S., & Jensen, M. (2007). The athlete stigma in higher education. *College Student Journal, 41*, 251–273.

Singh, A. A., Meng, S., & Hansen, A. (2013). It's already hard enough being a student: Developing affirming college environments for trans youth. *Journal of LGBT Youth, 19*, 208–223.

Steele, J., Salcedo, N., & Coley, J. (2010). *Service members in school: Military veterans' experiences using the Post-9/11 GI Bill and pursuing postsecondary education.* Santa Monica, CA: RAND Corporation.

Steinfeldt, J. A., Zakrajsek, R., Carter, H., & Steinfeldt, M. C. (2011). Conformity to gender norms among female student-athletes: Implications for body image. *Psychology of Men & Masculinity, 12*(4), 401–416.

Stevens, S. (2012). Meeting the substance abuse treatment needs of lesbian, bisexual and transgender women: Implication from research to practice. *Substance Abuse and Rehabilitation, 3*(Suppl. 1), 27–36.

Strickley, V. L. (2009). *Veterans on campus: A white paper from PaperClip Communications.* Little Falls, NJ: PaperClip Communications.

Sue, D. W., & Sue, D. (2015). *Counseling the culturally diverse: Theory and practice* (7th ed.). Hoboken, NJ: Wiley.

Sutherland, G. (1981). The origins of special education. In W. Swann (Ed.), *The practice of special education* (pp. 93–101). Oxford: Basil Blackwell/Open University Press.

Tanielian, T. L., & Jaycox, L. H. (2008). *Invisible wounds of war: Psychological and cognitive injuries, their consequences, and services to assist recovery.* Santa Monica, CA: RAND Corporation.

Thompson, R. A., & Sherman, R. T. (2007). *Managing student-athletes' mental health issues.* NCAA 57313-6/07.

Tidwell, R., & Hanassab, S. (2007). New challenges for professional counselors: The higher education international student population. *Counselling Psychology Quarterly, 20*(4), 313–324.

U.S. Department of Education, National Center for Education Statistics. (2012). *Digest of Education Statistics, 2011* (NCES 2012-001).

U.S. Department of Veterans Affairs. (2011). *Military sexual trauma.* Retrieved from http://www.mentalhealth.va.gov/msthome.asp

U.S. Department of Veterans Affairs. (2012). Who are today's student veterans? In *VA Campus Toolkit.* United States Department of Veterans Affairs. http://www.mentalhealth.va.gov/studentveteran/studentvets.asp

U.S. Department of Veteran Affairs. (2012a). *Characteristics of student veterans.* Retrieved from www.mentalhealth.va.gov

U.S. Department of Veteran Affairs. (2012b). *Who are today's women veterans? VA campus toolkit handout.* Retrieved from www.mentalhealth.va.gov

U.S. Department of Veteran Affairs. (2013). *VetSuccess on campus.* Retrieved from http://www.vetsuccess.gov/vetsuccess_on_campus

Walker, L., & Conyne, R. (2007). Group work with international students. In H. Singaravelu & M. Pope (Eds.), *Handbook for counseling international students* (pp. 299–310). Alexandria, VA: American Counseling Association.

Watson, J. C. (2005). College student-athletes attitudes toward help-seeking behavior and expectations of counseling. *Journal of College Student Development, 46*(4), 442–449.

Watson, J. C., & Kissinger, D. B. (2007). Athletic participation and wellness: Implications for counseling college student-athletes. *Journal of College Counseling, 10*(2), 153–162.

Weiner, E., & Weiner, J. (1996). Concerns and needs of students with psychiatric disabilities. *Journal of Postsecondary Education and Disability, 12,* 2–9.

Wendell, S. (1996). *The rejected body.* New York, NY: Routledge.

Whiteman, S. D., Barry, A. E., Mroczek, D. K., & Wadsworth, S. M. (2013). The development and implications of peer emotional support for student service members/veterans and civilian college students. *Journal of Counseling Psychology, 60*(2), 265–278.

Wolanin, T. R., & Steele, P. E. (2004). *Higher education opportunities for students with disabilities: A primer for policymakers.* Washington, DC: Institute for Higher Education Policy.

Wolfson, K., & Norden, M. E. (2000). Images of people with disabilities. In D. O. Braithwaite & T. L. Thompson (Eds.), *Handbook of communication and people with disabilities: Research and application* (pp. 289–305). Mahwah, NJ: Erlbaum.

World Professional Association for Transgender Health. (2012). Standards of care for the health of transsexual, transgender, and gender nonconforming people. *International Journal of Transgenderism, 13*(4), 165–232.

Yakushko, O., Davidson, M. M., & Sanford-Martens, T. C. (2008). Seeking help in a foreign land: International students' use patterns for a U.S. university counseling center. *Journal of College Counseling, 11*(1), 6–18.

Yi, J. K., Giseala, J., & Kishimoto, Y. (2003). Utilization of counseling services by international students. *Journal of Instructional Psychology, 30*(4), 333–342.

Yin, M., Shaewitz, D., & Megra, M. (2014). *An uneven playing field: The lack of equal pay for people with disabilities.* American Institutes for Research. Retrieved from http://www.air.org/resource/uneven-playing-field-lack-equal-pay-people-disabilities

Zhang, N., & Dixon, D. N. (2003). Acculturation and attitudes of Asian international students toward seeking psychological help. *Journal of Multicultural Counseling & Development, 31*(3), 205–222.

CHAPTER THIRTEEN

INTEGRATING THE COUNSELING CENTER INTO THE BROADER CAMPUS

Michelle M. King Lyn

In order for a college or university counseling center to successfully fulfill its mission, it is important that it fosters and maintains collaborative relationships with important campus stakeholders. Maintaining strong faculty relationships is considered essential to counseling center collaboration on campus. This chapter addresses the typical departments on campus that consult with the counseling center on a regular basis, including chief student affairs administrators and campus police. Important aspects of outreach and collaboration are also discussed as means of fully integrating the college counseling center into the broader campus community.

NEUTRALITY OF COUNSELING CENTER LEADERSHIP

The counseling center may be housed in student affairs, academic affairs, or integrated with student health, although most centers are located in the Division of Student Affairs. Regardless of the organizational structure of the institution of higher education, counseling centers accredited by the International Association of Counseling Services, Inc. (IACS) must be seen as a neutral entity on campus that provides services to students as well as provides direction on matters pertaining to student psychological well-being. The IACS accreditation standards state that counseling centers may provide mandated assessments and consultation to campus units, however, the center is not to make decisions about "admissions, disciplinary, curricular, or other administrative decisions involving students" (International Association of Counseling Services, Inc., 2011, p. 2). Thus, the neutral stance of the center is protected so that students feel safe disclosing to the counseling center without fear of termination from the university or other consequences. Even during consultations with other campus departments, confidentiality is maintained.

ISSUES OF CONFIDENTIALITY

Maintaining client confidentiality is of utmost importance in campus collaboration. Directors and clinical directors need to develop clear policies and procedures in keeping with state laws for mental health practitioners. They must also be mindful of the ethical principles of the American Psychological Association (APA), American Counseling Association (ACA), American Association for Marriage and Family Therapy (AAMFT), and National Association of Social Workers (NASW), and other professional standards in the mental health field. Most other higher education professionals may not be bound by the strict guidelines provided by state laws and professional associations associated with mental health information. As such, college counselors may inadvertently share privileged information. In most cases, there may be a lack of awareness about confidentiality in counseling centers. Other times, there may be pressure to disclose information that conflicts with mental health professional standards. Again, having clearly written guidelines that might be shared with interested parties and those in frequent collaboration with the center are important. Furthermore, staff should be trained and retrained in order to be competent and current with guidelines and expectations in their center.

Clear confidentiality guidelines also help foster relationships between the counseling center and students on campus. It is important for student to know the counseling they seek is confidential and not part of their official school record. For this reason, it is important to distinguish counseling center guidelines from the Family Educational Rights and Privacy Act (FERPA) guidelines. FERPA guidelines protect the academic information of students in a similar way medical and mental health records are protected. Although they may serve a similar purpose, the nature and method of such protection for mental health professionals is distinct.

The counseling center must take on the role of educating the campus about the limits of confidentiality. Students, faculty, and staff may not be aware of the role of and the importance of signing releases. A release of information (ROI) is a document created by mental health providers whereby a client gives permission to the counselor to share confidential information about the client's treatment. The signing of such a release is typically done in front of a witness other than just the student and counselor to validate that the student did not sign under duress and that it was actually the student's signature. It is considered a best practice to specify the reason for the release and the name of the person or agency to which the information is being released.

It is reasonable and expected that counseling center staff will consult with parents, peers, roommates, and other concerned individuals as long as confidentiality is maintained. For example, if a housing staff member calls the counseling center to say he or she would like to speak to the counselor who is seeing a particular student, information can only be taken and absorbed by a counselor. In this case, the counselor would specifically say "I cannot confirm or deny that student is being seen here by __ counselor, but I can give you general recommendations based on your concerns." If the student was an actual client, the call would be documented in the student file including the source of the call and the nature of the concern, for the counselor of record to review. This example illustrates how counseling center staff may often provide information and recommendations from a general position even when the student is known to be a client. Of course, in situations where an ROI is on file, counselors would still be mindful to share only the information about the student that is relevant to the consultation question at hand. When possible, the student is made aware of the specific information from his or her file to be shared with the authorized party.

KEY ASPECTS OF CAMPUS COLLABORATION WITH THE COUNSELING CENTER

Before discussing specific departments, offices, and campus stakeholders and their work with the counseling center, a context and framework for collaboration is important to consider.

Collaboration Models

The broader campus community is made up of departments, individuals, and programs that share a mission similar to the counseling center—to increase students' personal, social, and academic effectiveness and treat them respectfully as a whole person. It is critical to foster collaborative relationships with as many of the different campus entities as possible in order for counseling centers to be effective in this mission. Strong working relationships are especially needed given increased demands on college counseling centers and limited growth rate for counseling staff on most campuses.

Facilitators of Collaboration

Research on collaboration in health care has indicated that factors such as location of health services, commitment of leadership, institutional environment, and the experiences and attitudes of the health care providers themselves influence the quality of collaborative relationships (Bruner, Davey, & Waite, 2011). Bruner et al. (2011) conducted a focus group study in a large interdisciplinary and multidimensional health center to examine those factors that led to better collaboration among departments. Facilitators of collaboration were strong communication systems, respect among providers, patients presenting with greater needs, physical access to collaborators, and a shared vision with similar goals guided by the center's leadership. In addition, they found that the quality of the relationship among collaborators and greater frequency of collaboration are key variables associated with effective collaboration. Ongoing collaboration and commitment from all parties to the process of collaboration also fostered better results (Bruner et al., 2011).

In keeping with these findings, collaboration with counseling centers across the broader campus is likely to be successful with strong communication among departments. Having multiple modes of communication such as in-person meetings, phone calls, and e-mails as often as needed would foster consultation.

Mutual respect for the expertise and perspective of campus constituents and the counseling department is critical. Each collaborator should be able to appreciate the contribution of the other. A quick reference to programs and services offered by units across campus could be a way for counseling center staff to be made aware of research available for them and for their clients across campus.

Another important issue to consider is that students with multiple or complex needs may seek assistance from various offices on campus. These students, when presenting as needy or at risk, tend to get the attention of multiple departments and even upper administration. Due to the multifaceted nature of such students' concerns, interdepartmental collaboration may be facilitated both formally and informally. Furthermore, when upper administration values and encourages interdepartmental consultation, it is more likely to happen. For example, vice presidents of academic and student affairs might encourage collaboration among their respective divisions, resulting in new programs and services.

Barriers to Collaboration

In the study by Bruner et al. (2011), several barriers to collaboration were noted that may also be considered on a campus-wide consultation and collaboration model. Patients that were difficult to track were considered to be one type of barrier. Other barriers included poor follow-through among providers, hierarchical issues between providers (e.g., medical and mental health staff), demanding workloads of providers, and lack of access to consulting departments due to physical location constraints.

For optimal collaboration to occur in a broader campus context, these barriers would be eliminated. For example, a central tracking system for at-risk or problematic students, such as a Students of Concern Committee, would be used. Furthermore, the use of action lists and follow-up through various means of communication might help eliminate barriers to collaboration as well. The workload issue, especially for counseling center staff, is problematic during peak times of student traffic. These peak times tend to correspond with highly stressful periods in the semester such as midterms, drop/add dates, and final exams. During peak times, counseling center staff may have more difficulty attending meetings but may be more readily available for consultation by phone. Lastly, the physical location of campus offices does play a role. A counseling center that is located centrally on campus may be more visible. The opposite option for the center to be more remotely located, may help students feel a greater sense of privacy. The drawback to a remote location would be that counseling center staff potentially would feel more isolated from the larger campus and less accessible for consultation and collaboration.

THE BROADENING SCOPE OF COUNSELING CENTERS

Over the years, counseling center directors have continued to broaden the scope of services provided to the campus. The broadening of scope allows center directors to assert the importance of their centers and to advocate for the center in terms of funding and other means of institutional support. Bishop (2010) suggests that counseling centers are underutilized on most campuses with regard to ways the center can assist with recruitment of students, as well as assisting with risk management. Since more students come to college having received counseling before, parents and potential students want to know the college they are selecting has adequate mental health services on campus. Professional qualifications and adequate student-to-counseling center staff ratio would also be attractive to families who are considered consumers shopping for the best higher educational option. Bishop maintains that center directors should work with upper administrators to make information important to potential families about the counseling center readily available.

Furthermore, regarding retention, counseling centers have demonstrated their contribution in the literature. As such, institutions should value programs and services that contribute to the financial stability by helping to retain students. Bishop suggests that institutions pay attention to the needs of the counseling center in order to maintain and improve on services. Lastly, as others have noted, Bishop highlights how the counseling center plays a role in risk management for a college or university. One way is by the direct services offered to students in need of mental health treatment. Such students are being treated and evaluated appropriately and the level of risk for the students is lowered.

On a broader, campus-wide scale, counseling centers are more often participating in threat assessment teams on their respective campus. Counseling center directors or designees play a key role on these teams by providing recommendations about intervention for a given situation as well as educating the team about mental health and psychological issues.

RELATIONSHIPS WITH FACULTY

Faculty is considered critical to the process of integrating college counseling centers into the broader campus. Faculty is on the front lines in terms of their daily interactions with students. They have the opportunity to observe students across semesters and over the years of their matriculation period. Faculty are often the first to notice common signs of student distress such as missing class, difficulty concentrating during class, frequent tardiness in turning in assignments, poor hygiene, being disruptive to other students during class, dependency exhibited by frequent office visits, and social isolation from other classmates. Faculty can offer much when they are trained by counseling center staff to notice these signs and act on behalf of students. One of the ways they might help such students would be making a referral to the counseling center. This is usually most successful when the faculty member has knowledge and familiarity with the center and can provide reassurance to students that the center is a place that can help address their needs. Furthermore, it can be helpful if the faculty member can name counseling center staff to students or look on the website together with students to see specific information about services provided by the center and profiles of staff counselors. Faculty members also appreciate being able to pick up the phone and call the counseling center to ask for recommendations on how to handle student issues. For example, a faculty member may read disturbing information in a student paper and then decide to call the counseling center to get a professional opinion on whether there is cause for concern.

Since the mass shootings and suicides on the campus of Virginia Tech and other campuses, more faculty are likely to seek advice and direction to do their part to help students with mental health issues obtain the help and support they need. Faculty may also wish to accompany students to the counseling center when in distress. Again, the process is best facilitated by the faculty having adequate knowledge of the counseling center location, hours, staff, and crisis or walk-in procedures. In such cases, the faculty would be encouraged to speak directly to a staff counselor about their concerns for the student they are accompanying.

Faculty training is an integral way to build relationships with the counseling center. It is a good practice for counseling center staff to attend new faculty orientation where they present on recognizing distress in students and provide an overview of services and hours of the counseling center. It is helpful to review with faculty the process of consultation, making referrals, or walking students to the center in emergencies. Making presentations to faculty provides an opportunity for visibility on campus whereby faculty becomes accustomed to seeing counseling center staff around campus. It might also be important for faculty to be aware of licensed and terminal degree holders in the profession, thus developing respect for counseling center staff as highly trained professionals in their respective fields.

RELATIONSHIPS WITH STAFF AND KEY CONSTITUENTS ON CAMPUS

Chief Student Affairs Administrator and Dean of Students

The chief student affairs administrator oversees the counseling center. The vice president's office typically sets the tone for the entire student affairs division and the counseling center may have specific divisional directives. For example, a divisional focus might be on program evaluation or multicultural competence within student affairs. The counseling center would be expected to implement a review or training session according to the directives of the vice president's office. There may also be times the vice president's office may want the counseling center to be visible or have a presence at divisional and/or larger campus events. Maintaining a positive relationship and collaboration with the chief student affairs administrator tends to rest in the director's lap. The communication from the director to counseling center staff about greater divisional expectations is important for accountability and making sure staff is a part of and aware of the greater political climate for the center.

The role of the office of the dean of students is to assist students in resolving problems that are either academic or personal in nature. The office also helps students connect with campus resources that may provide support when students are having difficulties. As such, it is commonplace for the office of the dean of students to refer students to the counseling center for a variety of issues. A student may also be required to attend a meeting with the dean of students or designee when the student has been noncompliant with campus policies or guidelines with respect to his or her behavioral problems or disruption to the campus milieu. The dean of students may opt to mandate students to attend an evaluation or assessment at the counseling center. In such cases, it is imperative to outline the expectations of the referring dean and to ensure that the student understands the reason for the mandate, and consequences if the student is uncooperative with the counseling office.

RELATIONSHIPS WITH CAMPUS POLICE

The campus police are essential to any campus in providing safety and security to the community. Campus police may provide support to the counseling center in several ways. For example, students who may need transportation to an inpatient treatment facility for evaluation are often given the option of transport by the campus police. It may also be possible for some campus police departments to provide after-hours assistance to students since they work around the clock. Most counseling centers have a counselor on call after hours to respond to campus emergencies. Campus police may call the on-call counselor to consult about student situations that may require the opinion or expertise of a mental health provider.

An example might be a student who has made vague suicidal threats to his or her roommate and the roommate is concerned enough to call campus police for assistance. In a situation like this, the police officers responding to the scene may ask the distressed student themselves about suicidal ideation. Unless, a crime or act of violence to self or others has clearly occurred or may be in progress, they will call the counselor on call to also speak with the student. Depending on the campus culture, the on-call counselor may or may not be expected to evaluate the student in person or over the phone for threat of harming self or others. The police officers must be confident in the competence of the counseling center staff, and the counseling center staff must trust that officers will call when a true mental health emergency is taking place.

During regular business hours, campus police may be called by the counseling center or vice versa in a student crisis situation. Again, communication between department heads and mutual confidence in the professionalism of the other department is critical in order for the collaborative relationship to work. For example, when a student is being taken to the hospital, the counselor needs to feel comfortable releasing that student into the care of the officers. Officers who show caring and compassion while also demonstrating a feeling of control over the situation are most effective in these situations. It may also be helpful for campus police to send at least one female officer when a female student is being transported to the hospital. Clarity regarding the use of handcuffs, transporting students in the back of a squad car, or using plain-clothes officers are just a few issues to consider when the counseling center is seeking assistance.

Being aware of the policies and procedures of the police can help counselors adequately prepare their students for hospitalization.

Some campus police departments have one or more Crisis Intervention Team (CIT)-trained officers with specialized training in intervening in mental health emergencies. CIT officers are trained to recognize the signs and symptoms of mental illness and/or emotional distress, such as suicidal behavior, self-injurious behavior, homicidal behavior, psychosis, and mania. They are to protect the safety of all parties involved, including the officers themselves and the mentally ill individual. Campus police with these specially trained officers on their team will send such officers to respond to campus situations whether at the counseling center or elsewhere when mental illness is a suspected cause for the disturbance. Other than CIT officers, it is imperative for campus police officers to demonstrate compassion and concern for students in distress while simultaneously maintaining safety.

Threat Assessment Teams and Student of Concern Committees

Many colleges and universities have formed a committee that consists of representatives from many campus offices to prevent a campus crisis such as suicide or homicide. These initiatives were sparked by numerous statewide task forces that emerged after the Virginia Tech massacre in 2007 where a student killed himself and 32 other students and faculty members on campus. The various task forces that formed recommended improved communication among the counseling center office and other offices on campus. It was also recommended that the counseling center play a critical role in prevention efforts "in tandem with campus security staff in safeguarding our campuses from future homicidal acts" (Davenport, 2009). The counseling center, however, is not alone in this expectation, but it does require close communication and collaboration between the counseling center, campus police, and the office of the dean of students.

Davenport (2009) raises importance questions and concerns about these recommendations and how the role of the counseling center as "advocate" for students is shifting to that of "assessor" and "gatekeeper" (Davenport, 2009, p. 182). Furthermore, some centers feel burdened by the campus security expectations now placed on the counseling center staff. Staff traditionally concerned with assisting students with primarily developmental, social, or academic problems are now more often faced with trying to identify students that might pose a risk to others. As a part of this shift, Davenport (2009) suggests that some counselors may feel a conflict of interest in trying to be fully present with students and simultaneously acting in the role of threat assessor. Many college counseling center staff members may find themselves grappling with their professional identity and trying to find balance and satisfaction within this new role. Continued dialogue among counseling center administrators, college and university administrators, and campus police departments is needed to clearly define these roles and keep students' safety, protection, and best interests at the forefront of the conversation.

GREEK LIFE, STUDENT LEADERSHIP, AND STUDENT ACTIVITIES

Offices such as Greek life, student leadership, and student activities have the primary mission of supporting the educational goals of the institution by providing enrichment opportunities to enhance students' overall college experience. They also provide a variety of services, activities, and programs to meet the multifaceted needs of students. Some programs typically include those that promote social activities, cultural experiences, service learning, and leadership skills. The offices also usually engage students in leadership and peer mentoring opportunities.

Greek life challenges students who become leaders in their respective fraternities and sororities to provide programming to its members. Programs may include topics such as conflict resolution, diversity awareness, or Alcohol 101. Through such programs, counseling center staff can engage with students in small groups. The counseling center staff is also present with Greek leaders so students can tell one another about the counseling center staff and demystify the counseling center by connecting names with faces. The Greek life community on many campuses is tight-knit and closed to outsiders. Word of mouth from student to student may be the most powerful way of obtaining referrals from students who participate in Greek letter organizations.

The closed nature of the culture may also impact counselors' ability to address problematic issues within the Greek life system. Greek advisors or Greek life professional staff may be more open than students to bring in counselors to talk about issues such as sexual assault, alcohol or other drug abuse, and hazing activities. Scott-Sheldon, Carey, and Carey (2008) reported on a study comparing Greek and non-Greek students and their likelihood to engage in risky health behaviors. Results indicated Greek students were more likely to engage in more risky health behaviors such as alcohol use, cigarette smoking, high number of sexual partners, and having sex under the influence of alcohol or drugs. In light of this and similar studies (Buscemi, Murphy, Murphy, Yurasek, & Smith, 2011; Drout & Corsoro, 2003), counselors may be able to play an active role in prevention efforts regarding Greek students and alcohol use. Counseling center directors and Greek life professionals may seek out collaborative outreach opportunities for this target population.

In addition to fraternity and sorority members, student leaders are considered to be on the front line of campus life regarding their interactions and involvement with other students. Student leaders can be trained on how to recognize and approach students in distress. Many universities provide training for suicide prevention such as question, persuade, and refer (QPR) and other suicide gatekeeper training. Such training helps students in leadership positions to recognize the signs and symptoms of suicide and then to make appropriate referrals to the counseling center. They are also trained in the procedures for reporting up their chain of command for assistance with students, such as to organization advisors or student leadership directors and assistant directors. Student leaders have the confidence and connectedness on campus to comfortably interact with the counseling center staff. By doing so, they can help reduce stigma related to mental health and remove barriers to students receiving treatment.

Many counseling centers utilize a liaison system whereby staff counselors are paired with departments and services on campus and that counselor may be contacted directly for consultations, questions, and concerns. The liaison relationships are established according to counselor interests and expertise. It seems to work well for staff members to have a "go-to person" in mind when they need to make contact with the counseling center for a variety of reasons.

Academic Advising and Tutoring

Offices that provide academic support to students are ideal partners for the counseling center since most students with personal or mental health concerns may also experience some type of academic difficulties. In providing assistance to the total person, students may opt to sign a release allowing their academic advisor and counselor to consult. The academic advisor may find relief in knowing the student is seeking help for concerns that may come up in advising sessions. The counseling center in this situation can act as support for academic advisors when they become concerned that the issues of the student are beyond their scope of services.

Some counseling centers provide workshops to assist students with skill building such as study skills, test-taking skills, and time and stress management skills. Academic support offices may offer similar workshops along with academic tutoring. There may be some overlap in services between these offices and the counseling center. Close communication can help minimize overlapping services in order to maximize staff resources across campus.

Freshman Affairs and New Student Orientation

Starting college is a major developmental milestone for students in their transition from adolescence to adulthood. As such, much information about adjustment to college and accessing help for mental health concerns can be provided by the counseling center to freshman, new students, and transfers. The counseling center is often a partner during orientation programs, presenting to large groups of students and parents about transition and adjustment. This is also a good time for parents to ask questions about mental health resources on campus. Parents may also be curious about alcohol and other drug treatment and use on campus. The counseling center staff may be able to include alcohol and other drug information in their presentation as well.

Talking to students early in their college careers about potential problems and seeking help via the counseling center can help reduce stigma around mental health counseling. In addition to presentations, videos, brochures, and literature targeting new students and parents is often developed and disseminated by the counseling center. Various resources can provide information to different types of learners or consumers who may prefer to read and review counseling center information on their own. Similarly, it is important to emphasize the existence of the counseling center website as a resource to students and parents.

Graduate Student Resources

Graduate students make up a significant portion of the overall number of students seen at college counseling centers. While they utilize the services heavily, it important to note how their needs may be different from undergraduate students. They may not be as visible and have as much of a presence as a group, but making contact with offices on campus with graduate student access is imperative. For example, many graduate students may have partners and families and live in family housing. Sharing graduate student–specific resources with such a housing facility would be a good way of reaching the intended audience. The majority of graduate students has research and/or teaching assistantships and has to undergo some type of orientation as new employees. Being present at orientations for graduate students facilitates their knowledge of counseling center resources, both as students to use for themselves and as faculty/staff since they are interfacing with undergraduates. It would be important to present the policies around couples counseling and family counseling at this time as well in addition to normalizing help-seeking behaviors since many graduate students may suffer from imposter syndrome concerns or perfectionism.

A third way to gain access to graduate students would be through student groups and student leaders. It is critical to have working knowledge of the presidents of key student organizations and build bridges with them so they will refer other graduate students and/or colleagues. Student government leaders are trusted and well known among their peers. The peer-to-peer counseling center endorsement is certainly an effective way of marketing to students.

Women's Center

Joint programming between the women's center and the counseling center can be highly effective. Some popular programs include Take Back the Night and National Eating Disorders Awareness Week and corresponding screening days. These and other programs often take place in March each year as a part of Women's History Month. Take Back the Night is a program designed to raise awareness of the prevalence of violence and sexual crimes against women all over the world. Usually, students may give testimonials about their own experiences, which can be moving and emotionally triggering. Counseling center staff is usually present to debrief any audience member or participant who wants to talk to a professional. Follow-up may also occur in the days and weeks after the event. Again, having counselors present and available to students and interacting informally with students help break down potential barriers to treatment.

Collaboration between the counseling center and the women's center may also focus on preventive efforts for issues such as dating violence and sexual assault. Counselors may design programs to present in the women's center to raise awareness of these issues. One such program was discussed in an article by Schwartz, Magee, Griffin, and Dupuis (2004). A psychoeducational program was designed to impact attitudes of students regarding gender-role stereotypes, communication in relationships, anger management, and attitudes about entitlement. Students in the experimental group (N = 28) showed improved self-awareness, improved use of anger management skills to deescalate conflict, and reduced acceptance of stereotypical ideas about gender roles. The differences between the control group (N = 30) and the experiment group were significant in that the control group did not show change in these areas.

A group intervention such as the one used by Schwartz et al. (2004) in the experiment may also be adapted for an outreach program or used within the counseling center for a therapy group. The women's center may be willing to provide referrals for such a group or co-coordinate an outreach program. Women's History Month provides a connecting theme for joint programs between the counseling center and the women's center on campus. However, ongoing programming is necessary to impact the wider campus community.

For example, National Eating Disorders Awareness Week gives the entire campus community the opportunity to acknowledge a common issue for college students. Counseling center staff is usually present at tabling events or screenings to provide educational information and treatment resources. There are even more informal opportunities for collaboration between the counseling center and the women's center in the form of cross referrals, walk-overs, and phone consultations, among others. Similar to other interdepartmental collaboration, safety and confidentiality are important.

EDUCATIONAL OUTREACH AND CONSULTATION

Some studies have indicated that counseling centers are only seeing a small percentage of students in distress who may benefit from mental health counseling. Harrar, Affsprung, and Long (2010) found that approximately 29% of students in their research sample indicated significant levels of distress. However, only 7% of those students reported actually utilizing the counseling center. The results indicate that among those in need of assistance, many are not getting the help they need. The authors emphasize the role of counseling centers in partnering with student affairs professionals, faculty, staff, and students to recognize distressed students. It is simply not enough to recognize students, but campus community members must know what actions to take when the signs are present. Counseling centers with strong outreach and consultation programs are best equipped to lead the campus community in helping students find appropriate treatment.

Outreach can be an effective way of reaching students who are not otherwise seeking professional help. In terms of barriers, Martin (2010) maintains student who need help are not coming in because of existing stigma around mental health. The author proposes that stigma associated with counseling and mental health issues accounts for the discrepancy between those needing help and those seeking help. Stigma reduction is a major reason for conducting wide-reaching programming to the campus community. Training and discussions to reduce stigma may focus on Americans with Disabilities Act laws concerning students with mental health issues, actual statistics on the prevalence of mental health issues in college students, and dispelling commonly held myths and misperceptions about counseling in general and the counseling center specifically.

Ribeiro (2013) reported on outreach with staff and faculty where the focus was on exploring myths of mental illness and how this is another aspect of marginalization in our culture. Evaluations were used at the end of the workshop to assess participants' reactions to the outreach program. The participants found the information helpful and informative and felt more knowledgeable and aware of the issue. In addition, the experience of having the workshop in a group format where there was some sharing of personal insight was especially helpful to the participants. Outreach efforts focused on stigma reduction can clearly be useful for students and faculty alike.

Outreach and consultation efforts might also be synonymous with prevention efforts. Prevention of mental health issues may be accomplished by outreach efforts and knowledge and resource dissemination across campus. It is common for counseling centers to include prevention as an integral part of the mission of the center. Staff and financial resources of the center must be put toward prevention for it to be successful. Effective leadership of the outreach program is also critical to the success of the outreach goals.

Outreach Coordinating

College counseling centers usually have a senior staff counselor designated to coordinate and organize the major outreach and consultation efforts of the respective center. A good coordinator motivates the staff to participate in a variety of programs and offer their expertise and support to the overall goals of the outreach program. It is critical that counseling center staff be made aware of the expectation that everyone plays a part in providing outreach to the campus. A team effort is needed to adequately meet the needs of the campus because one person simply cannot meet the needs. It is quite helpful and facilitative for the outreach coordinator to be highly visible and known to the campus as a liaison and contact person if needed. The outreach coordinator might also obtain release time from other clinical duties if the coordinator presents often and has a small team of counselors to rely on.

In particular, engaging programs can draw in student allies and supporters. Outreach coordinators are constantly looking for new ways to engage students and design programs and workshops with a high level of interaction. Often the programming ideas are innovative and stretch beyond traditional counseling center activities. For example, Bigard (2009) wrote about an innovative program piloted on a campus where a classical labyrinth was used to engage the university community on multiple levels. The author explained the history of "walking the labyrinth" in many cultures in ancient and recent times. The process can be used as a metaphoric journey of self-reflection and understanding one's journey or purpose in life.

Human resources facilitated labyrinth walks to promote faculty and staff wellness. Faculty required it as a group activity in a class where students were to write a reflection piece on their experiences walking the labyrinth. Several other units on campus such as multicultural education, freshman orientation, academic success, and sexual assault peer educators utilized the labyrinth. According to Bigard (2009), the activity led by the counseling center outreach efforts facilitated new partnership and alliances between the counseling center and the campus. It was also a major initiative promoting self-reflection, wellness, and prevention of distress. It was recommended that counseling centers consider walking the labyrinth as a means of innovative outreach, but not without considering limitations and potential fit for each campus environment.

THE USE OF TECHNOLOGY IN INTEGRATING THE COUNSELING CENTER INTO THE BROADER CAMPUS

Video Links and YouTube

Given current trends of the utilization of technology, web-based materials are an optimal way of reaching a large audience of students, faculty, and staff. The center where this author works has produced video links on YouTube that provide such information to faculty and staff. Each senior staff member filmed a 7- to 10-minute video presenting psychoeducational information about common student concerns. The video links are housed on the counseling center website and can be accessed at any time by someone needing information about how to make a referral to the center as well as signs of a distressed student, multicultural issues, relationship issues, and a variety of other topics. The videos are designed to offer information as well as to allow counselors to express themselves and showcase their personality, therapy style, or clinical interest areas. The response to the senior staff videos by faculty, students, and staff has been very positive.

The videos demonstrate how helpful it might be for counseling centers to record staff counselors describing themselves or their approach to therapy. Many mental health clinicians in the community have websites that give information about their training and background. In a similar way, counseling center therapists can also talk about a common student-related problem such as accessing counseling center services, healthy relationships, diversity, cultural concerns, and so on. Students could not only gain helpful information for the video, but they can also become more familiar with the counseling center staff this way. Chapter 15 of this textbook contains more detailed information about web-based counseling and counseling center web design beyond the outreach theme of this section.

REFERENCES

Bigard, M. F. (2009). Walking the labyrinth: An innovative approach to counseling center outreach. *Journal of College Counseling, 12,* 137–148.

Bishop, J. B. (2010). The counseling center: An undervalued resource in recruitment, retention, and risk management. *Journal of College Student Psychotherapy, 24,* 248–260.

Bruner, P., Davey, M. P., & Waite, R. (2011). Culturally sensitive collaborative care models: Exploration of a community-based health center. *Families, Systems, & Health, 29,* 155–170.

Buscemi, J. M., Murphy, M. P., Murphy, J. G., Yurasek, A. M., & Smith, A. E. (2011). Moderators of the relationship between physical activity and alcohol consumption in college students. *Journal of American College Health, 59,* 503–509.

Davenport, R. (2009). From college counselor to "risk manager": The evolving nature of college counseling on today's campuses. *Journal of American College Health, 58,* 181–183.

Drout, C. E., & Corsoro, C. L. (2003). Attitudes toward fraternity hazing among fraternity members, sorority members, and non-Greek, students. *Social Behavior and Personality, 31,* 535–544.

Harrar, W. R., Affsprung, E. H., & Long, J. C. (2010). Assessing campus counseling needs. *Journal of College Student Psychotherapy, 24,* 233–240.

International Association of Counseling Services, Inc. (2011). *Standards for university and college counseling centers.* Retrieved from http://www.iacsinc.org

Martin, J. M. (2010). Stigma and student mental health in higher education. *Higher Education Research & Development, 29,* 259–274.

Ribeiro, M. D. (2013). Groups in college counseling centers. *The Group Psychologist.* Retrieved from http://www.apadivisions.org/division-49/publications/newsletter/group -psychologist/2013/04/college-counseling-groups.aspx

Schwartz, J. P., Magee, M., Griffin, L. D., & Dupuis, C. W. (2004). Effects of group preventative intervention on risk and protective factors related to dating violence. *Group Dynamics: Theory, Research, and Practice, 8,* 221–231.

Scott-Sheldon, L. A., Carey, K. B., & Carey, M. P. (2008). Health behavior and college students: Does Greek affiliation matter? *Journal of Behavioral Medicine, 31,* 61–70.

CHAPTER FOURTEEN

GRADUATE PRACTICUM AND INTERNSHIPS IN COLLEGE AND UNIVERSITY COUNSELING CENTERS

Kimber Shelton and Evelyn Hunter

The International Association of Counseling Services, Inc. (IACS), the accreditation body for college counseling centers, specifies training as a desirable responsibility and important focus of college counseling centers. There is a long and mutually beneficial relationship between clinical training and college counseling centers (Richardson & Massey, 1986). The college counseling center provides a diverse clinical experience to graduate trainees. For instance, the college population provides trainees with access to development-related issues such as identity exploration, relationship concerns, and adjustment, while also providing assessment and clinical experience working with more significant mental health concerns such as mood disorders, personality disorders, and substance use. Trainees are exposed to a variety of treatment modalities and theoretical orientations and receive formal and informal training through supervision, seminars, and consultations. Additionally, the campus environment and experiences of college students are easily relatable to trainees, which may assist in trainees' comfort in working within college counseling centers and also facilitate growth in professional identity.

Likewise, training programs are beneficial to the overall counseling centers and the clinical competence of center staff. The energy and intellectual stimulation of training programs grant staff a welcomed deviation from direct clinical work (Furr, 1999; IACS, 2010). Clinical staff are able to engage with trainees by providing supervision, leading seminars and training, and serving as mentors. Additionally, the diversity and experiences of trainees expose staff to innovative ideas, while also requiring staff to continue to enhance cultural competence and stay abreast of current research.

Training programs are also a cost-efficient means for increasing the number of clinicians available to see students and complete outreaches. Practica are typically unpaid learning experiences, and the cost of predoctoral interns and postdoctoral fellowships are significantly less than the cost of full-time staff. Research suggests that for every hour of training provided by clinical staff, approximately 3 hours and 30 minutes of services were returned by trainees

(Furr, 1999). Additionally, the services provided by trainees are of high quality. Although training programs provide competence-associated risks, particularly in cases of trainees with limited or no counseling experiences, client satisfaction surveys have shown no differences in clients' satisfaction levels between trainees and senior staff clinicians (Schauble, Murphy, Cover-Paterson, & Archer, 1989).

TYPES OF TRAINING EXPERIENCES

Counseling centers have the ability to provide training for a range of disciplines, including counselors, psychologists, social workers, psychiatrists, and other professionals. However, training cohorts within counseling centers are typically comprised of counseling master's students, counseling and clinical psychology doctoral students, and counseling and clinical postdoctoral fellows. Master's and doctoral students are generally trained within the confines of a practicum or predoctoral internship. Although the words practicum and internship are frequently used interchangeably, there are significant differences based on educational degree and clinical requirements.

Master's-Level Practicum and Internship

Practicum/Externship

Prior to beginning a practicum, master's-level students are expected to have taken courses on theoretical orientation, learned and role-played therapy skills, and conceptualized differing diagnoses. Practica are typically the first real-life experience trainees have in providing direct clinical services to individuals and groups, which can be both an exciting and anxiety-producing experience (Hodges, 2011). During practicum, counseling center trainees provide assessment, conceptualization, clinical intervention, and write case notes on mental health concerns previously learned about. Furthermore, practicum offers trainees an opportunity for professional identity exploration. Trainees are able to assess their fit for future entry-level positions in counseling centers, begin to develop clinical areas of interest, enhance their theoretical orientation, and enhance awareness of cohort group dynamics and conflict resolution. Typical responsibilities of practicum clinicians are providing individual counseling, group counseling, and outreach.

The Council for Accreditation of Counseling and Related Educational Programs (CACREP)–accredited counseling programs require master's students to complete a supervised practicum totaling a minimum of 100 clock hours over a minimum 10-week academic term and includes the following requirements (CACREP, 2009):

1. At least 40 clock hours of direct service with actual clients
2. One hour of weekly individual and/or triadic supervision throughout the practicum by a program faculty member, a student supervisor, or a

site supervisor who is working in biweekly consultation with a program faculty member in accordance with the supervision contract

3. An average of 1 hour and 30 minutes per week of regularly scheduled group supervision provided by a faculty memory or student supervisor

4. Provide audio/video recordings for use in supervision or live supervision of the student's interactions with clients

5. Evaluation of the student's counseling performance throughout the practicum, including documentation of a formal evaluation after the student completes the practicum

Internship

Master's-level internship experiences differ from practicum experiences in the number of hours required (trainees are typically engaged full time at internship sites), the comprehensive nature of training, and the building of a professional identity as a counselor (Hodges, 2011). The program requires completion of a supervised internship in the student's designated program area of 600 hours, begun after successful completion of the practicum. The internship is intended to reflect the comprehensive work experience of a professional counselor appropriate to the designated program area. Internship completion requires the following (CACREP, 2009):

1. At least 240 clock hours of direct service, including experience leading groups

2. Weekly interaction that averages 1 hour per week of individual and/or triadic supervision throughout the internship, usually performed by the onsite supervisor

3. An average of 1 hour and 30 minutes per week of group supervision provided on a regular schedule throughout the internship and performed by a program faculty member

4. The opportunity for the student to become familiar with a variety of professional activities and resources in addition to direct service (e.g., recordkeeping, assessment instruments, supervision, information and referral, in-service, and staff meetings)

5. The opportunity for the student to develop program-appropriate audio/video recordings for use in supervision or to receive live supervision of his or her interactions with clients

6. Evaluation of the student's counseling performance throughout the internship, including documentation of a formal evaluation after the student completes the internship by a program faculty member in consultation with the site supervisor

Completing a master's practicum and internship are necessary requirements to obtain licensure as a licensed professional counselor (LPC) or licensed mental health counselor (LMHC). Depending on the state, pursuing licensure typically requires additional supervised clinical experiences for 1 to 2 years postgraduation. For students continuing their education, certain doctoral programs require students to have completed a master's degree or to have had prior clinical experience. Given the necessity of master's practicum and internship, the role counseling centers play in producing practitioners is highly valued.

Doctoral Practicum and Internship

Practicum/Externship

A doctoral practicum may be the first clinical experience for some trainees, yet many doctoral trainees will have had prior clinical experiences through master's-level practicum and internship. The doctoral practicum is an opportunity for trainees to gain more clinical experience, greater exposure to different settings and different populations, and continue to refine clinical skills. The practicum is also an opportunity to amass clinical hours in preparation for applying to a predoctoral internship. Unlike master's-level practica, there are no specific hourly requirements for doctoral practica; however, American Psychological Association (APA)–accredited internships require applicants to have acquired a minimum of 400 direct clinical hours. As such, doctoral students typically complete several practica and often surpass the minimum 400 direct hour requirement. Individual counseling centers provide their own specifications regarding hour requirements and responsibilities, typically requiring approximately 10 hours of direct clinical contact weekly. This hour requirement is also somewhat dependent on the size of training cohorts in a particular counseling center, which is often dictated by the size and needs of the counseling center. Typical responsibilities of doctoral practicum clinicians in counseling centers include providing individual, couples, and group counseling, attending seminars and supervision, completing outreach, and maintaining clinical notes.

Dependent on the particular counseling center, general and/or advanced practicum training experiences may be offered. General practica are primarily focused on clinical work, whereas advanced practica provide opportunities to work with populations with increased acuity and more clinical responsibilities. Advanced practica may also have a specific concentration such as trauma, alcohol and other drugs, multiculturalism, or supervision.

Predoctoral Internship

For many psychology doctoral students, completing an internship is the final step in degree attainment. A predoctoral internship is required for licensure as a psychologist in all states, and has been described as a defining training moment that solidifies one's professional identity and prepares one for independent practice (Miville, Adams, & Juntunen, 2007).

Association of Psychology Postdoctoral and Internship Centers

The Association of Psychology Postdoctoral and Internship Centers (APPIC) organizes a database of registered predoctoral internships and runs the National Match Program. The purpose of registering internship training programs with APPIC is threefold: to confirm that training programs have the clinical staff, financial, and training resources in place to offer quality training; to ensure appropriate protection of the future intern with regard to adequate due-process procedures at the training site; and to ensure a cohort model of training such that a minimum of two interns complete internship training at a site in any given year (APPIC, 2013). Currently, there are approximately 709 internship sites registered with the APPIC database, and of these sites, approximately 163 are college counseling centers (APPIC, 2013). As stated previously, sites have a minimum of two internship training slots, with the largest training site offering 28 slots (APPIC, 2013).

Internship Application Process

Obtaining an internship is an intensive, costly, and at times confusing process. Potential predoctoral interns in clinical, counseling, and school psychology must register with the APPIC database and National Match Service to identify their interest in participating in the internship application process. After registration, potential interns complete a lengthy APPIC application for psychology internships (AAPI), which includes details on previous practicum experiences, self-reflection essays, recommendation letters, transcripts, and other training and education details relevant to predoctoral internship. The average applicant applies to approximately 13 to 14 internship sites, with an average application cost of $400 (APPIC, 2013). Though applicants are not limited and may apply to as many sites as they wish, application costs increase significantly as the number of sites increases (e.g., $25/application for up to 15 sites, $40/application for 16 to 20 sites, and $50/application for 21 or more sites; APPIC 2013).

After application submission, applicants are invited to interview with perspective sites interested in their application. While some sites allow for phone and/or electronic (e.g., Skype) interviews, many sites require in-person interviews, and potential interns incur the cost of traveling to internship interviews. Finally, applicants enter the APPIC match database and rank-order sites (typically only those at which they have interviewed) to be matched with an internship site. As most trainees approaching internship are aware, each year there is a significant disparity between the number of internship slots available and the number of applicants, making internship application a very competitive process.

Match Imbalance

The current disparity between internship placement sites and internship candidates makes the internship process competitive and stressful. Though the 2012 to 2013 match statistics showed an increase in internship sites (6%), the number of applicants in 2013 exceeded the number of positions by 1,105

(APPIC, 2013). Many organizations, including APPIC, APA, and student advocacy groups, are working to rectify this "match imbalance." Currently, APPIC has ruled that effective for the 2017 match year, only trainees from APA-accredited doctoral programs will be allowed to participate in the match service (APPIC, 2013). However, as relevant organizations work to rebalance the internship match process, it is important for counseling centers to ensure their practicum-level trainees are adequately prepared to be competitive in the internship match process.

Internship Accreditation

The most competitive of internship sites are those that are APA-accredited. The benefits of completing an APA-accredited internship include (a) meeting requirements of future employers (e.g., Veteran Affairs); (b) meeting state licensure requirements in some states; (c) needing less documentation for licensure in states not requiring an APA-accredited internship; (d) APA-accredited internships typically have higher stipends; and (e) APA-accredited internships are regularly evaluated to ensure the quality of training. The Commission on Accreditation (COA, 2009) has developed guidelines for APA-accredited sites:

1. The program requires of each intern the equivalent of 1-year full-time training to be completed in no fewer than 11 months (10 months for school psychology internships) and no more than 24 months.
2. Intern supervision is regularly scheduled and sufficient relative to the intern's professional responsibility ensuring at a minimum that a full-time intern will receive 4 hours of supervision per week, at least 2 hours of which will include individual supervision.
3. Interns are either in the process of completing a doctoral degree in professional psychology from a regionally accredited, degree-granting institution in the United States or have completed a doctoral degree in psychology in a field other than professional psychology and are certified by a director of graduate professional psychology training as having participated in an organized program in which the equivalent of preinternship training has been acquired at a regionally accredited degree-granting institution in the United States. In the case of Canadian programs, the institution is publicly recognized as a member in good standing by the Association of Universities and Colleges of Canada.

Counseling centers are highly desirable internship sites, particularly for counseling psychology students. Nearly 44% of counseling psychology students (versus 9% of clinical psychology students) complete university counseling center internships (Niemeyer, Rice, & Keilin, 2009). Counseling centers are sought over other internship sites as trainees consider counseling centers to have better supervision quality and more research opportunities, and trainees have greater comfort in working with the college client population than that offered at other internship sites (Brems & Johnson, 1996). Predoctoral intern responsibilities mirror more closely the responsibilities of full-time counseling center staff, however, interns are often provided with a number of resources and support to underscore their training. This additional support allows interns to experience each of the typical counseling centers responsibilities while adhering to the appropriate developmental level of the intern. These responsibilities can include providing individual counseling, group and/or couples counseling, supervising practicum clinicians, attending seminars and training, performing outreach and consultation, providing crisis intervention, on-call and after-hours crisis services, intake assessments, psychoeducational assessment, and report writing. Counseling centers may also provide internship rotations in which interns receive more intensive training in a particular area. Rotations may be clinically based, such as rotations in trauma work, alcohol and other drugs, multiculturalism, supervision, or consultation. Other rotations may be population-based, such as rotations focused on lesbian, gay, bisexual, and transgender (LGBT) students, women, or university faculty and staff.

Postdoctoral Fellowship

After completing the predoctoral internship and obtaining the doctorate of philosophy (PhD) degree, many psychologists chose to complete a postdoctoral fellowship. Obtaining a license to practice as a psychologist in most states requires a postdoctoral fellowship or supervised work experience (SWE). While some states do not hold this requirement for licensure (e.g., see Ohio Board of Examiners in Psychology), it is important to note that failure to complete a postdoctoral experience may limit an individual from moving and obtaining a license to practice in a state requiring the supervised experience. As such, many early career psychologists choose to complete this training whether required by law in their state or not.

Having completed multiple clinical experiences, the postdoctoral fellowship focuses on building clinical specialty, refinement of clinical skills, and a professional identity transition to that of an early career psychologist. Postdoctoral fellows continue to obtain supervision, yet in many ways, their role at the counseling center mirrors that of full-time clinical staff. There is typically a great level of autonomy with the expectation of skill acquisition and general treatment as an equal colleague within the counseling center.

Formal Versus Informal Postdoctoral Fellowships

Postdoctoral fellowships in counseling centers can be either formal or informal. While there should not be drastic differences in supervision and training received at an informal versus a formal postdoctoral position, there are general differences that warrant attention, as well as costs and benefits to each. A formal postdoctoral fellowship is one that has been reviewed and approved by APPIC, and is typically announced on the APPIC postdoctoral search website (APPIC, 2013). For counseling centers, there are benefits in having a formal postdoctoral fellowship. For instance, formal postdocs typically attract highly qualified candidates, and tend to ensure a continual placement in the postdoctoral position. Additionally, the formalized extension of this aspect of the training program solidifies a counseling center's presence as a formidable training center. Finally, formalized postdoctoral positions often encourage continued funding from higher administration, especially since the formalization includes recognition from a national organization (APPIC). For the early career psychologist, the benefit of a formal postdoctoral position includes the confidence in ensuring that the supervised experience received will adequately meet the requirements for state licensure, especially the number of supervision hours and direct clinical hours required. However, there are some drawbacks to the formal postdoctoral fellowship. First, many formal experiences pay less than informal SWEs. Additionally, there are currently very few formal postdoctoral fellowships at college counseling centers. In 2013, only 152 formal postdoctoral fellowships were listed on APPIC, 17 of which are college counseling centers sites. This creates an extremely competitive field for obtaining a position. For these reasons, some early career psychologists opt to seek out an informal postdoctoral experience in counseling centers.

Informal postdoctoral experiences are any experiences within counseling centers that can be used to fulfill the requirement of SWE. Informal experiences differ from the formal postdoctoral fellowship in that they are not regulated or assessed by an outside party. However, obtaining an informal position is typically more acceptable on the postdoctoral level than on the level of predoctoral intern. For many early career psychologists, the informal postdoctoral position may look very similar to a formal postdoctoral fellowship. For others, this may be a full-time staff position in a counseling centers in which the psychologist has negotiated supervision for licensure. Still others may complete only part of the postdoctoral requirement in the college counseling center, and then choose to complete the additional requirement in another setting, such as private practice. For counseling centers, the benefit of offering informal experiences is the ability to adapt the postdoctoral fellowship to the current needs of the center. For instance, a center can create a 6-month, part-time postdoctoral position to address heavy client volume. For the early career psychologist, informal postdoctoral positions hold the potential for greater income and greater flexibility with regard to timing of the postdoctoral position. However, there are drawbacks for both the counseling centers and supervisee alike in informal postdoctoral positions. For counseling centers, an informal postdoctoral position may make continual funding difficult, as higher administration may see this position as less stable within the center. Additionally, informal postdoctoral positions may prove difficult to fill, as the counseling centers may have difficulty spreading the word about the postdoctoral position, and some psychologists may opt for formal experiences. For the early career psychologists, there is also risk involved. Primarily, informal experiences are unregulated, and an unorganized experience may mean a supervisee does not collect the number of direct service hours needed, the supervision required, or another element of the experience does not meet the requirements of the state licensure board. Furthermore, individuals participating in informal experiences are often required to submit additional paperwork so that the state may ensure the experience was adequate. This is a large risk, and individuals and counseling centers alike engaging in informal postdoctoral experiences are encouraged to stay abreast of their specific state requirements with regard to the necessary components of the SWE prior to engaging in the postdoctoral year. Some states require early-career psychologists to submit a postdoctoral plan for approval prior to the postdoctoral year (e.g., see Georgia State Board of Examiners of Psychology). This can be a helpful method for early-career psychologists and counseling centers alike to ensure the informal postdoctoral program meets minimum requirements for state licensure.

ETHICAL CONSIDERATIONS

Training programs in college counseling centers are designed dependent on the needs of the counseling center and the college campus. Therefore, the types of seminars, rotations, size of cohorts, and training provided may be unique to the specific counseling center. Although there is variance in training programs and curricula, several universal issues exist for all college counseling centers. IACS expresses that training programs are implemented "where it is economically and functionally feasible" (p. 6). Physical facility recommendations related to training programs include adequate audio-visual recording capabilities used for supervision, and access to a telephone, computer, printer, and a library (IACS, 2010). Ethical considerations, the provision of supervision, best practices in training model, and selection of trainees are also important issues for training programs to consider.

There are a number of ethical considerations inherent in providing clinical training to master's and doctoral graduate students. Ethical considerations are integrated into the multiple roles counseling center staff must manage when providing training, particularly related to balancing the roles of teacher/trainer, mentor, and gatekeeper. Ethical considerations are also related to the individual trainee for issues related to competence, multiple relationships, and impairment. The following sections present several relevant ethical standards in conjunction with a description of the considerations for counseling centers' training programs and trainees.

Competence

2.01 Boundaries of Competence: (a) Psychologists provide services, teach and conduct research with populations and in areas only within the boundaries of their competence, based on their education, training, supervised experience, consultation, study or professional experience. (APA, 2002)

C.2.a. Boundaries of Competence: Counselors practice only within the boundaries of their competence, based on their education, training, supervised experience, state and national professional credentials, and appropriate professional experience. Counselors gain knowledge, personal awareness, sensitivity, and skills pertinent to working with a diverse client population. (ACA, 2005)

Training experiences at college counseling centers provide a means for building competence with particular clinical issues and populations, as well as identifying clinical strengths. Unfortunately, trainees entering college counseling center practica may lack basic clinical skills related to enhancing clinical competence. In a survey of over 300 doctoral-level clinical and counseling psychology trainees, a substantial number (up to 35% of students surveyed) reported that they did not receive the basic elements of training in their doctoral programs (e.g., primary and secondary supervision, client contact, assessment, and research; Gross, 2006), thus entered practicum and internship placement with clinical skill deficits and potential competence issues. This highlights the importance of counseling center staff to assess trainees' competence level at the beginning of the practicum or internship so that supervision is intentionally focused on building on the area of incompetence and/or quickly initiating remedial interventions. Assessing competence is also important as clinical supervisors engage in staffing cases for practicum and predoctoral trainees. Ethically, center staff must ensure that cases assigned to a trainee are within the bounds of the trainee's competence level. Consider the following vignette as an example of how center staff might adhere to ethical standards related to competence.

> Stacey is a first-year doctoral-level practicum student at an urban counseling center. She received a master's degree prior to entering her doctoral program, but her clinical experience to date has been limited to short-term psychoeducation with adolescent juvenile offenders. She has expressed an interest to her supervisor to gain experience working with trauma survivors of sexual abuse.

In adhering to the ethical standards related to competence, there are multiple considerations that Stacey's supervisor must make. First, the supervisor must assess and ensure his or her own competence level in working with and supervising cases related to sexual abuse. He or she must also ensure that Stacey has adequate education related to trauma work. This may include inquiring about Stacey's doctoral program training in trauma work, providing didactic seminars to Stacey and her cohort around trauma, and/or requiring Stacey to engage in additional readings to obtain adequate education. Finally, when the supervisor deems Stacey prepared for clinical work, he or she must carefully select the trauma case such that risk levels are low to ensure that Stacey can appropriately meet the client's needs, but that the case is challenging enough to give Stacey trauma experience.

Another consideration in the area of competence is the development of newly established or active research areas in psychology. Particularly in areas such as multiculturalism and evidence-based practice, trainees may have knowledge superior to that of counseling center staff (Babione, 2010). To provide appropriate supervision and training, staff employees must engage in continuing education in newer models and theory such that they are competent to instruct practicum and internship clinicians. This is not only important with regard to competence to supervise and train, but also with regard to a clinician's competence to engage in best practices in clinical work.

Multiple Relationships

3.05 Multiple Relationships

(a) A multiple relationship occurs when a psychologist is in a professional role with a person and (1) at the same time is in another role with the same person, (2) at the same time is in a relationship with a person closely associated with or related to the person with whom the psychologist has the professional relationship, or (3) promises to enter into another relationship in the future with the person or a person closely associated with or related to the person. (APA, 2002)

A psychologist refrains from entering into a multiple relationship if the multiple relationships could reasonably be expected to impair the psychologist's objectivity, competence or effectiveness in performing his or her functions as a psychologist, or otherwise risks exploitation or harm to the person with whom the professional relationship exists. (APA, 2002)

A.5.c. Nonprofessional Interactions or Relationships (Other Than Sexual or Romantic Interactions or Relationships) Counselor–client nonprofessional relationships with clients, former clients, their romantic partners, or their family members should be avoided, except when the interaction is potentially beneficial to the client. (ACA, 2005)

Literature is clear regarding sexual contact with clients as an ethical violation, yet many other multiple relationships are present at college counseling centers. Trainees in college counseling centers may serve in multiple roles on the college campus, such as graduate assistants, instructors, advisors, researchers, and students (Eberhardt, 2006). The many roles trainees serve on campus create an environment in which nonsexual multiple relationships may easily emerge between trainees and the students they serve and between trainees and center clinical staff. Harris (2002) summarized multiple relationships that trainees and students may present at college counseling centers: (a) trainees teaching undergraduate courses that clients are enrolled in; (b) trainees acting as a consultant to campus groups and departments; (c) trainees advising campus organization and groups; and (d) trainees completing committee work with clients. Multiple relationships between trainees and clinical staff can take the role of: (a) clinical staff teaching a course trainee is enrolled in; (b) clinical staff engaging in committee work or advising an organization with which trainee is involved; and (c) trainees and clinical staff having friendships within the same social circle. Considering that trainees may also be students at the counseling center's campus, there is also the possibility that trainees may be former therapy clients. To account for this and avoid ethical and privacy violations, some centers develop policies that restrict former clients from applying to practicum or internship at the counseling center site.

The APA Code of Conduct states that multiple relationships that would not reasonably be expected to cause impairment or risk exploitation or harm are not unethical (p. 6); thus, not all multiple relationships are negative and some may actually be beneficial. For example, Stacey's trauma supervisor may also invite Stacey to join the supervisor's trauma survivor research project. In this experience, Stacey's supervisor provides formal supervision, research guidance, and mentoring which furthers Stacey's clinical competence, research skill, and professional development. Dallesasse (2010) offers the following recommendations for addressing nonsexual multiple relationships on campus: (a) trainees should be aware of the frequency and nature of nonsexual multiple relationships; (b) trainees should engage in consultation with faculty and counseling centers staff when ethical dilemmas emerge; (c) counseling centers should provide seminars and training in resolving ethical decision making; and (d) trainees should document steps taken to address the multiple relationship and seek supervision.

Mentoring relationships have been hailed as not only beneficial, but critical in the development of professional counselors and psychologists (Lechuga, 2011); however, ethical issues related to mentoring relationships have received little attention in the counseling center literature. From the standpoint of the mentoring relationship, it is important that the onus is on the counseling center's staff, to ensure the mentoring relationship remains safe, appropriate, and beneficial for Stacey. It is also important that the task of the clinical director and the associated responsibilities are not lost within the mentoring relationship. In other words, the counseling centers staff must be clear with regard to specifying at which times they are acting in the role of a mentor, and at which times they are acting in the role of staff. While there are no specific ethical standards related to mentoring relationships in counseling centers' training settings, Johnson and Nelson (1999) suggest attending to the ethical principles of autonomy, nonmaleficence, beneficence, justice, and fidelity when engaging in mentoring relationships. Specifically, the authors suggest considering questions such as, "How can I strengthen my mentees knowledge, maturity, and independence?"; "How can I avoid unintentional harm to those I mentor?"; "How can I facilitate the growth of my mentee?"; "How can I ensure equitable treatment of my mentee and other trainees?"; and "How can I keep promises to those I mentor?" (Johnson & Nelson, 1999). The overarching ethical principles will likely ensure that the mentoring relationship remains ethically sound and that the quality of training is not sacrificed in preference of the mentoring.

Impairment

2.06 Personal Problems and Conflicts

(a) Psychologists refrain from initiating an activity when they know or should know that there is a substantial likelihood that their personal problems will prevent them from performing their work-related activities in a competent manner.

(b) When psychologists become aware of personal problems that may interfere with their performing work-related duties adequately, they take appropriate measures, such as obtaining professional consultation or assistance and determine whether they should limit, suspend or terminate their work-related duties. (APA, 2002)

C.2.g. Impairment

Counselors are alert to the signs of impairment from their own physical, mental, or emotional problems and refrain from offering or providing professional services when such impairment is likely to harm a client or others. They seek assistance for problems that reach the level of professional impairment, and, if necessary, they limit, suspend, or terminate their professional responsibilities until such time it is determined that they may safely resume their work. Counselors assist colleagues or supervisors in recognizing their own professional impairment and provide consultation and assistance when warranted with colleagues or supervisors showing signs of impairment and intervene as appropriate to prevent imminent harm to clients. (ACA, 2005)

One of the most difficult roles to manage in a counseling center training program is that of the gatekeeper. Counseling center staff report feeling discomfort with the role of addressing impairment and are underprepared in addressing impairment issues (Gizara & Forrest, 2004). Gizara and Forrest (2004) concretely delineate the difference between incompetence and impairment. Impairment exists if a trainee has reached and maintained a level of competence/ability and then experiences a decline in functioning. Whereas if a trainee has never reached a level of competence or appropriate level of functioning the trainee would be considered "not competent."

Difficulty addressing impairment exists because trainers do not see themselves in this role until remediation and/or expulsion from a practicum, internship, or training program is necessary. Additionally, the gatekeeper role is often assumed to belong to other parties. For instance, the program faculty believes the practicum trainers serve as the gatekeepers to the profession, the practicum trainers see the internship site as the gatekeepers to the profession, and the internship site looks to the program faculty. More concerning is the practice of some training sites to rely on the trainee to identify difficulties in his or her own interpersonal, professional, or health-related competencies (Schwartz-Mette, 2009). In an investigation of impairment in 118 predoctoral internship sites (29 college counseling centers) over the course of 10 years, 68% of internship sites identified at least one trainee who should have sought professional intervention for personal or mental health issues (Huprich & Rudd, 2004). The top five trainee impairments were anxiety, depression, personality disorder, adjustment disorder, and alcohol problems, and internship sites reported that the trainees' psychological impairment interfered with 75% of the trainees' clinical work (Huprich & Rudd, 2004).

This pattern of removed responsibility for the role of remediation and gatekeeping is not beneficial for the trainee, trainers, clients, or the profession as a whole. As such, it is important that counseling center staff engaged in training see themselves as gatekeepers at the start of the training relationship. For center staff having difficulty adopting this role, it is important to remember that staff are professionally, ethically, and most likely legally responsible for the actions of the trainee (Schwartz-Mette, 2009). Thus, there is liability involved in failing to serve in the role of gatekeeper, and counseling centers should readily adopt this role and implement policy and procedures relevant to adequately serve in this domain. Consider again the case of Stacey to better illustrate ethically resolving impairment issues.

> Stacey is currently in the second semester of her training experience. Her current supervisors, as well as other counseling center staff, have noticed recent changes in her behavior. Stacey has missed a number of days, failed to complete clinical notes in a timely manner, and her work attire has been questionable. Of greater concern is Stacey's recorded clinical work, which shows a clear decline in some of the most basic counseling skills.

Stacey's supervisors as well as other counseling centers staff have noticed possible signs of impairment. It is important that staff in a training program engage in formal, ongoing dialogue about trainees' progress, such that issues of note may be brought to the attention of the entire staff in a timely manner. At such time, it is important that the center maintain clear policies and procedures on how to identify and remediate impairment issues. It is likely that these policies and procedures begin with a clear and upfront conversation with the trainee regarding concerns, as noted in the APA Code of Conduct (2009). Subsequent policies and procedures should be written such that they protect clients, trainees, and the counseling center. Counseling centers should adhere to relevant ethical decision-making models when creating and following policy and procedures (see Knapp & VandeCreek, 2012, for a decision-making model).

Addressing issues of impairment serves the purpose of correcting/remediating problematic behaviors to prevent future, more serious consequences and also minimize future potential litigation taken by trainees or victimized clients. It is recommended that college counseling centers provide formal support and staff time in building the development and practice of supervisors, make use of collegial group relationships for consultation (Gizara & Forrest, 2004), have ongoing communication with the trainee's home university to address issues of impairment and to provide timely interventions (Forrest, Elman, Gizara, & Vacha-Haase, 1999), develop formal procedures and policies for addressing issues of impairment, and improve assessment of potential practicum and internship candidates beyond that of a simple interview (i.e., formal assessment; Huprich & Rudd, 2004).

SUPERVISION AND TRAINING

Supervision is one of the most critical aspects of counseling center training. Bernard and Goodyear (2004) define supervision as "an intervention provided by a more senior member of a profession to a more junior member or members of that same profession" (p. 8). Furthermore, they elaborate by explaining that the supervision relationship is evaluative, extends over time, and serves the primary purposes of fostering supervisee's professional development and ensuring client welfare. As well as enhancing professional functioning and monitoring client care, supervision is viewed as a valued experience by trainees. In a recent study on the quality of training, three of the top five attributes related to training quality were directly related to supervision, supervisory relationships, or feedback on the supervisory process (Gross, 2006). As such, it is important that counseling centers engaged in training be attentive to providing quality supervision.

Individual Supervision

An advantage of placement in a counseling center is the diversity of supervisory styles to which trainees are exposed. Although some counseling centers may have staff that ascribe to the same model, most counseling centers have staff that hold diverse theoretical orientations and supervision styles. Trainees may have the same supervisor during the entire academic year, or centers may operate by rotating supervisors midway through the semester. There are advantages and disadvantages to both approaches. Maintaining the same supervisor for an entire year provides for in-depth exploration of counseling concepts, models, and interpersonal processes, and allows for consistency in treatment for longer term clients. Switching supervisors is advantageous as it allows for greater exposure to different counseling models and a fresh perspective on clinical issues.

Clinical supervision is a complex task for both the supervisee and supervisor. Supervisees are required to report on the content of sessions, process countertransference issues, appropriately self-disclose, receive and provide feedback, and demonstrate ability to utilize feedback. Supervisors provide feedback on cases, facilitate supervisee's professional development, provide dyadic training as needed, monitor the supervisee's completion of tasks (i.e., case notes, outreach requirements), and attend to client needs if the supervisee is unavailable. In counseling centers, this likely involves watching therapy tapes, reviewing case notes, practicing new interventions during supervision, assignment and completion of book or journal readings, and processing the relationship between the supervisor/supervisee. In an effort to clarify the supervisory relationship and expectations, some centers or individual supervisors develop supervision contracts or informed consent contracts. An example of a supervision informed consent contract is provided in the appendix to this chapter.

A number of supervision models exist to help shape the supervision process. More recently, transtheoretical models have been applied to supervision. The transtheoretical model of clinical supervision (TMCS) identifies the stages of change that supervisees and supervisors undergo during their clinical development (Aten, Strain, & Gillespie, 2008). Supervisees' stages of change (SSC) involve supervisees working through precontemplation, contemplation, preparation, action, maintenance, and termination stages. Supervisees advance from a limited capacity and appreciation for change in their actions and the actions of their clients, to stages involving seeking change and creating change. Supervisors' processes of change (SPC) include interventions used by supervisors to produce experiential and behavioral changes in supervisees. A benefit of this model is that it allows supervisors to match interventions to the supervisees' readiness for change.

More traditional supervision models include the developmental, social role, and psychotherapy models. Developmental models have been specifically designed for supervision and focus on how supervisees learn, grow, and change through supervision (Bernard & Goodyear, 2004). The goal is to further the supervisees' competence and autonomy as they advance through different stages. These models include the integrated developmental model (IDM), the Ronnestad and Skovholt model, and the Longbill, Hardy, and Delworth model. Social role models incorporate different roles that occur during supervision and the different requirements of each role. For instance, at times, supervisors serve as teacher, counselor, or consultant (Bernard, 1979). These models include the Hawkins and Shohet model, the Holloway Systems model, and the Hess model. Similar to the manner in which clinicians conceptualize and develop interventions for their clients, psychotherapy models provide supervisors with a framework for conceptualizing supervision and appropriately intervening. Common psychotherapy models include cognitive behavioral therapy (CBT), client-centered, psychoanalytic, narrative, and solution-focused approaches.

> Stacey's current supervisor operates from a solution-focused supervision approach. Early into their supervisory relationship, Stacey's supervisor worked with Stacey to identify her strengths and competence, and identified how Stacey best adapts and learns novel ideas. Her supervisor then tailored interventions to utilize Stacey's strengths to assist in skill acquisition in areas of less competence. For example, Stacey identified empathy as a strength and challenging clients as a growth edge. Stacey's supervisor inquired about an exception in which Stacey was both empathetic and challenging. She followed up by asking her what it took for her to do this and inquired about how she can use her adaption strength to repeat this in the future. They also regularly used rating scales to monitor supervision effectiveness and the supervisory relationship, as well as her supervisor encouraging Stacey's use of rating scales with her clients. At each session, her supervisor begins discussing clinical issues by asking Stacey, "What is better in your clinical work (or professional development)?" which cues Stacey to acknowledge her strengths and solution-development skills.

Components of Successful Supervision

Research on supervision highlights the importance of a strong working alliance in supervision, so much so that the working alliance is considered to be the foundation of effective supervision (Ladany, Friedlander, & Nelson, 2005). As summarized by Ladany, Mori, and Mehr (2013), a strong supervision working alliance is associated with greater supervisor attractiveness and interpersonal sensitivity, goal setting and feedback, trainee satisfaction, supervisor self-disclosure, and supervisors and supervisees who were at advanced stages of racial identity. A strong working alliance requires the development of agreement on goals, agreement on task, and an emotional bond between the supervisor and supervisee (Bordin, 1983). Weak relationships are associated with greater trainee role conflict and ambiguity, lower supervisor multicultural competence, and poorer supervisor adherence to ethical behavior (Ladany et al., 2013).

Recently, Ladany et al. (2013) identified behaviors associated with effective and ineffective supervision. Effective supervision was provided by supervisors who provided (a) a strong supervisory relationship (e.g., supportive, encouraging, respectful, trustworthy); (b) demonstrated clinical knowledge and skill; (c) had positive personal and professional qualities (e.g., honest and friendly); (d) allowed for open discussion; (e) were engaged and valued supervision; (f) offered feedback and reinforcement; (g) encouraged autonomy; and (h) provided construct challenge. Ineffective supervision included supervisors (a) depreciating supervision; (b) having negative personal and professional qualities (e.g., judgmental and opinionated); (c) had a weak supervisor relationship; (d) demonstrated insufficient knowledge and skill development; (e) provided insufficient observation and feedback; (f) had ineffective client conceptualization and treatment; (g) emphasized evaluation and limitation; and (h) lacked application of theory.

There are also ethical issues related to supervisee disclosure that make it imperative for college counselors to focus on providing effective supervision. Clinical work and supervision can elicit feelings of anxiety, shame, resistance, attachment, and overreliance on the supervisor. Given the myriad of emotions a supervisee may experience, it is clear that supervision requires trainees to demonstrate a level of vulnerability. Although concerning, it is of little surprise that the majority of supervisees (97%) withhold information from their supervisor (Ladany, Hill, Corbutt, & Nutt, 1996). Supervisees in counseling centers may unintentionally or intentionally fail to disclose for the fear of making a clinical mistake, hold concerns regarding receiving a negative reaction or evaluation from the supervisor, have personal issues, do not identify certain information as important for sharing, hold negative feelings about what was not disclosed, or have safety concerns for sharing due to a poor supervisory relationship (Hess et al., 2008; Ladany, Hill, Corbutt, et al., 1996). With information intentionally or unintentionally withheld, the client's needs may go unmet and problems unresolved. A strong supervisory relationship allows supervisees to share sensitive issues (Webb & Wheeler, 1998) and provides a level of safety for processing difficult emotions. Walsh, Gillespie, Greer, and Eanes (2008) found that the quality of the supervisor relationship was the most important factor in trainees' willingness to disclose difficult material to their supervisors.

A number of supervision instruments are available to assist in the creation of a strong working alliance and also to evaluate components of supervision. These include the Supervision Questionnaire (Ladany, Hill, & Nutt, 2004), Supervisee Levels Questionnaire–Revised (Stoltenberg, 2004), Supervisee Perceptions of Supervision (Olk & Friedlander, 1992), Supervisory Working Alliance Inventory (Efstation, Patton, & Kardash, 1990), and Counselor Supervisor Self-Efficacy Scale (Barnes, 2004).

Multicultural Supervision

A significant contributor to a strong working relationship and supervision success is the supervisor's ability to provide multicultural competent supervision. Considering the already great diversity on college campuses and cultural differences between supervisors and supervisees, it is imperative for all supervision to be viewed as multicultural supervision (Chopra, 2013). Multicultural supervision is related to a positive working alliance, supervisee satisfaction, and increased supervisee multicultural counseling competence (Chopra, 2013; Inman, 2006).

Using a Delphi method, Dressel, Consoli, Kim, and Atkinson (2007) examined successful and unsuccessful multicultural supervisor behaviors in college counseling center supervision. Top behavioral components of successful multicultural supervision included: (a) creating a safe environment for discussion of multicultural values and ideas; (b) developing supervisors' own self-awareness about cultural/ethnic identity biases and limitations; (c) communicating acceptance of and respect for supervisees' culture and perspectives; (d) listing and demonstrating genuine respect for supervisees' ideas about how culture influences the clinician interaction; (e) providing openness, genuineness, empathy, warmth, and a nonjudgmental stance; and (f) discussing and validating integration of supervisees professional and racial/ethnic identities and helping to explore potential bias to this process. Among others, unsuccessful multicultural supervision behavioral components were: (a) lacking awareness regarding supervisors' own racial/ethnic/cultural biases and stereotyping; (b) overlooking or failing to discuss cultural issues in supervision; (c) becoming defensive around racial/ethnic/cultural issues; (d) failing to establish a working alliance and safe environment; and (e) not recognizing the power of the supervisor role.

The Multicultural Supervision Competencies Questionnaire (MSCQ; Wong & Wong, 2014) is a multicultural supervision instrument that can help with the supervision and development of multicultural competence. To aid in intern selection for a multiculturally competent internship site, Magyar-Moe et al. (2005) developed the Multicultural Internship Information Checklist for Prospective Interns. The MSCQ and the Multicultural Internship Information Checklist for Prospective Interns are provided in the appendix to this chapter.

Group Supervision

Bernard and Goodyear (2004) define group supervision as "the regular meeting of a group of supervisees with a designated supervisor, for the purpose of furthering their understanding of themselves as clinicians, of the clients with whom they work, and/or of service delivery in general, and who are aided in this endeavor by their interaction with each other in the context of group process" (p. 111). They also outline the numerous advantages of group supervision: (a) efficient use of time, money, and expertise; (b) minimizes supervisee dependence and diminishes hierarchical issues between the supervisor and supervisee as responsibility for feedback is dispersed; (c) provides opportunity for vicarious learning; (d) allows for exposure to a broader range of clients and clinical issues; (e) allows for greater quantity and diversity in feedback; (f) allows for feedback to be provided in a manner easily understood by the supervisee (i.e., peer to peer); (g) provides supervisor with a more comprehensive picture of the supervisee; (h) gives space to use action techniques such as role-plays and accountability; and (i) mirroring of the supervisee intervention. Limitations to group supervision have also been articulated and include limited time to address needs of all trainees.

Supervisees engaged in group counseling will also receive supervision of their group work. This supervision can occur on a one-on-one basis with the group cofacilitator, be completed as a part of individual counseling, or the supervisee may receive group supervision with peers. There are also several assessment and scale instruments available to aid in group supervision assessment including the Group Supervisory Behavior Scale (White & Rudolph, 2001) and Group Supervision Scale (Arcinue, 2002). The Group Supervision Scale is located in the appendix to this chapter.

Training Modalities

Training within university counseling centers is typically focused on providing individual and/or couples counseling, brief models, and group therapy (Stedman, Hatch, Schoefeld, & Keilin, 2005). While the primary training method utilized in the field is applied experience under the guidance of a supervisor with expertise in the applied area, counseling centers also utilize a number of modalities to support applied training experiences.

Training Seminars

Training seminars are didactic learning experiences that focus on specific training topics or skills. Training seminars may be structured as brief topic-based presentations (e.g., 1–2 hours in length), or longer-term skill-focused seminars (e.g., 1–2 hours weekly over 6–12 months). Topics may range from issues related to cultural differences (e.g., spirituality and religion), focus on specific psychopathology (e.g., posttraumatic stress disorder [PTSD]), or training on broader clinical content areas (e.g., trauma or substance use). In counseling centers, training seminars often include components of group supervision in conjunction with didactic learning components. For example, in a trauma seminar, trainees may receive group supervision on trauma cases currently in their case load. Likewise, in an alcohol or other drugs seminar, trainees may be required to maintain a caseload, and subsequently receive supervision on cases involving problematic substance use.

Case Conference/Staffing Meeting

Research suggests that counseling center clinicians deem consultation activities as one of the core functions of the counseling center environment (McWhirter, Palombi, & Garbin, 2000). These consultation activities include peer to peer, trainee to clinician, and counseling center to administration, faculty, and staff. As such, many counseling centers utilize a case conference or team meeting approach to facilitate and encourage consultation activities. These meetings may also include staffing of clinical cases as appropriate. Meetings may include the full counseling centers staff (or a subset of specific staff in larger counseling centers), other health-related clinicians in the university community (e.g., psychiatrists, nutritionists), relevant university administrators, and trainees. Case conferences allow senior clinicians to appropriately model consultative activities, including client presentation, development of the consulting question, practical use of ethical decision-making models, and appropriate engagement in difficult conversations when clinicians naturally disagree. Additionally, healthy consultative environments provide trainees the opportunity to engage in rewarding consultation experiences themselves.

Treatment Teams

Treatment teams are unique training opportunities within counseling centers that allow trainees to experience collaborative activities across the university community. Typically, treatment teams are focused on a specific clinical issue and include all university treatment providers that may work with clients around that issue. For instance, the eating disorder treatment team may include the counseling center clinicians, the university nutritionist, the university psychiatrist, and a medical doctor within the university community. These teams allow for coordinated and accurate care across the multiple treatment domains. Trainees' involvement in treatment teams creates understanding of the complexities involved in holistic treatment, builds clinical consultation skill, and develops expertise in a particular treatment area.

Professional Development Opportunities

Professional development opportunities within the context of counseling center training typically include participation in research with senior staff, presentation of workshops to university and local communities, and attendance at local, regional, or national conferences or networking events. These opportunities allow trainees to develop in their professional identities, connect with other trainees and professionals in the community, and build a framework for active postgraduate professional participation.

Supervision of Supervision

Historically, clinical psychologists have lacked formal training in supervision, with the majority of supervisors receiving no formal training prior to receiving the terminal degree (Falender & Shafranske, 2004). However, counseling center interns report positive experiences with regard to training related to providing supervision, and counseling centers have recently increased the availability of these experiences to interns (Crook-Lyon, Presnell, Suyama, & Mich, 2011). While supervision training varies among counseling centers, typical training includes formal didactic information, experience providing supervision to a less advanced trainee, and individual or group supervision of the supervision provided. These training experiences, which are typically limited to interns as the most advanced trainees in counseling centers, result in an extensive understanding of supervision models, and understanding of the differences in clinical versus supervisory work, an exploration of power, privilege, and cultural competency dynamics as they relate to holding an evaluative role, and a deepened understanding and use of self as a clinician and supervisor.

CONCLUSION

Ideally, practicum and internship experiences at college counseling centers are educative, enjoyable, and growth experiences for clinicians. Appropriate use of supervision and mentors in developing specific goals will assist trainees in making the most of their training experience and contribute to the development of an active, well-trained professional community. While the training aspects outlined in this chapter represent a brief overview of best practices in college counseling center training, the most effective training environments are those that are able to mold best-practice solutions to fit the specific needs of the counseling centers and trainees they serve. Additionally, it is important that all involved in the task of clinical and supervisory work incorporate elements of self-care into the framework of the clinical training model.

REFERENCES

American Counseling Association. (2005). *Code of ethics*. Alexandria, VA: Author.

American Psychological Association. (2002). Ethical principles of psychologists and code of conduct. *American Psychologist, 47*, 1597–1611.

Arcinue, F. (2002). Supervision scale. In J. M. Bernard & R. K. Goodyear (Eds.), *Fundamentals of clinical supervision* (p. 316). Boston, MA: Allyn & Bacon.

Association of Psychology Postdoctoral and Internship Centers. (2013). *2013 APPIC Match Statistics—Phase I*. Match Report from the APPIC Board of Directors February 22, 2013. Retrieved from http://www.appic.org/Match/MatchStatistics/MatchStatistics2013PhaseI.aspx

Aten, J. D., Strain, J. D., & Gillespie, R. E. (2008). A transtheoretical model of clinical supervision. *Training and Education in Professional Psychology, 2*(1), 1–9.

Babione, J. M. (2010). Evidence-based practice in psychology: An ethical framework for graduate education, clinical training, and maintaining professional competence. *Ethics & Behavior, 20*(6), 443–453.

Barnes, K. L. (2004). Counselor Supervisor Self-Efficacy Scale. In J. M. Bernard & R. K. Goodyear (Eds.), *Fundamentals of clinical supervision* (pp. 333–335). Boston, MA: Allyn & Bacon.

Bernard, J. M. (1979). Supervisor training: A discrimination model. *Counselor Education and Supervision, 19*, 60–68.

Bernard, J. M., & Goodyear, R. K. (2004). *Fundamentals of clinical supervision*. Boston, MA: Allyn & Bacon.

Bordin, E. S. (1983). Supervision in counseling: II. Contemporary models of supervision: A working alliance based model of supervision. *Counseling Psychologist, 11*, 35–42.

Brems, C., & Johnson, M. E. (1996). Comparison of PhD programs in clinical and counseling psychology. *Journal of Psychology, 130*, 485–498.

Chopra, T. (2013). All supervision is multicultural: A review of literature on the need for multicultural supervision in counseling. *Psychological Studies, 58*, 335–338.

Commission on Accreditation. (2009). *Guidelines and principles for accreditation of programs in professional psychology*. Washington, DC: Author.

Council for Accreditation of Counseling and Related Educational Programs. (2009). *2009 standards*. Retrieved from http://www.cacrep.org

Crook-Lyon, R. E., Presnell, J. S., Suyama, L., & Mich S. J. (2011). Emergent supervisors: Comparing counseling center and non-counseling center interns' supervisory training experiences. *Journal of College Counseling, 14*(1), 34–49.

Dallesasse, S. L. (2010). Managing nonsexual multiple relationships in university counseling centers: Recommendations for graduate assistants and practicum students. *Ethics & Behavior, 20*(6), 419–428.

Dressel, J. L., Consoli, A. J., Kim, B. S. K., & Atkinson, D. R. (2007). Successful and unsuccessful multicultural supervisory behaviors: A Delphi poll. *Multicultural Counseling and Development, 35*, 51–64.

Eberhardt, D. (2006). Do universities need to do more to prepare graduate students for ethical challenges? *Journal of College Character, 7*, 1–2.

Efstation, J. F., Patton, M. J., & Kardash, C. M. (1990). Measuring the working alliance in counselor supervision. *Journal of Counseling Psychology, 37*, 322–329.

Falender, C. A., & Shafranske, E. P. (2004). *Clinical supervision: A competency-based approach*. Washington, DC: American Psychological Association.

Forrest, L., Elman, N., Gizara, S., & Vacha-Haase, T. (1999). Trainee impairment: A review of identification, remediation, dismissal, and legal issues. *The Counseling Psychologist, 27*, 627–686. doi:10.1177/0011000099275001

Furr, S. R. (1999). Training graduate students in college counseling centers: Do the benefits outweigh the cost? *Journal of College Counseling, 2*, 42–48.

Gizara, S. S., & Forrest, L. (2004). Supervisors' experience of trainee impairment and incompetence at APA-accredited internship sites. *Professional Psychology: Research and Practice, 35*(2), 131–140.

Gross, S. M. (2006). The student perspective of psychology practica training. *Administration & Policy in Mental Health & Mental Health Services Research, 33*(3), 264–266. doi:10.1007/s10488-005-0023-1

Harris, R. S. (2002). Dual relationships and university counseling center environment. In A. Lazarus & O. Zur (Eds.), *Dual relationships and psychotherapy* (pp. 337–347). New York, NY: Springer Publishing Company.

Hess, S. A., Knox, S., Schultz, J. M., Hill, C. E., Sloan, L., Brandt, S., ... Hoffman, M. A. (2008). Predoctoral interns' nondisclosure in supervision. *Psychotherapy Research, 18,* 400–411.

Hodges, S. (2011). *The counseling practicum and internship manual: A resource for graduate counseling students.* New York, NY: Springer Publishing Company.

Huprich, S. K., & Rudd, M. D. (2004). A national survey of trainee impairment in clinical, counseling, and school psychology doctoral programs and internships. *Journal of Clinical Psychology, 60*(1), 43–52.

Inman, A. G. (2006). Supervisor multicultural competence and its relation to supervisory process and outcome. *Journal of Marital and Family Therapy, 32*(1), 73–85.

International Association of Counseling Services, Inc. (2010). *Standards for university and college counseling services.* Alexandria, VA: Author.

Johnson, W., & Nelson, N. (1999). Mentor-protégé relationships in graduate training: Some ethical concerns. *Ethics & Behavior, 9*(3), 189–210.

Knapp, S. J., & VandeCreek, L. D. (2012). *Practical ethics for psychologists: A positive approach* (2nd ed.). Washington, DC: American Psychological Association.

Ladany, N., Friedlander, M. L., & Nelson, M. L. (2005). *Critical events in psychotherapy supervision: An interpersonal approach.* Washington, DC: American Psychological Association.

Ladany, N., Hill, C. E., Corbutt, M. M., & Nutt, E. A. (1996). Nature, extent and importance of what psychotherapy trainees do not disclose to their supervisor. *Journal of Counseling Psychology, 43*(1), 10–24.

Ladany, N., Hill, C. E., & Nutt, E. A. (2004). Supervision questionnaire. In J. M. Bernard & R. K. Goodyear (Eds.), *Fundamentals of clinical supervision* (p. 316). Boston, MA: Allyn & Bacon.

Ladany, N., Mori, Y., & Mehr, K. E. (2013). Effective and ineffective supervision. *The Counseling Psychologist, 41*(1), 28–47.

Lechuga, V. (2011). Faculty-graduate student mentoring relationships: Mentors' perceived roles and responsibilities. *Higher Education, 62*(6), 757–771.

Magyar-Moe, J. L., Pedrotti, J. T., Edwards, L. M., Ford, A. I., Petersen, S. E., Rasmussen, H. N., & Ryder, J. A. (2005). Perceptions of multicultural training in predoctoral internship programs: A survey of interns and training directors. *Professional Psychology: Research and Practice, 36*(4), 446–450.

McWhirter, B. T., Palombi, B., & Garbin, C. P. (2000). University employees' perceptions of university counseling center services and consultation activities: A multidimensional scaling analysis. *Journal of College Counseling, 3*(2), 142–157.

Miville, M. L., Adams, E. M., & Juntunen, C. L. (2007). Counseling psychology perspectives on the predoctoral internship supply-demand imbalance: Strategies for problem definition and resolution. *Training and Education in Professional Psychology, 1*(4), 258–266.

Niemeyer, G. J., Rice, K. G., & Keilin, W. G. (2009). Internship placements: Similarities and differences between clinical and counseling psychology programs. *Training and Education in Professional Psychology, 3*(1), 47–52.

Olk, M., & Friedlander, M. L. (1992). Trainees' experience of role conflict and role ambiguity in supervision relationships. *Journal of Counseling Psychology, 39,* 389–397.

Richardson, M. S., & Massey, J. P. (1986). Counseling psychology training: Data and perceptions. *The Counseling Psychologist, 14*(2), 313–318.

Schauble, P. G., Murphy, M. C., Cover-Paterson, C. E., & Archer, J. (1989). Cost effectiveness of internship training programs: Clinical service delivery through training. *Professional Psychology: Research and Practice, 20*(1), 17–22.

Schwartz-Mette, R. A. (2009). Challenges in addressing graduate student impairment in academic professional psychology programs. *Ethics & Behavior, 19*(2), 91–102.

Stedman, J. M., Hatch, J. P., Schoenfeld, L. S., & Keilin, W. G. (2005). The structure of internship training: Current patterns and implications for the future of clinical and counseling psychologists. *Professional Psychology: Research and Practice, 36*(1), 3–8.

Stoltenberg, C. (2004). Supervisee Levels Questionnaire–Revised. In J. M. Bernard & R. K. Goodyear (Eds.), *Fundamentals of clinical supervision* (p. 319). Boston, MA: Allyn & Bacon.

Walsh, B. B., Gillespie, C. K., Greer, J. M., & Eanes, B. E. (2008). Influence of dyadic mutuality on counselor trainee willingness to self-disclose clinical mistakes to supervisors. *Clinical Supervisor, 21*(2), 83–98.

Webb, A., & Wheeler, S. (1998). How honest do counselors tend to be in the supervisory relationship?: An exploratory study. *British Journal of Guidance & Counselling, 26*(4), 509–524.

White, J. H. D., & Rudolph, B. (2001). A pilot investigation of the reliability and validity of the Group Supervisory Behavior Scale (GSBS). *The Clinical Supervisor, 19*(2), 161–171.

Wong, P. T. P., & Wong, L. C. J. (2014). Multicultural Supervision Competencies Questionnaire. In J. M. Bernard & R. A. Goodyear (Eds.), *Fundamentals of clinical supervision* (5th ed., pp. 334–337). Boston, MA: Pearson.

APPENDIX

Informed Consent for Supervision

Supervisor: [Name of Supervisor]
                       [Title and Licensed Number]

Supervisee: [Name of Supervisee]

Training Site: [Counseling Center Site]
                       [Address]

Logistics

We have agreed to commit to _____ hour(s) per week of individual supervision, beginning in August of _____ and continuing until December of _____. Tentative times of supervision sessions are on _____ (day of week) from _____ until _____ (times). In the event that there is a need to cancel or reschedule a supervision session due to any reason, supervisor and supervisee will reschedule during another mutually convenient time so that contracted supervision hours can be maintained. Supervision time may include the following: discussion and review of cases, conceptualization of cases, reviewing notes, listening to audio/video-tapes of client sessions, discussion of professional identity issues. Supervisor may provide supplementary readings to complement supervisee's conceptualization of cases.

Supervisor is available and accessible for emergency consultation, both during work hours and outside of the work day. If absent, supervisor will find an appropriate back-up supervisor. Supervisee is allowed and encouraged to seek out the assistance of supervisor if needed at any point during the workday, including, but not limited to, times that there may be a need to interrupt supervisor's own session with a client. Outside of the workday, if supervisor is not scheduled to be in the office or is working out of the office and supervisee needs assistance, supervisee is permitted to contact supervisor by telephone at _____ (mobile) or _____ (home).

Supervisor's Area of Competence and the Supervisory Relationship

[Include specific information about the supervisor such as number of years licensed, educational background, clinical experience and expertise, theoretical orientation, model of supervision, supervision expectations, etc.]

Prompt Example: I am a licensed psychologist with over _____ *years of experience working in several university counseling centers.*

(continued)

(*continued*)

I have experience providing therapy to [individuals, couples, and groups] who present with a wide range of clinical concerns.

I have over _____ years of experience supervising trainees at the [practicum, predoctoral internship, and postdoctoral fellowship] levels of training.

Multicultural competence is _____.

My specific clinical interests include _____.

My approach to supervision is _____.

As a supervisor, I will focus on _____.

Expectations for supervision include _____.

Supervision is not therapy. There is an expectation that the supervisory relationship will include open communication and two-way feedback in which growth is enhanced, and mentoring is accomplished.

Standards and Evaluation

The supervisee will adhere to the ethical and legal codes and principles of the training site as outlined in the Training Manual of the American Psychological Association (APA). Recordkeeping, including notes, is to be in compliance with APA recordkeeping or other established standards outlined by the training site. Supervisor will review and sign notes and bring to the attention of the supervisee any issues that need to be clarified. Supervisee will follow audio/videotape requirements as specified by the training site. The supervisor will model professionalism and will let supervisee know about procedures for evaluation, confidentiality, due process, and grievances in accordance with the guidelines of the training site.

The supervisor bears liability in supervision and thus it is essential that supervisee share complete information regarding clients, files, and abide by supervisor's final decisions as the welfare of the client is tantamount. Open and direct feedback will be provided on an ongoing basis, nestled in an atmosphere of support and care. Evaluation, both formative and summative, is based upon the details which are drawn from the supervision contract and from the training manual. Evaluation criteria are clearly defined and measurable, and occur at designated intervals as specified by the training site. The supervisor encourages supervisee to express disagreements and differences in opinion with the supervisor. The supervisor also expects that supervisee will be open to discuss any conflicts in the supervisory relationship.

(*continued*)

(*continued*)

Goals for Supervision

Goals will be jointly developed by the supervisor and the supervisee. The training site has outlined training goals and competencies for practicum/internship (see Practicum Manual/Pre-Doctoral Internship Manual). In addition, the supervisee has identified the following clinical goals that s/he would like to have addressed this semester:

1.
2.
3.
4.

Signature of Supervisee: _____ Date:

Signature of Supervisor: _____ Date:

Developed by T. Hughes-Troutman (2013). Unpublished document. Printed with permission of author.

Multicultural Supervision Competencies Questionnaire

This questionnaire is intended to evaluate the quality of multicultural supervision. If you have had a supervisor that is culturally or racially different from you, I would like you to complete this questionnaire with respect to this particular supervisor.

Your ethnic/racial background

_____

Your supervisor's ethnic/racial background

_____

Your gender_____ Your supervisor's gender_____

How long ago? _____ How long did you have him/her as supervisor _____

What was the level of your clinical training during this supervision?

_____

(*continued*)

(continued)

What was the nature of the clinical site where this supervision took place?

_____

Based on your experience and observation, rate the following statements according to the following scale:

1	2	3	4	5
Strongly disagree	Disagree	Undecided	Agree	Strongly agree

Circle the response code (e.g., 4 for Agree, or 2 for Disagree) at the end of each statement that most clearly reflects your opinion about this supervisor. Try to use 3 sparingly.

	1	2	3	4	5
1. Understands my culture and value systems	1	2	3	4	5
2. Shows openness and respect for culturally different supervisees	1	2	3	4	5
3. Actively avoids cultural biases and discriminatory practices in working with minority students	1	2	3	4	5
4. Understands the worldviews of supervisees and clients from other cultures	1	2	3	4	5
5. Understands the tendency and the problem of racial stereotyping	1	2	3	4	5
6. Makes an effort to understand and accommodate culturally different supervisees	1	2	3	4	5
7. Is able to avoid racial stereotypes by taking into account both the uniqueness of individuals as well as the known characteristics of the culture	1	2	3	4	5
8. Makes use of every opportunity to increase supervisees' multicultural competence in counseling	1	2	3	4	5
9. Is able to clarify presenting problems and arrives at culturally relevant case conceptualization with clients from different cultural backgrounds	1	2	3	4	5
10. Shows an understanding of how culture, ethnicity, and race influence supervision and counseling	1	2	3	4	5
11. Is able to overcome cultural and language barriers in relating to minority students and clients	1	2	3	4	5

(continued)

(*continued*)

12. Has never mentioned that race is an important consideration in supervision and counseling	1	2	3	4	5
13. Demonstrates skills to balance between the generic characteristic of counseling and the unique values of different cultural groups	1	2	3	4	5
14. Shows sensitivity and skills in supervising culturally different trainees	1	2	3	4	5
15. Shows unconditional acceptance of all supervisees, regardless of their race, ethnicity, and culture	1	2	3	4	5
16. Recognizes the limitations of models and approaches based on Western assumptions in working with culturally different individuals	1	2	3	4	5
17. Knows how to encourage discussion of cultural and racial issues in counseling and supervision	1	2	3	4	5
18 Shows interest in learning new skills and enhancing own multicultural competence in supervision and counseling	1	2	3	4	5
19. Recognizes that what is inappropriate from the standpoint of the majority culture may be appropriate for some minority cultures	1	2	3	4	5
20. Takes into account cultural biases in assessing supervisees and forming clinical judgments	1	2	3	4	5
21. Exhibits respect for other cultures without overly identifying self with minority culture or becoming paternalistic	1	2	3	4	5
22. Is willing to advocate for minorities who experience institutional discrimination	1	2	3	4	5
23. Understands the cultural reasons why minority students and clients tend to defer to authority figures	1	2	3	4	5
24. Communicates effectively with culturally different supervisees at both the verbal and nonverbal levels	1	2	3	4	5
25. Understands cultural differences in help-giving and help-seeking	1	2	3	4	5
26. Believes that Western models and approaches of counseling are equally generalizable to ethnic minorities	1	2	3	4	5

(*continued*)

(continued)

27. Gives emotional support and encouragement to minority students	1	2	3	4	5
28. Is very rigid and dogmatic regarding what constitutes the proper approach of counseling	1	2	3	4	5
29. Shows an interest in helping minority students to overcome systematic and institutional barriers	1	2	3	4	5
30. Welcomes my input even when I express different views and values	1	2	3	4	5
31. Knows how to consult or refer to resources available in ethnocultural communities	1	2	3	4	5
32. Takes into account racial biases and sociopolitical implications in counseling and supervision	1	2	3	4	5
33. Considers supervisees' cultural and linguistic backgrounds in giving them feedback and evaluation	1	2	3	4	5
34. Shows a genuine interest in learning about other cultures	1	2	3	4	5
35. Recognizes individual differences in ethnic/racial identity	1	2	3	4	5
36. Demonstrates a familiarity with the value systems of diverse cultural groups	1	2	3	4	5
37. Knows that biases and assumptions of Western counseling models can have a negative effect on culturally different supervisees and clients	1	2	3	4	5
38. Knows how to adapt knowledge of cultural differences to supervision and counseling	1	2	3	4	5
39. Does not seem to be aware of own limitations in working with culturally different supervisees or clients	1	2	3	4	5
40. Does not pay any attention to the demographics of supervisees	1	2	3	4	5
41. Is able to develop culturally appropriate treatment plans for clients from different cultural backgrounds	1	2	3	4	5
42. Makes an effort to establish a relationship of trust and acceptance with culturally different supervisees	1	2	3	4	5
43. Is flexible in adjusting his/her supervisory style to culturally different supervisees	1	2	3	4	5

(continued)

(*continued*)

44. Assists supervisees in formulating culturally appropriate assessment and treatment plans	1	2	3	4	5
45. Makes use of the support network of minorities	1	2	3	4	5
46. Does not seem to be aware of own implicit cultural biases in counseling and supervision	1	2	3	4	5
47. Acknowledges that his or her own life experiences, values, and biases may influence the supervision process	1	2	3	4	5
48. Actively interacts with minority students outside counseling and classroom settings	1	2	3	4	5
49. Knows something about gender, socioeconomic status, and religious issues are related to minority status	1	2	3	4	5
50. Shows some knowledge about the cultural traditions of various ethnic group	1	2	3	4	5
51. Is able to integrate own beliefs, knowledge, and skills in forming relationships with culturally different supervisees	1	2	3	4	5
52. Is able to reduce my defensiveness, suspicions, and anxiety about having a supervisor from a different culture	1	2	3	4	5
53. Shows no interest in understanding my cultural background and ethnic/racial heritage	1	2	3	4	5
54. Negatively evaluates supervisees who do not conform to supervisor's own theoretical orientation and approach to counseling	1	2	3	4	5
55. Has a tendency to abuse supervisory power (e.g., imposes view on supervisees)	1	2	3	4	5
56. Respects the worldview, religious beliefs, and values of culturally different supervisees	1	2	3	4	5
57. Demonstrates competence in a wide variety of methods of assessment and interventions, including nontraditional ones	1	2	3	4	5
58. Provides guidance to international students and new immigrants to facilitate their acculturation	1	2	3	4	5
59. Makes minority supervisees feel safe to share their difficulties and concerns	1	2	3	4	5
60. Is able to relate to culturally different supervisees while maintaining own cultural values	1	2	3	4	5

(*continued*)

(continued)

Scoring:	Before scoring, reverse the scoring of the following items: 12, 26, 28, 39, 40, 46, 53, 54, 55.
	Attitude and beliefs (how the supervisor feels about multicultural issues and culturally different supervisees): 2, 12, 16, 19, 21, 26, 34, 39, 40, 46, 47, 56
	Knowledge and understanding (what the supervisor knows about multicultural supervision): 1, 4, 5, 10, 23, 25, 36, 37, 49, 50
	Skills and practices (how the supervisor demonstrates multicultural competencies in actual practices of supervision): 7, 8, 9, 13, 14, 17, 18, 20, 24, 28, 31, 32, 33, 35, 38, 41, 43, 44, 45, 52, 54, 57
	Relationship (how the supervisor relates to culturally different supervisees): 3, 6, 11, 15, 22, 27, 29, 30, 42, 48, 51, 53, 55, 58, 59, 60

Multicultural Internship Information Checklist for Prospective Interns

POINTS TO CONISDER IN INTERNSHIP
SELECTION

Name of internship site = _____
Source(s) of information:
APPIC Directory only: yes _____ no _____
Training director/other senior staff: yes _____
Name of contact = _____
Current intern(s): yes _____
Name of current interns = _____

Site has a MAJOR multicultural rotation?
_____ yes _____ no

Notes:

Discrepancy between APPIC listing information
and information from training director/staff?
_____ yes _____ no

Site has a MINOR multicultural rotation?
_____ yes _____ no

Notes:

Discrepancy between APPIC listing information
and information from training director/staff?
_____ yes _____ no

Site's definition of "multicultural rotation?"
Definition provided? _____ yes _____ no

Notes:

Diverse clientele seen at this site?
_____ yes _____ no

Notes:

Percentages of types clients seen?

Information available?
_____ yes _____ no

(continued)

(*continued*)

Assessment strategies and evaluation criteria used to measure intern multicultural competence upon completion of the training program?

Notes:

Information available?
_____ yes _____ no

Seminars or specific training in multicultural topics available? _____ yes _____ no

Notes:

Number of hours devoted to such training?

Pertinent multicultural training/background of seminar leaders?

Types of diversity represented at site:
Race/ethnicity _____ yes _____ no
Religion _____ yes _____ no
Sexual orientation _____ yes _____ no
Disability _____ yes _____ no
Other _____ yes _____ no

Notes:

APPIC, Association of Psychology Postdoctoral and Internship Centers.

Source: Magyar-Moe et al. (2005). Copyright © 2005 by the American Psychological Association. Reproduced with permission. The use of APA information does not imply endorsement by APA.

Group Supervision Scale

Please answer the following items regarding your group supervisor. Assign a rating on a scale from 1 to 6, where 1 represents "**Strongly Disagree**" and 6 represents "**Strongly Agree**."

	1	2	3	4	5	6
The supervisor provides useful feedback regarding my skills and interventions.	O	O	O	O	O	O
The supervisor provided helpful suggestions and information related to treatment interventions.	O	O	O	O	O	O
The supervisor facilitates constructive exploration of ideas and techniques for working with clients.	O	O	O	O	O	O
The supervisor provides helpful information regarding case conceptualization and diagnosis.	O	O	O	O	O	O
The supervisor helps me comprehend and formulate clients' central issues.	O	O	O	O	O	O
The supervisor helps me to understand the thoughts, feelings, and behaviors of clients.	O	O	O	O	O	O

(*continued*)

(continued)

	1	2	3	4	5	6
The supervisor encourages trainee self-exploration appropriately.	O	O	O	O	O	O
The supervisor enables me to express opinions, questions, and concerns about my counseling.	O	O	O	O	O	O
The supervisor created a safe environment for group supervision.	O	O	O	O	O	O
The supervisor is attentive to group dynamics.	O	O	O	O	O	O
The supervisor effectively sets limits, and establishes norms and boundaries for the group.	O	O	O	O	O	O
The supervisor provides helpful leadership for the group.	O	O	O	O	O	O
The supervisor encourages supervisees to provide each other feedback.	O	O	O	O	O	O
The supervisor redirects the discussion when appropriate.	O	O	O	O	O	O
The supervisor manages time well between all the group members.	O	O	O	O	O	O
The supervisor provides enough structure in the group supervision.	O	O	O	O	O	O
Source: Arcinue (2002). Reprinted with permission from the author.						

CHAPTER FIFTEEN

21st-CENTURY CHALLENGES FOR THE COLLEGE COUNSELING CENTER

Shannon J. Hodges

College counseling has entered an era that promises to be radically different than any time in its previous 100-year history. College students in this 21st century are more technologically advanced than previous generations and more likely to take virtual classes than previous generations of college students (Patrick & Flanigan, 2012). Nationwide surveys have found 97% of college students owned a computer, 94% owned a cell phone, and over 90% had access to high-speed Internet (Junco & Cole-Avant, 2008). Several years ago, Ruffalo-Noel-Levitz (2008) found that over 70% of college applicants indicated an interest in exchanging instant messages with admissions counselors. This percentage has certainly gone up and any college campus will witness students scurrying to and from campus using their smartphones for texting.

Technology has impacted virtually every facet of collegiate life, including how students communicate with one another. In previous eras, the telephone was the primary means of high-tech communication on campus and in many cases each residence hall had only one phone for each floor. Today, it is the rare college student who does not have a cell phone, to say nothing of cell phones with Internet service, texting, e-mail, and Skype capabilities. Students walking and texting have become a ubiquitous sight on all collegiate campuses in the United States. In fact, landlines in college residence halls and pay phones in student unions are fast becoming an artifact of previous generations, much in the manner of phone booths. Students now receive a good portion of their mail through the Internet. Skype has also replaced traditional phone calls due to ease of use and cost-effectiveness, especially regarding overseas communication.

Then we have the emergence of virtual institutions, most notable of which is the University of Phoenix, which, with over 250,000 students, is one of the world's largest universities. Even traditional universities like the University of Maryland have very successful distance degree programs and even the venerable Harvard University offers web-based degrees. Essentially, colleges and universities have entered an entirely new era in their history and one that promises to both make education more available while creating more social distance in the process. Digital and online resources such as e-books and virtual libraries are common and will be the dominant method of storing scholarly information. Even today, an increasing number of students are selecting e-textbooks over traditional printed ones. Interactive software programs such as Blackboard have become commonplace, meaning the role of the professor is evolving. This rapid evolutionary process certainly has strong implications for college student services, most particularly counseling services.

Many researchers refer to today's college students, those born after 1982 as the millennial generation (Maples & Han, 2008). The key component of the millennial generation is that they grew up in a time of a technological revolution, involving personal computers, e-mail, the Internet, and later smartphones, texting, and so on. To the millennial generation, not only is technology a fact of life, it is completely intertwined with life. Cell phones that offer texting, e-mail, the Internet, video recording, a camera, and numerous additional applications are all at the tips of their fingers. Meeting in a chat room is as natural as in social groups, and through popular media such as Facebook, the term "friend" means something radically different to millennial students than previous generations. Regarding education, millennial generation students see web classes as a viable if not better alternative to traditional classes. For this reason, traditional mortar and brick campuses have added web classes and even degrees. As previously noted, virtual institutions such as the University of Phoenix have exploded in popularity and are likely to continue their expansion.

Clearly, anyone who has been around college campuses can attest to the fact that technology has totally revamped contemporary colleges and will continue to do so for the foreseeable future. A crucial question to examine is, "What do all the technological changes on college campuses mean for college counseling centers?" Interestingly, a database search through various scholarly search engines turned up very little information on this topic. Surprisingly, despite the explosion of technology and the revolutionary impact it has had on higher education, the literature on college and university counseling centers has had very little to report about the impact of technology on the college counseling center. One has to think this dearth of research represents a real concern for the profession. Most notably, will millennial generation students continue to see the campus counseling center as a viable resource? Given that many of these students prefer to communicate via technology (e.g., texting, Skype, the Internet), will face-to-face personal and career counseling become as passé as landline phones? Or will students begin reaching out to private providers on, say, Skype as it's likely that counseling professionals may see a market in counseling college students via cyberspace. After all, students can then sit on or lie in their own beds in their residence hall or in their apartment. This is not at all to suggest that Skype counseling with a distant counselor not connected to the institution is at all a "good" thing, but students may come to see such as more available to them given that they interact with the world through the medium of cyberspace. College counseling services already are adapting to millennial changes as many now offer online services (O'Neil, 2014) and few can doubt that online services will become as common as traditional in-person counseling.

Because college counseling centers exist within the "sea" of higher education, one has to wonder just what college counseling will look like given the growing movement away from residential education and toward virtual classes. In a national survey of over 2,500 U.S. colleges and universities, almost 6 million students were enrolled in at least one online course (Sloan Consortium, 2011). Combine this information with the explosion in enrollments in nontraditional virtual institutions such as the University of Phoenix, Capella University, Walden University, and others, and it's clear the trend toward nontraditional, virtual higher education is growing rapidly and shows no signs of abating. Growth in online classes is happening not only in maverick upstart colleges such as the University of Phoenix, but in small, traditionally residential colleges. Fort Hays State University in Fort Hays, Kansas, has experienced significant growth in enrollment largely due to its increase in online education (King, 2014). The phenomenon witnessed at Fort Hays State University can also be seen at numerous other traditionally residential colleges in the United States. Clearly, the trend toward online or at least hybrid coursework (hybrid classes are a blend of residential and online classes) is the future of higher education.

Therefore, the questions that must be posed for the college counseling profession are: "How will college counseling adapt to the movement toward online education given this will mean a less residential student population?" Another question to ponder is "How will college counseling be conducted in the future? Will it primarily be delivered via web-based technology with in-person counseling the exception?" "Will college counseling centers adapt and survive in a postmodern, virtual era or are they just one more dinosaur in higher education?"

These are the types of questions college counselors, professional organizations such as the American College Counseling Association (ACCA), the Association of University and College Counseling Center Directors, the International Association of Counseling Services, Inc., and others must begin to address. This author (Hodges) suggests a hybrid model for college counseling services utilizing both traditional, in-person counseling and counseling via the use of technology such as Skype. This author also wishes to stress he believes in-person counseling is not only preferable to counseling via Skype or the Internet, but in an era where students seem more detached than ever from peers, in-person counseling probably is better role-modeling. Nevertheless, the trends are moving in a radically different direction and survival of college counseling means the profession must adapt to changing demographics and trends else it will not survive. Charles Darwin, well over a century ago, wrote that it wasn't the smartest organisms that survived or the strongest, but the ones most willing to adapt to changing times (Darwin, 1859). College counseling centers must consider the great evolutionary biologist's words and apply them to their profession. As a former college counselor, and former director of a college counseling center, many changes will need to occur in the upcoming decade.

A MODEL FOR THE COLLEGE COUNSELING AND RESOURCE CENTER OF THE 21ST CENTURY

As mentioned in this text, the Internet has transformed society into a global marketplace (Freedman, 2004). The marketplace, higher education, and even social relationships (e.g., Facebook) have been forever altered due to the success and ubiquity of the Internet (Freedman, 2004). College counseling centers will be no exception especially as virtual education continues to take a larger share of the higher education pie (Sloan Consortium, 2011). Because the Internet, through virtual education, is beginning to transform the nature of higher education from "seat" time to "web" time, college counseling centers must also change. The following model for college counseling centers provides a rough outline for addressing some of the challenges of a high-tech age.

TRADITIONAL SERVICES

Traditional services provided by the college counseling center have included the following: individual and group counseling, psychoeducational groups, evaluation and assessment, career counseling, consultation to faculty and staff, medication management, resident advisor (RA) training, Project Safe-Haven training, and so on. Essentially, the college counseling center has provided on-site and even off-site counseling, assessment, and evaluation in mostly a face-to-face format. Admittedly, college counselors have often spoken with clients over the phone but the bulk of counseling services has been provided in person and at the counseling center. But as the student culture changes institutions must change as well. While in-person counseling is likely to remain a staple service provided by the college counseling center for the foreseeable future, it is likely to decline in the coming years due to a student population that increasingly interacts with the world through the medium of technology (e.g., smartphones, laptops, and texting). Nevertheless, college counseling centers will continue to provide on-site, in-person counseling. College counseling centers will also continue to provide consultation to faculty and staff on matters of student behavior and well-being.

VIRTUAL SERVICES

Although the traditional college counseling center services have been noted in the preceding section, nontraditional services will likely grow rapidly. Nontraditional services here are defined as virtual counseling, advising, and related services offered via distance technology (i.e., Skype, the Internet, virtual counseling chat and online, self-instructional, psychoeducational training). Admittedly, the definition of nontraditional services is somewhat vague due to the ever-expanding nature of technology. It is very difficult to accurately predict how technology will advance and what new forms it will take. Still, there are some current technologies that have become very popular and will be the subject of this section of the chapter.

College counseling centers will in the near future offer increased counseling, consultation, and outreach programming through the medium of the Internet. Some college counseling services may offer services primarily through the Internet due to staffing concerns and geographic distances. For example, Skype is a very popular and useful aspect of technology and many counselors are already utilizing it to provide counseling services (Hoffman, 2011; Maples & Han, 2008). Web-based counseling is rapidly becoming popular (Hoffman, 2011). Thus, it should come as no surprise that future college counseling centers will offer counseling and related services online through Skype and other web media. In fact, distance counseling offers several advantages, such as convenience and the ability to remain connected with clients from a distance. For example, say a student has gone on a study abroad experience to Chile, New Zealand, China, or another far-away country; with Skype, the student could continue to utilize counseling services. This ability offers real promise both for students in need of counseling services and college counseling centers as well. Instead of a student being cut off from needed services, the college counseling service could continue to treat the student. While students on study abroad or those enrolled in online programs could seek private providers, they would find such professionals far more expensive. Virtual counseling services enable the college counseling centers to market themselves in an era when traditional collegiate populations are declining.

SELF-INSTRUCTIONAL SYSTEMS

College counseling centers have long offered types of self-instructional services. Examples of self-instructional helping services can be viewed in the way of popular psychoeducational books like *Mind Over Mood*, *The Courage to Heal*, *The Relaxation and Stress Reduction Workbook*, and many others. Digital versatile disks (DVDs) addressing stress and anxiety management have been around for some time and many mental heal websites also offer tips to interested persons. Again, given that the Internet has become as popular as the phone and television did in the 20th century, interactive websites offered by college counseling centers will become standard as well. In fact, as most college counseling services are nonprofit departments, they may well have more credibility than private practitioners or for-profit websites. Naturally, such therapeutic websites must be very careful to inform whoever is using their website that such information is not a substitute for counseling.

College counseling center websites have been serving as information centers for well over a decade. But the future dictates that they will be more interactive and will offer psychoeducational services for students. An example of a psychoeducational service would be an interactive program on managing anxiety. Students interested in the service could simply use their student ID to access the system (this "closed" system would also provide more security). Another example of psychoeducational or even counseling services would be to offer group counseling through Skype in a manner where the counselor and all group members could see and interact with each other. This would provide convenience for working students, students on study abroad, and those living at a distance enrolled in online academic programs.

Disadvantages of Virtual Counseling

While advantages to virtual counseling and related services have been noted, disadvantages must also be acknowledged. Here are some disadvantages:

- Virtual counseling may not promote the same type of interaction as traditional, in-person counseling.
- For counselors providing addiction counseling virtual therapy means he or she cannot smell the client's breath or get a good look at the client's eyes to check for a relapse.
- Technology can fail. A counselor and a client may have reached a critical point in therapy only to lose the connection through a power failure or another similar problem.
- Security systems can be breached. Thus, informed consent during the intake process would mean making the prospective client aware of this significant issue.
- The quality of the video imaging is currently not the best. Certainly technology will improve but it may never be as defined as in-person interaction. Currently, dark shadows and blurry images are common with many virtual technologies such as Skype. This lack of image definition may reduce the quality of counseling.
- When using their smartphones, counselors may be held legally liable should they lose the phone and a hacker be able to obtain client information from it (Wheeler & Bertram, 2012).

STAFFING IN THE COLLEGE COUNSELING CENTER OF THE FUTURE

As a longtime professor, counselor, and student affairs professional (as director of a college counseling center, counseling center staff, career center, residence director, student activities staff, etc.) this author (Hodges) holds many concerns regarding staffing of future college counseling centers. The threat of outsourcing college counseling centers—as at Georgia State University—is a serious one for college counseling centers. In an era of high accountability, college counseling centers of the future must demonstrate an ability to be "lean" and at the same time flexible. Staffing at college counseling centers is almost certain to be reduced at many colleges as a means of curbing tuition. Thus, college counseling centers in the future will rely more on a hybrid of college staff and outside contractors. To keep the counseling center from being outsourced entirely, counseling staff must demonstrate why they would be more cost-effective and more effective in terms of services offered.

College counseling center staffing in the future will look somewhat like current staffing, with the exception that there will be fewer college staff and more private practitioners working on contracts. But the prediction here is that most colleges will keep some permanent staff in the counseling center as they will be needed for RA/resident director (RD) training, faculty and staff consultation, psychoeducational workshops, and even Skype counseling. College staff also will be more invested in the well-being of the institution they serve as opposed to a private contractor who may see the few hours a week he or she works for the college counseling center as simply another contract. Private contractors will also limit their services to what is billable through insurance; consultation, career counseling, psychoeducational workshops, support groups, and couples counseling usually are not billable and likely would be services private contractors would cut or limit.

College counseling center staff must work to develop additional areas of expertise that private contractors will be less likely to provide. In addition to some of the general services mentioned previously, college counselors may wish to expand into sports counseling, personal coaching, training and development through Human Resources, mediation services, and others. Certainly college counseling centers cannot be all things to the campus as overextending the parameters of service is neither realistic nor healthy for the center staff (Gilbert, 1989). But it is important to remember the 21st century appears to be the era of doing more with less and doing it in novel ways (e.g., virtual counseling). This new, postmodern era requires college counseling centers to make adaptations that previously they have not had to make.

THE IMPACT OF SOCIAL MEDIA

Given the popularity and ubiquity of Facebook, Twitter, LinkedIn, and numerous additional social media sites (not to mention new ones yet to come), students, faculty, and student affairs staff are utilizing these virtual websites to connect with friends, family, and colleagues. Social media sites, particularly Facebook, provide the vehicle to connect people with a wide audience. The advantage to social networks is they offer a window of opportunity for students to expand their circle of friends to those outside their geographic and social circle. A disadvantage of social media lies in the term "friend" itself. On today's campus, "friending" someone has begun to change the nature of the term *friend*. In point of fact, a "friend" on Facebook, for example, may not be an actual friend, or at least not a friendship in the conventional sense. This over reliance on social connections through cyberspace may leave students with fewer firmly rooted friendships.

College counseling centers will need to address social media in ways that are both ethically sound and also able to effectively engage college students in seeking counseling services. The American Psychological Association (APA), National Association for Social Workers (NASW), American Association for Marriage and Family Therapy (AAMFT), American Counseling Association (ACA), the ACCA, and similar professional counseling organizations are likely to create (or already have created) ethical policies addressing social media and ethical use thereof (see appendix to this chapter). It is likely that college counseling centers will make extensive use of social media in the near future though such use is likely to be limited. A basic parameter college counselor will be encouraged—if not ethically mandated—to respect is that of "friending." Counselors likely will be prohibited from "friending" clients and perhaps even former clients for a set period.

BLOGS

Blogs have become increasingly popular in avenues of society. A perusal of the Internet will reveal political, philosophical, spiritual, medical, and even psychologically-oriented blogs. College counseling centers are already using blogs and podcasts as a means of disseminating information to a wider campus audience much in the same way the campus newspaper was used in former collegiate eras. College counselors can use blogs to educate the campus on any number of mental health concerns (e.g., eating disorders, sexual assault, homesickness) and also use blogs as a means of supporting student organizations and special events (e.g., Pride Week, International Student Week, Depression screening). An advantage to blogs over the former print media is that blogs can be stored on the counseling center's website and remain available to students and their families for an extended period of time. Counselors writing blogs must take care to ensure any information they post on their blog is accurate and something the counselor is comfortable leaving in cyberspace. College counseling centers utilizing blogs are encouraged to form a peer-review system to read over and catch any potential issues prior to making the blog available on the counseling center website.

PODCASTS

Podcasts are similar in scope to blogs in that they can be made available to student listeners for an extended period of time. The counseling centers director, clinical or training director, or line counselor could deliver a podcast either with a prepared statement or through an interview with another party. Unlike blogs, which are written, podcasts are for the auditory delivery mode. Once again, counselors making use of this method of delivering information must ensure that what they say is accurate. Podcasts have become very popular in many arenas of society and especially on college campuses.

VIDEOS

YouTube has created a virtual explosion for home movies, informal films and performances, and capturing endeavors of a dubious nature. Like any medium, YouTube has the capacity to be utilized both for legitimate and nonlegitimate purposes. College counseling centers posting an educational talk by a staff person on posttraumatic stress disorder (PTSD), managing depression, and so forth would naturally fall into the former category. In partnership with perhaps the theater department, college counseling centers could also make engaging video skits to increase awareness of sexual assault, homophobia, racism, how to manage vacations in toxic home environments, and so on. In fact, given this digital era, educational videos, skits, and similar endeavors hold much potential for college counseling centers.

HOLISTIC APPROACHES TO COUNSELING

Many college students are coming to college with serious mental illnesses that strain college counseling services' resources. There has been much debate regarding how to provide proper services beyond traditional counseling, assessment, and medication. The Jed Foundation, for example, encourages a holistic approach that goes beyond traditional services. In 2013, the Foundation began offering a new certification program aimed at assisting colleges to create broader helping communities (Sander, 2013). The new program, known as Jed Campus, provides a seal of approval illustrating that the college's services are promoting optimal mental health. Jed offers to work with college counseling services struggling to measure up. The goal is to get everyone in the college system to think and care about campus mental health (Sander, 2013). Instead of waiting for students to present themselves to counseling services, Jed encourages early identification of potential students in crisis as well as developing mental health aids through social media. The foundation advocates teaching life skills to college students through psychoeducational classes and encourages students to learn to self-monitor their own mental and emotional well-being.

While the Jed Foundation represents an organizational approach to improving campus mental health, holistic approaches to mental health certainly are not new. The Wheel of Wellness presents a holistic model for emotional health and prevention across the life span (Myers, Sweeney, & Witmer, 2000) and the Wellness Evaluation Lifestyle (WEL) assists respondents in making healthy lifestyle choices based on responses to the five life tasks defined in the Wheel of Wellness. The life tasks are: spirituality, self-direction, work and leisure, friendship, and love. These life tasks interact with numerous life issues and events in the individual's life. The instrument consists of 131 items generated as self-statements to which respondent's reply using a five point Likert scale.

In addition to these efforts regarding holistic approaches to counseling, numerous workbooks regarding managing stress have been available for decades. "Wellness" centers likely have become more common on college campuses and may include a combination of traditional counseling and health services, physical therapy, massage, psychoeducational classes, meditation, yoga, acupuncture, and so on. The important point that these holistic approaches make is that the mind–body dichotomy is a false separation (Myers et al., 2000). Given an increasingly sophisticated college student population who interacts with their world via high-tech means, a holistic approach likely is prudent for college counseling services. Interestingly, holistic approaches have much in common with Eastern medicine and wholeness and are in fact older than traditional, Western, allopathic approaches to health care.

Positive approaches to counseling have been well documented in the last 15 years as Frankl (1988), Gladding (2013), Granello and Granello (2007), Seligman (2002), and others have written extensively on constructs of hope and meaning in the therapeutic encounter. Given that hope has been established as a critical mediating factor in preventing suicide attempts and helping keep addicts in treatment maintain sobriety (Beck, Wright, Newman, & Liese, 1993), establishing hope in college students is essential, especially when considering suicide is the second leading cause of death among college students (Granello & Granello, 2007). Hope may be operationally defined as "the belief that life is worthwhile and that life conditions will in some way improve over time." Because hope may be composed of many variables including cognitive and lifestyle changes (Adler & Seligman, 2016; Frankl, 1988), I have chosen to assess the construct by the creation of the subjective *Dimensions of a Healthy Lifestyle Scale* (DHLS), which assesses constructs related to hope. The DHLS is simply a brief assessment to provide the counselor and client with an approximate sense of functioning on 20 points. The DHLS is not intended as a diagnostic instrument but for the purposes of self-reporting information and to assist the university counselor and client in an ongoing discussion of creating a healthy lifestyle. The counselor can administer the DHLS to the client and then discuss the findings. Results from the DHLS can assist the counselor and client in forming a treatment plan, treatment goals, and avenues for future discussion.

THE DIMENSIONS OF A HEALTHY LIFESTYLE SCALE

1. Spirituality
"My spiritual life provides a sense of purpose and helps me address major life challenges."
(*Note:* An alternate for people professing no spiritual beliefs might be, "My sense of life meaning/purpose provides fulfillment and helps me address the challenges in my life.")
1   2   3   4   5   6   7   8   9   10
(1 = No help at all, 10 = Strongly helps)
If your score was less than five, how could you improve your situation?

2. Personal Vision
"I have a clear vision of my personal, spiritual, and professional life."
1   2   3   4   5   6   7   8   9   10
(1 = I lack a clear vision; 10 = I have a clear vision)
If you do not have a clear vision in these areas, how could you develop one? Visioning is a key component to success in all these areas. For nonspiritual clients, "life meaning/purpose" can be substituted.

3. Self-Worth

"I feel worthwhile as a human being and have a strong sense of self-acceptance. Though I am not perfect, I feel good about myself."

1   2   3   5   6   7   8   9   10

(1 = I am worthless, 10 = I have a strong sense of self-worth)

If you are experiencing low self-esteem, how could you begin to feel better about yourself? What actions could you take to begin to feel a stronger sense of self-worth?

4. Self-Direction

"I have a clear sense of direction in my personal, spiritual, and professional life."

1   2   3   4   5   6   7   8   9   10

(1 = No direction, 10 = I have a clear direction)

If you feel a lack of direction in one or more of these areas, how could you gain a sense of direction? (Or, "I could create a sense of direction by …"). Nonspiritual clients could substitute "life purpose" for "spiritual."

5. Goal Setting

"I feel self-confident about setting and meeting goals and demands in my life."

1   2   3   4   5   6   7   8   9   10

(1 = I lack confidence in my ability to meet demands and the goals I set; 10 = I feel very confident in setting, planning, and meeting goals and demands)

If you lack clear goals in your life, how could you begin to create some clear goals?

6. Rational Thinking

"I believe I perceive my life and life situations in a realistic fashion. I seldom engage in unrealistic thinking."

1   2   3   4   5   6   7   8   9   10

(1 = I frequently engage in unrealistic thinking; 10 = I am very realistic in my beliefs)

If you have rated yourself as frequently engaging in unrealistic beliefs, how could you begin to think in a more realistic manner? (Or, if you are unsure as to whether or not your beliefs are realistic, you might consider asking someone you trust for feedback on this issue.)

7. Emotional Understanding and Regulation

"I am in touch with my emotions and am able to express the full range of emotions appropriate to the situation. I also am not governed by my emotions."

1   2   3   4   5   6   7   8   9   10

(1 = I am unable to manage my emotions and often express emotions inappropriate to the situation; 10 = I am able to manage my emotions and experience emotions appropriate to the situation)

If you find you are not experiencing an appropriate range of emotions, or you find you are too often ruled by your emotions, how could you begin to change this?

8. Resilience

"I am a very resilient person, and able to analyze, synthesize, and make a plan to deal with challenges and projects that come my way."

1   2   3   4   5   6   7   8   9   10

(1 = I do not feel resilient; 10 = I am very confident in my resiliency)

If you do not feel resilient, or you are not as resilient as you would like to be, what could you do to develop more resilience? (*Note:* If you feel stuck on strategizing with this component, perhaps begin by making a list of ways you feel resilient. Or ask someone who knows you well to list ways he or she see you as being resilient.)

9. Sense of Humor

"I possess a healthy, appropriate sense of humor that helps me deal with the stresses of life."

1   2   3   4   5   6   7   8   9   10

(1 = I have no sense of humor; 10 = I have a healthy sense of humor)

If you do not feel your sense of humor is either strongly developed, appropriate, or provides an effective release of stress, what could you change to improve the situation?

10. Fitness or Recreation

"I have regular, weekly, fitness routine that helps me stay physically and emotionally fit."

1   2   3   4   5   6   7   8   9   10

(1 = I have no activity routine; 10 = I have an active physical routine)

If you do not have a regular weekly fitness routine, what could you do to change this? (Remember, you do not need to become a marathoner, competitive cyclist, swimmer, or dancer, and so on. It's simply about developing a regular routine of 20 minutes a day, at least 3 days a week.)

11. Healthy Diet

"I regularly eat a balanced diet, including healthy vegetables and fruits and restrict eating sweets and high-fat foods."

(*Note:* Healthy is not meant to imply you never eat sweets or fried food. Rather, it's about eating sweet or high-fat food in moderation.)

1   2   3   4   5   6   7   8   9   10

(1 = My diet is unbalanced and unhealthy; 10 = My diet is balanced and healthy)

If your diet is unhealthy (eating high-fat food, "junk" food, fast food, etc., too often), how could you begin to eat a healthier diet?

12. Mindful Living

"I maintain a healthy lifestyle by not abusing alcohol or other drugs, by wearing a seat belt, having regular medical exams, by refraining from high risk activities (casual sex, binge drinking, binge eating, restricting food, etc.), and by cultivating an awareness of self and healthy life choices."

1   2   3   4   5   6   7   8   9   10

(1 = I do not live a healthy mindful life; 10 = I maintain a healthy, mindful lifestyle)

If you find you are not living a healthy, mindful life, what steps could you take to address this?

13. Managing Stress and Anxiety

"Through my diet, workout routine, friendships, and so on. I have the ability to manage stress on a regular basis. When I find I am unable to manage the stress and anxiety in my life, I check in with close friends and family or if the need arises, I see a counselor."

1 2 3 4 5 6 7 8 9 10

(1 = I am regularly unable to manage the stress in my life; 10 = I am able to manage the stress in my life)

If you find you regularly have difficulty managing the stress and anxiety in your life, how could you begin to manage that stress and anxiety better?

14. Connection to Family and Culture

"I feel a strong connection to my cultural identity (or cultural identities) and value my cultural history."

1 2 3 4 5 6 7 8 9 10

(1 = I feel no connection to my cultural identity; 10 = I feel a strong and healthy connection to my culture or cultures)

In the event you feel no connection to your cultural identity, what would you say accounts for this? (Or, do you understand your cultural identity?) Also, how could you begin to make connections to your culture or cultures?

15. Career/Vocational Development

"I feel a sense of satisfaction in my career (or in the career/major I am pursuing)."

1 2 3 4 5 6 7 8 9 10

(1 = My career/academic major brings me no satisfaction; 10 = My career/academic major brings me maximum satisfaction)

If your career/academic major does not provide personal challenge and satisfaction, what steps could you take to create more satisfaction in your career? (Or, if you are unemployed, how could your job search become more fulfilling? Or, how could this period of unemployment be more productive?)

16. Hobbies

"My hobbies help me relax and provide a sense of enjoyment and emotional and personal renewal."

1 2 3 4 5 6 7 8 9 10

(1 = I have no hobbies or they provide no sense of enjoyment or relaxation; 10 = My hobbies are a pure joy)

If your hobbies provide little enjoyment or you lack hobbies or rewarding routines, how could you begin to change this situation?

17. Social Life

"I have healthy relationships that provide me a sense of emotional connection and help make life more rewarding."

1 2 3 4 5 6 7 8 9 19

(1 = I have no significant relationships or they are shallow, or provide little in the way of emotional connection; 10 = I have healthy and fulfilling personal relationships and they are an important part of my life)

If you lack significant personal connections or your relationships do not provide you a sense of emotional connection, how could you begin to address this? (Or, how could you begin to create fulfilling relationships?)

18. Intimacy

"Intimacy or love is a central part of my life and the intimacy of a close relationship provides the grounding, intimacy, and close connection I need." (*Note:* Love could involve sexual intimacy or a close, nonsexual relationship.)

1 2 3 4 5 6 7 8 9 10

(1 = Love is largely absent from my life'; 10 = Love is a large part of my life and provides me with great satisfaction)

If love seems absent from your life, or if that love seems unhealthy or unfulfilling, what do you need to do to change this situation?

19. Hope

"My life is hopeful and I believe things (e.g., school, career, relationships, etc.) can improve."

1 2 3 4 5 6 7 8 9 10

(1 = I feel hopeless and things will only get worse; 10 = I feel very hopeful and my situation will only get better)

If you feel less hopeful than you would like, what could you do to change this?

20. Meaning and Purpose

"I have discovered my life is full of meaning and that I have a strong sense of purpose in life."

1 2 3 4 5 6 7 8 9 10

(1 = My life is meaningless and purposeless; 10 = My life is rich with meaning and full of purpose)

If your life seems to lack meaning and purpose, what could you do to create more meaning and purpose in your life? Or, what would a meaningful, purposeful life look like?

There are additional standardized instruments to assess the trait of hope such as the Beck Depression Inventory II (BDI-II; Beck, Steer, & Brown, 1996), the Purpose in Life Test (Crumbaugh & Maholick, 1981), and the Rosenberg Self-Esteem Scale (Rosenberg, 1989), which measures the related construct of self-esteem. The important factor for the college counselor is to establish a dialogue on what role hope, life meaning, and purpose in life play in the student's life. Students who score high on the BDI-II generally score high on the inventory's hopelessness item (Beck et al., 1996). It is probably not a stretch to state that as clients improve in counseling, they are likely more hopeful.

SUMMARY

As colleges and universities have moved further into the 21st century, technological advances (e.g., web classes, degrees, and virtual universities) have been the most noticeable construct of change. As previously noted, the University of Phoenix has an enrollment that hovers around and above 250,000 students. Smartphones and their functions such as texting and Skype are quickly becoming the primary way college students stay socially connected. One can only wonder what changes the next 10 to 15 years will bring to the college campus, if indeed "campus" remains a relevant term. But, as depression, anxiety, and suicide ideation and attempts remain high, college counseling is certain to continue in some form. Clearly, many students will seek therapy from online providers, and that's likely to mean institutions contract much of their counseling service out to private providers, or colleges hire a counseling staff to provide virtual counseling. While change certainly is the one constant that will remain, college counseling will, in some form, continue to be a popular outlet and support service for college students. So, while college counseling services are certain to remain in some form, it is equally clear they will change and adapt to 21st-century marketplace demands. Such "demands" will include a global enrollment driven by technology and convenience.

REFERENCES

Adler, A., & Seligman, M. E. P. (2016). Using wellbeing for public policy: Theory, measurement, and recommendations. *International Journal of Wellbeing, 6*(1), 1–35. doi:10.5502/ijw.v6i1.1

Beck, A. T., Steer, R. A., & Brown, G. K. (1996). *Manual for Beck Depression Inventory-II.* San Antonio, TX: The Psychological Corporation.

Beck, A. T., Wright, F. D., Newman, C. F., & Liese, B. S. (1993). *Cognitive therapy of substance abuse.* New York, NY: Guilford Press.

Crumbaugh, J. C., & Maholick, L. T. (1981). *Manual for instructions for the Purpose-in-Life Test.* Murfreesboro, TN: Psychometric Affiliates.

Darwin, C. (1859). *The origin of the species.* Oxford, UK: Oxford World's Classics.

Frankl, V. E. (1988). *The will to meaning: Foundations and applications of logotherapy.* New York, NY: Penguin.

Freedman, T. (2004). *The world is flat: A brief history of the twenty-first century.* New York, NY: Farrar, Straus and Giroux.

Gilbert, S. P. (1989). The juggling act of the college counseling center. *The Counseling Psychologist, 17*(3), 477–489.

Gladding, S. T. (2013). *Counseling: A comprehensive profession* (7th ed.). New York, NY: Pearson.

Granello, D. H., & Granello, P. F. (2007). *Suicide: An essential guide for helping professionals and educators.* Boston, MA: Pearson.

Hoffman, J. (2011, September 23). When your therapist is only a click away. Fashion & Style section. *New York Times Online.* Retrieved from http://www.nytimes.com/2011/09/25/fashion/therapists-are-seeing-patients-online.html

Junco, R., & Cole-Avant, G. A. (2008). An introduction to technologies commonly used by college students. *New Directions for Student Services, 124*, 3–17.

King, D. (2014, March 13). How a Kansas regional school became one of the fastest-growing universities in the U.S. *Blackboard Blog.* Retrieved from http://blog.blackboard.com/regional-kansas-university-became-one-fastest-growing-institutions-u-s

Maples, M. F., & Han, S. (2008). Cybercounselling in the United States and South Korea: Implications for counseling college students of the millennial generation and the networked generation. *Journal of Counseling & Development, 86*(2), 178–183.

Myers, J., Sweeney, T. J., & Witmer, M. (2000). The wheel of wellness counseling for wellness: A holistic model for treatment planning. *Journal of Counseling & Development, 78*(3), 251–266.

O'Neil, M. (2014, January 13). Campus psychological counseling goes online for students at U. of Florida. *The Chronicle of Higher Education.* Retrieved from http://m.chronicle.com/article/Campus-Psychological/143963

Patrick, P. K. S., & Flanigan, A. Y. (2012). Computer technology (1995–2009). *Journal of Technology in Counseling, 5*(1). Retrieved from http://jtc.columbusstate.edu/Vol_1/Patrick.htm

Rosenberg, M. (1989). *Society and adolescent self-image* (Rev. ed.). Middletown, CT: Wesleyan University Press.

Ruffalo-Noel-Levitz. (2008). *Circling over enrollment: The e-expectations of the parents of college-bound students.* Retrieved from http://ruffalonl.com/documents/shared/Papers_and_Research/2008/EExpCirclingOverEnrollment08.pdf

Seligman, M. E. P. (2002). *Authentic happiness: Using the new positive psychology to realize your potential for lasting fulfillment.* New York, NY: Free Press.

Sloan Consortium. (2011). *Going the distance: Online education in the United States in 2011.* Retrieved from http://www.sloanconsortium.org/php

Wheeler, A. M. N., & Bertram, B. (2012). *The counselor and the law: A guide to legal and ethical practice* (6th ed.). Alexandria, VA: American Counseling Association.

APPENDIX

List of Professional Counseling Organizations Related to College and University Counseling

Note: The following is not a comprehensive list but represents sample organizations involved in college and university mental health care. Some of the following organizations are interdisciplinary (e.g., American College Counseling Association (ACCA), American College Health Association [ACHA]) while others represent a particular mental health profession (e.g., American Psychiatric Association [APA]).

American Counseling Association (ACA)

ACA is the flagship organization for counselors. www.counseling.org

American College Counseling Association (ACCA)

ACCA is an umbrella organization of college, community college, and university counseling professionals. ACCA membership is open to anyone involved in college counseling services (or desiring to be involved). www.college counseling.org

American College Health Association (ACHA)

The ACHA is a collaborative, interdisciplinary organization advocating, and promoting collegiate health and well-being. www.acha.org

American Psychiatric Association (APA)

The American Psychiatric Association represents the profession of psychiatry. Many psychiatrists staff large university counseling centers. www.psyc.org

American Psychological Association (APA)

APA is the professional organization for psychologists. www.apa.org

Association for University and College Counseling Center Directors (AUCCCD)

The AUCCCD is an organization composed of directors of college and university counseling centers.

Boosting Alcohol Consciousness Concerning the Health of University Students (BACCHUS)

BACCHUS is a national organization promoting alcohol education in college and universities. www.bacchusnetwork.org

Greeks Advocating Mature Management of Alcohol (GAMMA)

GAMMA is an educational organization to educate collegiate Greek organizations on alcohol education and abuse.

International Association of Counseling Services, Inc. (IACS)

IACS credentials college and university counseling services. www.iacsinc.org

Jed Foundation

The Jed Foundation works to educate college students, staff, faculty, administrators, and parents on suicide prevention. www.jedfoundation.org

National Association for Social Workersv (NASW)

NASW is the professional organization for social workers. www.naswdc.org

INDEX